THE SHORT
PROSE RE

THE SHORT PROSE READER

TWELFTH EDITION

Gilbert H. Muller
The City University of New York
LaGuardia

Harvey S. Wiener
The City University of New York
LaGuardia

Boston   Burr Ridge, IL   Dubuque, IA   New York   San Francisco   St. Louis
Bangkok   Bogotá   Caracas   Kuala Lumpur   Lisbon   London   Madrid   Mexico City
Milan   Montreal   New Delhi   Santiago   Seoul   Singapore   Sydney   Taipei   Toronto

Mc Graw Hill Higher Education

Published by McGraw-Hill, an imprint of The McGraw-Hill Companies, Inc., 1221 Avenue of the Americas, New York, NY 10020. Copyright © 2009, 2006, 2003, 2000, 1997, 1994, 1991, 1989, 1987, 1985, 1982, 1979. All rights reserved. No part of this publication may be reproduced or distributed in any form or by any means, or stored in a database or retrieval system, without the prior written consent of The McGraw-Hill Companies, Inc., including, but not limited to, in any network or other electronic storage or transmission, or broadcast for distance learning.

This book is printed on acid-free paper.

1 2 3 4 5 6 7 8 9 0 DOC/DOC 0 9 8

ISBN: 978-0-07-353314-8
MHID: 0-07-353314-9

Editor in Chief: *Michael Ryan*
Publisher: *David S. Patterson*
Senior Sponsoring Editor: *John Kindler*
Marketing Manager: *Allison Jones*
Developmental Editor: *Jesse Hassenger*
Production Editor: *Holly Paulsen*
Manuscript Editor: *Judith Brown*
Design Manager: *Margarite Reynolds*
Cover Designer: *Hiroko Chastain*

Senior Photo Research Coordinator: *Sonia Brown*
Production Supervisor: *Louis Swaim*
Media Project Manager: *Thomas Brierly*
Composition: *10.5/12 Times Roman by Macmillan Publishing Solutions*
Printing: *45# New Era Matte, R. R. Donnelley & Sons*

Cover: *Reader* (acrylic on canvas), Daniel Cacouault, (Contemporary Artist)/Private Collection/The Bridgeman Art Library.

Credits: The credits section for this book begins on page C-1 and is considered an extension of the copyright page.

Library of Congress Cataloging-in-Publication Data

The short prose reader / [compiled by] Gilbert H. Muller, Harvey S. Wiener. -- 12th ed.
    p. cm.
  Includes index.
  ISBN-13: 978-0-07-353314-8 (pbk. : acid-free paper)
  ISBN-10: 0-07-353314-9 (pbk. : acid-free paper) 1. College readers. 2. English language--Rhetoric--Problems, exercises, etc. 3. Report writing--Problems, exercises, etc. I. Muller, Gilbert H., 1941– II. Wiener, Harvey S.
  PE1417.S446 2009
  808'.0427--dc22

                                                    2008047503

The Internet addresses listed in the text were accurate at the time of publication. The inclusion of a Web site does not indicate an endorsement by the authors or McGraw-Hill, and McGraw-Hill does not guarantee the accuracy of the information presented at these sites.

www.mhhe.com

ABOUT THE AUTHORS

Gilbert H. Muller, who received a PhD in English and American literature from Stanford University, is currently professor emeritus of English at the LaGuardia campus of the City University of New York. He has also taught at Stanford, Vassar, and several universities overseas. Dr. Muller is the author of the award-winning study *Nightmares and Visions: Flannery O'Connor and the Catholic Grotesque, Chester Himes, New Strangers in Paradise: The Immigrant Experience and Contemporary American Fiction,* and *William Cullen Bryant: Author of America.* His essays and reviews have appeared in *The New York Times, The New Republic, The Nation, The Sewanee Review, The Georgia Review,* and elsewhere. He is also a noted author and editor of textbooks in English and composition, including *The McGraw-Hill Reader* and, with John Williams, *The McGraw-Hill Introduction to Literature.* Dr. Muller has received awards from the National Endowment for the Humanities, Fulbright Commission, and the Ford and Mellon foundations.

Harvey S. Wiener, professor Emeritus at LaGuardia Community College of the City University of New York, served as Vice President of Adult Programs and Community Outreach at Marymount Manhattan College. Previously University Dean for Academic Affairs at the City University of New York, he was founding president of the Council of Writing Program Administrators. Dr. Wiener is the author of many books on reading and writing for college students and their teachers, including *The Writing Room* (Oxford,

1981). He is coauthor of *The McGraw-Hill College Handbook,* a reference grammar and rhetorical text. Dr. Wiener has chaired the Teaching of Writing Division of the Modern Language Association (1987). He has taught writing at every level of education from elementary school to graduate school. A Phi Beta Kappa graduate of Brooklyn College, he holds a PhD in Renaissance literature. Dr. Wiener has won grants from the National Endowment for the Humanities, the Fund for the Improvement of Postsecondary Education, and the Exxon Education Foundation. His book *Any Child Can Write* was an alternate selection of the Book of the Month Club and was featured on the *Today* show. His writing has appeared in *Anglia, College English, College Composition and Communication,* and *WPA Journal,* as well as in the London *Times,* the New York *Daily News,* and *Gentleman's Quarterly.*

To the memory of George Groman

CONTENTS

CHAPTER 2

CHAPTER 3

CHAPTER 6

Illustration   216

CHAPTER 7

CHAPTER 8

CHAPTER 11

THEMATIC CONTENTS

Cultures and Ethnicities

School and Education

Men and Women

Nature and the Environment

Social Problems and Issues

Science and Technology

Psychology and Behavior

Language and Identity

Humor and Satire

PREFACE

The twelfth edition of *The Short Prose Reader* maintains the best features of the earlier editions: lively reading selections supported by helpful apparatus to integrate reading and writing in college composition and reading courses. In working through the text, the student progresses from key aspects of the writing and reading processes to chapters on the essential patterns of writing and then to more rigorous forms of analysis and argument. Each chapter provides diverse and lively prose models suited for discussion, analysis, and imitation.

New features of the twelfth edition include:

- **Eighteen new reading selections,** with essays by Nora Ephron, Norman Mailer, Anna Quindlen, Richard Rodriguez, Diane Ackerman, Thomas L. Friedman, and Susan Cheever. We balance these contemporary readings—all published since 2000—with favorites from earlier editions of *The Short Prose Reader,* such as Langston Hughes's "Salvation," George Orwell's "A Hanging," Amy Tan's "Mother Tongue," and Rachel Carson's "A Fable for Tomorrow."
- **New topics and issues** that will appeal to students, among them online writing styles, terrorism and torture, environmentalism, globalization, college life, and the roles of working women in society today.
- **A revised table of contents** that lets students move from easier rhetorical strategies to more challenging ones (like classification and definition) that stress synthetic and higher-order cognitive abilities.
- **New units in the thematic table of contents,** including Scenes and Places, Cultures and Ethnicities, Nature and the Environment, and Language and Identity.

- **A major revision of Chapter 11, Argumentation and Persuasion,** with a fresh pro/con pair on torture and a new unit on the "Mommy Wars."
- **New visuals** throughout *The Short Prose Reader* that encourage students to move from seeing to writing.
- **An updated Guide to Research and Documentation,** with an expanded student paper and examples of current citation practice.
- **Links to the online learning center (OLC)** integrated throughout the text. The OLC provides students with links to more information about some of the writers in this collection, as well as access to *Catalyst*—McGraw-Hill's premier writing, editing, and research resource. Through *Catalyst,* students can find over 3,000 grammar and usage exercises; tips on effective revision strategies; Bibliomaker software that formats source information in one of five documentation styles, including MLA and APA; an online source evaluation tutorial; and much more.

These features enhance the key elements of *The Short Prose Reader* that have made the previous eleven editions so enduringly popular.

ORGANIZATION

The organization of *The Short Prose Reader* is one of its major strengths. Chapter 1, On Writing, and Chapter 2, On Reading, offer students brief overviews of these two interdependent skills; each chapter offers four unique views on the crafts of writing or reading by well-known writers. Each of the following eight chapters contains four short essays that illustrate clearly a specific pattern or technique—description, narration, process analysis, illustration, comparison and contrast, causal analysis, classification, or definition. The final chapter is on argumentation. Students learn to build upon earlier techniques and patterns as they progress through the book.

READABILITY

From the beginning, we have chosen selections for *The Short Prose Reader* that are readable yet substantial and representative of many different types of writers. The essays, which range typically between 300 and 1,200 words, achieve their goals succinctly and clearly and are easy to understand. They exemplify both the types of college writing expected of students and the length of essay that is frequently assigned. The detailed questions that follow each essay can be used in reading as well as writing classes, since they ask the student to analyze both the content and the form of the prose selections.

APPARATUS

The questions and activities we have included for each piece are comprehensive and integrated—designed to develop and reinforce the key critical-thinking skills required in college writing.

- **Extensive biographical notes:** The headnotes preceding the selections provide valuable information about each writer, giving students more tools for reading the essays critically.
- **Prereading questions:** Before each essay, students encounter an activity called Prereading: Thinking About the Essay in Advance, which encourages them to think and talk about the topic before reading what the writer says about it. Studies show that such prior discussion arouses interest and holds the reader's attention.
- **Vocabulary exercises:** Each selection includes two vocabulary exercises. Words to Watch alerts students to words they will read in context, and Building Vocabulary uses other effective methods of teaching vocabulary, including attention to prefixes and suffixes, context clues, synonyms and antonyms, and abstract versus concrete words.
- **Questions that emphasize critical thinking:** To emphasize critical thinking as the main reason for questioning and discussion, we have grouped our conversational prods and probes under the heading Thinking Critically About the Essay. The questions titled Understanding the Writer's Ideas reinforce reading comprehension. The questions titled Understanding the Writer's Techniques and Exploring the Writer's Ideas provide excellent bases for class discussion and independent reading and analysis.
- **Prewriting prompts:** These sections help students record informal thoughts for writing in advance of producing an essay.
- **Guided Writing Activities:** A key exercise for each essay and a novel feature of *The Short Prose Reader,* the Guided Writing

activities offer a dynamic approach to writing projects. These activities tie the writing project to the reading selection, but instead of simply being told to write an essay on a certain topic, students can use the Guided Writing segment to move from step to step in the composing process.

- **Collaborative activities:** Thinking and Writing Collaboratively activities encourage students to work together in groups on essays and ideas for writing.
- **Reader response activities:** Writing About the Text asks students to examine closely the language and ideas in each selection and to write thoughtfully about them.
- **Additional writing projects:** More Writing Projects provides students with additional ideas for writing on the topic of the selection.

At the end of each chapter is a **Summing Up** section, a means for students to focus their attention on issues raised by several of the chapter's selections and on more writing topics, and a **From Seeing to Writing** activity, an engaging visual assignment that gives students another means of coming up with ideas for writing. And at the end of the text is an **appendix on research and documentation,** including a step-by-step guide to the research process, a section on using MLA style to document sources, and a sample student research paper on body image and advertising that uses a visual as support.

FLEXIBILITY

Students and teachers alike can use *The Short Prose Reader* flexibly and effectively. An alternate table of contents suggests thematic groupings of readings. The text is simple yet sophisticated, inviting students to engage in a multiplicity of cultural and traditional topics through essays and exercises that are easy to follow but never condescending. Weighing the needs and expectations of today's first-year students, we have designed a rhetoric/reader that can serve as the primary text for almost any composition course.

ANCILLARIES

- **The Instructor's Manual** provides teaching approaches for each chapter and essay, along with answers to the vocabulary and critical-thinking questions that follow each essay.

- **The text's companion Web site at www.mhhe.com/muller/ shortprose** offers three types of links—cultural, bibliographical, and biographical—to further information on selected authors within *The Short Prose Reader,* as well as access to *Catalyst,* McGraw-Hill's premier writing, editing, and research software.
- **Teaching Composition Faculty Listserv (www.mhhe.com/ tcomp),** moderated by Chris Anson at North Carolina State University, brings together senior members of the college composition community with newer members—junior faculty, adjuncts, and teaching assistants—in an online newsletter and accompanying discussion group to address issues of pedagogy, in theory and in practice.

ACKNOWLEDGMENTS

For this edition of *The Short Prose Reader,* we enjoyed the support of John Kindler, our sponsoring editor, who has brought a fresh perspective and calm persistence to the project. We are also deeply grateful for the patient and extraordinary efforts of Jesse Hassenger, our development editor. We also owe a debt of gratitude to Scott Smith, who assisted us throughout the revision process and produced the instructor's manual. Finally, we want to thank Meg Botteon, whose invaluable efforts helped bring the research appendix from an idea to an accomplishment.

We wish to thank our colleagues across the country for their support and are especially grateful to those who reviewed the manuscript for this edition:

Christy Burns, *Jacksonville State University*
Yvonne Cassidy, *Alfred State College*
Aniko Constantine, *Alfred State College*
Joseph Couch, *Montgomery College*
Carmine Di Biase, *Jacksonville State University*
Mary Evans, *Hudson Valley Community College*
Scott Hathaway, *Hudson Valley Community College*
Robin Havenick, *Linn Benton Community College*
William Hug, *Jacksonville State University*
Theodore Johnston, *El Paso Community College*
Lawrence Kaiser, *Bergen Community College*
Jesse Kavaldo, *Maryville University*

Denise Lagos, *Union County College*
Ellen Laird, *Hudson Valley Community College*
Richard Nordquist, *Armstrong Atlantic State University*
Elizabeth Rogers, *Central Piedmont Community College*
Dean Roughton, *College of the Albemarle*
Barbara Urban, *Central Piedmont Community College*
Kelli Wood, *El Paso Community College*

Gilbert H. Muller
Harvey S. Wiener

CHAPTER 1

On Writing

WHAT IS WRITING?

Writing helps us to record and communicate ideas. It is a definitive and essential part of daily human experience. Whether we write a shopping list or a great novel, we use a tool without which we would find ourselves isolated. Without writing we cut ourselves off from vital processes like the expression of political opinions, the description of medical emergencies, and the examination of our feelings in diaries and letters.

Writing crosses many cultures. Whether we consider historic cave drawings or the transmission of fax messages after the World Trade Center disaster, we find evidence of the human instinct to communicate ideas to other people.

In the past, writing brought about change. African American slaves were frequently forbidden to learn to read or write, but some managed to find ways to gain literacy anyway. Their narratives of slave life helped fire the abolition movement. Women in the nineteenth century used writing to advance the cause of suffrage, winning votes with passionate speeches and articles in newspapers. Immigrants struggled to learn English in order to find a better life in the New World.

Writing celebrates human achievement. In religion, in love, in wartime and in peace, in astronomy and medicine and archaeology, in the arts and humanities, writing reminds us of our shared human identity. From the Song of Solomon in the Bible to the words of Martin Luther King Jr.'s "I Have a Dream," from the Declaration of Independence to song lyrics by Bruce Springsteen or Alicia Keys, writing helps us to come to terms with who we are and what we want.

What is writing, exactly? For most of us, writing is so familiar that the question seems silly. We all know what writing is. Yet when we try to write ourselves, we may find that asking and answering the question are vital.

Writing is both a product and a process. Writing is, of course, *what* we write: a letter, a law brief, a term paper, an inaugural address. Since it is a product, we must think of writing as having a public as well as a private purpose. While some writing, like shopping lists or a diary, may be meant only for our own eyes, most writing is intended for an audience. In learning what writing is, we need to think about who the audience is, and what the purpose of the writing is.

Writing is also a process; it is *how* we write. In learning to write well, we examine the process of transferring ideas from head to hand. We realize that the actual, mechanical practice of writing out ideas helps us to think more carefully, to plan and arrange ideas, to analyze our vague thoughts into solid words on a page.

HOW DO WE WRITE?

The process of writing is not absolute; there is no one sure way to learn to write well. However, there are some common elements in this process that will help anyone getting started as a writer.

Warming Up: Prewriting

Like an athlete, the writer benefits from warm-up exercises. Usually called prewriting, these steps help a writer prepare gradually and thoughtfully for the event of writing a long essay. Writers stretch their intellectual muscles by thinking about a topic before they write about it. They talk to friends and colleagues. They visit a library and flip through reference books, newspapers, magazines, and books. Sometimes, they make notes and lists as a way of putting pen to paper for the first time. Some writers brainstorm: they use free association to jot down ideas as thoroughly as possible in an unedited form. Others use "timed writing": they write nonstop whatever comes to mind in a set time period—fifteen or twenty minutes, say. Freewriting like this loosens up ideas without the worry of correctness in language too early in the writing process.

After these preliminary warm-ups, many writers try to group or classify ideas by making a rough outline or drawing boxes or making lists to try to bring some plan or order to their rough ideas.

Once the writer has a rough topic area outlined, he or she may return to the audience and purpose for the essay. Who will read the essay? What material would best suit this audience? What language would be most appropriate for this audience? What is the purpose of the essay? A thesis sentence is important here. The thesis is your main point, the essential idea you want to assert about your subject. It's always a good idea to write out your thesis whether or not you ultimately use it in your essay.

Often the purpose or intent becomes clearer as the writer continues to think and write. Choosing the audience and purpose carefully—and stating the thesis succinctly—make the writer's as well as the reader's task easier.

Look at the following prewriting by a student who wanted to write about her impressions of a hospital. She made a list of free associations with the intent of using her notes to prepare the draft of an essay.

Roller skating accident
Go to the hospital for tests
My mother drops me off and has to go to work in the supermarket
I'm alone, I never stayed in a hospital before
I did visit my aunt in Atlanta when she was in the hospital and I was there
    for the summer
Doctors and nurses whispering
Tray drops suddenly and scares me out of my wits
A nurse helps a girl but she pulls the curtain & I can't see
My third grade class wrote letters to one of the children who was in the
    hospital but we never saw the hospital room
I can't sleep, there's too much noise
The nurse takes my temperature, I have 102 she gives me pills
Nobody tells me anything about what's happening or what to expect they
    just do things to me
The nurse's heels squeak on the floor and give me the shivers
A red lite goes on and off in the opposite room

As she reviewed her prewriting list, the student realized that her purpose was to write about her own short stay in the hospital after an accident. Most of the items recorded relate directly to that incident.

She saw that she had included on the list a number of impressions that, although hospital related, did not suit her purpose for this essay. She wanted to write about her own particular experiences, and so she ultimately rejected the items about her aunt in Atlanta, her mother going to work, and the third-grade classmate. With a clearer sense of how to proceed, she thought about a thesis sentence. The essay needed focus: exactly what point did she want to make in her essay? Simply presenting descriptive details might give readers a picture of the hospital but would not make an assertion about the experience. In fact she intended to write about how uncomfortable she felt and how the sights and sounds of the hospital contributed to that discomfort. She developed this thesis sentence:

I was uncomfortable in the hospital after my accident.

This thesis states an opinion, and so it helps the writer narrow her topic. Yet it is very broad, and some of the details on the list suggest a thesis that could more accurately express the writer's main point. After several more tries, she developed the thesis which includes, as you can see, an error in spelling and verb use, that appears in the draft:

There I layed stiff and silent in the night listening to the noises outside my room in the long corridors and watching everything that went on around me.

www.mhhe.com/
shortprose

For more help with prewriting, click on
Writing > Prewriting

First Draft

Prewriting leads to the first draft. Drafts are usually meant for the writer's eyes only; they are messy with rethinking, rewriting, and revision. Drafts help the writer figure out what to write by giving him or her a place to think on paper before having to make a public presentation of the writing. Everyone develops a personal style of draft writing, but many writers find that double-spacing, leaving wide margins, and writing on only one side of the paper are steps that make rewriting easier. If you write on a computer, you'll find you can easily revise and produce several drafts without discarding earlier versions of the essay.

In a first draft, a writer begins to shape paragraphs, to plan where to put each piece of the essay for maximum effect. Sometimes, a first draft doesn't have an introduction. The introduction can be written after the writer has finished the draft and has a better sense of what the essay is about. The audience will see only the final draft, after all, and will never know when the writer wrote the introduction.

Having finished the first draft, the writer tries to become the audience. How will the essay sound to someone else? Does it make sense? Are the ideas and expression clear? Is there a main point? Do all the ideas in the essay relate to this main point? Is there a coherent plan to the essay? Do ideas follow logically one from the next? Would someone unfamiliar with the topic be able to follow the ideas? Should more information be added? What should be left out?

In attempting to answer these questions, writers often try to find a friendly reader to look over the draft and give advice. Whatever else they may look for at this stage, they do not pay too much attention to spelling or grammar. A helpful reader will enable the writer to see the essay as the audience will see it, and suggest ways to reorganize and clarify ideas.

| www.mhhe.com/ **shortprose** | For more help with drafting, click on **Writing > Drafting and Revising** |

Here is an early draft of the essay written from the prewriting sample you observed on page 3.

DRAFT

ALL ALONE

There I sat all alone in my hard bed at the hospital. This was the place I most definitely did not want to be in. But because of my rollerskating accident I had no choice. I had to listen to the doctors and go for the necessary tests. There I layed stiff and silent in the night listening to the noises
5 outside my room in the long corridors and watching everything that went on around me.

As I layed there bundled up in my white sheets and the cold, hard steel bars of the bed surrounding me. I could hear everything that was

happening on my ward. Nurses would pass up and down the corridor with
their white rubber heal shoes squeeking on the white freshly polished   **10**
floors. The squeaking would send shrieking chills up my spin. Soft whispers were heard as doctors and nurses exchanged conversations. If
they only knew how disturbing it was for me to hear these slight mutters.
The most startling noise, though, was when a tray must have accidentally
slipped out of a nurses hand. The clatter of the tray echoed down the long, **15**
endless white corridors setting my nerves on end, I must have sat there
shaking for at least five minutes.

    Watching what was going on outside and inside my room was no
picnic either. In the hall a bright light shown enabling me to view the room
next door. As I was peering out my door, I noticed the little red light above **20**
the opposite door light flash along with a distantly faint ringing of a bell
down the hall. The nurse, in a clean white uniform, was there in an instant
to help the young curly haired girl. With a sturdy thrust of her hand the
nurse pulled the white cloth divider across the room concealing the two of
them in the corner.   **25**

    Two other nurses were making their rounds when they noticed I was
awake. One was in her mid forties, had brown hair, brown eyes and was
slim. The other nurse looked slightly older, taller than the first one, had
white streaks throughout her dark hair and was of medium build. The first
nurse said to me, "What are you doing up at this hour." I told her I could   **30**
not sleep. They noticed that I was perspiring and decided to take my
temperature. The first nurse left and returned with the thermometer. She
placed the cold, thin piece of glass into my warm mouth and put her cool
fingers around my wrist to take my pulse. They discovered I had a fever of
a hundred and two. The second nurse disappeared this time and returned **35**
holding a little silver packet with two tylonal aspirins in it. I took out the
two white tablets and swallowed them with water. Every so often until the
following morning either one of the nurses would saunter into my room to
check on me. All this happened in one night.

    Hospital visits can be very frightening. Nobody realizes the trauma   **40**
patients go threw.

    After discussing her draft with students in the class and with
her teacher, the writer of the hospital essay knew how to make revi-
sions. As she weighed her options, she knew that an even more
clearly stated thesis would help her readers understand what she
was trying to accomplish, and so she revised it further. The thesis
from the revised draft appears below:

I was supposed to be in the hospital to recuperate; instead of
sleeping, though, I lay there all night stiff and silent, uncomfortably
listening to the noises outside my room off the long hallway and
watching everything that happened around me.

Friendly readers suggested further that the writer needed to
fill in more information about the reason for her hospital stay and
also to provide more snapshots of the scene around her. If in fact
her objective was to portray the hospital as producing further discomfort, she needed to offer more sensory details than she had presented to her readers. (See pages 5–6.) Some readers felt that the
writer should better organize these details, perhaps considering the
sights and the sounds separately or pointing out first the activity in
the room and then the activity in the hallway, both places apparently contributing to the writer's unhappiness. And to improve the
coherence of the essay, the writer knew that in revising she should
look carefully at sentence transitions, particularly from paragraph
to paragraph.

Several readers felt that the conclusion was flat and that somehow the writer had to figure out a way to raise the issue of the
hospital's indifference to her discomfort. It was not enough to record
the unpleasantness; she also wanted to recommend some ways hospitals could avoid distressing their patients, and she decided that the
conclusion might be a good place to raise those issues.

Errors distracted readers even at the draft stage. These included
the sentence fragment on lines 7 and 8 and the comma splice
on line 17. Some spelling, usage, and grammar errors needed
attention–*layed* in line 7 (the correct verb form needed here is *lay*)
and *squeeking* for *squeaking* in line 10, for example. The use of
the passive voice in line 12 does not help the descriptive and narrative flow, and the writer knew to change the passive to active as
she revised. Simply by revising sentences some errors vanish and
others appear, and attentive writers know that a careful editing
prior to producing the final draft is critical.

Additional Drafts

After getting responses from a reader, the writer begins the second
draft. And the third. And maybe the fourth. No one can predict how
many drafts are necessary for a final essay, but very few writers get

by with fewer than two or three drafts. Revision usually involves working first on the clear expression of ideas and later on editing for spelling, grammatical correctness, and good sentence structure.

Here is a revised draft of the essay "All Alone." Note the comments in the margin.

REVISED DRAFT

ALL ALONE

Introductory paragraph: fills in accident details; leads comfortably to the thesis.

Thesis: last sentence of the first paragraph.

Concrete sensory details ("white sheets," "cold steel bars," "rubber heels squeaking," etc.): heighten readers' awareness of hospital room scene.

Frustration at disturbing room noises now clear; readers perceive essay's unity with repeated references to sounds.

"Perhaps the most startling noise"—effective link to thesis.

Transition from paragraph 2 to paragraph 3: "All the noises aside" links the topic of paragraph 3 to the topic of paragraph 2 and to the thesis.

I spent a long, unpleasant weekend in a bed at University Hospital, the result of a bad roller skating accident I had one Saturday afternoon last October. There might be a concussion; there might he broken bones—and so I had no choice but to listen to the doctors and go for necessary tests. I was supposed to be in the hospital to recuperate; instead of sleeping, though, I lay there all night, stiff and silent, uncomfortably listening to the noises outside my room off the long hallway and watching everything that happened around me.

Bundled up in my white sheets and surrounded by the cold steel bars of my bed I heard every little sound in my ward all night long. Nurses, their rubber heels squeaking on the freshly polished floors, passed up and down the corridor. I heard soft whispers as one doctor in a green shirt spoke to two orderlies leaning against the wall with their arms folded. Occasionally one of them would laugh and the other two would giggle and say, "Sh! Sh!" If they only knew how disturbing it was for me to hear their muttering! At one point I almost shouted "Would you all get out of here!" but I didn't have the courage, and I pulled the blanket over my head instead. Perhaps the most startling noise, though, was the sound of a tray that must have accidentally slipped out of a nurse's hand far beyond my view. I jumped up as the clatter echoed down the long, endless white corridors, setting my nerves on end. Perspiration streaming down my face, I must have sat there in my bed shaking for at least five minutes.

All the noises aside, watching the activity outside and inside my room disturbed me, too. Across the hall a little red light above the door of the opposite room suddenly flashed on and off. A nurse in a clean white uniform was there in an instant to help a young, curly haired girl twisting and crying on her bed. A bright light in the hall enabled me to see the actions clearly. With a sturdy thrust of her hand the nurse pulled the white cloth divider across the room, concealing the two of them in the corner. However, I saw the nurse's shadow moving up and down, back and forth, until the child quieted down.

Soon after I noted all this, two other nurses making their rounds saw that I was still awake. One, a slim woman in her mid forties with brown eyes, said in a loud voice, "What are you doing up at this hour, dear? It's after two AM." When I said I couldn't sleep, they saw how clammy I was, and the one who spoke to me rushed off for a thermometer. Placing the rigid glass rod in my mouth, she took my pulse with cool fingers at my wrist. "A hundred and two," she said. "Wanda, bring this girl something for her fever." The second nurse disappeared this time and returned holding a silver packet of Tylenol, and I swallowed the pills with water from the drinking glass on my bedstand. Every so often until morning one of the nurses would saunter in, touch my brow, and make cheerful but noisy conversation. I knew they were trying to help, but all this activity did not make me feel any better. It made me feel worse.

Because hospital stays can be very frightening, hospital employees must realize the trauma patients go through just lying in their beds wondering what will happen to them next. The slightest sound, the barest visible action magnifies a million times in a tense person's mind. Couldn't the admitting clerk, a floor nurse, or an intern explain to patients about what to expect at the hospital? I would have liked knowing all about the tests I'd have to go through, but also would have liked knowing not to expect much sleep. If I knew in advance of all the noise and activity I might have relaxed.

The words "watching the activity outside and inside my room disturbed me, too" set the topic of the next part of the essay.

Concrete sensory detail holds readers' interest and brings scene to life: "red light above the door"; "clean white uniform"; "curly haired girl twisting and crying on her bed"; "nurse's shadow moving up and down, back and forth."

Clear connection to previous paragraph; "Soon after I noted all this" provides transition, helping to build essay's coherence.

Nurses' spoken words add life to the essay.

Short, succinct final sentence very effective in this paragraph.

Conclusion adds depth to the essay; it places narrative and descriptive details in a larger, more profound framework.

www.mhhe.com/
shortprose

For more help with revising, click on
Writing > Drafting and Revising

We call attention particularly to the greatly improved last paragraph in the revised draft, the writer's conclusion. This is no mere restatement of the topic. The writer has used the experience that she revealed in the rest of the essay to establish a new context for the topic. What did her unpleasant stay in University Hospital tell her? Hospitals don't realize the trauma even a short stay can produce in a patient, and if only hospital staff would explain what to expect in advance, patients might not have such a rough time. We can see how the body paragraphs lead her to reach this conclusion and feel satisfied that the writer has led us to new insights based on her experiences.

www.mhhe.com/
shortprose

For more help with conclusions, click on
Writing > Conclusions

Throughout the revised essay, the writer has tightened her sentences by combining a number of them and by eliminating unnecessary words and phrases. In addition, we note a reduction of distracting errors in sentence structure and spelling. Efforts to eliminate errors and improve language and sentences will continue as the writer moves toward producing a final draft and formally edits her paper.

www.mhhe.com/
shortprose

For more help with editing, click on
**Editing > Coordination and
          Subordination**
**Editing > Eliminating
          Redundancies**
Editing > Spelling

Final Draft

The final draft is intended for public, rather than private, reading. It must be the writer's best effort. Most editors and teachers require final drafts to be double-spaced, with wide margins, and printed by means of a computer; and clearly identified with the writer's name, the date, and information to locate the writer (such as class code or home address). The four writers in this chapter represent a variety of approaches to both the craft and the inspiration of writing.

Jennifer Lee investigates the relation between standard written English and instant-messaging language created by the online population of computer users. Kurt Vonnegut Jr. sees style as the defining essence of good writing. Amy Tan finds her writer's voice when she realizes that her mother is the ideal audience. Like William Zinsser pleading for the preciseness that comes only with simplicity, Tan advises us to aim for direct and simple language instead of academic jargon or pretentious style.

The four writers represented here also introduce expository techniques discussed in subsequent chapters. Careful examination of their sources of inspiration *and* their revelations about the nuts and bolts of how to get the writing done prepares the way for later chapters and writing assignments.

www.mhhe.com/
shortprose

For more help mixing the patterns, click on
**Writing > Writing Tutor:
Blended Essay**

Finally, though the Internet and CD-ROMs increasingly replace the printed page, the basic medium of communication is still words. Whether we scratch them onto stone tablets, draw them on parchment with turkey feathers, or type them into a computer, we still use words. Without writing, we risk the loss of our political freedom and our personal history. With words, we pass ideas and values on from one generation to the next. The words of Henry Miller will always ring true: "Writing, like life itself, is a voyage of discovery."

USING AND MIXING PATTERNS

Essay writing presents a challenge to beginning writers. Even for an accomplished and experienced writer, facing a blank page can be scary. However, attention to the writing process and some careful thought about what you are trying to accomplish can make the task more manageable. Discovering and exploring the purpose for a piece of writing will help you decide what your essay should be and what organizing techniques you can use.

We call these organizing techniques *patterns,* or rhetorical modes. The four major modes, or patterns, of writing are narration, description, exposition, and argumentation-persuasion. To tell a story, a writer uses narration. To bring to life a situation or scene, a writer draws on description, vivid words, and phrasing that "paint a picture" for the reader. To explain an idea or situation, a writer uses exposition.

We can further break exposition down into six different writing patterns: illustration, in which the use of examples makes an idea clearer; comparison and contrast, which exposes two or more objects or ideas in relation to each other; definition, which explains the meaning of certain words; classification, which establishes categories for a subject; process analysis, which outlines the methods for doing or making something; and cause-and-effect analysis, which examines a subject for its origins or results.

The final, and perhaps most important, writing pattern is argumentation-persuasion, in which a writer makes a claim concerning a controversial topic and/or encourages the reader to engage in a course of action. The following chart gives an overview of these rhetorical modes, what purpose they serve in an essay, and an example of what kind of essay you might find them in.

Rhetorical Mode	*Purpose*	*Example*
Description	To give the reader the texture of reality, to evoke images and other sensations through words	A travel essay
Narration	To tell a story	A personal essay recounting an important event from one's childhood
Process Analysis	To show how something is done or how something happens	Written instructions for how to create a movie on your computer
Illustration	To give examples to support an important idea	An essay about victims of drug abuse in a community
Comparison/ Contrast	To set two or more subjects side by side to show their similarities or differences	A critical article explaining why one movie is better than another movie

Rhetorical Mode	Purpose	Example
Cause-and-Effect Analysis	To explain the reason for an event or the effects of an event	An essay about the effects of the 2004 tsunami on tourism in Southeast Asia
Classification	To categorize information to show relationships between items or concepts	A humorous essay about the many kinds of men women meet when Internet dating
Definition	To explain the meaning of a word or concept	An essay exploring the various meanings of the word *bad* in slang
Argumentation and Persuasion	To convince readers to change their views or to act in a certain way	An opinion piece in a newspaper about drug sentencing legislation before Congress

Choosing a mode of writing can help you focus your thoughts, but essays would be impoverished if you were forced to choose just one of these patterns and stick to it. Thus, writers often choose a dominant mode for an essay but then draw on other modes to achieve their goals. For example, suppose you want to write an essay about the time your girlfriend or boyfriend broke up with you. You would use narration as the dominant mode, unfolding the events as they occurred. But your essay would be ineffective if you didn't at least include some physical description of your lost love, and to explain what went wrong and why your relationship fell apart, you'd need to draw on cause-and-effect analysis. Or imagine that you want to write a persuasive essay to convince your readers to adopt a pet from an animal shelter. Your essay would fall flat without an emotional appeal, so in addition to drawing on persuasion, you'd also want to describe a cute puppy or kitten; you might also want to lead your reader through the process of adopting an animal, classify the kinds of animals that end up in shelters, analyze the causes of pet abandonment, or tell a personal narrative based on your own experience adopting a pet.

Mixing rhetorical modes can improve any essay. Consider this paragraph by acclaimed essayist Scott Russell Sanders. The dominant mode in Sanders's essay is classification, but there are several patterns at work here.

Sanders is using narration here. This an event that happened, and he is going to tell it as it happened.

The author uses vivid description, pointing out visual images that will make this scene more real in the mind's eye of the reader.

Comparison and contrast will be an important part of any classification essay, and this is true of Sanders's essay as well.

The author's main idea is dependent on a certain definition of manhood, and here he offers a couple of preliminary definitions—he will offer more later.

The first men, besides my father, I remember seeing were black convicts and white guards, in the cottonfield across the road from our farm on the outskirts of Memphis. I must have been three or four. The prisoners wore dingy gray-and-black zebra suits, heavy as canvas, sodden with sweat. Hatless, stooped, they chopped weeds in the fierce heat, row after row, breathing the acrid dust of boll-weevil poison. The overseers wore dazzling white shirts and broad shadowy hats. The oiled barrels of their shotguns flashed in the sunlight. Their faces in memory are utterly blank. Of course, those men, white and black, have become for me an emblem of racial hatred. But they have also come to stand for the twin poles of my early vision of manhood—the brute toiling animal and the boss.

We discuss all major rhetorical patterns at length in subsequent chapters. Moreover, the last essay in each chapter in this book demonstrates a blending of patterns and is followed by a "Mixing Patterns" assignment that asks you to identify how the writer of that essay combines the various rhetorical modes. Use the questions to develop your understanding of the importance and power of drawing on a range of strategies and staying flexible after you ask yourself that original question—What is this essay for?

This overview sketches in some of the important steps and strategies in the writing process. But you don't want to lose the idea that writing is a process both of inspiration and of craft. Many writers have tried to explain how the two connect in their own particular efforts to create. The novelist and short story writer Katherine Anne Porter, for example, tells how inspiration becomes communication in her writing: "Now and again thousands of memories converge, harmonize, and arrange themselves around a central idea in a coherent form, and I write. . . ." Jean Cocteau, the playwright, asserts the need to shape inspiration into language for a page of writing: "To write, to conquer ink and paper, accumulate letters and paragraphs, divide them with periods and commas, is a different matter from carrying around the dream of a play or a book." The point made by Porter and Cocteau is that writing emerges from both creativity and skill, instruction and technique, talent and effort. As we said, writing is a process *and* a craft.

I Think, Therefore IM

Jennifer Lee

Jennifer Lee was born in New York City in 1976 and grew up there. Lee attended Harvard University, where she majored in applied mathematics and economics, but she developed an interest in current affairs while working with low-income students. After graduation in 1999, Lee became a reporter for the *New York Times,* covering the metropolitan desk and cultural affairs. Her book, *The Fortune Cookie Chronicles* (2008), explores the history of Chinese food as well as its role in American culture. In the following selection, which appeared in the September 19, 2002, issue of the *New York Times,* Lee examines the impact of instant-messaging shorthand on students' writing styles.

PREREADING: THINKING ABOUT THE ESSAY IN ADVANCE

Reflect on your online writing habits. Does online writing have a style of its own? How does online writing differ from "standard" writing that appears in newspapers, magazines, and books—as well as essays you compose for college courses?

Words to Watch

lingua franca (par. 8)   a hybrid or mixed language used for communication
errant (par. 11)   straying from what is right; wrong
riddled (par. 14)   shot through; made holes in
milieu (par. 18)   surroundings; environment

1   Each September Jacqueline Harding prepares a classroom presentation on the common writing mistakes she sees in her students' work.

2   Ms. Harding, an eighth-grade English teacher at Viking Middle School in Guernee, Ill., scribbles the words that have plagued generations of schoolchildren across her whiteboard:

3   There. Their. They're.

4   Your. You're.

5   To. Too. Two.

6   Its. It's.

7   This September, she has added a new list: u, r, ur, b4, wuz, cuz, 2.

When she asked her students how many of them used shortcuts 8
like these in their writing, Ms. Harding said, she was not surprised
when most of them raised their hands. This, after all, is their online
lingua franca: English adapted for the spitfire conversational style
of Internet instant messaging.

Ms. Harding, who has seen such shortcuts creep into student 9
papers over the last two years, said she gave her students a warning: "If I see this in your assignments, I will take points off."

"Kids should know the difference," said Ms. Harding, who 10
decided to address this issue head-on this year. "They should know
where to draw the line between formal writing and conversational
writing."

As more and more teenagers socialize online, middle school 11
and high school teachers like Ms. Harding are increasingly seeing
a breezy form of Internet English jump from e-mail into schoolwork. To their dismay, teachers say that papers are being written
with shortened words, improper capitalization and punctuation,
and characters like &, $ and @.

Teachers have deducted points, drawn red circles and tsk-tsked 12
at their classes. Yet the errant forms continue. "It stops being funny
after you repeat yourself a couple of times," Ms. Harding said.

But teenagers, whose social life can rely as much these days 13
on text communication as the spoken word, say that they use
instant-messaging shorthand without thinking about it. They write
to one another as much as they write in school, or more.

"You are so used to abbreviating things, you just start doing 14
it unconsciously on schoolwork and reports and other things,"
said Eve Brecker, 15, a student at Montclair High School in New
Jersey.

Ms. Brecker once handed in a midterm exam riddled with 15
instant-messaging shorthand. "I had an hour to write an essay on
Romeo and Juliet," she said. "I just wanted to finish before my
time was up. I was writing fast and carelessly. I spelled 'you' 'u.'"
She got a C.

Even terms that cannot be expressed verbally are making their 16
way into papers. Melanie Weaver was stunned by some of the term
papers she received from a 10th-grade class she recently taught as
part of an internship. "They would be trying to make a point in a
paper, they would put a smiley face in the end," said Ms. Weaver,
who teaches at Alvernia College in Reading, Pa. "If they were
presenting an argument and they needed to present an opposite
view, they would put a frown."

17   As Trisha Fogarty, a sixth-grade teacher at Houlton Southside School in Houlton, Maine, puts it, today's students are "Generation Text."

18   Almost 60 percent of the online population under age 17 uses instant messaging, according to Nielsen/NetRatings. In addition to cellphone text messaging, Weblogs and e-mail, it has become a popular means of flirting, setting up dates, asking for help with homework and keeping in contact with distant friends. The abbreviations are a natural outgrowth of this rapid-fire style of communication.

19   "They have a social life that centers around typed communication," said Judith S. Donath, a professor at the Massachusetts Institute of Technology's Media Lab who has studied electronic communication. "They have a writing style that has been nurtured in a teenage social milieu."

20   Some teachers see the creeping abbreviations as part of a continuing assault of technology on formal written English. Others take it more lightly, saying that it is just part of the larger arc of language evolution.

21   "To them it's not wrong," said Ms. Harding, who is 28. "It's acceptable because it's in their culture. It's hard enough to teach them the art of formal writing. Now we've got to overcome this new instant-messaging language."

22   Ms. Harding noted that in some cases the shorthand isn't even shorter. "I understand 'cuz,' but what's with the 'wuz'? It's the same amount of letters as 'was,' so what's the point?" she said.

23   Deborah Bova, who teaches eighth-grade English at Raymond Park Middle School in Indianapolis, thought her eyesight was failing several years ago when she saw the sentence "B4 we perform, ppl have 2 practice" on a student assignment.

24   "I thought, 'My God, what is this?'" Ms. Bova said. "Have they lost their minds?"

25   The student was summoned to the board to translate the sentence into standard English: "Before we perform, people have to practice." She realized that the students thought she was out of touch. "It was like 'Get with it, Bova,'" she said.

26   Ms. Bova had a student type up a reference list of translations for common instant-messaging expressions. She posted a copy on the bulletin board by her desk and took another one home to use while grading.

27   Students are sometimes unrepentant.

28   "They were astonished when I began to point these things out to them," said Henry Assetto, a social studies teacher at Twin

Valley High School in Elverson, Pa. "Because I am a history teacher, they did not think a history teacher would be checking up on their grammer or their spelling," said Mr. Assetto, who has been teaching for 34 years.

But Montana Hodgen, 16, another Montclair student, said she 29 was so accustomed to instant-messaging abbreviations that she often read right past them. She proofread a paper last year only to get it returned with the messaging abbreviations circled in red.

"I was so used to reading what my friends wrote to me on 30 Instant Messenger that I didn't even realize that there was something wrong," she said. She said her ability to separate formal and informal English declined the more she used instant messages. "Three years ago, if I had seen that, I would have been 'What is that?'"

The spelling checker doesn't always help either, students say. 31 For one, Microsoft Word's squiggly red spell-check lines don't appear beneath single letters and numbers such as u, r, c, 2 and 4. Nor do they catch words which have numbers in them such as "l8r" and "b4" by default.

Teenagers have essentially developed an unconscious "accent" 32 in their typing, Professor Donath said. "They have gotten facile at typing and they are not paying attention."

Teenagers have long pushed the boundaries of spoken language, 33 introducing words that then become passe with adult adoption. Now teenagers are taking charge and pushing the boundaries of written language. For them, expressions like "oic" (oh I see), "nm" (not much), "jk" (just kidding) and "lol" (laughing out loud), "brb" (be right back), "ttyl" (talk to you later) are as standard as conventional English.

"There is no official English language," said Jesse Sheidlower, 34 the North American editor of the Oxford English Dictionary. "Language is spread because not anyone dictates any one thing to happen. The decisions are made by the language and the people who use the language."

Some teachers find the new writing style alarming. "First of 35 all, it's very rude, and it's very careless," said Lois Moran, a middle school English teacher at St. Nicholas School in Jersey City.

"They should be careful to write properly and not to put these little 36 codes in that they are in such a habit of writing to each other," said Ms. Moran, who has lectured her eighth-grade class on such mistakes.

Others say that the instant-messaging style might simply be a 36 fad, something that students will grow out of. Or they see it as an opportunity to teach students about the evolution of language.

38   "I turn it into a very positive teachable moment for kids in the class," said Erika V. Karres, an assistant professor at the University of North Carolina at Chapel Hill who trains student teachers. She shows students how English has evolved since Shakespeare's time. "Imagine Langston Hughes's writing in quick texting instead of 'Langston writing,'" she said. "It makes teaching and learning so exciting."

39   Other teachers encourage students to use messaging shorthand to spark their thinking processes. "When my children are writing first drafts, I don't care how they spell anything, as long as they are writing," said Ms. Fogarty, the sixth-grade teacher from Houlton, Maine. "If this lingo gets their thoughts and ideas onto paper quicker, the more power to them." But during editing and revising, she expects her students to switch to standard English.

40   Ms. Bova shares the view that instant-messaging language can help free up their creativity. With the help of students, she does not even need the cheat sheet to read the shorthand anymore.

41   "I think it's a plus," she said. "And I would say that with a + sign."

BUILDING VOCABULARY

Lee sprinkles her article with words, abbreviations, and terms drawn from online communication. Prepare a list of the "instant communication" forms that appear in the essay, and offer definitions or explanations for them.

THINKING CRITICALLY ABOUT THE ESSAY

Understanding the Writer's Ideas

1. In what ways, according to Lee, do instant messaging and other forms of social communication on the Internet affect students' classroom writing?
2. How do teachers respond to student writing that shows the effects of online communication? Do all teachers respond the same way? Justify your response.
3. What does Lee mean by "language evolution"? Where does this term appear in the essay? What is the effect of technology on this evolution?
4. Why do some students resist teachers' attempts to purge their essays of online writing styles?

5. According to some observers, how might online writing styles influence critical and creative thinking?

Understanding the Writer's Techniques

1. What is the thesis of Lee's essay? Does she state her main idea or imply it? Explain your response.
2. Lee jumps right into her subject without any formal introduction. Do you find this opening effective? Why or why not?
3. What elements of a journalistic style do you detect in this essay? How do these features make the article accessible to a reading audience or literate public? What assumptions does Lee make about her audience?
4. Why does Lee use so many examples drawn from online communication? What is the effect?
5. What comparisons and contrasts does Lee draw between students' online communication styles and teachers' expectations? What tone or attitude does she adopt? What is her purpose? What does she hope to accomplish?
6. How does the conclusion of the essay affect your overall response to the article?

Exploring the Writer's Ideas

1. Lee suggests that the connections between online writing and school writing are more complicated than one might originally think. What do you think about this issue?
2. The writer focuses, in large part, on the responses of teachers to student writing that is "riddled," as one instructor contends, with terrible forms of online style. What is your opinion of such teachers? Do they have a valid concern?
3. Based on your reading of Lee's essay, what is the best approach to the implicit clash between instant online writing styles and the expectations of teachers that their students compose essays in standard English?

IDEAS FOR WRITING

Prewriting

Spend a few minutes jotting down abbreviations and images (for example, *OMG, btw,* ☺) that you or friends use when communicating

online. Share these abbreviations and their meanings during classroom discussion.

Guided Writing

Write your own essay titled "I Think, Therefore IM."

1. Begin briskly, as Lee does, by reciting some of the online
    abbreviations that you use when blogging, instant messaging,
    or employing other online communication styles. Establish
    your thesis based on these examples.
2. Next, recount the ways in which you think these online commu-
    nication forms help or hinder students when writing for courses.
3. As you develop the essay, support your own observations by
    referring to some of the teachers and experts who appear in
    Lee's article.
4. Throughout the essay, try to maintain a balanced tone, laying
    out the pros and cons of online communication styles.
5. Write a conclusion that circles back to your introduction and
    adds substance to it.

Thinking and Writing Collaboratively

In groups of three or four, combine your lists of online abbreviations
from the prewriting exercise, and then compose (like Ms. Bova in
Lee's essay) a reference list of translations for common instant-
messaging expressions.

Writing About the Text

Write an essay in which you analyze Lee's journalistic style.
Explain the ways she develops her article and tries to appeal to a
specific audience of *New York Times* readers. What assumptions
does she make about her primary audience?

More Writing Projects

1. In a journal entry, recount your online social interactions for
    the day and the ways you communicated with various people.
2. In an extended paragraph, write about one blog that you find
    appealing for its style and format.
3. Write an essay in which you argue for or against the idea
    that instant-messaging styles can enhance a student's critical
    thinking and writing ability.

How to Write with Style
Kurt Vonnegut Jr.

Kurt Vonnegut, born in 1922 in Indianapolis, Indiana, is one of America's most imaginative writers. Called by some a modern-day Mark Twain, he frequently draws on science fiction to cast a fresh light on earthly life. In so doing, he highlights the powerful presence of randomness and coincidence in human society, but he also discovers reasons for wonder and, not least, humor. Some of his best-known books, such as *Slaughterhouse-Five* (1969) and *Breakfast of Champions* (1973), are biting satires on American politics. Vonnegut continued his attack on American society in a 2004 essay online called "Cold Turkey" <www.inthesetimes.com/site/main/article/733/>. Vonnegut said that he owed his outlook, at least in part, to the sometimes dismaying facts of his biography, such as that his mother committed suicide on Mother's Day 1942 or that, during World War II, he had to live through the firebombing of Dresden by the United States and Britain because he was being held there by the Germans as a prisoner of war. Vonnegut died in 2007. In this iconoclastic selection, Vonnegut, who was not shy about creating an interesting persona for himself as a hook for his readers, recommends the same to young writers and shares other secrets of his trade.

PREREADING: THINKING ABOUT
THE ESSAY IN ADVANCE

What are your thoughts about "writing with style"? What does the phrase mean? What qualities of writing do you admire? What qualities of writing do you not admire?

Words to Watch

piquant (par. 10)   pleasantly disturbing
galvanized (par. 10)   coated
locutions (par. 11)   speaking style
higgledy-piggledy (par. 15)   in disorder or confusion
egalitarian (par. 20)   equal rights for all citizens
aristocrats (par. 20)   members of the nobility

Newspaper reporters and technical writers are trained to reveal   1
almost nothing about themselves in their writings. This makes
them freaks in the world of writers, since almost all of the other

ink-stained wretches in that world reveal a lot about themselves to readers. We call these revelations, accidental and intentional, elements of literary style.

2   These revelations are fascinating to us as readers. They tell us what sort of person it is with whom we are spending time. Does the writer sound ignorant or informed, crazy or sane, stupid or bright, crooked or honest, humorless or playful—? And on and on.

3   When you yourself put words on paper, remember that the most damning revelation you can make about yourself is that you do not know what is interesting and what is not. Don't you yourself like or dislike writers mainly for what they choose to show you or make you think about? Did you ever admire an empty-headed writer for his or her mastery of the language? No.

4   So your own winning literary style must begin with interesting ideas in your head. Find a subject you care about and which you in your heart feel others should care about. It is this genuine caring, and not your games with language, which will be the most compelling and seductive element in your style.

5   I am not urging you to write a novel, by the way—although I would not be sorry if you wrote one, provided you genuinely cared about something. A petition to the mayor about a pothole in front of your house or a love letter to the girl next door will do.

6   Do not ramble, though.

7   As for your use of language: Remember that two great masters of our language, William Shakespeare and James Joyce, wrote sentences which were almost childlike when their subjects were most profound. "To be or not to be?" asks Shakespeare's Hamlet. The longest word is three letters long. Joyce, when he was frisky, could put together a sentence as intricate and glittering as a necklace for Cleopatra, but my favorite sentence in his short story "Eveline" is this one: "She was tired." At that point in the story, no other words could break the heart of a reader as those words do.

8   Simplicity of language is not only reputable, but perhaps even sacred. The Bible opens with a sentence well within the writing skills of a lively fourteen-year-old: "In the beginning God created the heavens and the earth."

9   It may be that you, too, are capable of making necklaces for Cleopatra, so to speak. But your eloquence should be the servant of the ideas in your head. Your rule might be this: If a sentence no matter how excellent does not illuminate my subject in some new and useful way, scratch it out. Here is the same rule paraphrased

to apply to storytelling, to fiction: Never include a sentence which does not either remark on character or advance the action.

The writing style which is most natural for you is bound to echo speech you heard when a child. English was the novelist Joseph Conrad's third language, and much that seems piquant in his use of English was no doubt colored by his first language, which was Polish. And lucky indeed is the writer who has grown up in Ireland, for the English spoken there is so amusing and musical. I myself grew up in Indianapolis, Indiana, where common speech sounds like a band saw cutting galvanized tin, and employs a vocabulary as unornamental as a monkey wrench. 10

In some of the more remote hollows of Appalachia, children still grow up hearing songs and locutions of Elizabethan times. Yes, and many Americans grow up hearing a language other than English, or an English dialect a majority of Americans cannot understand. 11

All these varieties of speech are beautiful, just as the varieties of butterflies are beautiful. No matter what your first language, you should treasure it all your life. If it happens not to be standard English, and if it shows itself when you write standard English, the result is usually delightful, like a very pretty girl with one eye that is green and one that is blue. 12

I myself find that I trust my own writing most, and others seem to trust it most, too, when I sound most like a person from Indianapolis, which is what I am. What alternatives do I have? The one most vehemently recommended by teachers has no doubt been pressed on you, as well: that I write like cultivated Englishmen of a century or more ago. 13

I used to be exasperated by such teachers, but am no more. I understand now that all those antique essays and stories with which I was to compare my own work were not magnificent for their datedness or foreignness, but for saying precisely what their authors meant them to say. My teachers wished me to write accurately, always selecting the most effective words, and relating the words to one another unambiguously, rigidly, like parts of a machine. The teachers did not want to turn me into an Englishman after all. They hoped that I would become understandable—and therefore understood. 14

And there went my dream of doing with words what Pablo Picasso did with paint or what any number of jazz idols did with 15 music. If I broke all the rules of punctuation, had words mean whatever I wanted them to mean, and strung them together higgledy-piggledy, I would simply not be understood. So you, too, had better avoid Picasso-style or jazz-style writing, if you have something worth saying and wish to be understood.

16   If it were only teachers who insisted that modern writers stay close to literary styles of the past, we might reasonably ignore them. But readers insist on the very same thing. They want our pages to look very much like pages they have seen before.

17   Why? It is because they themselves have a tough job to do, and they need all the help they can get from us. They have to identify thousands of little marks on paper, and make sense of them immediately. They have to *read,* an art so difficult that most people do not really master it even after having studied it all through grade school and high school—for twelve long years.

18   So this discussion, like all discussions of literary styles, must finally acknowledge that our stylistic options as writers are neither numerous nor glamorous, since our readers are bound to be such imperfect artists. Our audience requires us to be sympathetic and patient teachers, ever willing to simplify and clarify—whereas we would rather soar high above the crowd, singing like nightingales.

19   That is the bad news. The good news is that we Americans are governed under a unique Constitution, which allows us to write whatever we please without fear of punishment. So the most meaningful aspect of our styles, which is what we choose to write about, is unlimited.

20   Also: We are members of an egalitarian society, so there is no reason for us to write, in case we are not classically educated aristocrats, as though we were classically educated aristocrats.

21   For a discussion of literary style in a narrower sense, in a more technical sense, I commend to your attention *The Elements of Style* by William Strunk, Jr., and E. B. White (Macmillan, 1979). It contains such rules as this: "A participial phrase at the beginning of a sentence must refer to the grammatical subject," and so on. E. B. White is, of course, one of the most admirable literary stylists this country has so far produced.

22   You should realize, too, that no one would care how well or badly Mr. White expressed himself, if he did not have perfectly enchanting things to say.

BUILDING VOCABULARY

Use *context clues* (see Glossary) to determine the meanings of the words below. Use a dictionary to check your definitions.

a. intentional (par. 1)
b. compelling (par. 4)
c. intricate (par. 7)
d. reputable (par. 8)
e. eloquence (par. 9)
f. illuminate (par. 9)
g. exasperated (par. 14)

THINKING CRITICALLY ABOUT THE ESSAY

Understanding the Writer's Ideas

1. What is the difference between newspaper reporters and technical writers and the "ink-stained wretches," as Vonnegut puts it?
2. According to the writer, what is the best way to begin a "winning literary style" (par. 4)?
3. Why does Vonnegut believe that simple writing is best, and how does he try to prove his point?
4. What is the writer's attitude toward standard language versus the language "you heard when a child" (par. 10)?
5. For Vonnegut, writers should avoid "jazz-style" writing. Why?
6. How does the writer come to the conclusion that reading is "an art so difficult that most people do not really master it" (par. 17)?
7. Why does Vonnegut say it is good news that writers in America are "governed under a unique Constitution" (par. 19)?
8. What is the benefit of being a writer in an "egalitarian society" as opposed to an aristocratic one, according to Vonnegut (par. 20)?

Understanding the Writer's Techniques

1. What is the thesis of this essay? Who is Vonnegut's audience here? How can you tell?
2. Why does Vonnegut begin his essay with references to newspaper reporters and technical writers if he does not mention them in the rest of the text?

3. Why is the *transition* (see Glossary) at the beginning of paragraph 3 effective, given the title of this essay?

4. Vonnegut suggests that writers use sentences that are almost "childlike." How can you tell that he follows his own advice?

5. What purpose does using direct quotes from William Shakespeare and James Joyce serve?

6. What is the effect of Vonnegut's switching to the first person in paragraph 13, pointing to the Indianapolis speech in his own writing?

7. How does the question "Why?" (par. 17) serve as a clear shift in the idea development of the essay?

8. The word "Also" in paragraph 20 is followed by a colon to signal a transition. Check a grammar handbook. Is this the way transitions should be punctuated?

9. Why does Vonnegut recommend the book *The Elements of Style?* Hasn't he already instructed us in these matters himself?

10. Explain how and why Vonnegut's last paragraph returns the reader to the essay's main idea in paragraph 3.

Exploring the Writer's Ideas

1. Vonnegut believes that since newspaper reporters and technical writers reveal almost nothing about themselves, they are less fascinating to us. Based on your experiences as a reader, do you agree? Why or why not?

2. If you care deeply about a subject, Vonnegut claims this will make your writing more interesting to others. Has this been true in your experiences as a writer? Explain.

3. Vonnegut makes the case (par. 12) that using nonstandard English can make a writer's work "beautiful." Do you agree with him? Why or why not?

4. Vonnegut says you should use the speech you heard as a child (par. 10) to achieve a successful writing style. Then he says that if he broke all the rules of language, he "would simply not be understood" (par. 15). Is Vonnegut contradicting himself? What if a person's childhood language is not understandable outside his or her community?

5. Vonnegut reminds us that we live in an "egalitarian" society. What implications does this have for the development of your writing style?

6. Given a choice, which writers would you rather read—those that reveal "nothing about themselves" or those whose "revelations are fascinating"? Explain your preferences.

IDEAS FOR WRITING

Prewriting

Make a list of the steps you take in the process of doing something that you have excelled in (for example, gardening, cooking, playing sports, making friends, and so on).

Guided Writing

Write an essay called "How to _____ with Style." Fill in the blank with something you do well, such as skiing, painting a room, and so on. Instruct the reader on how and why he or she should also do this activity and what you mean by doing it with style.

1. Begin by defining the most important quality you think someone needs to be successful at this activity.
2. In the next two or three paragraphs, elaborate on how and why this quality will help ensure a person's success in this activity.
3. Describe another quality needed to be a success at this activity. Give two or three paragraphs of supporting detail to show how others have been successful at this activity because they too have had the quality you just described. Here you should make clear what doing the activity "with style" means.
4. Tell if there is any reason why this activity can or cannot be done by most people. Is a special quality needed? Is this something a child can do? Why or why not?
5. Give personal testimony of how and why being a success at this activity is simple or complicated for you. What personal traits have you relied on to be a success at this activity?
6. Warn readers about the most common mistakes made by those who do not succeed at this activity, and suggest how to avoid such mistakes.
7. End with why you think this activity might (or might not) be well suited for people living in a society where they have the constitutional right to live freely. (Consider recommending a book that might assist the reader with this activity.)

Thinking and Writing Collaboratively

Write a short letter using the words of love you would share with someone close to you. Then write out a dictionary definition of *love*. Form groups of three students each and share your letters and definitions with the members of the group, asking them: Which words would most appeal to you? Why? Note the responses and write an essay on how to write a love letter.

Writing About the Text

Here is an essay on style that argues "genuine caring" about the subject is the secret of style. Do you think this is true of Vonnegut himself in this essay? What evidence would you cite, for and against? Write an essay about this selection in which you examine whether Vonnegut himself actually applies the ideas he prescribes for young writers.

More Writing Projects

1. In your journal, write a short entry in language that you heard as a child. Try to capture the sounds and traits that will amuse and delight readers.
2. Write two paragraphs that contrast your language use. In paragraph one, describe with examples the kind of language you use with your friends and family. In paragraph two, describe with examples the kind of language you use with your professors or strangers.
3. Write an essay on something you care strongly about, using the language you feel best reveals something personal about yourself, as Vonnegut suggests.

Simplicity

William Zinsser

This selection is a chapter from one of the most successful books about writing, titled *On Writing Well*. The *New York Times* has compared William Zinsser's book, first published in 1976, with the classics in the field, saying it "belongs on any shelf of serious reference works for writers." From 1959 to 1987 Zinsser, the author of fifteen books, was general editor of the Book-of-the-Month Club. He now teaches in New York City at the New School and the Columbia University Graduate School of Journalism. In this selection, Zinsser begins with a fairly pessimistic analysis of the clutter that pervades and degrades American writing, and he offers many examples to prove his point. Zinsser deals with almost all major aspects of the writing process—thinking, composing, awareness of the reader, self-discipline, rewriting, and editing—and concludes that simplicity is the key to them all.

| www.mhhe.com/ **shortprose** | To learn more about Zinsser, click on **More Resources > Chapter 1 > William Zinsser** |

PREREADING: THINKING ABOUT THE ESSAY IN ADVANCE

Do you find writing difficult or easy? Why? What is there about the act of writing that annoys, frustrates, or satisfies you?

Words to Watch

decipher (par. 2)   to make out the meaning of something obscure
adulterants (par. 3)   added substances that make something impure or inferior
mollify (par. 4)   to appease; to soothe
spell (par. 4)   a short period of time
assailed (par. 8)   attacked with words or physical violence
tenacious (par. 10)   stubborn; persistent
rune (par. 10)   character in an ancient alphabet
bearded (par. 12)   approached or confronted boldly

Clutter is the disease of American writing. We are a society stran- 1
gling in unnecessary words, circular constructions, pompous frills
and meaningless jargon.

2   Who can understand the clotted language of everyday American commerce: the memo, the corporation report, the business letter, the notice from the bank explaining its latest "simplified" statement? What member of an insurance or medical plan can decipher the brochure explaining his costs and benefits? What father or mother can put together a child's toy from the instructions on the box? Our national tendency is to inflate and thereby sound important. The airline pilot who announces that he is presently anticipating experiencing considerable precipitation wouldn't think of saying it may rain. The sentence is too simple—there must be something wrong with it.

3   But the secret of good writing is to strip every sentence to its cleanest components. Every word that serves no function, every long word that could be a short word, every adverb that carries the same meaning that's already in the verb, every passive construction that leaves the reader unsure of who is doing what—these are the thousand and one adulterants that weaken the strength of a sentence. And they usually occur in proportion to education and rank.

4   During the 1960s the president of my university wrote a letter to mollify the alumni after a spell of campus unrest. "You are probably aware," he began, "that we have been experiencing very considerable potentially explosive expressions of dissatisfaction on issues only partially related." He meant the students had been hassling them about different things. I was far more upset by the president's English than by the students' potentially explosive expressions of dissatisfaction. I would have preferred the presidential approach taken by Franklin D. Roosevelt when he tried to convert into English his own government's memos, such as this blackout order of 1942:

> Such preparations shall be made as will completely obscure all
> Federal buildings and non-Federal buildings occupied by the
> Federal government during an air raid for any period of time from
> visibility by reason of internal or external illumination.

5   "Tell them," Roosevelt said, "that in buildings where they have to keep the work going to put something across the windows."

6   Simplify, simplify. Thoreau said it, as we are so often reminded, and no American writer more consistently practiced what he preached. Open *Walden* to any page and you will find a man saying in a plain and orderly way what is on his mind:

> I went to the woods because I wished to live deliberately, to front
> only the essential facts of life, and see if I could not learn what it had
> to teach, and not, when I came to die, discover that I had not lived.

How can the rest of us achieve such enviable freedom from 7
clutter? The answer is to clear our heads of clutter. Clear thinking becomes clear writing; one can't exist without the other. It's
impossible for a muddy thinker to write good English. He may get
away with it for a paragraph or two, but soon the reader will be
lost, and there's no sin so grave, for the reader will not easily be
lured back.

Who is this elusive creature, the reader? The reader is some- 8
one with an attention span of about 30 seconds—a person assailed
by many forces competing for attention. At one time those forces
were relatively few: newspapers, magazines, radio, spouse, children, pets. Today they also include a "home entertainment center"
(television, VCR, tapes, CDs), e-mail, the Internet, the cellular
phone, the fax machine, a fitness program, a pool, a lawn, and that
most potent of competitors, sleep. The man or woman snoozing in
a chair with a magazine or a book is a person who was being given
too much unnecessary trouble by the writer.

It won't do to say that the reader is too dumb or too lazy to 9
keep pace with the train of thought. If the reader is lost, it's usually
because the writer hasn't been careful enough. The carelessness
can take any number of forms. Perhaps a sentence is so excessively cluttered that the reader, hacking through the verbiage, simply doesn't know what it means. Perhaps a sentence has been so
shoddily constructed that the reader could read it in several ways.
Perhaps the writer has switched pronouns in midsentence, or has
switched tenses, so the reader loses track of who is talking or when
the action took place. Perhaps Sentence B is not a logical sequel
to Sentence A; the writer, in whose head the connection is clear,
hasn't bothered to provide the missing link. Perhaps the writer has
used a word incorrectly by not taking the trouble to look it up. He or
she may think "sanguine" and "sanguinary" mean the same thing,
but the difference is a bloody big one. The reader can only infer
(speaking of big differences) what the writer is trying to imply.

Faced with such obstacles, readers are at first tenacious. They 10
blame themselves—they obviously missed something, and they go
back over the mystifying sentence, or over the whole paragraph,
piecing it out like an ancient rune, making guesses and moving on.
But they won't do this for long. The writer is making them work
too hard, and they will look for one who is better at the craft.

Writers must therefore constantly ask: What am I trying to say? 11
Surprisingly often they don't know. Then they must look at what

they have written and ask: have I said it? Is it clear to someone encountering the subject for the first time? If it's not, some fuzz has worked its way into the machinery. The clear writer is someone clearheaded enough to see this stuff for what it is: fuzz.

12   I don't mean that some people are born clearheaded and are therefore natural writers, whereas others are naturally fuzzy and will never write well. Thinking clearly is a conscious act that writers must force upon themselves, as if they were working on any other project that requires logic: making a shopping list or doing an algebra problem. Good writing doesn't come naturally, though most people seem to think it does. Professional writers are constantly bearded by strangers who say they'd like to "try a little writing sometime"—meaning when they retire from their real profession, like insurance or real estate, which is hard. Or they say, "I could write a book about that." I doubt it.

13   Writing is hard work. A clear sentence is no accident. Very few sentences come out right the first time, or even the third time. Remember this in moments of despair. If you find that writing is hard, it's because it *is* hard.

Two pages of the final manuscript of this chapter from the First Edition of *On Writing Well*. Although they look like a first draft, they had already been rewritten and retyped—like almost every other page—four or five times. With each rewrite I try to make what I have written tighter, stronger and more precise, eliminating every element that is not doing useful work. Then I go over it once more, reading it aloud, and am always amazed at how much clutter can still be cut. (In later editions I eliminated the sexist pronoun "he" denoting "the writer" and "the reader.")

```
is too dumb or too lazy to keep pace with the ~~writer's~~ train
of thought.  My sympathies are ~~entirely~~ with him.)  ~~He's not~~
~~so dumb~~.  (If the reader is lost, it is generally because the
writer ~~of the article~~ has not been careful enough to keep
him on the ~~proper~~ path.

    (This carelessness can take any number of ~~different~~ forms.
Perhaps a sentence is so excessively ~~long and~~ cluttered that
the reader, hacking his way through ~~all~~ the verbiage, simply
```

doesn't know what *it* ~~the writer~~ means. Perhaps a sentence has

been so shoddily constructed that the reader could read it in

any of *several* ~~two or three different~~ ways. ~~He thinks he knows what~~

~~the writer is trying to say, but he's not sure.~~ Perhaps the

writer has switched pronouns in mid-sentence, or ~~perhaps he~~

has switched tenses, so the reader loses track of who is

talking ~~to whom~~, or ~~exactly~~ when the action took place. Per-

haps Sentence B is not a logical sequel to Sentence A — the

writer, in whose head the connection is ~~perfectly~~ clear, has

bothered to provide
not ~~given enough thought to providing~~ the missing link. Per-

haps the writer has used an important word incorrectly by not

taking the trouble to look it up ~~and make sure~~. He may think

that "sanguine" and "sanguinary" mean the same thing, but)

~~I can assure you that~~ (the difference is a bloody big one ~~to the~~

The reader
~~reader.~~ ~~He~~ can only ~~try to~~ infer ~~xhxx~~ (speaking of big differ-

ences) what the writer is trying to imply.

these
 (Faced with ~~such a variety of~~ obstacles, the reader

is at first a remarkably tenacious bird. He ~~tends to~~ blame *s*

himself, ~~he~~ He obviously missed something, ~~he thinks~~, and he goes

back over the mystifying sentence, or over the whole paragraph,

piecing it out like an ancient rune, making guesses and moving

on. But he won't do this for long.) ~~He will soon run out of~~

~~patience.~~ (The writer is making him work too hard,) ~~harder~~

~~than he should have to work~~ — (and the reader will look for

one
a ~~writer~~ who is better at his craft.

 (The writer must therefore constantly ask himself: What am

I trying to say? ~~in this sentence?~~ (Surprisingly often, he

doesn't know.) ~~And~~ Then he must look at what he has ~~just~~

written and ask: Have I said it? Is it clear to someone

encountering
~~who is coming upon~~ the subject for the first time)? If it's

not, ~~clear~~, it is because some fuzz has worked its way into the

machinery. The clear writer is a person ~~who is~~ clear-headed

enough to see this stuff for what it is: fuzz.

⌐ I don't mean ~~to suggest~~ that some people are born

clear-headed and are therefore natural writers, whereas

others
~~other people~~ are naturally fuzzy and will ~~therefore~~ never write

                                    a
well. Thinking clearly is, ~~an entirely~~ conscious act that the

              force
writer must ~~keep forcing~~ upon himself, just as if he were

embarking   *requires*
~~starting out~~ on any other ~~kind of~~ project that ~~falls for~~ logic:

adding up a laundry list or doing an algebra problem ~~or playing~~

~~chess.~~ Good writing doeesn't ~~just~~ come naturally, though most
                        it does.
people obviously think ~~it's as easy as walking~~. The professional

BUILDING VOCABULARY

1. Zinsser uses a number of words and expressions drawn from areas other than writing; he uses them to make interesting combinations or comparisons in such expressions as "elusive creature" (par. 8) and "hacking through the verbiage" (par. 9). Find other such expressions in this essay. Write simple explanations for the two above and the others that you find.
2. List words or phrases in this essay that pertain to writing—the process, the results, the faults, the successes. Explain any with which you are unfamiliar.

THINKING CRITICALLY ABOUT THE ESSAY

Understanding the Writer's Ideas

1. State simply Zinsser's meaning in the opening paragraph. What faults of "bad writing" does he mention in this paragraph?
2. To what is Zinsser objecting in paragraph 2?
3. What, according to the author, is the "secret of good writing" (par. 3)? Explain this "secret" in a few simple words of your own. What does Zinsser say detracts from good writing? Why does Zinsser write that these writing faults "usually occur, in proportion to education and rank"?
4. What was the "message" in the letter from the university president to the alumni (par. 4)? Why does the writer object to it? Was it more objectionable in form or in content?

5. Who was Thoreau? What is *Walden?* Why are references to the two especially appropriate to Zinsser's essay?
6. What, according to Zinsser, is the relation between clear thinking and good writing? Can you have one without the other? What is meant by a "muddy thinker" (par. 7)? Why is it "impossible for a muddy thinker to write good English"?
7. Why does the author think most people fall asleep while reading? What is his attitude toward such people?
8. Look up and explain the "big differences" between the words *sanguine* and *sanguinary; infer* and *imply.* What is the writer's point in calling attention to these differences?
9. In paragraph 11, Zinsser calls attention to a writer's necessary awareness of the composing process. What elements of the *process* of writing does the author include in that paragraph? In that discussion, Zinsser speaks of *fuzz* in writing. What does he mean by the word as it relates to the writing process? To what does Zinsser compare the writer's thinking process? Why does he use such simple comparisons?
10. Explain the meaning of the last sentence. What does it indicate about the writer's attitude toward his work?

Understanding the Writer's Techniques

1. What is the writer's thesis? Is it stated or implied?
2. Explain the use of the words *disease* and *strangling* in paragraph 1. Why does Zinsser use these words in an essay about writing?
3. For what purpose does Zinsser use a series of questions in paragraph 2?
4. Throughout this essay, the writer makes extensive use of examples to support general opinions and attitudes. What attitude or opinion is he supporting in paragraphs 2, 4, 5, 6, and 9? How does he use examples in each of those paragraphs?
5. Analyze the specific structure and organization of paragraph 3:
    a. What general ideas about writing does Zinsser propose?
    b. Where does he place that idea in the paragraph?
    c. What examples does he offer to support his general idea?
    d. With what new idea does he conclude the paragraph? How is it related to the beginning idea?
6. Why does Zinsser reproduce exactly portions of the writings of a past president of a major university, President Franklin D. Roosevelt, and Henry David Thoreau? How do these sections

make Zinsser's writing clearer, more understandable, or more important?

7. What is the effect on the reader of the words "Simplify, simplify," which begin paragraph 6? Why does the writer use them at that particular point in the essay? What do they indicate about his attitude toward his subject? Explain.

8. Why does the author begin so many sentences in paragraph 9 with the word "Perhaps"? How does that technique help to *unify* (see Glossary) the paragraph?

9. For what reasons does the writer include the two pages of rough manuscript as a part of the finished essay? What is he trying to show the reader in this way? How does seeing these pages help you to understand better what he is writing about in the completed essay?

10. Overall, how would you describe the writer's attitude toward the process and craft of writing? What would you say is his overall attitude toward the future of American writing? Is he generally optimistic or pessimistic? On what does his attitude depend? Refer to specifics in the essay to support your answer.

11. Do you think Zinsser expected other writers, or budding writers, to be the main readers of this essay? Why or why not? If so, with what main ideas do you think he would like them to come away from the essay? Do you think readers who were not somehow involved in the writing process would benefit equally from this essay? Why?

Exploring the Writer's Ideas

1. Do you think that Zinsser is ever guilty in this essay of the very "sins" against writing about which he is upset? Could he have simplified any of his points? Select one of Zinsser's paragraphs in the finished essay and explain how you might rewrite it more simply.

2. In the reading that you do most often, have you noticed overly cluttered writing? Or, do you feel that the writing is at its clearest level of presentation and understanding for its audience? Bring to class some examples of this writing, and be prepared to discuss it. In general, what do you consider the relation between the simplicity or complexity of a piece of writing and its intended readership?

3. In the note to the two rough manuscript pages included with this essay, the writer implies that the process of rewriting and simplifying may be endless. How do you know when to stop trying

to rewrite an essay, story, or poem? Do you ever really feel satisfied that you've reached the end of the rewriting process?

4. Choose one of the rough manuscript paragraphs, and compare it with the finished essay. Which do you feel is better? Why? Is there anything Zinsser deleted from the rough copy that you feel he should have retained? Why?

5. Comment on the writer's assertion that "Thinking clearly is a conscious act that writers must force upon themselves" (par. 12). How does this opinion compare with the opinions of the three other writers in this chapter?

6. Reread Kurt Vonnegut Jr.'s essay "How to Write with Style" (pages 22–25). What similarities and differences do you note in Zinsser's and Vonnegut's approaches to writing and language?

IDEAS FOR WRITING

Prewriting

For the most part, teachers have called upon you to put your thoughts in writing from your elementary school days onward. Make a list of your writing "problems"—the elements of writing or the elements of your personality that create problems for you whenever you try to produce something on paper.

Guided Writing

In a 500- to 750-word essay, write about what you feel are some of the problems that you face as a writer.

1. In the first paragraph, identify the problems that you plan to discuss.

2. In the course of your essay, relate your problems more generally to society at large.

3. Identify what, in your opinion, is the "secret" of good writing. Give specific examples of what measures to take to achieve that secret process and thereby to eliminate some of your problems.

4. Try to include one or two accurate reproductions of your writing to illustrate your composing techniques.

5. Point out what you believe are the major causes of your difficulties as a writer.

6. Toward the end of your essay, explain the type of writer that you would like to be in order to succeed in college.

Thinking and Writing Collaboratively

Form groups of two and exchange drafts of your Guided Writing essay. Do for your partner's draft what Zinsser did for his own: edit it in an effort to make it "stronger and more precise, eliminating every element that is not doing useful work." Return the papers and discuss whether or not your partner made useful recommendations for cutting clutter.

Writing About the Text

Teachers of writing tend to stress two, apparently contradictory, philosophies about writing. The first is that clear thinking makes for clear writing. This point of view assumes that thinking precedes writing, that you need to get your thoughts in order before you can write. The second is that you don't really know what you think until you write it down. This point of view assumes that writing is a process of discovery and that thinking and writing occur more or less simultaneously. Write an essay to explain which position you think Zinsser would take. What evidence does he present to support this position? Then explain your position on the matter. Draw on your own experience as a writer.

More Writing Projects

1. Over the next few days, listen to the same news reporter or talk-show host on television or radio. Record in your journal at least ten examples that indicate the use of "unnecessary words, circular constructions, pompous frills, and meaningless jargon." Or compile such a list from an article in a newspaper or magazine you read regularly. Then write an essay presenting and commenting on these examples.

2. Respond in a paragraph to Zinsser's observation, "Good writing doesn't come naturally."

3. In preparation for a writing assignment, collect with other class members various samples of junk mail and business correspondence that confirm Zinsser's statement that these tend to be poorly written. Write an essay describing your findings. Be certain to provide specific examples from the documents you have assembled.

Mother Tongue

Amy Tan

Amy Tan is a fiction writer and essayist who was born in California several years after her parents emigrated from China to the United States. Her first book, *The Joy Luck Club* (1989), is a collection of related short stories (often assumed to be a novel) that depicts the conflicted relationship of Chinese mothers and their American-born daughters. This extremely popular book was followed by *The Kitchen God's Wife* (1991), *The Hundred Secret Senses* (1995), *The Bonesetter's Daughter* (2001), *The Opposite of Fate* (2003), and, most recently, *Saving Fish from Drowning* (2005), a novel about a group of American tourists lost in the jungles of Burma. Like *The Joy Luck Club,* the first three books explore intercultural relationships between Chinese-born mothers and their American-born daughters, or, in the case of *The Hundred Secret Senses,* between Chinese- and American-born half sisters. *The Opposite of Fate,* Tan's first work of nonfiction, collects essays about Tan's life and experience and provides rich detail of her personal challenges and triumphs.

Although she is a writer whose work has enjoyed impressive commercial success, Tan chose to publish this selection in 1990 in a small West Coast literary magazine, *The Threepenny Review,* edited by the writer Wendy Lesser. You might want to ask why she made this choice. The essay's title is a pun, referring at once to the language that nurtures us and, literally, to the language spoken by Tan's mother. Tan presents herself here as a writer and not a student of language, although she holds an MA in linguistics from San Jose State University. Speaking and writing in standard English is essential, Tan argues, but the diversity of cultures in America requires that we acknowledge the different "Englishes" spoken by immigrants. As you read her essay, think about your own experience in learning English and about how you respond to the other Englishes you may have heard spoken by your family or neighbors. Consider why Tan chooses to write in standard English.

www.mhhe.com/
shortprose

To learn more about Tan, click on
**More Resources > Chapter 1 >
Amy Tan**

PREREADING: THINKING ABOUT
THE ESSAY IN ADVANCE

What varieties of English do you speak? In other words, do you speak different kinds of English in different situations and to different individuals or groups of people? Why or why not?

Words to Watch

intersection (par. 3)   crossroad
wrought (par. 3)   made; worked
belies (par. 7)   misrepresents; disguises
wince (par. 8)   cringe; shrink
empirical (par. 9)   relying on observation
guise (par. 10)   outward appearance
benign (par. 14)   not harmful
insular (par. 15)   like an island; isolated

1   I am not a scholar of English or literature. I cannot give you much more than personal opinions on the English language and its variations in this country or others.

2   I am a writer. And by that definition, I am someone who has always loved language. I am fascinated by language in daily life. I spend a great deal of my time thinking about the power of language—the way it can evoke an emotion, a visual image, a complex idea, or a simple truth. Language is the tool of my trade. And I use them all—all the Englishes I grew up with.

3   Recently, I was made keenly aware of the different Englishes I do use. I was giving a talk to a large group of people, the same talk I had already given to half a dozen other groups. The nature of the talk was about my writing, my life, and my book, *The Joy Luck Club*. The talk was going along well enough, until I remembered one major difference that made the whole talk sound wrong. My mother was in the room. And it was perhaps the first time she had heard me give a lengthy speech, using the kind of English I have never used with her. I was saying things like, "The intersection of memory upon imagination" and "There is an aspect of my fiction that relates to thus-and-thus"—a speech filled with carefully wrought grammatical phrases, burdened, it suddenly seemed to me, with nominalized forms, past perfect tenses, conditional phrases, all the forms of standard English that I had learned in

school and through books, the forms of English I did not use at home with my mother.

Just last week, I was walking down the street with my mother, 4 and I again found myself conscious of the English I was using, the English I do use with her. We were talking about the price of new and used furniture and I heard myself saying this: "Not waste money that way." My husband was with us as well, and he didn't notice any switch in my English. And then I realized why. It's because over the twenty years we've been together I've often used that same kind of English with him, and sometimes he even uses it with me. It has become our language of intimacy, a different sort of English that relates to family talk, the language I grew up with.

So you'll have some idea of what this family talk I heard 5 sounds like, I'll quote what my mother said during a recent conversation which I videotaped and then transcribed. During this conversation, my mother was talking about a political gangster in Shanghai who had the same last name as her family's, Du, and how the gangster in his early years wanted to be adopted by her family, which was rich by comparison. Later, the gangster became more powerful, far richer than my mother's family, and one day showed up at my mother's wedding to pay his respects. Here's what she said in part:

"Du Yusong having business like fruit stand. Like off the 6 street kind. He is Du like Du Zong—but not Tsung-ming Island people. The local people call putong, the river east side, he belong to that side local people. That man want to ask Du Zong father take him in like become own family. Du Zong father wasn't look down on him, but didn't take seriously, until that man big like become a mafia. Now important person, very hard to inviting him. Chinese way, came only to show respect, don't stay for dinner. Respect for making big celebration, he shows up. Mean gives lots of respect. Chinese custom. Chinese social life that way. If too important won't have to stay too long. He come to my wedding. I didn't see. I heard it. I gone to boy's side, they have YMCA dinner. Chinese age I was nineteen."

You should know that my mother's expressive command of 7 English belies how much she actually understands. She reads the *Forbes* report, listens to *Wall Street Week,* converses daily with her stockbroker, reads all of Shirley MacLaine's books with ease—all kinds of things I can't begin to understand. Yet some of my friends tell me they understand 50 percent of what my mother says. Some say they understand 80 to 90 percent. Some say they understand none of it, as if she were speaking pure Chinese. But to me, my mother's English is perfectly clear, perfectly natural. It's my mother tongue. Her language, as I hear it, is vivid, direct, full of observation and imagery. That was the language that helped shape the way I saw things, expressed things, made sense of the world.

8 Lately, I've been giving more thought to the kind of English my mother speaks. Like others, I have described it to people as "broken" or "fractured" English. But I wince when I say that. It has always bothered me that I can think of no way to describe it other than "broken," as if it were damaged and needed to be fixed, as if it lacked a certain wholeness and soundness. I've heard other terms used, "limited English," for example. But they seem just as bad, as if everything is limited, including people's perceptions of the limited English speaker.

9 I know this for a fact, because when I was growing up, my mother's "limited" English limited *my* perception of her. I was ashamed of her English. I believed that her English reflected the quality of what she had to say. That is, because she expressed them imperfectly her thoughts were imperfect. And I had plenty of empirical evidence to support me: the fact that people in department stores, at banks, and at restaurants did not take her seriously, did not give her good service, pretended not to understand her, or even acted as if they did not hear her.

10 My mother has long realized the limitations of her English as well. When I was fifteen, she used to have me call people on the phone to pretend I was she. In this guise, I was forced to ask for information or even to complain and yell at people who had been rude to her. One time it was a call to her stockbroker in New York. She had cashed out her small portfolio and it just so happened we were going to go to New York the next week, our very first trip outside California. I had to get on the phone and say in an adolescent voice that was not very convincing, "This is Mrs. Tan."

11 And my mother was standing in the back whispering loudly, "Why he don't send me check, already two weeks late. So mad he lie to me, losing me money."

12 And then I said in perfect English, "Yes, I'm getting rather concerned. You had agreed to send the check two weeks ago, but it hasn't arrived."

Then she began to talk more loudly. "What he want, I come 13
to New York tell him front of his boss, you cheating me?" And I
was trying to calm her down, make her be quiet, while telling the
stockbroker, "I can't tolerate any more excuses. If I don't receive
the check immediately, I am going to have to speak to your manager when I'm in New York next week." And sure enough, the following week there we were in front of this astonished stockbroker,
and I was sitting there red-faced and quiet, and my mother, the
real Mrs. Tan, was shouting at his boss in her impeccable broken
English.

We used a similar routine just five days ago, for a situation 14
that was far less humorous. My mother had gone to the hospital
for an appointment, to find out about a benign brain tumor a CAT
scan had revealed a month ago. She said she had spoken very good
English, her best English, no mistakes. Still, she said, the hospital
did not apologize when they said they had lost the CAT scan and
she had come for nothing. She said they did not seem to have any
sympathy when she told them she was anxious to know the exact
diagnosis, since her husband and son had both died of brain tumors.
She said they would not give her any more information until the
next time and she would have to make another appointment for
that. So she said she would not leave until the doctor called her
daughter. She wouldn't budge. And when the doctor finally called
her daughter, me, who spoke in perfect English—lo and behold—
we had assurances the CAT scan would be found, promises that
a conference call on Monday would be held, and apologies for
any suffering my mother had gone through for a most regrettable
mistake.

I think my mother's English almost had an effect on limiting 15
my possibilities in life as well. Sociologists and linguists probably
will tell you that a person's developing language skills are more
influenced by peers. But I do think that the language spoken in
the family, especially in immigrant families which are more insular, plays a large role in shaping the language of the child. And I
believe that it affected my results on achievement tests, IQ tests,
and the SAT. While my English skills were never judged as poor,
compared to math, English could not be considered my strong suit.
In grade school I did moderately well, getting perhaps B's, sometimes B-pluses, in English and scoring perhaps in the sixtieth or
seventieth percentile on achievement tests. But those scores were
not good enough to override the opinion that my true abilities lay

in math and science, because in those areas I achieved A's and scored in the ninetieth percentile or higher.

16   This was understandable. Math is precise; there is only one correct answer. Whereas, for me at least, the answers on English tests were always a judgment call, a matter of opinion and personal experience. Those tests were constructed around items like fill-in-the-blank sentence completion, such as, "Even though Tom was _____, Mary thought he was _____." And the correct answer always seemed to be the most bland combinations of thoughts, for example, "Even though Tom was shy, Mary thought he was charming," with the grammatical structure "even though" limiting the correct answer to some sort of semantic opposites, so you wouldn't get answers like, "Even though Tom was foolish, Mary thought he was ridiculous." Well, according to my mother, there were very few limitations as to what Tom could have been and what Mary might have thought of him. So I never did well on tests like that.

17   The same was true with word analogies, pairs of words in which you were supposed to find some sort of logical, semantic relationship—for example, "*Sunset* is to *nightfall* as _____ is to _____." And here you would be presented with a list of four possible pairs, one of which showed the same kind of relationship: *red* is to *stoplight, bus* is to *arrival, chills* is to *fever, yawn* is to *boring.* Well, I could never think that way. I knew what the tests were asking, but I could not block out of my mind the images already created by the first pair, "*sunset* is to *nightfall*"— and I would see a burst of colors against a darkening sky, the moon rising, the lowering of a curtain of stars. And all the other pairs of words—red, bus, stoplight, boring—just threw up a mass of confusing images, making it impossible for me to sort out something as logical as saying: "A sunset precedes nightfall" is the same as "a chill precedes a fever." The only way I would have gotten that answer right would have been to imagine an associative situation, for example, my being disobedient and staying out past sunset, catching a chill at night, which turns into feverish pneumonia as punishment, which indeed did happen to me.

18   I have been thinking about all this lately, about my mother's English, about achievement tests. Because lately I've been asked, as a writer, why there are not more Asian Americans represented in American literature. Why are there few Asian Americans enrolled

in creative writing programs? Why do so many Chinese students go into engineering? Well, these are broad sociological questions I can't begin to answer. But I have noticed in surveys—in fact, just last week—that Asian students, as a whole, always do significantly better on math achievement tests than in English. And this makes me think that there are other Asian-American students whose English spoken in the home might also be described as "broken" or "limited." And perhaps they also have teachers who are steering them away from writing and into math and science, which is what happened to me.

Fortunately, I happen to be rebellious in nature and enjoy the challenge of disproving assumptions made about me. I became an English major my first year in college, after being enrolled as pre-med. I started writing nonfiction as a freelancer the week after I was told by my former boss that writing was my worst skill and I should hone my talents toward account management. 19

But it wasn't until 1985 that I finally began to write fiction. And at first I wrote using what I thought to be wittily crafted sentences, sentences that would finally prove I had mastery over the English language. Here's an example from the first draft of a story that later made its way into *The Joy Luck Club,* but without this line: "That was my mental quandary in its nascent state." A terrible line, which I can barely pronounce. 20

Fortunately, for reasons I won't get into today, I later decided I should envision a reader for the stories I would write. And the reader I decided upon was my mother, because these were stories about mothers. So with this reader in mind—and in fact she did read my early drafts—I began to write stories using all the Englishes I grew up with: the English I spoke to my mother, which for lack of a better term might be described as "simple"; the English she used with me, which for lack of a better term might be described as "broken"; my translation of her Chinese, which could certainly be described as "watered down"; and what I imagined to be her translation of her Chinese if she could speak in perfect English, her internal language, and for that I sought to preserve the essence, but neither an English nor a Chinese structure. I wanted to capture what language ability tests can never reveal: her intent, her passion, her imagery, the rhythms of her speech and the nature of her thoughts. 21

Apart from what any critic had to say about my writing, I knew I had succeeded where it counted when my mother finished reading my book and gave me her verdict: "So easy to read." 22

BUILDING VOCABULARY

Tan uses technical words to distinguish standard English from the English her mother speaks. Investigate the meanings of the following terms, and find examples to illustrate them for your classmates.

a. scholar (par. 1)
b. nominalized forms (par. 3)
c. transcribed (par. 5)
d. imagery (par. 7)
e. linguists (par. 15)
f. semantic opposites (par. 16)
g. word analogies (par. 17)
h. freelancer (par. 19)
i. quandary (par. 20)
j. nascent (par. 20)

THINKING CRITICALLY ABOUT THE ESSAY

Understanding the Writer's Ideas

1. Why does Tan start her essay by identifying who she is *not?* What does she see as the difference between a scholar and a writer?

2. What does Tan mean when she says, "Language is the tool of my trade"? What are the four ways she says language can work?

3. Tan speaks of "all the Englishes I grew up with" in paragraph 2, and later of the "different Englishes" she uses. Why does her mother's presence in the lecture room help her recall these Englishes? Why does she give us examples of what was "wrong" with her talk in paragraph 3?

4. In paragraph 4, Tan recognizes that she herself shifts from one English to another. Which English is "our language of intimacy"? Why?

5. Tan describes how she recorded her mother's words. Why does she give us her technique in paragraph 5 before presenting her mother's exact words in paragraph 6?

6. What do we know about Tan's mother when we learn she reads the *Forbes* report and various books? Why is it important for

Tan to understand the way her mother sees the world? What connection does Tan make between the way we use language and the way we see the world?

7. In paragraph 8, Tan tries to find a suitable label for her mother's language. Why is she unwilling to use a description like "broken" or "limited" English? What does her mother's English sound like to you?

8. In what ways did outsiders (like bankers and waiters) make judgments of Tan's mother because of her language? Were the judgments deliberate or unconscious on their part?

9. How does Tan use humor as she contrasts the two Englishes in the telephone conversations she records? How does the tone change when Tan shifts to the hospital scene? Why do the authorities provide different service and different information when the daughter speaks than they do when the mother speaks?

10. How does Tan connect her math test scores with her mother's language? Why does she think she never did well on language tests? Why does she think the tests do not measure a student's language use very well? Why does Tan ultimately become an English major (par. 19)?

11. In paragraph 20, why does Tan show us the sentence: "That was my mental quandary in its nascent state"? How does it compare with the other sentences in her essay? What is wrong with this "terrible" sentence? What does it mean?

12. In her two final paragraphs, Tan returns to her mother. Why does selecting her mother as her reader help Tan learn to become a better writer? What are the elements of good writing her mother recognizes, even if she herself cannot write standard English?

Understanding the Writer's Techniques

1. What is the thesis statement in Tan's essay? Where does it appear?

2. Throughout her essay, Tan uses *dialogue,* the written reproduction of speech or conversation. Why does she do this? What is the effect of dialogue? Which sentences of dialogue do you find especially effective, and why?

3. In paragraph 3, Tan writes fairly long sentences until she writes, "My mother was in the room." Why is this sentence shorter? What is the effect of the short sentence on the reader?

4. How does identifying her mother as her intended audience help Tan make her own language more effective? Does Tan suggest that all writing should be "simple"? Is her writing always "simple"? Why does her mother find it "easy" to read?

5. Why does Tan put quotation marks around "broken" and "limited"? What other words can describe this different English?

✳ MIXING PATTERNS

Narration (see Chapter 4) is the telling of a story or series of events. *Anecdotes* are very short narrations, usually of an amusing or autobiographical nature. Point out uses of narration and anecdote in Tan's essay. Why does she use narration in this essay? How does the technique of narration interact with description here?

Exploring the Writer's Ideas

1. Why is an awareness of different kinds of English necessary for a writer? Why are writers so interested in "different Englishes"? Should all Americans speak and write the same English?

2. What is the role of parents in setting language standards for their children? How did your parents or other relatives influence your language use?

3. Reread Tan's essay, and look more carefully at her *point of view* (see Glossary) about other Englishes. How do we know what her point of view is? Does she state it directly or indirectly? Where?

4. Listen to someone who speaks a "different" English. Try to record a full paragraph of the speech, as Tan does in paragraph 6. Use a tape recorder and (or) a video camera so that you can replay the speech several times. Explain what the difficulties are in capturing the sound of the speech exactly. Write a "translation" of the paragraph into standard English.

5. Tan explores the special relation between mothers and daughters. How would you describe the author's relation with her mother?

IDEAS FOR WRITING

Prewriting

Free-associate on a sheet of paper about the language you use in daily communication, its delights, difficulties, problems, confusions, humor—in short, anything that comes to mind about the language you use in your daily life.

Guided Writing

Write a narrative essay using first-person point of view in which you contrast your language with the language of someone who speaks differently from you.

1. Begin by making some notes on your own language and by deciding whom you will choose as your other subject. It should be someone you can spend time with so that you can record his or her speech.
2. Following Tan's model, create a narrative to frame your subject's language. Tell who you are and why you speak the way you do. Introduce the other speaker, and tell why his or her speech is different.
3. Use dialogue to provide examples of both Englishes.
4. Analyze how listeners other than yourself respond to both types of speech. What are the social implications of speech differences?
5. Show how listening to the other speaker and to yourself has helped you shape your own language and write your essay. What can you learn about good writing from this project?
6. Be sure the essay has a clear thesis in the introduction. Add a strong conclusion that returns to the idea of the thesis.

Thinking and Writing Collaboratively

Exchange a draft version of your Guided Writing essay with another writer in the class. As you read each other's work, make suggestions to help the writer produce the next draft. Is the thesis clear? Is the introduction focused? Is the conclusion linked to the thesis idea? Is the dialogue realistic?

Writing About the Text

Write a critique of the language and style of this selection as though you were Tan's mother. Before writing, look carefully at what the selection tells us about Tan's mother—about what sort of person she is, about her likes and dislikes, about her reading. Write the essay in standard English.

More Writing Projects

1. In your journal, record examples of new words you have heard recently. Divide the list into columns according to whether the words are standard English or a different English. How many different Englishes can you find in your community and in college?
2. Reread question 1 in Exploring the Writer's Ideas, and write a one-paragraph response to it.
3. Tan's experience as a daughter of recent immigrants has clearly shaped her life in fundamental ways. She writes about the "shame" she once felt for her mother's speech. Write about a personal experience in which you were once embarrassed by someone close to you who was "different." Tell how you would feel about the same encounter if it happened today.

SUMMING UP: CHAPTER 1

1. It sounds simple enough. Many writers, famous and unknown, have tried it at one time or another. Now, it's your turn. Write an essay simply titled "On Writing." Develop the essay in any way you please: you may deal with abstract or concrete ideas, philosophical or practical issues, emotional or intellectual processes, and so forth. Just use this essay to focus your own thoughts and to give your reader a clear idea of what writing means to you.

2. William Zinsser ("Simplicity") tells writers to simplify their writing. Select any writer from this section, and write an essay about whether you think the writer achieved (or did not achieve) simplicity. How did the writer achieve it? Where in the selection would you have preferred even more simplicity? Make specific references to the text.

3. Think of how, in their essays, Amy Tan implies that her mother is her ideal audience and Jennifer Lee suggests that today's online generation of young people have their own unique audience. Find your own ideal listener. Then write a letter to that person in which you discuss your reactions to becoming a writer. Include observations you think your listener or reader will enjoy, such as your everyday life as a student, daydreams, descriptions of teachers, or cafeteria food, or of interesting people you have met.

4. Write a letter from Kurt Vonnegut Jr. to Amy Tan on how style affects good writing. Draw on what you understand of Vonnegut's philosophy of writing from his essay "How to Write with Style" and what Amy Tan says in "Mother Tongue."

5. Many writers (including many represented in this book) feel that writing entails a certain social responsibility. For example, when French writer Albert Camus received the 1957 Nobel Prize for Literature, the Nobel Committee cited his efforts in "illuminating the problems of the human conscience of our time." And, in his acceptance speech, he stated, "[T]he writer's function is not without arduous duties. By definition, he cannot serve today those who make history; he must serve those who are subject to it."

    What do you believe are writers' responsibilities to themselves and to others? Do you agree with Camus? Do you prefer writing that deals primarily with an individual's experience or with more general social issues? Write an essay concerning the social responsibility of writers. As you consider the issue, refer to points made by writers in this section.

6. Kurt Vonnegut says that good writing comes from the heart; William Zinsser says that good writing comes from the head. Write an essay based on your experience that explores how each of these pieces of advice is useful to the student of writing.

7. In a variety of ways, the writers in this chapter stress the importance of finding your own voice as central to writing, including as a motive for writing. Explore the idea of writing as a way to be yourself (think of the meaning of writing to Amy Tan or Kurt Vonnegut, for example). How can you write in your own voice and yet meet the expectations of different audiences—teachers, employers, peers? What have you learned about writing in your own voice from the selections in this chapter?

8. The writers in this chapter urge clarity and simplicity of style. Simplicity can be deceiving, however; usually an artist (a writer, a dancer, a painter) achieves simplicity only after spending a career working in his or her discipline and honing his or her craft. Is simplicity too ambitious a goal for students, then? Explain.

✳ FROM SEEING TO WRITING

Examine the cartoon and consider what it says about writing. What does Calvin say about creativity? What role does creativity play in writing? Why does Calvin say that he has to wait for his mood to be "last-minute panic" before he can write? What role does last-minute panic play in your writing? What are the advantages of last-minute panic? The disadvantages? What advice would you offer Calvin to help prevent this mood? Write an essay in which you analyze the cartoon by addressing some of these questions.

Calvin and Hobbes   by Bill Watterson

CALVIN AND HOBBES © 1992 Watterson. Reprinted with permission of Universal Press Syndicate. All rights reserved.

CHAPTER 2

On Reading

WHAT IS READING?

"Reading had changed forever the course of my life," writes Malcolm X in one of the essays in this chapter. For many of us, the acquisition of reading skills may not have been quite as dramatic as it was for the author of "Prison Studies," but if we are to understand the value of literacy in today's society, Malcolm X's analysis of the power of the written word is vital. Reading allows us to engage actively with the minds of many writers who have much to tell us and to hear a variety of viewpoints not always available on television, radio, and other forms of media that vie for our attention. Even the ever-present computer and its brainchild, the Internet, demand active reading for maximum benefit. Learning to read well opens new universes, challenges your opinions, enhances your understanding of yourself and others as well as of your past, present, and future. Knowledge of books is the mark of a literate person.

But how do we learn this complex skill? Eudora Welty's essay on reading as a child may remind you of your own early experiences with printed words. Or, if you are a parent, you may be reading stories to your own children to help them learn to read. As we become mature readers, we read not just as we once did, for the story and its magical pleasures, but also for information and for pleasure in the *style* of writing. We learn not to be passive readers but active ones.

That early love of stories, and the self-esteem that came with mastery of a once impossible task, is, however, only the first step in understanding the power of reading. Malcolm X's "Prison Studies" extends our understanding of what reading is beyond the personal into the cultural sphere. He explores not only the power of reading to excite and inspire, but also the ways in which language connects to social identity. Malcolm X uses reading, and later writing, to challenge existing assumptions and find a place as an alert and engaged member of society. He argues that his reading outside of school made him better educated than most formally educated citizens in America.

Reading gives us access to many printed stories and documents, old and new. It lets us see beyond the highly edited sound bites and trendy video images that tempt us. With print, we can read what we want when we want to read it. We can reread difficult passages to be sure we understand them. We have time to question the author's point—and we have time to absorb and analyze ideas not only from contemporary life but also from ancient cultures and distant places. The diverse materials in libraries allow us to select what we read rather than be channeled into one point of view. On the Web we can access stories, poems, essays, even books, and can create a home library for use on a computer monitor.

Reading lets us share ideas. Reading can teach us practical skills that we need for survival in our complex world, such as how to repair a computer or how to become a biology teacher or a certified public accountant. Good reading can inspire us or entertain us. It can enrich our fantasy lives. Reading critically also helps us analyze how society operates, how power is distributed, how we can improve our local community or the global environment. And reading can lead us to discoveries about the world; it can make us "educated." But more than this, reading can show us the beauty of the written word; it can stir the imagination and create in us a vision of what is and what should be. That is what reading can produce; that is reading.

HOW DO WE READ?

To become a good reader, we need to think about what we read just as we think about what and how we write. In other words, we need to read *self-consciously* and *critically*. Reading, like writing, is a *process*. If we break this process down, we can say that reading involves three large steps or stages. To begin with, we want to grasp the writer's main point and the general outline of what he or she says. Then second, we reflect on what's being said: we probe, analyze, look more deeply, think things through. Finally, we make a judgment—"Wow!" or "Yes, I agree," or "What a lot of rubbish!"

We can focus these three stages of the reading process and enhance our understanding by pursuing certain strategies as we read. It's useful, for example, after reading a chapter to go back through it and then to *summarize* the main idea. A summary is a drastically condensed version of a piece of writing that aims to state the writer's main points by retaining only essential arguments, facts, and statements. A summary is usually brief, a sentence or two. Composing a summary, then, is one good way to help us get a clearer picture of the writer's main idea.

No essay contains just one idea, of course. In addition to the main idea, the writer usually includes a variety of supporting points in her essay. And most writers will support big ideas with facts, arguments, observations, quotations—the writer, in other words, tries to *substantiate* her major points in order to persuade you to see things her way.

Throughout the reading process, we can make sure that we are reading critically by asking ourselves a series of questions about the material in order to arrive at a fair assessment of its significance. The word *critically* here does not mean negatively, in the sense of criticizing what we read for what it's doing wrong. Rather, *critically* is intended to suggest a curious but questioning attitude, an alertness to what is being said and how it is being said, and a certain self-awareness about our responses to what is being said and how it is being said. Here are some questions we might ask ourselves as we start to read:

- What is it that we're reading? (In other words, what *genre,* or type of writing, does it belong to?)

We should first examine what we are about to read to determine what it is: Is it a romance? a history book? a religious tract? Why was it written? How do the answers to these questions shape our attitude toward the material? As readers of novels, for instance, we soon learn that a book with a cover featuring a heroine snatched from a fiery castle belongs to a particular genre of literature: the gothic romance. As potential readers, we might prepare ourselves to be skeptical about the happy ending we know awaits us, but at the same time we are prepared for a romantic tale. In contrast, if we face a hard-covered glossy textbook entitled *Economics,* we prepare ourselves to read with far more concentration. We might enjoy the gothic romance, but if we skip whole chapters it may not matter much. If, however, we skip chapters of the textbook, we may find ourselves confused. The first book *entertains* us, while the second *informs* us. In other words, our initial clue to what we might find as we read further is provided by the *kind* of book, essay, or article that we are reading. Our expectations of a romance novel are different from our expectations of a textbook.

- Who is the writer? For whom is he or she writing? When did he or she write it?

Clues to a writer's identity can often help us establish whether the material we are reading is reliable. Would we read a slave owner's account of life in slave quarters the same way we would read a slave's diary, for instance? If a Sioux writes about the effects of a treaty on Native American family life, we might read the essay one way; if the writer were General Custer we surely would read it another way. The *audience* is also important. If we are reading a handbook on immigration policies in the United States, we might read it differently if we knew it was written for officials at Ellis Island in 1890 from the way we would read it if it were written for Chinese men arriving to work on the railroads in the nineteenth century.

Sometimes we may not know more about a writer than when he wrote. This knowledge can itself be crucial. An essay written in the sixteenth century will be different in important ways from an essay written yesterday. Not only will the sixteenth-century author use a vocabulary that is likely to diverge from ours, but he also will make allusions to people, places, and books that may be unfamiliar to us. Moreover, he will certainly have ideas and beliefs that reflect this unfamiliar world. Today, for example, we wonder only how much interest a bank will charge us on our loan; in the sixteenth century people looked on charging interest as a doubtful if not an outright wicked practice. One of the challenges in reading work from the past, then, is to read it on its own terms, remembering that what we think and what we know are different from—rather than necessarily better than—what people thought and knew in the past. The date of writing also matters with writing published closer to our own day. A writer assessing Bill Clinton before he was impeached, for example, may well have written something significantly different had she put pen to paper after Clinton was impeached. In these ways the date of writing provides important information about what to expect.

• What is the precise issue or problem that the writer treats?

During the first and second stages of the reading process, we seek to identify the writer's *exact* topic. A writer's general topic might be the Battle of Gettysburg, for instance, but if she is writing about the women at Gettysburg, then her precise topic is narrower. What is she saying, we next ask, about these women?

• What information, conclusions, and recommendations does the writer present?

The reader may find that note taking is helpful in improving understanding of a text. Creating an outline of materials after reading can help identify the writer's aims. Both note taking and outlining will help us when we want to make a summary or when we want to pinpoint the subtopics and supporting evidence of an essay.

• How does the writer substantiate, or "prove," his case?

The reader must learn the difference between a writer who merely *asserts* an idea and one who effectively *substantiates* an idea. The writer who only asserts that the Holocaust never happened will be read differently from the writer who substantiates claims that the Holocaust did exist with photographs of Germany in the 1940s, interviews with concentration camp survivors, military records of medical experiments, and eyewitness accounts of gas chambers.

As in the example of the Holocaust, most essays aim to persuade you to see things in a certain way. Most essays, in other words, make what is formally known as an *argument*. An *argument* is not a quarrel but rather a more-or-less formal way of making a point. Often a writer begins an essay by introducing the topic or problem in the opening paragraph or paragraphs— *the introduction*—and then offers a *thesis statement*. The *thesis statement* presents the writer's position; that is, it tells what the writer has to say about the topic or problem. It usually comes early in an essay, at the close of the introduction, frequently at the close of the first paragraph.

After stating a *thesis,* the writer will try to *prove* or *substantiate* it through use of supporting *details* and *facts,* or *reasons.* In the case of the Holocaust, a writer may use a photograph or an eye-witness account to support the position that the Holocaust did in fact occur. It is not enough, though, to see that support has been provided. We also need to assess whether this support is accurate, credible, and relevant.

Usually a writer combines generalities and specifics, facts and reasons. The writer uses reasoning. You'll find a more detailed look at reasoning in Chapter 11, Argumentation and Persuasion. Here it will be enough to say that we want to be sure that the reasoning the writer uses is sound. If the writer says that event A caused event B, we want to be sure that A and B really are related as cause and effect—that they're not two separate events. In a more general way, we want to be comfortable that a writer's conclusions are valid. Does the essay really add up to the conclusions claimed?

• Is the total message successful, objective, valid, or persuasive?

Once you have answered all of the above questions, you are ready to *assess* the work you have read. As you make your evaluation, find specific evidence in the text to back up your position.

Assessment or *evaluation* is not an exact science—assessments and evaluations are ultimately opinions. But this does not mean that we can make them recklessly—"Don't bother me with the facts!" An opinion should not be prejudice in another form. Rather, an opinion should itself be a kind of *argument,* based on fact or reason. Sometimes our deeply held beliefs are refuted by new evidence or by reasons we have not before encountered. In such cases we as educated thinkers cannot say, "Well, that may be so, but I still stick to my opinion." If the facts or reasons contradict our opinions, we have no choice but to reexamine our beliefs. That's what education is all about.

By reading critically—by reading to understand, analyze, and evaluate—you respond to an author's ideas, opinions, and arguments in an informed way. In a sense you enter into a conversation with the author. You agree or disagree with the author, "talk back," and try to understand the author's perspective on the subject. To become a critical reader, you may wish to employ a strategy, called annotation, in which you literally mark up the essay.

Here are the basic elements of this method:

- Underline important ideas in an essay. You can also, for example, use an asterisk, star, or vertical lines in the margins next to the most important information or statements.
- Pose questions in the margins. Place question marks next to the points that you find confusing.
- Take notes in the margins.
- Use numbers in the margins to highlight the sequence of major ideas that the author presents.
- Circle key words and phrases.

Examine the annotations made by one student as she read an essay by Leonid Fridman titled "America Needs Its Nerds."

America Needs Its Nerds

Leonid Fridman

nice title! Is he serious or being funny?

1 ✳   There is something very wrong with the system of values in a society that has only derogatory terms like nerd and geek for the intellectually curious and academically serious.

Intro/Thesis?

2   A geek, according to "Webster's New World Dictionary," is a street performer who shocks the public by biting off heads of live chickens. It is a telling fact about our language and our culture that someone dedicated to pursuit of knowledge is compared to a freak biting the head off a live chicken.

Key definition

3   Even at a prestigious academic institution like Harvard, anti-intellectualism is rampant: Many students are ashamed to admit, even to their friends, how much they study. Although most students try to keep up their grades, there is but a minority of undergraduates for whom pursuing knowledge is the top priority during their years at Harvard. Nerds are ostracized while athletes are idolized.

?? Is this true? Where is the evidence?

Meaning?

4   The same thing happens in U.S. elementary and high schools. Children who prefer to read books rather than play football, prefer to build model airplanes rather than get wasted at parties with their

He mentions athletes several times. Must they be separated from intellectuals?

Note comparison and contrast throughout essay

classmates, become social outcasts. Ostracized for their intelligence and refusal to conform to society's anti-intellectual values, many are deprived of a chance to learn adequate social skills and acquire good communication tools.

*Call to action?

✳   Enough is enough.   5

Why this fragment?

Geeks must rebel?

Nerds and geeks must stop being ashamed of who they are. It is high time to face the persecutors who   6 haunt the bright kid with thick glasses from kindergarten to the grave. For America's sake, the anti-intellectual values that pervade our society must be fought.

U.S. vs rest of world

There are very few countries in the world where   7 anti-intellectualism runs as high in popular culture as it does in the U.S. In most industrialized nations, not least of all our economic rivals in East Asia, a kid who studies hard is lauded and held up as an example to other students.

In many parts of the world, university professorships are the most prestigious and materially rewarding positions. But not in America, where average professional ballplayers are much more respected and better paid than faculty members of the best universities.

look up

Anti-intellectualism has negative impact on America's political and economic future. Does he prove his point?

How can a country where typical parents are   9 ashamed of their daughter studying mathematics instead of going dancing, or of their son reading Weber while his friends play baseball, be expected to compete in the technology race with Japan or remain a leading political and cultural force in Europe? How long can America remain a world-class power if we constantly emphasize social skills and physical prowess over academic achievement and intellectual ability?

Note series of questions. Are answers self evident?

Do we really expect to stay afloat largely by import-   10 ing our scientists and intellectuals from abroad, as we have done for a major portion of this century, without making an effort to also cultivate a pro-intellectual culture at home? Even if we have the political will to spend substantially more money on education than we do now, do we think we can improve our schools if we deride our studious pupils and debase their impoverished teachers?

11   Our fault lies not so much with our economy or
with our politics as within ourselves, our values and our
image of a good life. America's culture has not adapted
to the demands of our times, to the economic realities
that demand a highly educated workforce and innovative intelligent leadership.

12   If we are to succeed as a society in the 21st
century, we had better shed our anti-intellectualism
and imbue in our children the vision that a good life is
impossible without stretching one's mind and pursuing
knowledge to the full extent of one's abilities.

*Essay comes full
circle—reread intro.*

13   And until the words "nerd" and "geek" become
terms of (approbation) and not (derision,) we do not stand
a chance.

**Idea for essay:
"My Favorite
Nerd"*

The process that this student follows reflects the sort of active,
critical reading expected of you in college courses. Through annotation, you actually bring the acts of reading and writing together
in a mutually advantageous way. Reading critically and responding to texts through annotation prepares you for the more sustained
writing assignments presented in this anthology.

These steps will help you engage in an active conversation,
or dialogue, with the writer, sharing ideas and debating issues.
At the same time, becoming a better reader will help you become
a better writer. Judith Ortiz Cofer, a well-known writer, tells how
reading comic books as a child liberated her imagination. Malcolm X tells us how reading was so powerful for him that it
allowed him to break down prison walls. He became a reader
as part of his apprenticeship to becoming a writer. For Eudora
Welty, reading remains, as it does for most of us, a personal
achievement. Welty reminds us that parents can assure a comfortable reading environment for children. And Norman Mailer
warns us that reading is a skill that can be compromised by the
power of television.

"READING" VISUALS

Living in this era of information technology, we are immersed in a
world in which we are constantly confronted by images. To swim
through this world successfully, we must learn to think critically

about all the images we encounter. From advertising to film to the Internet, we must understand the purpose of the minds behind these works, and we must understand the methods used to move us and to persuade us visually. Even in college textbooks, we are required to come to grips, not only with the words on the page, but also with the photographs, tables, and graphics (like charts and graphs) the authors use to reinforce their message.

Frequently, textbooks for courses in psychology, biology, political science, and other disciplines use tables, charts, and graphs to show relationships discussed in words in the text. When you encounter such graphics, look at them carefully. Just as you often have to reread a verbal text, you also might have to return to charts, graphs, and tables, perhaps from a fresh perspective, to comprehend them fully.

For example, consider the graph below:

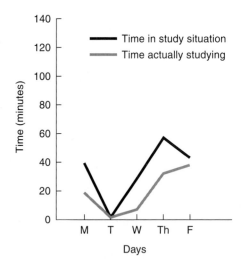

This graph shows the relationship between the amount of time a student spent in a "study situation" (sitting at a desk or in a study carrel in the library, for example) and the amount of time the student actually spent studying, by day of the week. It appeared in an introductory psychology textbook, in a section discussing how to represent data graphically. Consider this graphic. What can you infer about this student's study habits based on this graph? Do you see a change over the course of the week?

When studying a table, chart, or graph in context, ask yourself the following questions:

- What is the purpose of the graphic? What thesis or point of view does it suggest?
- How does the design or structure of the graphic help the author achieve this purpose?
- What information is provided? Is the information appropriate and verifiable? Does the information support the point the visual is trying to make?
- How does the visual support or reinforce the verbal text surrounding it?

When responding to visuals like charts, tables, and graphs that reinforce the message of a verbal text, you must take nothing for granted; you must sift through the evidence and the images with a critical eye in order to understand the strategies the author or graphic artist has used to reinforce the message conveyed by the verbal text.

When visual elements stand alone, as in a painting or a photograph, they often make profound statements about human experience and frequently reflect a persuasive purpose as skillfully composed as an argumentative essay. Consider, for example, the photograph on the next page of three children sleeping, taken by the photographer and social reformer Jacob Riis. Riis, a late-nineteenth-century photojournalist, was determined to alert well-to-do New Yorkers to the conditions in which the poor were living. He took artfully composed photographs, like this one, to show "as no mere description could, the misery and vice that [Riis] had noticed in [his] ten years of experience . . . and suggest[ed] the direction in which good might be done."

Look at the photograph and consider Riis's purpose, focusing your attention on the following features:

- The color, light, and shadow in the item depicted.
- The number and arrangement of objects or people and the relationships among them.
- The foregrounding and backgrounding of images within the frame.
- The inferences and values that you draw from the overall composition.

Jacob Riis, Children Sleeping in Mulberry Street *(1890)*

Although the primary purpose of a work of visual art may not always be persuasive, that is not the case with advertisements. In most cases, advertisements are designed to persuade you to spend money; in the case of public service announcements or political campaign ads, the purpose is to influence your behavior or even change your mind.

How do they achieve their purpose? Frequently, advertisers take advantage of our innate capacity to be affected by symbols. The president framed by American flags, a bottle of Coca-Cola beneath the word "America"—such visual emblems represent ideals and have enormous emotional power that is being drawn on to promote products, personalities, and ideas. Consider, for example, the public service advertisement on the following page.

This advertisement uses a potent emotional appeal to "sell" viewers on the idea that gun manufacturers should be required to include safety locks on all weapons.

When confronted by an ad, whether it is selling a product or an idea, consider the following:

• What is the advertisement designed to get me to do, think, or buy?
• How is the advertisement designed to achieve this goal?
• Does the advertisement work by appealing to my ideals or my emotions?

At the end of each chapter, throughout this text, you will find From Seeing to Writing exercises that will prompt you to look critically at a visual—a photograph, an advertisement, a cartoon—and interpret its meaning and purpose. The skills you will develop by analyzing these images will help you as you confront images not only in your textbooks but in your day-to-day lives as well.

Volar

Judith Ortiz Cofer

A poet, novelist, and essayist, Judith Ortiz Cofer has explored the triumphs, discoveries, and costs of hyphenated Americanism in an impressive variety of highly regarded publications. Born in Puerto Rico and reared in Paterson, New Jersey, Ortiz Cofer identifies herself as "a daughter of the Puerto Rican diaspora," or dispersion, for whose writing nevertheless "a sense of place has been very important." Her collection of autobiographical essays, *Silent Dancing,* was awarded the 1990 Pushcart Prize for Non-Fiction, and her story "Nada" won the prestigious O'Henry Prize for the Short Story in 1994. Her books of poetry include *Peregrina* (1986) and *A Love Story Beginning in Spanish* (2005). Other of her publications are *The Latin Deli: Prose and Poetry* (1993), *Woman in Front of the Sun: On Becoming a Writer* (2000), and *Call Me Maria* (2006), a young adult novel. Ortiz Cofer received her BA from Augusta College, Georgia, in 1974 and is the Franklin Professor of English and the Director of the Creative Writing Program at the University of Georgia. In this selection, she recounts how reading—in this case, reading *Supergirl* comics—can feed a young person's hunger to live. This deftly structured essay also shows how art and life mysteriously—and often, ironically—flow into one another.

www.mhhe.com/
shortprose

To learn more about Cofer, click on
**More Resources > Chapter 2 >
Judith Ortiz Cofer**

PREREADING: THINKING ABOUT THE ESSAY IN ADVANCE

What is *volar?* What expectations are raised by a title in Spanish? What sort of flying are we talking about?

Words to Watch

volar   Spanish for "to fly"
aerodynamic (par. 1)   relating to bodies in motion
supersonic (par. 1)   speed greater than sound
ermine (par. 1)   fur of a weasel, sometimes used to trim judge's robes as a symbol of honor and purity

incongruous (par. 1)   not in harmony, unsuitable
dismal (par. 2)   gloomy, depressing

1   At twelve I was an avid consumer of comic books—*Supergirl* being my favorite. I spent my allowance of a quarter a day on two twelve-cent comic books or a double issue for twenty-five. I had a stack of *Legion of Super Heroes* and *Supergirl* comic books in my bedroom closet that was as tall as I. I had a recurring dream in those days: that I had long blond hair and could fly. In my dream I climbed the stairs to the top of our apartment building as myself, but as I went up each flight, changes would be taking place. Step by step I would fill out: my legs would grow long, my arms harden into steel, and my hair would magically go straight and turn a golden color. Of course I would add the bonus of breasts, but not too large; Supergirl had to be aerodynamic. Sleek and hard as a supersonic missile. Once on the roof, my parents safely asleep in their beds, I would get on tip-toe, arms outstretched in the position for flight and jump out my fifty-story-high window into the black lake of the sky. From up there, over the rooftops, I could see everything, even beyond the few blocks of our barrio; with my X-ray vision I could look inside the homes of people who interested me. Once I saw our landlord, whom I knew my parents feared, sitting in a treasure-room dressed in an ermine coat and a large gold crown. He sat on the floor counting his dollar bills. I played a trick on him. Going up to his building's chimney, I blew a little puff of my super-breath into his fireplace, scattering his stacks of money so that he had to start counting all over again. I could more or less program my Supergirl dreams in those days by focusing on the object of my current obsession. This way I "saw" into the private lives of my neighbors, my teachers, and in the last days of my childish fantasy and the beginning of adolescence, into the secret room of the boys I liked. In the mornings I'd wake up in my tiny bedroom with the incongruous—at least in our tiny apartment—white "princess" furniture my mother had chosen for me, and find myself back in my body; my tight curls still clinging to my head, skinny arms and legs and flat chest unchanged.

2   In the kitchen my mother and father would be talking softy over a café con leche. She would come "wake me" exactly forty-five minutes after they had gotten up. It was their time together at the beginning of each day and even at an early age I could feel

their disappointment if I interrupted them by getting up too early. So I would stay in my bed recalling my dreams of flight, perhaps planning my next flight. In the kitchen they would be discussing events in the barrio. Actually, he would be carrying that part of the conversation; when it was her turn to speak she would, more often than not, try shifting the topic toward her desire to see her *familia* on the Island: *How about a vacation in Puerto Rico together this year, Querido? We could rent a car, go to the beach. We could. . . .* And he would answer patiently, gently. *Mi amor, do you know how much it would cost for all of us to fly there? It is not possible for me to take the time off. . . . Mi vida, please understand. . . .* And I knew that soon she would rise from the table. Not abruptly. She would light a cigarette and look out the kitchen window. The view was of a dismal alley that was littered with refuse thrown from windows. The space was too narrow for anyone larger than a skinny child to enter safely, so it was never cleaned. My mother would check the time on the clock over her sink, the one with a prayer for patience and grace written in Spanish. A birthday gift. She would see that it was time to wake me. She'd sigh deeply and say the same thing the view from her kitchen window always inspired her to say: *Ay, si yo pudiera volar.*

BUILDING VOCABULARY

Writing American English often involves using words from other languages, or words that originated in other languages but have been adopted (sometimes also adapted) into English. If you watch a Woody Allen movie, for example, you will hear characters use Yiddish words or expressions that have become commonplace in New York. This essay includes some words in Spanish. Translate these words into English. Which, if any, do you think have become commonplace, part of contemporary American usage?

a. barrio (par. 1)
b. café con leche (par. 2)
c. Querido (par. 2)
d. Mi amor (par. 2)
e. Mi vida (par. 2)
f. Ay, si yo pudiera volar. (par. 2)

THINKING CRITICALLY ABOUT THE ESSAY

Understanding the Writer's Ideas

1. How old was Cofer at the time of the essay? What clues suggest roughly the calendar year in question?
2. What kinds of stories are found in the comics the writer "consumes"? How do the main characters in these stories differ from the writer?
3. In what kind of community does the writer live?
4. How does the writer use her fantastic powers to affect her everyday world?
5. Why does Cofer describe her bedroom furniture as "incongruous" (par. 1)?
6. Why were the writer's parents "disappointed" if she woke too early (par. 2)?
7. What did the writer's father discuss over breakfast? the writer's mother?
8. Why does Cofer say that when her mother rises from the breakfast table it is "Not abruptly" (par. 2)?
9. What did the writer's mother see outside the kitchen window?
10. What is the connection between the writer's dreams and what the view from the kitchen window "always inspired" her mother to say?

Understanding the Writer's Techniques

1. Does this essay have a thesis statement? If so, what is it? If not, express the essay's main idea in one or two sentences.
2. Compare and contrast the essay's two paragraphs—look, for example, at the similarities and differences in *setting, point of view,* and *theme.*
3. How does Cofer achieve unity in a two-paragraph essay?
4. Show how *incongruity* serves as an organizing principle for each paragraph.
5. What is the role of *irony* in the essay? (See Glossary.)

Exploring the Writer's Ideas

1. The writer, at age twelve, seems attracted to reading as a way of escaping the harsh reality of her barrio existence. What do

you think is the adult writer's attitude toward her youthful habits? And what is your view: is reading or, say, watching television as an "escape" a good thing? a bad thing? neither?

2. Do you think the essay aims to contrast two kinds of "flying"— that of daughter and mother; or does the essay want to suggest *analogies* between the outlook of daughter and mother? Explain.

3. Is this an essay about a certain reaction to poverty, or does the essay have implications beyond the barrio? Explain.

IDEAS FOR WRITING

Prewriting

Think about what you read at age twelve or thirteen that fed your fantasies. List a few book or magazine or comic book titles. Or, if you prefer, list movies or television shows that played this role.

Guided Writing

Write a two-paragraph essay that illustrates the differences between your reality at twelve or thirteen and the fantasy life you led then, as stimulated by your reading or television or movie watching or the Internet.

1. In the first paragraph identify the source of your fantasies.

2. In the same paragraph, describe how the fantasy imitates your reading or viewing and how you apply it to your life.

3. End the paragraph as you come back to reality and discover the incongruity between your fantasy and your true situation.

4. In the second paragraph, identify in a narrative fashion a situation that triggers your mother's or father's (or some other relative's) desire for escape, or that person's refusal to resort to escapism.

5. Conclude with a clinching last sentence that serves as a kind of punch line, linking your fantasizing and that of your relative or your fantasizing and your relative's lack of fantasizing.

Thinking and Writing Collaboratively

In a small group of three or four, explore the ways childhood reading and childhood fantasies work together. List some of the group members' favorite things to read as children that triggered childhood fantasies. On the basis of your discussion, write a paragraph or two about the kinds of things children like to read, and why.

Writing About the Text

Write an essay that shows how Ortiz Cofer achieves the essay's delicate and economical character portrayals—of herself, of her father, of her mother, of the family.

More Writing Projects

1. Are all fantasies of power benign? Pick up an assortment of comics that a young teenager might read and in your journal explore the kinds of fantasies these comics might induce.
2. Children's reading strongly tends toward imaginary worlds. Some of these imaginary worlds, as Ortiz Cofer shows, offer an escape from severe limits into unlimited power. But others are less directly escapist. In an extended paragraph, contrast the imaginary world invoked by *Supergirl* and the world invoked by a children's classic, such as *Winnie the Pooh* or *Alice in Wonderland* or *Little Women* or *The Little House on the Prairie*.
3. By doing some research into children's literature, expand into an essay the topic that is given in an extended paragraph in Thinking and Writing Collaboratively.

Prison Studies
Malcolm X

Born Malcolm Little in Omaha, Nebraska, Malcolm X (1925–1965)
was a charismatic leader of the black power movement and founded
the Organization of Afro-American Unity. In prison, he became a
Black Muslim. (He split with this faith in 1963 to convert to orthodox
Islam.) "Prison Studies" is excerpted from the popular and fascinating
Autobiography of Malcolm X, which he co-wrote with *Roots* author
Alex Haley. The selection describes the writer's struggle to learn to
read as well as the joy and power he felt when he won that struggle.

PREREADING: THINKING ABOUT
THE ESSAY IN ADVANCE

Reflect on what you know about prison life. Could someone interested in reading and learning find a way to pursue these interests
in such a setting? Why or why not?

Words to Watch

emulate (par. 2)   imitate, especially from respect
motivation (par. 2)   reason to do something
tablets (par. 3)   writing notebooks
bunk (par. 9)   small bed
rehabilitation (par. 10)   the process of restoring to a state of use-
    fulness or constructiveness
inmate (par. 10)   prisoner
corridor (par. 13)   hallway; walkway
vistas (par. 15)   mental overviews
confers (par. 15)   bestows; gives ceremoniously
alma mater (par. 15)   the college that one has attended

Many who today hear me somewhere in person, or on television, 1
or those who read something I've said, will think I went to school
far beyond the eighth grade. This impression is due entirely to my
prison studies.

It had really begun back in the Charlestown Prison, when 2
Bimbi first made me feel envy of his stock of knowledge. Bimbi
had always taken charge of any conversation he was in, and I had

tried to emulate him. But every book I picked up had few sentences which didn't contain anywhere from one to nearly all of the words that might as well have been in Chinese. When I just skipped those words, of course, I really ended up with little idea of what the book said. So I had come to the Norfolk Prison Colony still going through only book-reading motions. Pretty soon, I would have quit even these motions, unless I had received the motivation that I did.

3   I saw that the best thing I could do was get hold of a dictionary— to study, to learn some words. I was lucky enough to reason also that I should try to improve my penmanship. It was sad. I couldn't even write in a straight line. It was both ideas together that moved me to request a dictionary along with some tablets and pencils from the Norfolk Prison Colony school.

4   I spent two days just riffling uncertainly through the dictionary's pages. I'd never realized so many words existed! I didn't know which words I needed to learn. Finally, to start some kind of action, I began copying.

5   In my slow, painstaking, ragged handwriting, I copied into my tablet everything printed on that first page, down to the punctuation marks.

6   I believe it took me a day. Then, aloud, I read back, to myself, everything I'd written on the tablet. Over and over, aloud, to myself, I read my own handwriting.

7   I woke up the next morning, thinking about those words— immensely proud to realize that not only had I written so much at one time, but I'd written words that I never knew were in the world. Moreover, with a little effort, I also could remember what many of these words meant. I reviewed the words whose meanings I didn't remember. Funny thing, from the dictionary first page right now, that "aardvark" springs to my mind. The dictionary had a picture of it, a long-tailed, long-eared, burrowing African mammal, which lives off termites caught by sticking out its tongue as an anteater does for ants.

8   I was so fascinated that I went on—I copied the dictionary's next page. And the same experience came when I studied that. With every succeeding page, I also learned of people and places and events from history. Actually the dictionary is like a miniature encyclopedia. Finally the dictionary's A section had filled a whole tablet—and I went on into the B's. That was the way I started copying what eventually became the entire dictionary. It went a

lot faster after so much practice helped me to pick up handwriting speed. Between what I wrote in my tablet, and writing letters, during the rest of my time in prison I would guess I wrote a million words.

I suppose it was inevitable that as my word-base broadened, 9 I could for the first time pick up a book and read and now begin to understand what the book was saying. Anyone who has read a great deal can imagine the new world that opened. Let me tell you something; from then until I left that prison, in every free moment I had, if I was not reading in the library, I was reading on my bunk. You couldn't have gotten me out of books with a wedge. Between Mr. Muhammad's teachings, my correspondence, my visitors—usually Ella and Reginald—and my reading of books, months passed without my even thinking about being imprisoned. In fact, up to then, I never had been so truly free in my life. . . .

As you can imagine, especially in a prison where there was 10 heavy emphasis on rehabilitation, an inmate was smiled upon if he demonstrated an unusually intense interest in books. There was a sizable number of well-read inmates, especially the popular debaters. Some were said by many to be practically walking encyclopedias. They were almost celebrities. No university would ask any student to devour literature as I did when this new world opened to me, of being able to read and *understand*.

I read more in my room than in the library itself. An inmate 11 who was known to read a lot could check out more than the permitted maximum number of books. I preferred reading in the total isolation of my own room.

When I had progressed to really serious reading, every night 12 at about ten P.M. I would be outraged with the "lights out." It always seemed to catch me right in the middle of something engrossing.

Fortunately, right outside my door was a corridor light that 13 cast a glow into my room. The glow was enough to read by, once my eyes adjusted to it. So when "lights out" came, I would sit on the floor where I could continue reading in that glow.

At one-hour intervals the night guards paced past every room. 14 Each time I heard the approaching footsteps, I jumped into bed and feigned sleep. And as soon as the guard passed, I got back out of bed onto the floor area of that light-glow, where I would read for another fifty-eight minutes—until the guard approached again. That went on until three or four every morning. Three or four hours of sleep a night was enough for me. Often in the years in the streets I had slept less than that.

15   I have often reflected upon the new vistas that reading opened to me. I knew right there in prison that reading had changed forever the course of my life. As I see it today, the ability to read awoke inside me some long dormant craving to be mentally alive. I certainly wasn't seeking any degree, the way a college confers a status symbol upon its students. My homemade education gave me, with every additional book that I read, a little bit more sensitivity to the deafness, dumbness, and blindness that was afflicting the black race in America. Not long ago, an English writer telephoned me from London, asking questions. One was, "What's your alma mater?" I told him, "Books." You will never catch me with a free fifteen minutes in which I'm not studying something I feel might be able to help the black man. . . .

16   Every time I catch a plane, I have with me a book that I want to read—and that's a lot of books these days. If I weren't out here every day battling the white man, I could spend the rest of my life reading, just satisfying my curiosity—because you can hardly mention anything I'm not curious about. I don't think anybody ever got more out of going to prison than I did. In fact, prison enabled me to study far more intensively than I would have if my life had gone differently and I had attended some college. I imagine that one of the biggest troubles with colleges is there are too many distractions, too much panty-raiding, fraternities, and boola-boola and all of that. Where else but in prison could I have attacked my ignorance by being able to study intensely sometimes as much as fifteen hours a day?

BUILDING VOCABULARY

1. Throughout the selection, the writer uses *figurative* and *colloquial language* (see Glossary). As you know, figurative language involves imaginative comparisons, which go beyond plain or ordinary statements. Colloquial language involves informal or conversational phrases and expressions.

    The following are examples of some of the figurative and colloquial usages in this essay. Explain each italicized word group in your own words.

    a. *going through only book-reading motions* (par. 2)
    b. I *was lucky enough* (par. 3)
    c. *Funny thing* (par. 7)
    d. can imagine *the new world that opened* (par. 9)
    e. *You couldn't have gotten me out of books with a wedge* (par. 9)
    f. an inmate was *smiled upon* (par. 10)
    g. to be practically *walking encyclopedias* (par. 10)
    h. ask any student *to devour literature* (par. 10)
    i. changed forever *the course of my life* (par. 15)
    j. *some long dormant craving to be mentally alive* (par. 15)
    k. *the deafness, dumbness, and blindness that was afflicting* the black race in America (par. 15)
    l. Every time I *catch a plane* (par. 16)
    m. every day *battling the white man* (par. 16)
    n. just *satisfying my curiosity* (par. 16)
    o. *boola-boola and all of that* (par. 16)
    p. I have *attacked my ignorance* (par. 16)

2. Find the following words in the essay. Write brief definitions for them without using a dictionary. If they are unfamiliar to you, try to determine their meaning based on the context in which they appear.
    a. riffling (par. 4)
    b. painstaking (par. 5)
    c. ragged (par. 5)
    d. burrowing (par. 7)
    e. inevitable (par. 9)
    f. emphasis (par. 10)
    g. distractions (par. 16)

THINKING CRITICALLY ABOUT THE ESSAY

Understanding the Writer's Ideas

1. What was the highest level of formal education that the writer achieved? How is this different from the impression most people got from him? Why?

2. Who was Bimbi? Where did Malcolm X meet him? How was Bimbi important to the writer?

3. What does the writer mean by stating that when he tried to read, most of the words "might as well have been in Chinese"?

What happened when he skipped over such words? What motivated him to change his way of reading?

4. Why did Malcolm X start trying to improve his handwriting? How was it connected to his desire to improve his reading ability? Briefly describe how he went about this dual process. How did he feel after the first day of this process? Why?

5. How is the dictionary "like a miniature encyclopedia"?

6. Judging from this essay and his description of his "homemade education," how much time did Malcolm X spend in prison? Does the fact that he was in prison affect your appreciation of his learning process? How?

7. What is a "word-base" (par. 9)? What happened once the author's word-base expanded? How did this give him a sense of freedom?

8. Who is "Mr. Muhammad"?

9. Why did the prison officials like Malcolm X? What special privileges came to him as a result of this favorable opinion?

10. Why was Malcolm X angered with the "lights out" procedure? How did he overcome it?

11. What does the following sentence tell you about Malcolm X's life: "Often in the years in the streets I had slept less than that" (par. 14)?

12. Characterize the writer's opinion of a college education. How does he compare his education to a college degree? How did his education influence his understanding of his place and role in American society?

13. In your own words, describe the writer's attitude toward American blacks. Toward the relation between blacks and whites?

14. To what main purpose in life does the writer refer? What was the relation between this purpose and his feelings about reading? Use one word to describe Malcolm X's attitude toward reading.

15. What does the conclusion mean?

Understanding the Writer's Techniques

1. What is the thesis? Where does the writer place it?

2. In Chapters 5 and 8, you will learn about the techniques of *process analysis* and *cause-and-effect analysis*. Briefly, process analysis tells the reader *how* something is done;

cause-and-effect analysis explains *why* one thing leads to or affects another.

For this essay, outline step-by-step the process whereby Malcolm X developed his ability to read and enthusiasm for reading. Next, for each step in your outline, explain why one step led to the next.

3. *Narration* (see Chapter 4) is the telling of a story or the orderly relating of a series of events. How does Malcolm X use narration in this essay? How does he order the events of his narration?

4. What is the effect of the words "Let me tell you something" in paragraph 9?

5. How is the writer's memory of the first page of the dictionary like a dictionary entry itself? What does this say about the importance of this memory to the author?

6. *Tone* (see Glossary) is a writer's attitude toward his or her subject. Characterize the tone of this essay. What elements of the writing contribute to that tone? Be specific.

7. Which paragraphs make up the conclusion of this essay? How does the writer develop his conclusion? How does he relate it to the main body of the essay? Do you feel that there is a change in tone (see question 6) in the conclusion? Explain, using specific examples.

8. What is Malcolm X's main purpose in writing this essay? For whom is it intended? How do you know?

Exploring the Writer's Ideas

1. Malcolm X writes about his newly found love of reading and ability to read: "In fact, up to then, I never had been so truly free in my life." Has learning any particular skill or activity ever given you such a feeling of freedom or joy? Explain.

2. What do you feel was the source of Malcolm X's attitude toward a college education? Do you think any of his points here are valid? Why? What are your opinions about the quality of the college education you are receiving?

3. The writer also implies that, in some ways, the educational opportunities of prison were superior to those he would have had at college. What is his basis for this attitude? Have you ever experienced a circumstance in which being restricted actually benefited you? Explain.

4. Malcolm X held very strong opinions about the relations between blacks and whites in America. Do some library research on him to try to understand his opinions. You might begin by reading *The Autobiography of Malcolm X,* from which this essay was excerpted. Do you agree or disagree with his feelings? Why?

5. Following Malcolm X's example, handwrite a page from a dictionary (a pocket dictionary will be fine), copying everything— including punctuation—exactly!

   How long did it take you? How did it make you feel? Did you learn anything from the experience?

IDEAS FOR WRITING

Prewriting

Brainstorm on a difficult activity that you learned how to perform. What problems did the activity present? Why did you want to learn how to do it?

Guided Writing

Write an essay in which you tell about an activity that you can now perform but that once seemed impossible to you.

1. Open your essay with an example in which you compare what most people assume about your skill or background in the activity to what the reality is.

2. Mention someone who especially influenced you in your desire to master this activity.

3. Tell what kept you from giving up on learning this activity.

4. Explain, step by step, the *process* by which you learned more and more about the activity. Explain how and why one step led to the next.

5. Use *figurative* and *colloquial* language where you think it appropriate in your essay.

6. Describe in some detail how you overcame an obstacle, imposed by others, which could have impeded your learning process.

7. Use your conclusion to express a deeply felt personal opinion and to generalize your learning of this skill to the population at large.

Thinking and Writing Collaboratively

Exchange a draft version of your Guided Writing essay with another writer in the class. After you read your partner's essay, make recommendations for helping the writer produce the next draft. Use the items numbered 1–7 above to guide your discussion.

Writing About the Text

In this essay, Malcolm X directly connects literacy and power, words and politics. Do you think that if Malcolm were alive today—in the era of the image, of TV and video—he would have been just as likely to have needed and have valued literacy? Write an essay that explores this question, drawing as much as seems appropriate on the selection.

More Writing Projects

1. Select any page of a standard dictionary and copy in your journal at least ten words, with definitions, that are new or somewhat unfamiliar to you. Then jot down some thoughts on the process.
2. Ask yourself formal, journalistic questions about Malcolm X's essay: *What* happened? *Who* was involved? *How* was it done? *Where* did it occur? *When* did it occur? *Why* did it happen? Write out answers to these questions, and then assemble them in a unified, coherent paragraph.
3. Form a group with three other classmates. Focus on the context of Malcolm X's essay and on his comment on "the deafness, dumbness, and blindness that was afflicting the black race in America" (par. 15). Discuss this issue and its connection to education. Then prepare a collaborative essay on the topic.

One Writer's Beginnings
Eudora Welty

Mixing Patterns

Eudora Welty, one of America's most revered twentieth-century writers, was born in 1909 on North Congress Street in Jackson, Mississippi, in the house that she would live in almost all her long life. Although she attended the University of Wisconsin at Madison, studied business for a year at Columbia University, and traveled widely, Welty always returned to the family home in Jackson. She never married. Her brief autobiography, *One Writer's Beginnings* (1980), from which this selection is drawn, ends with these words: "I am a writer who came of a sheltered life. A sheltered life can be a daring life as well. For all serious daring starts from within." The sheltered life to which Welty alludes is the life of a white woman in the Deep South in the first decades of the twentieth century. The ways of life in rural Mississippi are the subject of most of her acclaimed writing. Her novel *The Optimist's Daughter* won the 1972 Pulitzer Prize, and her total work has been collected in two volumes for the authoritative Library of America series. But as this selection shows, her sheltered life was not limited or narrow. Rather, it was rich in sensations and emotions, and through reading she reached out to the ends of the earth and the depths of the heart. Eudora Welty died in 2001.

PREREADING: THINKING ABOUT THE ESSAY IN ADVANCE

What attitudes did your family have toward reading when you were a child? Did books surround you? Which books did your parents or other relatives read to you or suggest that you read? How did you feel about books as a child growing up?

Words to Watch

disposed (par. 4)   inclined; receptive
vignettes (par. 5)   charming literary sketches
roué (par. 7)   lecherous, wasted man
interlocutor (par. 9)   partner in a dialogue
quoth (par. 9)   archaic form of word *quoted*
wizardry (par. 15)   magic
sensory (par. 18)   pertaining to the senses

reel (par. 19)   fast dance
constellations (par. 20)   positions of star groups in sky, consid-
    ered to look like (and named for) mythological characters

I learned from the age of two or three that any room in our house, 1
at any time of day, was there to read in, or to be read to. My
mother read to me. She'd read to me in the big bedroom in the
mornings, when we were in her rocker together, which ticked in
rhythm as we rocked, as though we had a cricket accompanying
the story. She'd read to me in the diningroom on winter after-
noons in front of the coal fire, with our cuckoo clock ending the
story with "Cuckoo," and at night when I'd got in my own bed. I
must have given her no peace. Sometimes she read to me in the
kitchen while she sat churning, and the churning sobbed along
with *any* story. It was my ambition to have her read to me while
I churned; once she granted my wish, but she read off my story
before I brought her butter. She was an expressive reader. When
she was reading "Puss in Boots," for instance, it was impossible
not to know that she distrusted *all* cats.

It had been startling and disappointing to me to find out that 2
story books had been written by *people,* that books were not natural wonders, coming up of themselves like grass. Yet regardless of
where they came from, I cannot remember a time when I was not
in love with them—with the books themselves, cover and bind-
ing and the paper they were printed on, with their smell and their
weight and with their possession in my arms, captured and carried
off to myself. Still illiterate, I was ready for them, committed to all
the reading I could give them.

Neither of my parents had come from homes that could afford 3
to buy many books, but though it must have been something of
a strain on his salary, as the youngest officer in a young insurance company, my father was all the while carefully selecting and
ordering away for what he and Mother thought we children should
grow up with. They bought first for the future.

Besides the bookcase in the livingroom, which was always 4
called "the library," there were the encyclopedia tables and dictionary stand under windows in our diningroom. Here to help us grow up
arguing around the diningroom table were the Unabridged Webster,
the Columbia Encyclopedia, Compton's Pictured Encyclopedia,
the Lincoln Library of Information, and later the Book of Knowledge.
And the year we moved into our new house, there was room to

celebrate it with the new 1925 edition of the Britannica, which my father, his face always deliberately turned toward the future, was of course disposed to think better than any previous edition.

5   In "the library," inside the mission-style bookcase with its three diamond-latticed glass doors, with my father's Morris chair and the glass-shaded lamp on its table beside it, were books I could soon begin on—and I did, reading them all alike and as they came, straight down their rows, top shelf to bottom. There was the set of Stoddard's Lectures, in all its late nineteenth-century vocabulary and vignettes of peasant life and quaint beliefs and customs, with matching halftone illustrations: Vesuvius erupting, Venice by moonlight, gypsies glimpsed by their campfires. I didn't know then the clue they were to my father's longing to see the rest of the world. I read straight through his other love-from-afar: the Victrola Book of the Opera, with opera after opera in synopsis, with portraits in costume of Melba, Caruso, Galli-Curci, and Geraldine Farrar, some of whose voices we could listen to on our Red Seal records.

6   My mother read secondarily for information; she sank as a hedonist into novels. She read Dickens in the spirit in which she would have eloped with him. The novels of her girlhood that had stayed on in her imagination, besides those of Dickens and Scott and Robert Louis Stevenson, were *Jane Eyre, Trilby, The Woman in White, Green Mansions, King Solomon's Mines.* Marie Corelli's name would crop up but I understood she had gone out of favor with my mother, who had only kept *Ardath* out of loyalty. In time she absorbed herself in Galsworthy, Edith Wharton, above all in Thomas Mann of the *Joseph* volumes.

7   *St. Elmo* was not in our house; I saw it often in other houses. This wildly popular Southern novel is where all the Edna Earles in our population started coming from. They're all named for the heroine, who succeeded in bringing a dissolute, sinning roué and atheist of a lover (St. Elmo) to his knees. My mother was able to forgo it. But she remembered the classic advice given to rose growers on how to water their bushes long enough: "Take a chair and *St. Elmo.*"

8   To both my parents I owe my early acquaintance with a beloved Mark Twain. There was a full set of Mark Twain and a short set of Ring Lardner in our bookcase, and those were the volumes that in time united us all, parents and children.

9   Reading everything that stood before me was how I came upon a worn old book without a back that had belonged to my

father as a child. It was called *Sanford and Merton*. Is there anyone left who recognizes it, I wonder? It is the famous moral tale written by Thomas Day in the 1780s, but of him no mention is made on the title page of *this* book; here it is *Sanford and Merton in Words of One Syllable* by Mary Godolphin. Here are the rich boy and the poor boy and Mr. Barlow, their teacher and interlocutor, in long discourses alternating with dramatic scenes—anger and rescue allotted to the rich and the poor respectively. It may have only words of one syllable, but one of them is "quoth." It ends with not one but two morals, both engraved on rings: "Do what you ought, come what may," and "If we would be great, we must first learn to be good."

This book was lacking its front cover, the back held on by 10 strips of pasted paper, now turned golden, in several layers, and the pages stained, flecked, and tattered around the edges; its garish illustrations had come unattached but were preserved, laid in. I had the feeling even in my heedless childhood that this was the only book my father as a little boy had had of his own. He had held onto it, and might have gone to sleep on its coverless face: he had lost his mother when he was seven. My father had never made any mention to his own children of the book, but he had brought it along with him from Ohio to our house and shelved it in our bookcase.

My mother had brought from West Virginia that set of Dickens; 11 those books looked sad, too—they had been through fire and water before I was born, she told me, and there they were, lined up—as I later realized, waiting for *me*.

I was presented, from as early as I can remember, with books 12 of my own, which appeared on my birthday and Christmas morning. Indeed, my parents could not give me books enough. They must have sacrificed to give me on my sixth or seventh birthday— it was after I became a reader for myself—the ten-volume set of Our Wonder World. These were beautifully made, heavy books I would lie down with on the floor in front of the diningroom hearth, and more often than the rest volume 5, *Every Child's Story Book,* was under my eyes. There were the fairy tales—Grimm, Andersen, the English, the French, "Ali Baba and the Forty Thieves"; and there was Aesop and Reynard the Fox; there were the myths and legends, Robin Hood, King Arthur, and St. George and the Dragon, even the history of Joan of Arc; a whack of *Pilgrim's Progress* and a long piece of *Gulliver*. They all carried their classic illustrations.

I located myself in these pages and could go straight to the stories and pictures I loved; very often "The Yellow Dwarf" was first choice, with Walter Crane's Yellow Dwarf in full color making his terrifying appearance flanked by turkeys. Now that volume is as worn and backless and hanging apart as my father's poor *Sanford and Merton*. The precious page with Edward Lear's "Jumblies" on it has been in danger of slipping out for all these years. One measure of my love for Our Wonder World was that for a long time I wondered if I would go through fire and water for it as my mother had done for Charles Dickens; and the only comfort was to think I could ask my mother to do it for me.

13   I believe I'm the only child I know of who grew up with this treasure in the house. I used to ask others, "Did you have Our Wonder World?" I'd have to tell them The Book of Knowledge could not hold a candle to it.

14   I live in gratitude to my parents for initiating me—as early as I begged for it, without keeping me waiting—into knowledge of the word, into reading and spelling, by way of the alphabet. They taught it to me at home in time for me to begin to read before starting to school. I believe the alphabet is no longer considered an essential piece of equipment for traveling through life. In my day it was the keystone to knowledge. You learned the alphabet as you learned to count to ten, as you learned "Now I lay me" and the Lord's Prayer and your father's and mother's name and address and telephone number, all in case you were lost.

15   My love for the alphabet, which endures, grew out of reciting it but, before that, out of seeing the letters on the page. In my own story books, before I could read them for myself, I fell in love with various winding, enchanted-looking initials drawn by Walter Crane at the heads of fairy tales. In "Once upon a time," an "O" had a rabbit running it as a treadmill, his feet upon flowers. When the day came, years later, for me to see the Book of Kells, all the wizardry of letter, initial, and word swept over me a thousand times over, and the illumination, the gold, seemed a part of the word's beauty and holiness that had been there from the start.

16 Learning stamps you with its moments. Childhood's learning is made up of moments. It isn't steady. It's a pulse.

17   In a children's art class, we sat in a ring on kindergarten chairs and drew three daffodils that had just been picked out of the yard; and while I was drawing, my sharpened yellow pencil and the cup

of the yellow daffodil gave off whiffs just alike. That the pencil doing the drawing should give off the same smell as the flower it drew seemed part of the art lesson—as shouldn't it be? Children, like animals, use all their senses to discover the world. Then artists come along and discover it the same way, all over again. Here and there, it's the same world. Or now and then we'll hear from an artist who's never lost it.

In my sensory education I include my physical awareness of the *word*. Of a certain word, that is; the connection it has with what it stands for. At around age six, perhaps, I was standing by myself in our front yard waiting for supper, just at that hour in a late summer day when the sun is already below the horizon and the risen full moon in the visible sky stops being chalky and begins to take on light. There comes the moment, and I saw it then, when the moon goes from flat to round. For the first time it met my eyes as a globe. The word "moon" came into my mouth as though fed to me out of a silver spoon. Held in my mouth the moon became a word. It had the roundness of a Concord grape Grandpa took off his vine and gave me to suck out of its skin and swallow whole, in Ohio. 18

This love did not prevent me from living for years in foolish error about the moon. The new moon just appearing in the west was the rising moon to me. The new should be rising. And in early childhood the sun and moon, those opposite reigning powers, I just as easily assumed rose in east and west respectively in their opposite sides of the sky, and like partners in a reel they advanced, sun from the east, moon from the west, crossed over (when I wasn't looking) and went down on the other side. My father couldn't have known I believed that when, bending behind me and guiding my shoulder, he positioned me at our telescope in the front yard and, with careful adjustment of the focus, brought the moon close to me. 19

The night sky over my childhood Jackson was velvety black. I could see the full constellations in it and call their names; when I could read, I knew their myths. Though I was always waked for eclipses, and indeed carried to the window as an infant in arms and shown Halley's Comet in my sleep, and though I'd been taught at our diningroom table about the solar system and knew the earth revolved around the sun, and our moon around us, I never found out the moon didn't come up in the west until I was a writer and Herschel Brickell, the literary critic, told me after I misplaced it in a story. He said valuable words to me about my new profession: "Always be sure you get your moon in the right part of the sky." 20

BUILDING VOCABULARY

1. Identify the following references to authors, books, and stories from Welty's essay:
   a. Charles Dickens
   b. Robert Louis Stevenson
   c. *Jane Eyre*
   d. *The Woman in White*
   e. Edith Wharton
   f. Thomas Mann
   g. Mark Twain
   h. Ring Lardner
   i. *Pilgrim's Progress*
   j. *Gulliver*
2. Write definitions and your own sentences for the following words:
   a. quaint (par. 5)
   b. hedonist (par. 6)
   c. dissolute (par. 7)
   d. allotted (par. 9)
   e. garish (par. 10)
   f. heedless (par. 10)
   g. gratitude (par. 14)
   h. essential (par. 14)
   i. keystone (par. 14)
   j. reigning (par. 19)

THINKING CRITICALLY ABOUT THE ESSAY

Understanding the Writer's Ideas

1. Why does the writer say of her mother, "I must have given her no peace" (par. 1)?
2. Why was it "startling and disappointing" for Welty to find out that storybooks were written by *people*? Where did she think they came from? Aside from the stories themselves, what is it that the author loves so much about books?
3. How did the way Welty's mother felt toward books affect her child's attitude toward reading? In what ways did the conditions in Welty's home contribute to her attitude toward books?
4. What is it, exactly, that Welty loved about books as a child?

5. Why did Welty's parents make sacrifices to buy books for the household? What were their hopes for their children? What kinds of books did the parents choose to buy and to read? What, if anything, do these choices tell us about the parents' characters?

6. For what reasons does the writer feel that learning the alphabet is so important? To what other learning processes does she compare it? Before she learned to recite her alphabet, why was it so important to her?

7. Explain in your own words what the writer considers to be the relation between physical sensations and learning words. According to the author why is it important for parents to read to their children?

8. What does Welty mean when she says a child's learning "Isn't steady. It's a pulse"?

9. Explain the significance of Welty's description of her experience of the moon at age six.

10. What, if anything, do we learn from Herschel Brickell's advice?

Understanding the Writer's Techniques

1. What is the main idea of Welty's essay? Is there any point at which she directly states that main idea? Explain.

2. A *reminiscence* is a narrative account of a special memory. How does the writer use reminiscence in this essay?

3. The *tone* (see Glossary) of an essay is the expression of the writer's attitude toward the topic. State the tone of this essay. What specifically about the writing contributes to that tone?

4. Placing words in italics emphasizes them. Where does the author use italics in this essay? Why does she use them?

5. What does the writer mean by stating that the set of Dickens books "had been *through fire and water* before I was born" (par. 11)? How does the image contribute to the point she's making?

6. In paragraph 1, Welty employs a technique called *personification* (see Glossary) in stating that "the churning sobbed along with any story." Consider the effect of this technique, along with her description of her mother's reading style ("it was impossible not to know that she distrusted all cats") in the same paragraph. What does Welty seem to suggest about the connection between emotion (or expressiveness) and reading?

7. Why does Welty make a point of vividly describing books' physical characteristics, as in paragraphs 2, 10, and 15? What

do her descriptions contribute to our understanding of her relationship to reading?

8. *Similes* (see Glossary) are imaginative comparisons using the word *like* or *as*. Use of similes often enlivens the writing and makes it memorable.

   In your own words, explain what is being compared in the following similes (in italics) drawn from Welty's essay, and tell how they contribute to the essay:

   a.   ... we were in her rocker together, which ticked in rhythm as we rocked, *as though we had a cricket accompanying the story.* (par. 1)

   b.   ... books were not natural wonders, coming up of themselves like grass. (par. 2)

   c.   The word "moon" came into my mouth *as though fed to me out of a silver spoon.* (par. 18)

9. Welty makes a number of references to other writers, artists, and books, in addition to those listed in the "Building Vocabulary" section: for example, Nellie Melba, Enrico Caruso, Amelita Galli-Curci, and Geraldine Farrar; Sir Walter Scott, *Green Mansions,* and John Galsworthy; Walter Crane and Edward Lear—there are many others too.

   a.   See if you can find some information on each of these references. When did the writers and artists live? When were the books written?

   b.   Why do you think Welty makes these references? Do you think she expects her readers to recognize them? (Keep in mind that *One Writer's Beginnings* was first published in book form in 1984.) Do the references in any way contribute to your understanding of her piece, even if they were unfamiliar to you?

✳ MIXING PATTERNS

Description helps the reader to "see" objects and scenes and to feel their importance through the author's eyes. *Narration*—the telling of a story—helps the reader follow a sequence of events. (See Chapters 3 and 4.) Both techniques rely on the writer's skill in choosing and presenting details. In what way does Welty make use of description and narration in this essay? How would you evaluate her use of details?

Exploring the Writer's Ideas

1. The writer believes that it is very important for parents to read to their children. Some specialists in child development even advocate reading to infants still in the womb and to babies before they've spoken their first words. For what reasons might such activities be important? Do you personally feel they are important or useful? Would you read to an unborn infant? Why or why not? If you would, *what* would you read?

2. Welty was born in 1909 and obviously belongs to a different generation from the vast majority of college students today. Do you feel that her type of love and advocacy of reading are as valid for the current generation, raised on television, video, CDs, cable, MTV, and the Internet? Explain.

3. Welty describes her love of books as going beyond the words and stories they contain to their physical and visual attributes. What objects—not other people—do you love or respect with that intensity? Tell a little about why and how you have developed this feeling.

IDEAS FOR WRITING

Prewriting

In the visual and auditory age in which we live—we watch and listen to television, tune in the radio, see movies regularly—what is the proper role for reading? Talk to friends, teachers, and fellow students about the matter. Record their observations and try to classify their responses.

Guided Writing

Write an essay that indicates your own attitude toward reading.

1. In order to set the stage for the discussion of your attitude, begin by recalling details about a moment with a parent or other adult.

2. Use dialogue as part of this scene.

3. Go as far back in your childhood as you can possibly remember, and narrate two or three incidents that help explain the formation of your current attitude toward reading.

4. Use sensory language (color, sound, smell, touch, and taste) to show how the environment of the home where you grew up helped shape your attitude.
5. Tell about a particular, special childhood fascination with something you *saw*—not read—in a book.
6. Try to describe the first time you were conscious of the *meaning* of a particular word.
7. Use at least one *simile* in your essay.
8. Create and keep a consistent *tone* throughout the essay.
9. End your essay with an explanation of how a particular book has been continually influential to you as well as to others of your generation.
10. Give your essay an unusual title that derives from some description in your essay.

Thinking and Writing Collaboratively

Form groups of three to five students and read the essays you each prepared for the Guided Writing assignment. Together, make a list of the various attitudes expressed about reading by group members. Report to the class as a whole on the reading attitudes of your group.

Writing About the Text

This selection is written by someone whom many critics consider to be a great writer, a notch above the group of excellent, admirable, or fine writers. What qualities in Welty's writing support this high praise? How do these qualities square with the prescriptions for good writing offered in Chapter 1?

More Writing Projects

1. Enter in your journal early memories of people who read to you or of books that you read on your own. Try to capture the sensation and importance of these early reading experiences.
2. Return to question 2 in Exploring the Writer's Ideas, and write a one-paragraph response to it.
3. Write an essay on the person who most influenced your childhood education. Did this person read to you, give you books, make you do your homework? Assess the impact of this person on your life.

One Idea

Norman Mailer

Norman Mailer, born in Long Branch, New Jersey, in 1923, was a controversial writer, producer, director, actor, and political gadfly who influenced American letters for almost sixty years. After graduating from Harvard in 1943 and serving in the Pacific theater during World War II, Mailer published *The Naked and the Dead* (1948). The critic Orville Prescott hailed Mailer's first book as "the most impressive novel about the Second World War that I have ever read." At the age of twenty-five, Mailer suddenly enjoyed public fame—a heightened celebrity that the writer never relinquished during a long and frequently combative career. Married six times, preoccupied with sex and violence, critical of American culture and power, and given to grandiose literary projects, Mailer produced more than three dozen novels, nonfiction narratives, plays, and essay collections. Some of his more significant works are *The Armies of the Night* (1968), *Miami and the Siege of Chicago* (1968), *The Executioner's Song* (1979), *Harlot's Ghost* (1991), and *The Castle in the Forest* (2007), the first part of a cycle of novels on Hitler that Mailer completed before his death in 2007. During his career, Mailer received many of the nation's major literary awards, including two National Book Awards and two Pulitzer Prizes. The following selection is part of a longer essay that appeared in the January 23, 2005, issue of *Parade*. In this piece, Mailer responds to a question posed by the editors of the magazine: "If you could do one thing to change America for the better, what would it be?" Mailer provides a typically opinionated answer, focusing on reading and television commercials.

PREREADING: THINKING ABOUT THE ESSAY IN ADVANCE

It apparently is a truism that children should read more and watch television less. In fact, experts contend that very young children should be limited to no more than two hours of television viewing daily. But might reading and television watching (as well as reading and viewing on computer screens) actually be complementary activities? In this age of split screens, multitasking, and googling, could reading actually benefit from exposure to various media forms? What do *you* think?

Words to Watch

diminishes (par. 1)   reduces in size, importance, proportion, or degree

analogy (par. 1)   similarity between things otherwise unlike; partial resemblance

advent (par. 2)   a coming or arrival

rebuke (par. 4)   harsh criticism

kaleidoscope (par. 5)   a constantly changing pattern or collection

stagnation (par. 5)   without motion or current, hence dull, sluggish

1   If the desire to read diminishes, so does one's ability to read. The search for a culprit does not have to go far. There are confirming studies all over academia and the media that too many hours are devoted each day to the tube. Television is seen as the culprit, since the ability to read well is directly related to one's ability to learn. If it is universally understood that the power to concentrate while reading is the royal road to knowledge, what may not be perceived as clearly is how much concentration itself is a species of psychic strength. It can be developed or it can go soft in much the manner that body muscle can be built up or allowed to go slack. The development of physical ability is in direct relation to use. Reading offers its analogy. When children become interested in an activity, their concentration is firm—until it is interrupted. Sixty years ago, children would read for hours. Their powers of concentration developed as naturally as breathing. Good readers became very good readers, even as men and women who go in for weight-lifting will bulk up. The connection between loving to read and doing well in school was no mystery to most students.

2   With the advent of television, the nature of concentration was altered. Yet children could still develop such powers by watching TV. Video and books had a common denominator then—narrative.

3   In the early years of television, it was even hoped that the attention children gave to TV would improve their interest in reading. Indeed, it might have if TV, left to itself, consisted of uninterrupted narratives. That, of course, was soon not the case. There were constant interruptions to programs—the commercials.

4   Every parent has had the experience of picking up a 2- or 3-year-old who is busy at play. All too often, a tantrum occurs. Even as adults, we have to learn to contain our annoyance when

our thoughts are broken into. For a child, an interruption to one's concentration can prove as painful as a verbal rebuke.

Yet this is what we do to our children for hours every day. On 5 the major networks, the amount of time given to commercials and other promotional messages increased by 36 percent from 1991 to 2003. Each of the four major networks now offers 52 minutes of commercials in the three hours from 8 P.M. to 11 P.M. every day. It is equal to saying that every seven, 10 or 12 minutes, our attention to what is happening on the tube is cut into by a commercial. It is as bad for most children's shows. Soon enough, children develop a fail-safe. Since the child knows that any interesting story will soon be amputated by a kaleidoscope of toys, food, dolls, clowns, new colors and the clutter of six or seven wholly different products all following one another in 10-, 20- and 30-second spots all the way through a three-minute break, the child also comes to recognize that concentration is not one's friend but is treacherous. For soon enough, attention will be turned inside out. The need to get up and move can become a frantic if routine response for highly keyed children. Other kids, stupefied by the onslaught of a quick series of ads that have nothing to do with each other, suffer a dire spiritual product—stagnation. They sit on the couch in a stupor, they eat and drink, and alarms are sounded through the nation. Our children are becoming obese.

What then, is to be done? . . . We have an economy that is 6 stimulated by TV advertising. Yet the constant interruption of concentration it generates not only dominates much of our lives, but over the long run also is bound to bleed into our prosperity. The rest of the world is getting into position to do far better than us with future economic conditions.

If we want to have the best of all possible worlds, we had 7 better recognize that we cannot have all the worlds. I believe that television commercials have got to go. Let us pay directly for what we enjoy on television rather than pass the spiritual cost on to our children and their children.

BUILDING VOCABULARY

1. Use the items in Words to Watch in sentences of your own.
2. Explain in the context of the essay "royal road to knowledge" (par. 1), "species of psychic strength" (par. 1), "amputated by

a kaleidoscope" (par. 5), "highly keyed children" (par. 5), and "bleed into our prosperity" (par. 6).

THINKING CRITICALLY ABOUT THE ESSAY

Understanding the Writer's Ideas

1. Is this essay about reading, television, or both? Justify your answer.
2. Explain in your own words the *analogy* (see Glossary) that Mailer develops in paragraph 1.
3. What does Mailer mean when he writes that "concentration . . . is a form of psychic strength" (par. 1)? What aspects of "concentration" does he focus on?
4. What does Mailer say about commercials in paragraphs 4–7? What is his purpose in focusing on them?
5. To what and to whom does Mailer refer when he talks about "a dire spiritual product" (par. 5) and "spiritual cost" (par. 7)? What is his intention here? Do you agree or disagree with his argument?

Understanding the Writer's Techniques

1. What is Mailer's thesis? Where does he state his main idea most clearly and forcefully?
2. Mailer wrote this piece for a popular magazine with a fairly conventional readership. What elements of style, content, and organization in this essay would appeal to a general audience?
3. In what ways does the analogy in paragraph 1 extend to the entire essay? Do you think that Mailer intended this effect? Why or why not?
4. How might Mailer's writing reflect a problem–solution approach to essay organization and development? Cite specific details to support your response.
5. What types of evidence does Mailer provide to support his key ideas? Do you think that he provides sufficient evidence? Why or why not?
6. How does Mailer develop his conclusion? Without the last paragraph, how would the essay be different?

✳ MIXING PATTERNS

Mailer's essay relies heavily on principles that we associate with *causal analysis* (see Chapter 8) and *argumentation and persuasion* (see Chapter 11). What is the relation between these two strategies as Mailer employs them? How does Mailer use both techniques in the essay, and toward what goal?

Exploring the Writer's Ideas

1. Mailer makes several sweeping generalizations—reading is "the royal road to knowledge," commercials produce spiritual poverty in children, excessive television viewing makes kids obese, and so forth. Do you agree or disagree with Mailer's opinions, and why?
2. Mailer creates an opposition between reading and television viewing. How well does he make his case? Are you convinced? Explain your response.
3. What would Mailer have us do about the problem he outlines in this essay? Does his argument appeal to you in terms of logic, ethics, or emotion? (See Chapter 11 for an introduction to argumentation.) Could he succeed in moving readers to action? Why or why not?

IDEAS FOR WRITING

Prewriting

Make two lists titled "Reading Pleasures" and "Viewing Pleasures" (or "Viewing Distractions"). Provide at least five entries for each column.

Guided Writing

Write an essay that either supports Mailer's main idea or takes issue with it. Feel free to include television, film, e-books, and the Internet in your response.

1. State your thesis in a well-organized introductory paragraph.
2. Imagine that you are writing for a general audience—not exclusively for your instructor. Adjust your style accordingly.

3. Adopt a problem–solution approach to the organization of your essay.
4. As you develop the body of the essay, try to maintain a balance in coverage between or among your key subjects.
5. Make certain that you provide specific evidence to support your more general ideas.
6. Write a concluding paragraph that contains a call to action.

Thinking and Writing Collaboratively

Share with another class member the lists that you developed for the Prewriting exercise. Discuss with your classmate the details in the list and how they influenced the direction and scope of the essay you composed (or are planning to write).

Writing About the Text

Much of the energy of this essay comes from Mailer's willingness to state his opinions sharply and forcefully. Write an essay in which you analyze his opinionated style and how it contributes to his thesis.

More Writing Projects

1. In your journal, write your own entry about your television viewing habits, and whether or not they have compromised or harmed your reading abilities.
2. In a 100-word paragraph, explain how television viewing *might* make children obese.
3. Write an essay explaining why today's generation of college students is better prepared than earlier ones to multitask, manage, and "read" the flow of information coming from a variety of print, visual, and digital sources.

SUMMING UP: CHAPTER 2

1. In one way or another, most of the writers in this chapter explain how reading has provided them with emotional ease or intellectual stimulation at some point in their lives. Which of these writers, alone or in combination, best reflects your own view of reading? Write an essay in which you address this question.

2. On the average, Americans are said to read less than one book per person annually. Take a survey of several people who are not students to find out how often and what kinds of books they read. In an essay, analyze the results. Indicate the types of people you interviewed, and explain why your results either conformed to or differed from the norm. Indicate the types of books each person read.

3. List all the books you have read in the past six months. For each, write a brief two- or three-sentence reaction. Compare your list with those of your classmates. What reading trends do you notice? Do you find patterns in the reactions to reading? What generalizations can you draw about the reading habits of students at your school?

4. The United States ranks forty-ninth among nations in literacy. People often ask, "Why is there such a low rate of literacy in such an advanced country?" What is your answer to this question? Write an essay that explains your response. Refer to the opinions on reading of Ortiz Cofer, Malcolm X, Welty, and Mailer. Suggest some ways to reverse this trend in American reading.

5. Using Ortiz Cofer as an example, write an essay in which you reflect on your early memories of reading. Describe when you learned to read, when you experienced pleasure at being read to, or when you started appreciating a particular kind of reading. Call your essay, "Reading When I Was Young."

6. Several writers represented in this chapter speak about reading in a distinctly personal way. In each case reading is vital to their sense of personal identity. But it is through the discovery of the world beyond the self, the great world found in books, that the writers find themselves. Write an essay that explores this paradox of reading.

7. Compare and contrast the essays by Ortiz Cofer and Mailer on the subject of reading. Predict at least one disagreement that they might likely have about reading and popular media.

8. Malcolm X goes through the dictionary learning words because he sees vocabulary as power. How does ambition in reading relate to ambition in life? Explain your response in an essay.

✳ FROM SEEING TO WRITING

Examine the photograph below and write an essay in which you analyze the reasons that the Read Across America program chose to present such an image in the national media. Why did the organization use a photograph of Gwyneth Paltrow reading from the book *One Fish Two Fish Red Fish Blue Fish* by Dr. Seuss? Why and how does the photo link celebrity and reading? Is this a good idea? Why or why not? Try to address these questions in your analysis.

CHAPTER 3

Description

WHAT IS DESCRIPTION?

Description is a technique for showing readers what the writer sees: objects, scenes, characters, ideas, and even emotions and moods. Good description relies on the use of *sensory language*—that is, language that evokes our five senses of sight, touch, taste, smell, and sound. In writing, description uses specific *nouns* and *adjectives* to create carefully selected vivid details. The word *vehicle* is neutral, but a "rusty, green 1959 Pontiac convertible" creates a picture. Description is frequently used to make abstract ideas more *concrete*. While the abstract word *liberty* may have a definition for each reader, a description of the Statue of Liberty gleaming in New York's harbor at twilight creates an emotional description of liberty. Description, then, is used by writers who want their readers to *see* what they are writing about. A writer like Diane Ackerman uses description in order to capture the passing of summer. Annie Dillard uses description of the natural world to reflect on our life on earth. Maxine Hong Kingston uses description of her mother's collection of turtles, catfish, pigeons, skunks, and other unexpected food sources to re-create for her readers a culture different from their own. Suzanne Berne describes the former site of the World Trade Center to sort out her feelings about 9/11. Each writer, then, uses description to help us, as readers, *see* the material about which he or she is writing. As writers, we can study their techniques to improve our own essays.

HOW DO WE READ DESCRIPTION?

Reading a descriptive essay requires us to

- Identify what the writer is describing, and ask why he or she is describing it.
- Look for the concrete nouns, supportive adjectives, or other sensory words that the writer uses to create vivid pictures.
- Find the perspective or angle from which the writer describes: Is it top to bottom, left to right, front to back? Or is it a mood description that relies on feelings? How has the writer *selected* details to create the mood?
- Determine how the writer has organized the description. Here we must look for a "dominant impression." This arises from the writer's focus on a single subject and the feelings that the writer brings to that subject. Each one should be identified.
- Identify the purpose of the description. What is the *thesis* of the writing?
- Determine what audience the writer is aiming toward. How do we know?

HOW DO WE WRITE DESCRIPTION?

After reading some of the selections of descriptive writing in this chapter, you should be ready to write your own description. Don't just read about Kingston's animals, though, or Dillard's Napo River jungle. Think critically about how you can adapt their methods to your needs.

Select a topic and begin to write a thesis statement, keeping in mind that you will want to give the reader information about what you are describing and what angle you are taking on the topic.

Sample thesis sentence:

> For a first-time tourist in New York City, the subway trains can seem confusing and threatening, but the long-time resident finds the train system a clever, speedy network for traveling around the city.

Here, we see the thesis statement sets out a purpose and an audience. The purpose is to demonstrate the virtues of the New York transit system, and the audience is not the well-traveled New Yorker, but a visitor.

Collect a list of sensory words.

New York City's subway trains are noisy and crowded, labeled with brightly colored letters, made of shiny corrugated stainless steel, travel at 90 miles per hour, display colorful graffiti and advertising signs, run on electricity.

Use the five senses:

What are subway sounds? Music by street musicians, the screech of brakes, conductors giving directions over scratchy loudspeakers, people talking in different languages.

What are subway smells? Pretzels roasting, the sweaty odor of human bodies crowded together on a hot summer day.

What are subway textures? Colored metal straps and poles for balance, the crisp corner of a newspaper you're reading.

What are subway tastes? A candy bar or chewing gum you buy at the newsstand.

What are subway sights? Crowds of people rushing to work; the colorful pillars freshly painted in each station; the drunk asleep on a bench; the police officer in a blue uniform; the litter on the ground; the subway system maps near each token booth; the advertising posters on the walls and trains.

Plan a dominant impression and an order for arranging details. You might look at the subway from a passenger's point of view and describe the travel process from getting onto the train to arriving at the destination. Your impression might be that to the uninitiated, the subway system seems confusing, but to the experienced New Yorker, trains are the fastest and safest way to get around town.

Express a *purpose* for the description. The purpose might be to prepare a visitor from out of town for her first subway ride by writing a letter to her before she arrives in New York.

Identify the audience: Who will read the essay?

If you were writing to the Commissioner of Transportation in New York, or to a cousin from Iowa whom you know well, you would write differently in each case. Awareness of audience can help you choose a level of diction and formality. Knowing your audience can also help you decide which details to include and which your readers might know. It is always best to assume that the audience knows less than you do and to include details even if they seem obvious to you.

For example, even if you, as a native New Yorker, know that subway trains run twenty-four hours a day, your cousin from Iowa would not be expected to know this, so you should include it as part of your description of how efficient the system is.

Writing the Draft

Use the thesis statement to set up an introductory paragraph. Then plan the body paragraphs so that they follow the order you decided on—from beginning the journey to arriving, from the top of a subway car to the bottom, or from the outside of the train to the inside. Include as many details in the first draft as possible; it is easier to take them out in a second or third draft than to add them later. Then plan the conclusion to help the reader understand what the purpose of the description has been.

Reading and Revising the Draft

Read your first draft, circling each description word. Then go back and add *another* description word after the ones already in the essay. If you can't think of any more words, use a *thesaurus* to find new words.

If possible, read your essay aloud to a classmate. Ask him or her to tell you if the details are vivid. Have your classmate suggest where more details are needed. Check to see that you have included some description in each sensory category: sight, sound, taste, touch, and smell.

Proofread your essay for correctness.
Make a clean, neat final copy.

A STUDENT PARAGRAPH: DESCRIPTION

Read the student paragraph below about the New York City subway. Look for descriptive elements that can help you write your own paper on description. Comments in the margin highlight important features of descriptive writing.

A first-time visitor to the New York City subway system will probably find the noise overwhelming, at least at first. The variety of sounds, and their sheer volume, can send most unprepared tourists running for the exit; those who remain tend to slip into a state of deep shock. As I wait for the Number 4 train at the Lexington

Topic sentence announces purpose

Supporting detail

Supporting detail

Supporting detail

Supporting detail

Concluding sentence returns to topic; providing *coherence*

Avenue station, the passing express cars explode from the tunnel in a blur of red and gray. Sometimes as many as three trains roar by at the same time. A high-pitched squeal of brakes adds powerfully to the din. A few passengers heave sighs or mutter under their breath as the crackle and hiss of an unintelligible announcement coming over the public address system adds to the uproar. As I continue to wait for the local, I can hear fragments of the shouted exchanges between weary booth attendants and impatient customers trying to communicate through the bulletproof glass. Irritably, I watch one of the many subway musicians, an old bald man who sings "O Solo Mio" off-key as a battered tape recorder behind him plays warped-sounding violin music. Once in a while some goodhearted passenger tosses a crumpled dollar bill into an old straw hat at the singer's feet. Why are they encouraging these horrible sounds, I wonder to myself? I obviously haven't been here long enough to tune them out.

www.mhhe.com/
shortprose

To learn more about description, click on
**Writing > Writing Tutor:
Description
Writing > Paragraph Patterns**

Farewell to Summer and Its Buzzing Creatures

Diane Ackerman

Diane Ackerman is a prize-winning poet and writer of nonfiction
for adults and children. Born in Waukegan, Illinois, in 1948, she
received her BA, MA, and PhD from Cornell University, where she
has served as writer-in-residence. Ackerman has varied personal and
literary interests, writing about her life on a cattle ranch, learning
to fly, gardening, creativity, neuroscience, endangered species, crisis counseling, and more. In both poetry and prose, she probes the
worlds of science, nature, and human behavior with exquisite detail.
Ackerman's poetry collections include *Jaguar of Sweet Laughter:
New and Selected Poems* (1991) and *I Praise My Destroyer* (1998).
Among her many nonfiction books are the best-selling *A Natural
History of the Senses* (1990), *A Natural History of Love* (1994),
and *The Zookeeper's Wife: A War Story* (2007). Ackerman has been
praised for her fine eye for detail, as this essay, which appeared in the
September 7, 2002, issue of the *New York Times,* confirms.

PREREADING: THINKING ABOUT THE ESSAY IN ADVANCE

When you think about the end of summer, what comes to mind?
Do you have images or recollections of summer's departure?
What are your emotions as you experience the passing of this
season?

Words to Watch

alcove (par. 1)   a recessed area of a room, as a breakfast nook
spiked (par. 2)   [slang], to add alcohol or another strong sub-
stance to a drink
treacle (par. 5)   molasses
sodden (par. 6)   filled with moisture; soaked through
emissaries (par. 7)   persons or agents sent on a special mission
commotion (par. 9)   violent motion; turmoil; agitation; disturbance

1   It's 6:45 A.M. Sitting in an alcove near the back window, I watch
summer packing to leave—the yard's hummingbirds busily feeding. Any day now they'll migrate to their winter homes. But at the

moment, they're gobbling sugar to build the fat reserves they need for long solo flights.

I've spiked their drink, sweetened their water 3-to-1, since putting on weight is so urgent. Trees and flowers only dispense nectar in doses (to encourage pollinators to move to other blooms), but feeders provide a steady source of sweetness, and where in life can any creature find that? So I tend the feeder carefully—change the water every other day, keep ants and wasps at bay if I can.

I saw a baby hummer at the feeder for the first time this week, a late visitor I mistook for a bumblebee until I noticed the helicopter blur of its wingbeats. Here it is again. Smaller, darker and jerkier than the adults, it sips, elevates, swallows, sips six times more, then angles backward in a reverse swan dive. Yesterday morning it squawked a faint tearing-cardboard sound when a yellow jacket vexed it. One or two wasps a hummer can keep an eye on, joust with, and usually drive off. But three become gangland dangerous.

(Yellow jackets plagued the adult hummers all month. Yesterday I learned why: the wasps had built a hive inside the back wall of the house.)

The three humming residents of the yard—male, female, baby—take turns at the red plastic feeder. Why waste valuable energy chasing each other around the yard? So they line up. The menu is always the same—treacle. Sometimes treacle laced with raisin-like ants.

In these precious last days with the hummingbirds, I sit quietly on the ledge of the morning, watching the sodden darkness lift like a stage curtain, and the tiny players arrive one by one, do their dance, engage in a little swordplay, and leave in fast arcing backdives.

At nightfall, I see them darken and linger, sip seven or 10 times in a row, hovering backward after each sip to lift swordlike beaks, slowly swallow the liqueur, then belly up to the feeder again for their last nightcaps. I'll miss these small emissaries from the natural world.

Light rain begins. The hummers will be reluctant to fly, and yet they must feed every 15 minutes to survive. At least it's not a pelting rain. Still, the soggy flowers will droop and the falling raindrops may feel like artillery.

Even the yellow jackets are gone now. The other day, 50 poured into the house all at once with more emerging every minute, so I reluctantly phoned an exterminator and asked him to relocate the wasps. After he stopped laughing, he suggested ripping the nest out of the wall, which he did a few hours later, producing big-time commotion.

10   I feared the hummingbirds might be scared off. But they returned at sunset, hungry, vigilant and bold. They don't seem to mind danger, which they confront or wait out. Yellow jackets fly faster and are armed, but they can't angle around the way hummers can.

11   I wonder if the adults are leaving today? Last year a baby stayed a few days longer, to fatten up before traveling. They'll fly alone, on the most dangerous journey of their lives, then arrive famished to feast among tropical flowers, perhaps in the company of other humans. Next summer they'll return early, separately, while the nights are still cool. Whichever direction they're heading, they always leave too soon.

BUILDING VOCABULARY

Denotation refers to the dictionary definition of a word; *connotation* refers to the various shades of meaning and feelings readers bring to a word or phrase (see Glossary). Look up and write dictionary definitions for each of the words in italics. Then explain in your own words the connotative meaning of each word.

a. I watch summer *packing* to leave (par. 1)
b. So I *tend* the feeder carefully (par. 2)
c. But three became *gangland* dangerous (par. 3)
d. In these *precious* last days (par. 6)
e. At nightfall, I see them darken and *linger* (par. 7)
f. At least it's not a *pelting* rain (par. 8)

THINKING CRITICALLY ABOUT THE ESSAY

Understanding the Writer's Ideas

1. What is the connection between the late summer day and the writer "[s]itting in an alcove by the window"?
2. How much does Ackerman seem to know about nature? Explain.

3. Why does Ackerman move from morning to nightfall, from the present to the past, and back again to the present? What is her purpose?

4. What, if anything, would Ackerman have us learn through careful attention to the processes of nature? By describing a small slice of nature, might she (and the reader) see the world anew? Justify your response.

Understanding the Writer's Techniques

1. What is this essay's thesis? Is it stated or implied? Explain.

2. How does the window that Ackerman sits by at the start of the day serve as an organizational or framing device for the essay?

3. Which senses does Ackerman invoke in her essay? Which descriptive details do you find most effective, and why? What mood or atmosphere does she create? How does Ackerman manage to create a dominant impression based on these details?

4. What "poetic" attributes can you identify in the essay—in other words, where does Ackerman use *imagery, simile, metaphor, personification*, and other types of *figurative language*? (See Glossary.) What is the overall effect?

5. How would you describe the words that Ackerman uses in this essay? Are they *concrete* or *abstract;* specific or general? (See Glossary.)

6. Explain your response to the last paragraph. What does the concluding paragraph contribute to the essay?

Exploring the Writer's Ideas

1. Ackerman writes elsewhere: "I try to give myself passionately, totally, to whatever I'm observing . . . as a means to understanding a little better what being human is." In this essay, how does the writer's "passion" manifest itself, and what does she actually inform us about being human?

2. Do you think that Ackerman captures the essence of the scene that she describes? Why or why not?

3. Ackerman admits that she tries to write about Nature (a word she capitalizes) in "its widest sense," because to do otherwise "is not only reprehensible and philistine, it bankrupts the

experience of living, it ignores much of life's fascination and variety." Consider her observation in relation to "Farewell to Summer and Its Buzzing Creatures."

IDEAS FOR WRITING

Locate and identify a specific animal, bird, or insect, and observe it carefully. For five to ten minutes, jot down as many details about this object—and the scene or environment surrounding it—as possible.

Guided Writing

Write an essay titled "Farewell to _____." You might want to focus on a month or a season, or perhaps even a place that you know intimately and think you can describe in detail.

1. Begin, as Ackerman does, by identifying your subject and describing your setting. Pay close attention to your surroundings.
2. Position yourself in relation to the creatures, objects, and scene you plan to describe. Place yourself strategically within the scene (close up, from a distance, by a window, or from some other vantage point) so that the reader senses or understands your relationship to the situation, the things in it, and the moment.
3. Carefully describe the most important objects and details within the frame or scene that you create.
4. Use both concrete and figurative language, along with compelling images, to create a dominant impression.
5. Develop a solid concluding paragraph implying (without stating it in so many words) that Nature can reveal to us important things about the human condition.

Thinking and Writing Collaboratively

Form groups of three or four students, and read your descriptive essays aloud. Discuss the relative success of each classmate's attempt to create a dominant impression, drawn from nature, and designed to illuminate some aspect of the human condition.

Writing About the Text

Critics have called Ackerman a "sensuous" writer. Analyze and evaluate this claim in "Farewell to Summer and Its Buzzing Creatures," discussing those aspects of Ackerman's style that produce a sensuous effect.

More Writing Projects

1. Is Ackerman's essay basically about the end of summer, or about something else? Respond to this question in a journal entry.
2. Write a paragraph describing what you sense or learn about Ackerman herself from this essay.
3. Write an essay of extended description in which you try to capture the essence of a single object drawn from nature. Use all five senses to create a dominant impression.

In the Jungle
Annie Dillard

Essayist, novelist, and poet Annie Dillard, best known for her reflec-
tive, critically acclaimed writing about nature, was born in Pittsburgh,
Pennsylvania, in 1945. She attended Hollins College in Virginia. Her
book *Pilgrim at Tinker Creek* (1974), a collection of lyrical observations and meditations on the natural world of Virginia's Blue Ridge
Mountains, was awarded the Pulitzer Prize for general nonfiction.
Among Dillard's many books are *Teaching a Stone to Talk* (1982),
a collection of essays; *An American Childhood* (1987), an autobiography; and *The Living* (1992), a novel. Her most recent book is
The Maytrees (2007). This selection, from *Teaching a Stone to Talk,*
illustrates Dillard's gift for evocative description that at the same
time is a form of meditation on our residence on earth.

www.mhhe.com/
shortprose

To learn more about description, click on
**More Resources > Chapter 3 >
Annie Dillard**

PREREADING: THINKING ABOUT
THE ESSAY IN ADVANCE

What do you associate with the word *jungle*? What is nature like in
the jungle? Do you expect to meet people in the jungle? If so, what
sort of people? How do they live? Why might someone from the
postmodern world of video and cities travel to a jungle?

Words to Watch

headwaters (par. 1)   sources of a river
tributaries (par. 9)   streams that feed larger streams
fronds (par. 14)   large, fernlike leaves
boles (par. 14)   trunks of trees
flanges (par. 14)   supporting rims or ribs
iridescent (par. 14)   shimmering with colors (as in a soap bubble)
dinghies (par. 14)   small boats
reciprocate (par. 19)   repay

Like any out-of-the-way place, the Napo River in the Ecuadorian 1
jungle seems real enough when you are there, even central. Out of
the way of *what?* I was sitting on a stump at the edge of a bankside
palm-thatch village, in the middle of the night, on the headwaters
of the Amazon. Out of the way of human life, tenderness, or the
glance of heaven?

A nightjar in a deep-leaved shadow called three long notes, 2
and hushed. The men with me talked softly in clumps: three North
Americans, four Ecuadorians who were showing us the jungle. We
were holding cool drinks and idly watching a hand-sized taran-
tula seize moths that came to the lone bulb on the generator shed
beside us.

It was February, the middle of summer. Green fireflies spat- 3
tered lights across the air and illumined for seconds, now here,
now there, the pale trunks of enormous, solitary trees. Beneath us
the brown Napo River was rising, in all silence; it coiled up the
sandy bank and tangled its foam in vines that trailed from the forest and roots that looped the shore.

Each breath of night smelled sweet, more moistened and sweet 4
than any kitchen, or garden, or cradle. Each star in Orion seemed
to tremble and stir with my breath. All at once, in the thatch house
across the clearing behind us, one of the village's Jesuit priests
began playing an alto recorder, playing a wordless song, lyric, in a
minor key, that twined over the village clearing, that caught in the
big trees' canopies, muted our talk on the bankside, and wandered
over the river, dissolving downstream.

This will do, I thought. This will do, for a weekend, or a sea- 5
son, or a home.

Later that night I loosed my hair from its braids and combed it 6
smooth—not for myself, but so the village girls could play with it
in the morning.

We had disembarked at the village that afternoon, and I had 7
slumped on some shaded steps, wishing I knew some Spanish or
some Quechua so I could speak with the ring of little girls who
were alternately staring at me and smiling at their toes. I spoke
anyway, and fooled with my hair, which they were obviously dying
to get their hands on, and laughed, and soon they were all braid-
ing my hair, all five of them, all fifty fingers, all my hair, even my
bangs. And then they took it apart and did it again, laughing, and
teaching me Spanish nouns, and meeting my eyes and each other's
with open delight, while their small brothers in blue jeans climbed

down from the trees and began kicking a volleyball around with one of the North American men.

8   Now, as I combed my hair in the little tent, another of the men, a free-lance writer from Manhattan, was talking quietly. He was telling us the tale of his life, describing his work in Hollywood, his apartment in Manhattan, his house in Paris. . . ."It makes me wonder," he said, "what I'm doing in a tent under a tree in the village of Pompeya, on the Napo River, in the jungle of Ecuador." After a pause he added, "It makes me wonder why I'm going *back.*"

9   The point of going somewhere like the Napo River in Ecuador is not to see the most spectacular anything. It is simply to see what is there. We are here on the planet only once, and might as well get a feel for the place. We might as well get a feel for the fringes and hollows in which life is lived, for the Amazon basin, which covers half a continent, and for the life that—there, like anywhere else— is always and necessarily lived in detail: on the tributaries, in the riverside villages, sucking this particular white-fleshed guava in this particular pattern of shade.

10   What is there is interesting. The Napo River itself is wide (I mean wider than the Mississippi at Davenport) and brown, opaque, and smeared with floating foam and logs and branches from the jungle. White egrets hunch on shoreline deadfalls and parrots in flocks dart in and out of the light. Under the water in the river, unseen, are anacondas—which are reputed to take a few village toddlers every year—and water boas, stingrays, crocodiles, manatees, and sweet-meated fish.

11   Low water bares gray strips of sandbar on which the natives build tiny palm-thatch shelters, arched, the size of pup tents, for overnight fishing trips. You see these extraordinarily clean people (who bathe twice a day in the river, and whose straight black hair is always freshly washed) paddling down the river in dugout canoes, hugging the banks.

12   Some of the Indians of this region, earlier in the century, used to sleep naked in hammocks. The nights are cold. Gordon MacCreach, an American explorer in these Amazon tributaries, reported that he was startled to hear the Indians get up at three in the morning. He was even more startled, night after night, to hear them walk down to the river slowly, half asleep, and bathe in the water. Only later did he learn what they were doing: they were getting warm. The cold woke them; they warmed their skins in the river, which was

always ninety degrees; then they returned to their hammocks and slept through the rest of the night.

The riverbanks are low, and from the river you see an unbro- 13 ken wall of dark forest in every direction, from the Andes to the Atlantic. You get a taste for looking at trees: trees hung with the swinging nests of yellow troupials, trees from which ant nests the size of grain sacks hang like black goiters, trees from which seven-colored tanagers flutter, coral trees, teak, balsa and bread-fruit, enormous emergent silk-cotton trees, and the pale-barked *samona* palms.

When you are inside the jungle, away from the river, the trees 14 vault out of sight. It is hard to remember to look up the long trunks and see the fans, strips, fronds, and sprays of glossy leaves. Inside the jungle you are more likely to notice the snarl of climbers and creepers round the trees' boles, the flowering bromeliads and epi-phytes in every bough's crook, and the fantastic silk-cotton tree trunks thirty or forty feet across, trunks buttressed in flanges of wood whose curves can make three high walls of a room—a shady, loamy-aired room where you would gladly live, or die. Butterflies, iridescent blue, striped, or clear-winged, thread the jungle paths at eye level. And at your feet is a swath of ants bearing triangular bits of green leaf. The ants with their leaves look like a wide fleet of sailing dinghies—but they don't quit. In either direction they wobble over the jungle floor as far as the eye can see. I followed them off the path as far as I dared, and never saw an end to ants or to those luffing chips of green they bore.

Unseen in the jungle, but present, are tapirs, jaguars, many 15 species of snake and lizard, ocelots, armadillos, marmosets, howler monkeys, toucans and macaws and a hundred other birds, deer, bats, peccaries, capybaras, agoutis, and sloths. Also present in this jungle, but variously distant, are Texaco derricks and pipe-lines, and some of the wildest Indians in the world, blowgun-using Indians, who killed missionaries in 1956 and ate them.

Long lakes shine in the jungle. We traveled one of these in dug- 16 out canoes, canoes with two inches of freeboard, canoes paddled with machete-hewn oars chopped from buttresses of silk-cotton trees, or poled in the shallows with peeled cane or bamboo. Our part-Indian guide had cleared the path to the lake the day before; when we walked the path we saw where he had impaled the lopped head of a boa, open-mouthed, on a pointed stick by the canoes, for decoration.

17   The lake was wonderful. Herons, egrets, and ibises plodded the sawgrass shores, kingfishers and cuckoos clattered from sunlight to shade, great turkeylike birds fussed in dead branches, and hawks lolled overhead. There was all the time in the world. A turtle slid into the water. The boy in the bow of my canoe slapped stones at birds with a simple sling, a rubber throng and leather pad. He aimed brilliantly at moving targets, always, and always missed; the birds were out of range. He stuffed his sling back in his shirt. I looked around.

18   The lake and river waters are as opaque as rain-forest leaves; they are veils, blinds, painted screens. You see things only by their effects. I saw the shoreline water roil and the sawgrass heave above a thrashing *paichi,* an enormous black fish of these waters; one had been caught the previous week weighing 430 pounds. Piranha fish live in the lakes, and electric eels. I dangled my fingers in the water, figuring it would be worth it.

19   We would eat chicken that night in the village, and rice, yucca, onions, beets, and heaps of fruit. The sun would ring down, pulling darkness after it like a curtain. Twilight is short, and the unseen birds of twilight wistful, uncanny, catching the heart. The two nuns in their dazzling white habits—the beautiful-boned young nun and the warm-faced old—would glide to the open cane-and-thatch schoolroom in darkness, and start the children singing. The children would sing in piping Spanish, high-pitched and pure; they would sing "Nearer My God to Thee" in Quechua, very fast. (To reciprocate, we sang for them "Old MacDonald Had a Farm"; I thought they might recognize the animal sounds. Of course they thought we were out of our minds.) As the children became excited by their own singing, they left their log benches and swarmed around the nuns, hopping, smiling at us, everyone smiling, the nuns' faces bursting in their cowls, and the clear-voiced children still singing, and the palm-leafed roofing stirred.

20   The Napo River: it is not out of the way. It is *in* the way, catching sunlight the way a cup catches poured water; it is a bowl of sweet air, a basin of greenness, and of grace, and, it would seem, of peace.

BUILDING VOCABULARY

1. An important tool of description is *diction,* the word choices a writer makes. In the sentences below, substitute your own words for those in italics:

   a. Beneath us the brown Napo River was rising . . . it *coiled* up the *sandy* bank and *tangled* its *foam* in vines that *trailed* from the forest and roots that *looped* the shore (par. 3).

   b. [O]ne of the village's Jesuit priests began playing . . . a wordless song, lyric, in a minor key, that *twined* over the village clearing, that *caught* in the big trees' *canopies, muted* our talk on the *bankside,* and *wandered* over the river, *dissolving* downstream (par. 4).

2. One way the writer suggests the jungle is out of the way is to name its inhabitants. Look up the animal or plant names you don't know that appear in pars. 13, 14, 15, and 17.

THINKING CRITICALLY ABOUT THE ESSAY

Understanding the Writer's Ideas

1. The writer begins by saying that the jungle is out of the way. Out of the way of what? She ends, however, by saying that the jungle river is "*in* the way." Of what? What is the implication of these apparently opposite points of view?
2. Why does the writer go to the jungle?
3. Where is the jungle that Dillard writes about?
4. At what time of year, and in what season, does she visit the jungle?
5. Who inhabits the village where Dillard disembarks?
6. What does the writer mean when she says, "This will do" (par. 5)? Who else that is there evidently agrees with her?
7. The writer says that what she finds in the jungle is "interesting." How is it interesting for her?
8. What does Dillard mean by saying "it would be worth it" when she dangles her fingers in water that is supposed to contain piranha—flesh-eating jungle fish?
9. Are the writer and her companions at home in the jungle? How are they viewed by the natives?
10. Dillard concludes by saying that Napo River is a place "of grace, and, it would seem, of peace." What evidence can you find in the essay to support this conclusion? What evidence is there that seems to support a different conclusion? Does the writer simply ignore this contrary evidence, or does she incorporate it into her view of the jungle? Explain.

Understanding the Writer's Techniques

1. What is the main idea of this essay? Where is it stated?

2. What is the effect of the opening paragraph of the essay? What is the relation of the opening paragraph to the thesis of the essay?

3. How does Dillard establish that the jungle is "out of the way"?

4. The essay's introduction takes up five paragraphs. In what ways does the rest of the essay amplify the introduction?

5. How does the writer convey her attitude toward the natives?

6. What is the connection between the concluding sentence of par. 17—"I looked around"—and the theme of the essay? Why do you think this sentence appears at this point of the essay?

7. What aspects of the final two paragraphs contribute to an effective conclusion for the essay?

Exploring the Writer's Ideas

1. The writer ends her introduction with this sentence: "This will do, for a weekend, for a season, for a home." Do you find this progression of commitments believable—that is, are you persuaded that the writer is actually considering making the Napo River her home? If so, what evidence in the essay supports such a reading? If not, what evidence do you find to the contrary?

2. The writer says that, since we are "on the planet only once," we "might as well get a feel for the place." Does the writer persuade you that going to the jungle offers a significantly different "feel for the place" than staying at home (wherever home may be)? The nineteenth-century poet Emily Dickinson, who is considered one of the greatest American poets, is said almost never to have left her home village—Amherst, Massachusetts. What do you think she might have said to the writer about the pointlessness of traveling to the jungle? What might Dillard have said to persuade Emily Dickinson to come along to the Napo River?

3. The natives of this region, the writer reports, have eaten people in the past. One native boy in her party aims at birds with

stones, and the part-native guide puts a snake's head on a pole for decoration. What is Dillard's attitude toward these "out-of-the-way" behaviors? Do you share her attitude? If so, why? If not, why not?

IDEAS FOR WRITING

Prewriting

Think about an experience of yours that was "out-of-the-way" and whose "strangeness" seemed full of lessons or richness of experience. Write down some of the things you particularly remember about that experience.

Guided Writing

Write an essay describing a place or experience that is as "out-of-the-way" of your usual lifestyle as possible, but which you can show as "interesting" in itself and instructive about what to value in your usual everyday life. (You might think of a neighborhood completely different from your own, or, say, a meal—Thanksgiving dinner at the soup kitchen—completely different from what to you is "usual.")

1. Begin, as Dillard does, by identifying where you are, and catching yourself thinking what an out-of-the-way place or experience this is.
2. Give a graphic description of the place—but not yet of the people who inhabit it.
3. Suggest, through more description, how this place has features deeper, richer, more intense than the places where you usually spend your days.
4. Now pause to reflect: hmm, is this a place where I might want to live?
5. Describe the people in this place through your interaction with them.
6. Write about what you notice in the place upon better acquaintance, maybe later in the day or just before leaving.
7. End by thinking back, now that you have returned to your routine, about how the out-of-the-way place is *in* the way of . . .

Thinking and Writing Collaboratively

In small groups discuss your impressions of places you have been that are different from those you are used to and people you have known who are completely different from you. What qualities of these other places and other people most impress you? What do other places and people make you miss most about your usual life? What do they make you want most to add to your usual life?

Writing About the Text

Dillard tells us, through many details, about the jungle. She contrasts the jungle with an implicit picture of the nonjungle where she lives. Write an essay that looks at those implicit contrasts and that explores her essay not in terms of *description* but rather in terms of *argument* or *persuasion*. Is the jungle a place rich in things and values that are absent from the nonjungle? Does Dillard "romanticize" the jungle? Does Dillard make you want to go to the jungle? If yes, why? If not, why not?

More Writing Projects

1. In your journal write about traveling as a nuisance, a bore, a rip-off . . .
2. Spend a day in a place that is as close to being wild as you can find near where you live. For at least an hour of that day, sit still in one spot. Write a descriptive paragraph about your day.
3. Who are the nuns and priests in the jungle? Why do the boys wear blue jeans? On the basis of some outside reading, or online research, write an essay that discusses some aspect of the encounter, in the Amazon, between the old and new worlds and between the "first world" and the "third."

Catfish in the Bathtub

Maxine Hong Kingston

Born in 1940 in Stockton, California, Maxine Hong Kingston is the daughter of Chinese immigrants. Her first language was Say Yup, a dialect of Cantonese. She was named "Maxine" after a lucky blonde gambler who frequented the gambling house where her scholarly father was forced to find work. She received a BA from the University of California at Berkeley, where she taught for many years. Her first book, *The Woman Warrior* (1976), vividly depicts her experience growing up as a girl and young woman in the United States but within an intensely Chinese American home and culture. *China Men* (1980) is a sequel to *The Woman Warrior,* exploring the experience of being Chinese American males. Kingston has also published a collection of prose writing about her residence in Hawaii—*Hawaii One Summer* (1987)—and the novel *Tripmaster Monkey: His Fake Book* (1989). Her more recent work includes *To Be the Poet* (2002) and *The Fifth Book of Peace* (2006). This selection from *The Woman Warrior* is one of many vignettes in that book about Kingston's mother, a larger-than-life figure. Through a colorful evocation of the strange food her mother served up, Kingston portrays a world of difference that is at once rich and weird, powerful and repelling. She brings that world to life by means of a style that is characteristically fierce, poetic, and tender all at the same time.

www.mhhe.com/ **shortprose**

To learn more about Kingston, click on
More Resources > Chapter 3 > Maxine Hong Kingston

PREREADING: THINKING ABOUT THE ESSAY IN ADVANCE

What unusual foods have you eaten? What unusual dish can you remember one of your relatives preparing when you were a child? How did you feel about eating this food?

Words to Watch

dromedaries (par. 1) one-humped camels
sensibility (par. 1) ability to receive sensations
perched (par. 1) resting on a bird's roost

scowls (par. 1)   expressions of displeasure
dismembering (par. 1)   taking apart bodily limbs and innards
sprains (par. 2)   sudden twists of joints such as ankles or wrists
unsettle (par. 3)   make uneasy or uncomfortable
tufts (par. 4)   forms into small patches of hair
awobble (par. 6)   unsteady; teetering
toadstools (par. 7)   mushrooms
revulsion (par. 8)   a strong reaction away from something

1   My mother has cooked for us: raccoons, skunks, hawks, city pigeons, wild ducks, wild geese, black-skinned bantams, snakes, garden snails, turtles that crawled about the pantry floor and sometimes escaped under refrigerator or stove, catfish that swam in the bathtub. "The emperors used to eat the peaked hump of purple dromedaries," she would say. "They used chopsticks made from rhinoceros horn, and they ate ducks' tongues and monkeys' lips." She boiled the weeds we pulled up in the yard. There was a tender plant with flowers like white stars hiding under the leaves, which were like the flower petals but green. I've not been able to find it since growing up. It had no taste. When I was as tall as the washing machine, I stepped out on the back porch one night, and some heavy, ruffling, windy, clawed thing dived at me. Even after getting chanted back to sensibility, I shook when I recalled that perched everywhere there were owls with great hunched shoulders and yellow scowls. They were a surprise for my mother from my father. We children used to hide under the beds with our fingers in our ears to shut out the bird screams and the thud, thud of the turtles swimming in the boiling water, their shells hitting the sides of the pot. Once the third aunt who worked at the laundry ran out and bought us bags of candy to hold over our noses; my mother was dismembering skunk on the chopping block. I could smell the rubbery odor through the candy.

2   In a glass jar on a shelf my mother kept a big brown hand with pointed claws stewing in alcohol and herbs. She must have brought it from China because I do not remember a time when I did not have the hand to look at. She said it was a bear's claw, and for many years I thought bears were hairless. My mother used the tobacco, leeks, and grasses swimming about the hand to rub our sprains and bruises.

3   Just as I would climb up to the shelf to take one look after another at the hand, I would hear my mother's monkey story. I'd take my fingers out of my ears and let her monkey words enter my brain. I

did not always listen voluntarily, though. She would begin telling the story, perhaps repeating it to a homesick villager, and I'd overhear before I had a chance to protect myself. Then the monkey words would unsettle me; a curtain flapped loose inside my brain. I have wanted to say, "Stop it. Stop it," but not once did I say, "Stop it."

"Do you know what people in China eat when they have the 4 money?" my mother began. "They buy into a monkey feast. The eaters sit around a thick wood table with a hole in the middle. Boys bring in the monkey at the end of a pole. Its neck is in a collar at the end of the pole, and it is screaming. Its hands are tied behind it. They clamp the monkey into the table; the whole table fits like another collar around its neck. Using a surgeon's saw, the cooks cut a clean line in a circle at the top of its head. To loosen the bone, they tap with a tiny hammer and wedge here and there with a silver pick. Then an old woman reaches out her hand to the monkey's face and up to its scalp, where she tufts some hairs and lifts off the lid of the skull. The eaters spoon out the brains."

Did she say, "You should have seen the faces the monkey made"? 5 Did she say, "The people laughed at the monkey screaming"? It was alive? The curtain flaps closed like merciful black wings.

"Eat! Eat!" my mother would shout at our heads bent over 6 bowls, the blood pudding awobble in the middle of the table.

She had one rule to keep us safe from toadstools and such: "If 7 it tastes good, it's bad for you," she said. "If it tastes bad, it's good for you."

We'd have to face four- and five-day-old leftovers until we ate 8 it all. The squid eye would keep appearing at breakfast and dinner until eaten. Sometimes brown masses sat on every dish. I have seen revulsion on the faces of visitors who've caught us at meals.

"Have you eaten yet?" the Chinese greet one another. 9

"Yes, I have," they answer whether they have or not. "And 10 you?"

I would live on plastic. 11

BUILDING VOCABULARY

1. Go through this essay again and list every animal mentioned. Then, write a short description of each, using the dictionary or encyclopedia if necessary.
2. Use any five of the Words to Watch in sentences of your own.

THINKING CRITICALLY ABOUT THE ESSAY

Understanding the Writer's Ideas

1. What is Kingston saying about her childhood? How does her opening catalog of foods that her mother prepared, combined with further descriptions of foods, support this point? What are some of the "strange" foods that she ate but that are not mentioned in this first paragraph?

2. Who are "the emperors" mentioned in paragraph 1? What were some of their more unusual dishes?

3. What attacks and frightens the young Kingston on her back porch? Where did they come from? How do we know that she was a young girl at the time? Explain the meaning of "even after getting chanted back to sensibility."

4. At the end of the first paragraph, the writer mentions methods that she and her siblings used to shut out unpleasant sensory input. What were they?

5. For what purpose did her mother keep a bear's claw in a glass jar? Where did Kingston think it came from? Why?

6. What are the "monkey words"? Summarize the "monkey words" in your own language. Kingston says that she wanted to say "Stop it" to the monkey words, but didn't. Why didn't she?

7. What was Kingston's mother's attitude toward the taste of things in relation to their healthfulness?

8. Why would there sometimes be "revulsion on the faces of visitors" who watched the author's family eating?

9. What is the traditional Chinese greeting?

10. What is the writer's overall attitude toward her mother? Explain.

Understanding the Writer's Techniques

1. Does Kingston ever make a direct *thesis statement?* Why or why not?

2. In this essay, Kingston seems to shift in and out of various tenses deliberately. For example, in paragraph 3, she writes: "... a curtain *flapped* loose inside my brain. I *have wanted* to say ..." Why do you think that Kingston uses such a technique? List three other examples of such tense shifts.

3. Comment on Kingston's use of transitions. How do they contribute to the overall *coherence* (see Glossary) of the essay?

4. How does Kingston use the five senses to create descriptive imagery? Give examples of her use of sounds, tastes, smells, sights, and feelings. Which are the most effective?

5. Eliminating the specific references to China, how do we know that the writer is of Chinese background? Which details or references contribute to this understanding?

6. Evaluate the use of *dialogue* (records of spoken words or conversations) in this essay. What effect does it have on the flow of the writing? on our understanding of Kingston's main point?

7. In paragraph 1, why does the writer give so much attention to the white flower stars with no taste? Is she merely describing yet another thing she ate, or does she have some other purpose? Explain.

8. Although other incidents or ideas are described rather briefly, Kingston devotes a full, detailed paragraph to a description of the monkey feast. Why?

9. Throughout the essay, Kingston combines very realistic description (the bear's claw, the turtles thudding against the cook pot, the monkey feast) with various *similes* and *metaphors* (see Glossary). Explain the meaning of the following uses of *figurative language* (see Glossary):
   a. a curtain flapped loose inside my brain (par. 3)
   b. The curtain flaps closed like merciful black wings. (par. 5)
   c. Sometimes brown masses sat on every dish. (par. 8)

10. What is the effect of the series of questions in paragraph 5? Why are some in quotations and others not?

11. Explain the meaning of the last sentence. How does it relate to Kingston's *purpose* (see Glossary) in this essay?

Exploring the Writer's Ideas

1. Kingston certainly describes some "strange" foods and eating habits in this essay. But what makes particular foods "strange"? What are some of the strangest foods you have ever eaten? Where did they come from? Why did you eat them? How did you react to them? What foods or eating habits that are common to your everyday life might be considered strange by people from other cultures?

2. In this essay, Kingston concentrates on her mother, mentioning her father only once. Speculate on why she excludes her father in this way, but base your speculation on the material of the essay.

3. As we all know, different cultures have very different customs. In this essay, for example, the writer describes the Chinese way of greeting one another as well as the monkey feast, both of which are quite foreign to American culture. Describe different cultural customs that you have observed in your school, among your friends, in places around your city or town. How do you feel when you observe customs different from the ones you are familiar with? Do you believe that any particular custom is "right" or "wrong"? Why? Which custom among your own culture's would you most like to see changed? Why?

4. Describe your reaction to the monkey feast description.

5. For what reason do you think the Chinese greet each other with the words "Have you eaten yet?" Attempt to do further research on this custom. List as many different ways as you know of people greeting one another.

IDEAS FOR WRITING

Prewriting

Write the words "Family Food" on top of a sheet of paper and write everything that comes to mind about the topic. Give yourself about five minutes or so. Do not edit your writing: put as many of your ideas as you can on paper.

Guided Writing

Write an essay entitled "Food" in which you describe its importance to you, your family, and your cultural background.

1. Begin with a list of important foods related to your family's lifestyle.

2. Show the role of your parents or other relatives in relation to these foods.

3. Briefly tell about an incident involving food that affected you deeply.

4. Create strong sensory imagery. Attempt to use at least one image for each of the five senses.
5. If possible, relate food customs to your family's ethnic or cultural background.
6. Use dialogue in your essay, including some of the dialogue of your "inner voice."
7. Use transitions to make the parts of your essay cohere.
8. Mention how outsiders experienced this custom.
9. End your essay with a direct statement to summarize your current attitude toward the food you have described and those times in your life.

Thinking and Writing Collaboratively

Read a draft of the Guided Writing essay by one of your classmates. Then, write a paragraph to indicate what you learned about the importance of food to the writer and to his or her family and cultural background. What parts of the essay stand out most in your mind? Where do you think the writer might have included further details?

Writing About the Text

The power of Kingston's writing derives in part from the power of her descriptions. These are often startling, even bizarre. Write an essay that takes a close, careful look at some of her descriptions. Aim to weigh the question of whether she has painted an exaggerated picture in order to shock, or whether her pictures reflect a complex reality, one aspect of which is indeed shocking.

More Writing Projects

1. In your journal, write a description of an interesting custom or activity that you witnessed, a custom coming from outside your own cultural or social background. Include vivid sensory details.
2. Write a paragraph describing in detail the most wonderful meal you have ever eaten.
3. Research and write a short report about the food and eating customs of a culture other than your own.

My Ticket to the Disaster
Suzanne Berne

Mixing Patterns

Suzanne Berne is the author of *A Crime in the Neighborhood* (1997) and *A Perfect Arrangement* (2002), popular novels in both the United States and Great Britain. She has published fiction and essays in many publications, including the *New York Times.* In this essay, she describes an emotional trip to the site of the World Trade Center in early 2002.

PREREADING: THINKING ABOUT THE ESSAY IN ADVANCE

People from all over the world come to see the sixteen acres where the World Trade Center used to stand before 9/11. Why do people come to peer at a location that has been cleared of the rubble from the attacks? Should the place be a tourist spot? Why or why not?

Words to Watch

shearling (par. 2)   skin of a lamb with short wool attached
periphery (par. 8)   the area around the edge
welter (par. 9)   messy pile
swags (par. 9)   hung-up ornaments
kiosk (par. 15)   a stand where items are sold
reverence (par. 20)   feeling of profound respect

1 On a cold, damp March morning, I visited Manhattan's financial district, a place I'd never been, to pay my respects at what used to be the World Trade Center. Many other people had chosen to do the same that day, despite the raw wind and spits of rain, and so the first thing I noticed when I arrived on the corner of Vesey and Church Streets was a crowd.

2 　　Standing on the sidewalk, pressed against aluminum police barricades, wearing scarves that flapped into their faces and woolen hats pulled over their ears, were people apparently from everywhere. Germans, Italians, Japanese. An elegant-looking Norwegian family in matching shearling coats. People from Ohio and California and Maine. Children, middle-age couples, older people. Many of them

were clutching cameras and video recorders, and they were all craning to see across the street, where there was nothing to see.

At least, nothing is what it first looked like, the space that is now   3
ground zero. But once your eyes adjust to what you are looking at,
"nothing" becomes something much more potent, which is absence.

But to the out-of-towner, ground zero looks at first simply like   4
a construction site. All the familiar details are there: the wooden
scaffolding; the cranes, the bulldozers and forklifts; the trailers
and construction workers in hard hats; even the dust. There is the
pound of jackhammers, the steady beep-beep-beep of trucks back-
ing up, the roar of heavy machinery.

So much busyness is reassuring, and it is possible to stand   5
looking at the cranes and trucks and feel that mild curiosity and
hopefulness so often inspired by construction sites.

Then gradually your eyes do adjust, exactly as if you have   6
stepped from a dark theater into a bright afternoon, because what
becomes most striking about this scene is the light itself.

Ground zero is a great bowl of light, an emptiness that seems   7
weirdly spacious and grand, like a vast plaza amid the dense tan-
gle of streets in lower Manhattan. Light reflecting off the Hudson
River vaults into the site, soaking everything—especially on an
overcast morning—with a watery glow. This is the moment when
absence begins to assume a material form, when what is not there
becomes visible.

Suddenly you notice the periphery, the skyscraper shrouded   8
in black plastic, the boarded windows, the steel skeleton of the
shattered Winter Garden. Suddenly there are the broken steps and
cracked masonry in front of Brooks Brothers. Suddenly there are
the firefighters, the waiting ambulance on the other side of the pit,
the police on every corner. Suddenly there is the enormous cross
made of two rusted girders.

And suddenly, very suddenly, there is the little cemetery   9
attached to St. Paul's Chapel, with tulips coming up, the chapel
and grounds miraculously undamaged except for a few plastic-
sheathed gravestones. The iron fence is almost invisible beneath
a welter of dried pine wreaths, banners, ribbons, laminated poems
and prayers and photographs, swags of paper cranes, withered
flowers, baseball hats, rosary beads, teddy bears. And flags, flags
everywhere, little American flags fluttering in the breeze, flags
on posters drawn by Brownie troops, flags on T-shirts, flags on
hats, flags streaming by, tied to the handles of baby strollers.

10   It takes quite a while to see all of this; it takes even longer to come up with something to say about it.

11   An elderly man standing next to me had been staring fixedly across the street for some time. Finally he touched his son's elbow and said: "I watched those towers being built. I saw this place when they weren't there." Then he stopped, clearly struggling with, what for him, was a double negative, recalling an absence before there was an absence. His son, waiting patiently, took a few photographs. "Let's get out of here," the man said at last.

12   Again and again I heard people say, "It's unbelievable." And then they would turn to each other, dissatisfied. They wanted to say something more expressive, more meaningful. But it is unbelievable, to stare at so much devastation, and know it for devastation, and yet recognize that it does not look like the devastation one has imagined.

13   Like me, perhaps, the people around me had in mind images from television and newspaper pictures: the collapsing buildings, the running office workers, the black plume of smoke against a bright blue sky. Like me, they were probably trying to superimpose those terrible images onto the industrious emptiness right in front of them. The difficulty of this kind of mental revision is measured, I believe, by the brisk trade in World Trade Center photograph booklets at tables set up on street corners.

14   Determined to understand better what I was looking at, I decided to get a ticket for the viewing platform beside St. Paul's. This proved no easy task, as no one seemed to be able to direct me to South Street Seaport, where the tickets are distributed. Various police officers whom I asked for directions, waved me vaguely toward the East River, differing degrees of boredom and resignation on their faces. Or perhaps it was a kind of incredulousness. Somewhere around the American Stock Exchange, I asked a security guard for help and he frowned at me, saying, "You want tickets to the disaster?"

15   Finally I found myself in line at a cheerfully painted kiosk, watching a young juggler try to entertain the crowd. He kept dropping the four red balls he was attempting to juggle, and having to chase after them. It was noon; the next available viewing was at 4 p.m.

16   Back I walked, up Fulton Street, the smell of fish in the air, to wander again around St. Paul's. A deli on Vesey Street advertised a view of the World Trade Center from its second-floor dining area.

I went in and ordered a pastrami sandwich, uncomfortably aware that many people before me had come to that same deli for pastrami sandwiches who would never come there again. But I was here to see what I could, so I carried my sandwich upstairs and sat down beside one of the big plate-glass windows.

And there, at last, I got my ticket to the disaster. 17

I could see not just into the pit now, but also its access ramp, 18 which trucks had been traveling up and down since I had arrived that morning. Gathered along the ramp were firefighters in their black helmets and black coats. Slowly they lined up, and it became clear that this was an honor guard, and that someone's remains were being carried up the ramp toward the open door of an ambulance.

Everyone in the dining room stopped eating. Several people 19 stood up; whether out of respect or to see better, I don't know. For a moment, everything paused.

Then the day flowed back into itself. Soon I was outside once 20 more, joining the tide of people washing around the site. Later, as I huddled with a little crowd on the viewing platform, watching people scrawl their names or write "God Bless America" on the plywood walls, it occurred to me that a form of repopulation was taking effect, with so many visitors to this place, thousands of visitors, all of us coming to see the wide emptiness where so many were lost. And by the act of our visiting—whether we are motivated by curiosity or horror or reverence or grief, or by something confusing that combines them all—that space fills up again.

BUILDING VOCABULARY

In her descriptive essay, Berne chooses words carefully to bring the World Trade Center (WTC) site to life and to further her argument. Define each of the following, using the context of the essay to develop your definition. Explain for each what makes the use of the word effective.

a. raw (par. 1)
b. craning (par. 2)
c. shrouded (par. 8)
d. cracked (par. 8)
e. plume (par. 13)
f. superimpose (par. 13)

THINKING CRITICALLY ABOUT THE ESSAY

Understanding the Writer's Ideas

1. Why does Berne go to the site of the WTC?
2. From where are most of the people at the site visiting?
3. What is special to Berne about the light at the WTC site?
4. What does Berne mean in paragraphs 8 and 9 when she says that she noticed the area surrounding the site, including the cemetery "suddenly"?
5. Why does Berne find the sight of the WTC "unbelievable" (par. 12)?
6. Why in paragraph 14 does the security guard frown at Berne and answer her rudely?
7. Why does Berne want to visit the viewing platform?
8. What does Berne see when she views the site from the deli's dining room?
9. Berne ends her essay by saying that by visiting the WTC, the "space fills up again." What does she mean by this?

Understanding the Writer's Techniques

1. What is the main idea of this essay? Where does the writer best express it?
2. Is the description of the crowd in paragraph 2 effective? Why or why not?
3. How does Berne create the feeling of the financial district in New York City?
4. How does she create the geography for readers who might never have been to New York?
5. In what way does Berne describe the weather? Why does she describe it?
6. In paragraphs 6 through 8, Berne uses the second person, writing that "your eyes adjust" and "you notice the periphery." Why does she make this switch? Is this effective? At what point does she switch back to first person, and why?
7. What is effective about the scene in the deli?
8. What does Berne mean when she writes that "the day flowed back into itself"?
9. Do you think the last paragraph is effective? Why or why not?

✳ MIXING PATTERNS

Description is the basic mode of development in this essay, but Berne also uses narrative. In what ways does narrative help advance her point?

Exploring the Writer's Ideas

1. In this essay, Berne shows the frustration some New Yorkers feel about tourism around the 9/11 site. Why does she focus on this frustration, in your opinion? What are your feelings about tourism at a place of such terrible destruction? Explain your answer fully.

2. There is a certain spiritual, almost religious, aspect to Berne's pilgrimage to the WTC site. How is this spiritualism conveyed by the text? Why do you think Berne develops this aspect of the essay? How did you react to it, and why?

3. Berne implies that in part, the disbelief people feel in looking at the WTC site is that it conflicts with their memories of the site on 9/11. How does Berne deal with the disbelief? How have you dealt with the same feelings? In what other ways might people deal with this disbelief?

IDEAS FOR WRITING

Prewriting

Think about a historical event, such as a Civil War battle or a civil rights march, that occurred in your community and that is commemorated by a monument or plaque. Something momentous happened there, something that people wanted to remember and wanted others to remember. Jot down your experience of the site. If you have no particular memories, visit the site, think about its historical and emotional significance to you and others, and make a note of your reactions.

Guided Writing

Write an essay describing a historical site. If the site of the 9/11 attack seemed to Berne to be disconnected from the event itself while rescue workers were still pulling bodies out of the rubble, very likely your chosen place has a different atmosphere from the original event's importance. Write about your attempt to connect with the feelings you *should* be feeling.

1. Begin by identifying the location you will describe.
2. Next, describe the people you see at the site.
3. Describe in clear, vivid terms the site itself.
4. Explain next how the feelings attached to the site as it exists now do not match the importance of the original event.
5. End with your attempt to reconcile the current state of the site with the event.

Thinking and Writing Collaboratively

In groups of three, exchange your Guided Writing paper so that you end up reading at least two papers other than your own. Write a short report in an extended paragraph for each author, explaining what is effective or ineffective in each paper. Collect the reports on your paper, and rewrite your essay in light of the suggestions you receive.

Writing About the Text

Berne uses the concepts of absence and emptiness and their opposite to make several points. Write an essay that explains how Berne uses these concepts to be argumentative and persuasive. What meaning, finally, does she associate with those concepts, and how effective is she in using them?

More Writing Projects

1. Do some research on the origins of the phrase "ground zero," and write a journal entry explaining why the phrase is used to describe the World Trade Center site.
2. Spend an hour in a public place near your home sitting in one spot. In an extended paragraph, describe the relation between the location and the people you see.
3. The city of New York is in the process of rebuilding the World Trade Center site. Do some research on the arguments over what should be built there, and write an essay on your findings. Focus on either the 9/11 memorial, the tower, the fight over arts organizations relocating there, or transportation.

SUMMING UP: CHAPTER 3

1. As you have discovered in this chapter, one of the keys to writing effective description is the selection and creation of vivid and relevant images. How do the writers in this chapter use imagery? Which writer's images do you find most concrete, original, vivid, and creative? For each of the four descriptive essays in this chapter, write a paragraph in which you evaluate the writer's use of imagery. Save the last paragraph for the writer you think has used imagery most effectively.

2. All the writers in this chapter provide vivid descriptions of people, places, and objects. What general guidelines for such descriptions do you derive from reading these writers? Write a short essay called "How to Write Description," basing your observations on at least two of the writer's techniques.

3. The essays by Ackerman and Berne focus on the meaning of life in the face of death or the passing of a season. How does each writer approach the issue? Which essay do you find most effective and why?

4. Both Dillard and Ackerman write about the relation between the human and nonhuman worlds. Compare and contrast their observations and discoveries. How do you think their outlook on nature affects the way they write?

5. A common complaint about fiction is that it contains too much description, which readers sometimes find boring. Write a note to such a complainer. Encourage that person to reconsider his view of description, making your case on the basis of the essays in this chapter.

6. As these essays show, description is rarely an end in itself. The writer usually uses description to make an abstract point concrete, to advance an argument by using vivid imagery, or to offer an example that can help the reader understand something better. But one thing is clear: description works best when it is enjoyable; a dull description is worse than no description at all. Find examples in these essays where you sense that the writer enjoys writing and thus is writing lively descriptions. Discuss what qualities these lively passages share.

7. Compare and contrast how Amy Tan (pp. 41–46) and Maxine Hong Kingston (pp. 123–124) describe their mothers.

✳ FROM SEEING TO WRITING

Examine the photograph below of the busy marketplace and write a descriptive essay about it, drawing on sensory impressions implied by the scene. Remember to avoid description for its own sake. Develop a thesis about what you see in the photograph, and present descriptive details to support that thesis.

CHAPTER 4

Narration

WHAT IS NARRATION?

Narration is the telling of a story. As a technique in essay writing, it normally involves a discussion of events that are "true" or real, events that take place over a period of time. Narration helps a writer explain things and, as such, it is an important skill for the kind of writing often required of you.

Narration often includes the use of *description* in order to make the *purpose* of the story clear. A good narrative, then, must have a *thesis*. The thesis tells the reader that the narrative goes beyond just telling a story for entertainment. Like description, the narrative has a purpose, and an audience. The writer puts forth a main idea through the events and details of the story. For example, a writer might decide to *narrate* the events that led her to leave her native country and come to the United States as an immigrant. She would establish her thesis—her main point—quickly, and then use the body of the essay to tell about the event itself. She would use narration as the means to an end—to make a significant statement about the important decision that changed her life.

Writer Elizabeth Wong uses narrative to explore the pitfalls of divorcing herself from her cultural heritage as she discusses events in her youth to point out the dangers of becoming "All-American." In his comic narrative "Salvation," Langston Hughes reveals the disillusionment he feels when he cannot find Jesus as his family expects him to. Essayist David Sedaris uses his own brand of humorous narrative to raise questions about the nature of childhood. The renowned writer George Orwell narrates events at a hanging he witnessed in Burma to call attention to how, all too often, we take the value of life for granted. Each writer, then, whose work you will read in this chapter, uses narrative to tell a story of events that take place over a period of time, but also to put forward a thesis or main idea that comes directly out of events in the story.

HOW DO WE READ NARRATIVE?

Reading narrative requires us to look for more than the story, but not to overlook the story. So, as we read, we should ask ourselves:

- What are the main events in the narrative or story?
- What is the writer's purpose in telling us about these events, as stated in the thesis?
- How is the story organized? Is it chronological? Does the writer use *flashback* (see Glossary)? How much time is covered in the narrative?
- Does the author use description to make the narrative more vivid for a reader?
- What point of view does the author use? Are events told through his or her own eyes, or from a detached and objective point of view? Why did the writer make this choice about point of view? How would altering the point of view alter the purpose of the narrative?
- What transitions of time does the writer use to connect events? Look for expressions that link events: *next, soon after, a day later, suddenly, after two years.* These expressions act like bridges to connect the various moments in the narrative pattern.
- Does the writer use dialogue? What is the effect of dialogue in the narrative?
- What audience is the author aiming at? How do we know?

HOW DO WE WRITE NARRATIVE?

After reading the selections of narrative writing in this chapter, you should be ready to try narrative writing on your own. Fortunately, most individuals have a basic storytelling ability and know how to develop stories that make a point. Once you master narration as a writing pattern, you will be able to use it in a variety of situations.

Select the event you want to tell a story about. Begin with a thesis statement that gives the reader the purpose of the narrative.

Sample thesis statement:

My year studying abroad in Paris was an adventure that taught
me not only skills in a foreign language but also a new respect for
people with cultural values different from my own.

Decide which point of view you will use: first person? third
person? Think about who your audience is, and choose the point
of view best suited for that audience. If you are writing to a friend,
first person may be more informal. If you are writing to address a
wider public audience, as Orwell is, third person might be more
effective.

First person: I saw a man hanged, and the experience changed my
     views on capital punishment.
Third person: Spending a day at a Planned Parenthood clinic
     would help opponents of abortion understand the other side's
     fervent commitment to choice.

Determine the purpose of the narrative in relation to your
audience. If you were writing for a Roman Catholic newspaper,
for instance, your audience would be different from the audience
you'd address in a feminist magazine like *Ms.:* the purpose would
be different as well. In one case, you might be trying to get readers
to change their views through your description. In another case,
you might be showing how weak the opposition was by the way
you described them.

Plan the scope of the piece: How much time will events cover?
Can you describe all the events within the required length of the
essay?

Plan to include dialogue. For example, you might include a
few fragments of conversation between lost or confused freshmen
to give a "first day at school" story real-life flavor:

"Did you buy your books yet?"

"No, I couldn't find the bookstore!"

"Well, I already spent $125, and that was only for two courses.
I'm going to have to ask my Mom for more money."

"Yeah, I'm thinking maybe I'm going to need a part-time
job."

"Yeah, maybe we can work in the bookstore and get a
discount."

Make a list of *transitions* that show the passage of time and use
(without overusing) as many as you need to help your reader follow

the narrative sequence. Check that there are transitions between events: *after that, a few hours later, by the time the day ended.*

State your *thesis*. Write out the thesis statement so that you know the *subject* and the *purpose* of the essay. Then make a list of the major events in the story. You might begin with why you chose the college you did, and how you felt when you got accepted. Or you might begin with your arrival on the first day of classes, and go through the main events of the day—going to class, buying books, meeting other new students, evaluating teachers, having lunch, and so forth.

Plan an arrangement of events. Most narratives benefit from a clear chronological sequence. All the writers here pay careful attention to the march of events over time, and you should follow their lead. As in Orwell's focused narrative, integrate commentary, analysis, or assessment, but keep your eye on the order of events.

Writing the Draft

Once you have structured your essay, build your ideas by including descriptive details. Insert as many descriptive words as possible to help a reader *see* the campus, the students, the cafeteria, and so on:

the bright-colored sofas in the student lounge, filled with cigarette burns

the smells of French fries from the cafeteria, with its long rows of orange tables

the conversations of the biology majors at the next table, who were talking about cutting up frogs

the large, imposing library, with its rows of blue computer terminals and its hushed whispered sounds

Discuss how these events made you feel about your decision. Did you choose the right college?

Write a conclusion that reinforces the purpose of the essay. Make a direct statement of the way the events in the narrative changed you, or how your expectations for the day compare with what really happened.

Reading and Revising the Draft

Read the essay aloud to a classmate who is also a new freshman. Ask your listener if his or her day was the same as yours. Did you put the events in a logical sequence? Can your listener suggest more ideas to add? Have you included enough details so that a reader who was not a member of the college community could see the events as you saw them?

Proofread carefully for correctness and make a neat final copy.

A STUDENT PARAGRAPH: NARRATION

In preparation for the essay on narration, one student wrote a narrative paragraph to tell part of the story of his first day on campus. Look at the selection and the annotations, which highlight important elements of narrative writing.

Topic sentence	It was my first official day as a student here at State;
Statement of time and place helps set narrative scene.	the September morning had hardly begun, and I was already in a sweat. The crisp, colorful map I'd picked up shortly after passing through the iron gates had collapsed into a moist crumpled ball in my fist. Now I was
"I" sets narrative point of view (first person).	flushed, panting, and miserable, as I tried to decide which seemingly endless line of students I needed to join next in order to fix the financial mess the university's
Supporting detail	computers had put me in. Standing in the middle of the quad, hemmed in on all sides by towering brick and
Transitions ("now," "next") promote chronological sequence.	marble buildings, I gazed helplessly around me. Suddenly, I caught a glimpse of a familiar face: Dan Merritt, a tall, skinny kid with bright red hair who had quit the Westmont High football team in his sophomore year, a
Supporting detail	few weeks before I did. Springing into action, I virtually tackled the poor guy, frantic lest he should escape and
Supporting detail	leave me alone with my rapidly disappearing self-confidence. I felt a real jolt of pleasure, though, when
Dialogue adds real-life flavor.	I saw relief flood <u>his</u> face. "Boy, am I glad to see you," Dan said. "I was beginning to think I wouldn't get out of here alive."

The Struggle to Be an All-American Girl

Elizabeth Wong

Elizabeth Wong is an award-winning Chinese American playwright. *Letters to a Student Revolutionary* (1991), her best-known work to date, has been produced around the world. Her other plays include *Kimchee and Chitlins* (1990), about relations between Korean Americans and African Americans, and *The Happy Prince* (1997). A new play, *China Doll,* debuted in Los Angeles in 2004 and came to New York City in 2005. Wong was a staff writer for the ABC sitcom *All-American Girl,* the first network series to feature an Asian American woman as its central character. In this selection, which originally appeared in the *Los Angeles Times,* Wong effectively blends concrete description and imaginative comparisons. She uses her storytelling gifts to give the reader a vivid look into the life of a child who felt that she had a Chinese exterior but an American interior.

PREREADING: THINKING ABOUT THE ESSAY IN ADVANCE

America prides itself on its ability to assimilate cultures, yet the process of assimilation is not without difficulties, particularly for children. What problems do you foresee for a child of one cultural background growing up in the midst of another culture?

Words to Watch

stoically (par. 1)   without showing emotion
dissuade (par. 2)   to talk out of doing something
ideographs (par. 7)   Chinese picture symbols used to form words
disassociate (par. 8)   to detach from association
vendors (par. 8)   sellers of goods
gibberish (par. 9)   confused, unintelligible speech or language
pidgin (par. 10)   simplified speech that is usually a mixture of two or more languages

1   It's still there, the Chinese school on Yale Street where my brother and I used to go. Despite the new coat of paint and the high wire fence, the school I knew 10 years ago remains remarkably, stoically the same.

Every day at 5 P.M., instead of playing with our fourth- and 2
fifth-grade friends or sneaking out to the empty lot to hunt ghosts
and animal bones, my brother and I had to go to Chinese school.
No amount of kicking, screaming, or pleading could dissuade my
mother, who was solidly determined to have us learn the language
of our heritage.

Forcibly, she walked us the seven long, hilly blocks from our 3
home to school, depositing our defiant tearful faces before the
stern principal. My only memory of him is that he swayed on his
heels like a palm tree, and he always clasped his impatient twitch-
ing hands behind his back. I recognized him as a repressed maniacal child killer, and knew that if we ever saw his hands we'd be in
big trouble.

We all sat in little chairs in an empty auditorium. The room 4
smelled like Chinese medicine, an imported faraway mustiness.
Like ancient mothballs or dirty closets. I hated that smell. I favored
crisp new scents. Like the soft French perfume that my American
teacher wore in public school.

There was a stage far to the right, flanked by an American flag 5
and the flag of the Nationalist Republic of China, which was also
red, white and blue but not as pretty.

Although the emphasis at the school was mainly language— 6
speaking, reading, writing—the lessons always began with an
exercise in politeness. With the entrance of the teacher, the best
student would tap a bell and everyone would get up, kowtow, and
chant, "Sing san ho," the phonetic for "How are you, teacher?"

Being ten years old, I had better things to learn than ideo- 7
graphs copied painstakingly in lines that ran right to left from the
tip of a *moc but,* a real ink pen that had to be held in an awkward
way if blotches were to be avoided. After all, I could do the mul-
tiplication tables, name the satellites of Mars, and write reports on
"Little Women" and "Black Beauty." Nancy Drew, my favorite
book heroine, never spoke Chinese.

The language was a source of embarrassment. More times than 8
not, I had tried to disassociate myself from the nagging loud voice
that followed me wherever I wandered in the nearby American
supermarket outside Chinatown. The voice belonged to my grandmother, a fragile woman in her seventies who could outshout the
best of the street vendors. Her humor was raunchy, her Chinese
rhythmless, patternless. It was quick, it was loud, it was unbeauti-
ful. It was not like the quiet, lilting romance of French or the gentle

refinement of the American South. Chinese sounded pedestrian. Public.

9   In Chinatown, the comings and goings of hundreds of Chinese on their daily tasks sounded chaotic and frenzied. I did not want to be thought of as mad, as talking gibberish. When I spoke English, people nodded at me, smiled sweetly, said encouraging words. Even the people in my culture would cluck and say that I'd do well in life. "My, doesn't she move her lips fast," they would say, meaning that I'd be able to keep up with the world outside Chinatown.

10   My brother was even more fanatical than I about speaking English. He was especially hard on my mother, criticizing her, often cruelly, for her pidgin speech—smatterings of Chinese scattered like chop suey in her conversation. "It's not 'What it is,' Mom," he'd say in exasperation. "It's 'What *is* it, what *is* it, what *is* it!' Sometimes Mom might leave out an occasional "the" or "a," or perhaps a verb of being. He would stop her in mid-sentence: "Say it again, Mom. Say it right." When he tripped over his own tongue, he'd blame it on her: "See, Mom, it's all your fault. You set a bad example."

11   What infuriated my mother most was when my brother cornered her on her consonants, especially "r." My father had played a cruel joke on Mom by assigning her an American name that her tongue wouldn't allow her to say. No matter how hard she tried, "Ruth" always ended up "Luth" or "Roof."

12   After two years of writing with a *moc but* and reciting words with multiples of meanings, I finally was granted a cultural divorce. I was permitted to stop Chinese school.

13   I thought of myself as multicultural. I preferred tacos to egg rolls; I enjoyed Cinco de Mayo more than Chinese New Year.

14   At last, I was one of you; I wasn't one of them.

15   Sadly, I still am.

BUILDING VOCABULARY

For each of the words in italics, choose the letter of the word or expression that most closely matches its meaning.

1. the *stern* principal (par. 3)
  a. military
  b. very old
  c. immoral
  d. strict

2. *repressed* maniacal child killer (par. 3)
   a. quiet
   b. ugly
   c. held back
   d. retired
3. an imported faraway *mustiness* (par. 4)
   a. country
   b. mothballs
   c. chair
   d. staleness
4. a *fragile* woman (par. 8)
   a. elderly
   b. frail
   c. tall
   d. inconsistent
5. her humor was *raunchy* (par. 8)
   a. obscene
   b. unclear
   c. childish
   d. very funny
6. quiet, *lilting* romance of French (par. 8)
   a. musical
   b. tilting
   c. loving
   d. complicated
7. thought of as *mad* (par. 9)
   a. foreign
   b. angry
   c. stupid
   d. crazy
8. what *infuriated* my mother most (par. 11)
   a. angered
   b. humiliated
   c. made laugh
   d. typified

THINKING CRITICALLY ABOUT THE ESSAY

Understanding the Writer's Ideas

1. What did Elizabeth Wong and her brother do every day after school? How did that make them different from their friends?

What was their attitude toward what they did? How do you know?

2. What does Wong mean when she says of the principal "I recognized him as a repressed maniacal child killer"? Why were she and her brother afraid to see his hands?

3. What was the main purpose of going to Chinese school? What did Wong feel she had learned at "regular" American school? Which did she feel was more important? What are *Little Women, Black Beauty,* and Nancy Drew?

4. In the first sentence of paragraph 8, what language is "the language"?

5. What was Wong's grandmother like? What was Wong's attitude toward her? Why?

6. When Wong spoke English in Chinatown, why did the others think it was good that she moved her lips quickly?

7. What was her brother's attitude toward speaking English? How did he treat their mother when she tried to speak English? Why was it unfortunate that the mother had the American name *Ruth?* Who gave her that name? Why?

8. Explain the expression "he tripped over his own tongue" (par. 10).

9. In paragraph 13, Wong states, "I thought of myself as multicultural." What does that mean? What are tacos, egg rolls, and Cinco de Mayo? Why is it surprising that Wong includes those items as examples of her multiculturalism?

10. Who are the "you" and "them" of paragraph 14? Explain the significance of the last sentence. What does it indicate about Wong's attitude toward Chinese school from the vantage point of being an adult?

Understanding the Writer's Techniques

1. Wong does not state a thesis directly in a thesis sentence. How does her title imply a thesis? If you were writing a thesis sentence of your own for this essay, what would it be?

2. What is Wong's purpose in writing this narrative? Is the technique of narration an appropriate one to her purpose? Why or why not?

3. This narrative contains several stories. The first one ends after paragraph 7 and tells about Wong's routine after 5 P.M. on school days. Paragraphs 8 and 9, 10 and 11, and 12 and 13 offer other related narratives. Summarize each of these

briefly. How does Wong help the reader shift from story to story?

4. The writer of narration will present *time* in a way that best fulfills the purpose of the narration. This presentation may take many forms: a single, personal event; a series of related events; a historical occurrence; an aging process. Obviously Wong chose a series of related events. Why does she use such a narrative structure to make her point? Could she have chosen an alternative plan, do you think? Why or why not?

5. Writers of narration often rely upon descriptive details to flesh out their stories. Find examples of sensory language here that make the scene come alive for the reader.

6. Writers often use figurative comparisons to enliven their writing and to make it more distinctive. A *simile* is an imaginative form of figurative comparison using *like* or *as* to connect two items. One thing is similar to another in this figure. A *metaphor* is a figure of speech in which the writer compares two items not normally thought of as similar, but unlike in a simile, the comparison is direct—that is, it does not use *like* or *as*. (See Glossary for *simile* and *metaphor*.) In other words, one thing is said to be the other thing, not merely to be like it. For example, if you wanted to compare love to a rose, you might use these two comparisons:

Simile:
    My love is *like* a red, red rose.
Metaphor:
    My love *is* a red, red rose.

In Wong's essay, find the similes and metaphors in paragraphs 2, 3, 4, 10, and 12. For each, name the two items compared and explain the comparison in your own words.

7. Narratives often include lines of spoken language—that is, one person in the narrative talking alone or to another. Wong uses quoted detail sparsely here. Why did she choose to limit the dialogue? How effective is the dialogue that appears here? Where do you think she might have used more dialogue to advance the narrative?

8. The last two paragraphs are only one sentence each. Why do you think the author chose this technique?

9. What is the *irony* (see Glossary) in the last sentence of the essay? How would the meaning of the last sentence change if

you eliminated the word "sadly"? What is the irony in the title of the essay?

10. What is the *tone* (see Glossary) of this essay? How does Wong create that tone?

Exploring the Writer's Ideas

1. Wong and her brother deeply resented being forced to attend Chinese school. When children very clearly express displeasure or unhappiness, should parents force them to do things anyway? Why or why not?

2. On one level this essay is about a clash of cultures, here the ancient Chinese culture of Wong's ancestry and the culture of twentieth-century United States. Is it possible for someone to maintain connections to his or her ethnic or cultural background and at the same time to become an All-American girl or boy? What do people of foreign backgrounds gain when they become completely Americanized? What do they lose?

3. Because of their foreign ways, the mother and grandmother clearly embarrassed the Wong children. Under what other conditions that you can think of do parents embarrass children? Children, parents?

IDEAS FOR WRITING

Prewriting

Do timed writing—that is, write nonstop for fifteen or twenty minutes without editing or correcting your work—on the topic of your grade school or high school. What experience stands out most in your mind? What moment taught you most about yourself?

Guided Writing

Write a narration in which you tell about some difficult moment that took place in grade school or high school, a moment that taught you something about yourself, your needs, or your cultural background.

1. Provide a concrete description of the school.
2. Tell in correct sequence about the event.

3. Identify people who play a part in this moment.
4. Use concrete, sensory description throughout your essay.
5. Use original similes and metaphors to make your narrative clearer and more dramatic.
6. Use dialogue (or spoken conversation) appropriately in order to advance the narrative.
7. In your conclusion, indicate what your attitude toward this moment is now that you are an adult.
8. Write a title that implies your thesis.

Thinking and Writing Collaboratively

In groups of two or three, read aloud drafts of each other's essays, looking particularly at the use of concrete sensory detail and figures of speech—metaphors and similes. Which images strike you as most clear, original, and easy to visualize?

Writing About the Text

Write an essay that explores the ambivalence of the concluding two sentences. Why is Wong sad? Is the mixed emphasis of these final sentences, for example, felt throughout the essay? Is the ending a surprise?

More Writing Projects

1. Did you have any problems in grade school or high school because of your background or ancestry? Did you know someone who had such problems? Record a specific incident in your journal.
2. Write a narrative paragraph explaining some basic insights about your heritage or culture.
3. Get together with other classmates in a small group and brainstorm or bounce ideas off one another on troubling ethnic, racial, or cultural issues on campus. Write down all the incidents. Then write a narrative essay tracing one episode or connecting a series of them.

Salvation

Langston Hughes

One of the great American writers of the twentieth century, Langston Hughes was born in 1902 in Joplin, Missouri. His parents divorced while he was still an infant, and he was reared by his maternal grandmother, Mary Langston. His grandmother, whose first husband died in the raid on Harpers Ferry as a follower of John Brown, was an abiding influence on Hughes. Nonetheless, he suffered from parental absence; he later said that it was childhood loneliness that led him to books "and the wonderful world in books." Hughes studied for a year at Columbia University and later completed his college education at the historically black Lincoln University in Pennsylvania.

In 1926 Hughes published "The Negro Artist and the Racial Mountain," an essay that served as a manifesto for the Harlem Renaissance, of which he was a leading figure—as a poet, an essayist, a novelist, and a playwright. His poetry brilliantly employed the sounds of African American speech and of jazz, as suggested by the titles of two of his books of poems, *The Weary Blues* (1926) and *Montage of a Dream Deferred* (1951). In 1942 Hughes began to write a weekly column for the *Chicago Defender.* For two decades the column featured an offbeat Harlem character, Jesse B. Simple, Hughes's best-known and most-loved creation. Simple appears in five collections that Hughes edited, beginning with *Simple Speaks His Mind* (1950). This selection, from Hughes's autobiography, *The Big Sea* (1940), tells the story of his "conversion" to Christ. Salvation was a key event in the life of his community, but Hughes tells comically, and poignantly, of how he bowed to pressure by permitting himself to be "saved from sin." Hughes died in 1967.

www.mhhe.com/
shortprose

To learn more about Hughes, click on
**More Resources > Chapter 4 >
Langston Hughes**

PREREADING: THINKING ABOUT THE ESSAY IN ADVANCE

What is the role of religion today in the lives of most Americans? What role does religion play in your life? In what ways do the religious values of your family compare and contrast with your own?

Words to Watch

dire (par. 3)   terrible; disastrous
gnarled (par. 4)   knotty; twisted
rounder (par. 6)   watchman; policeman
deacons (par. 6)   members of the clergy or laypersons who are
    appointed to help the minister
serenely (par. 7)   calmly; tranquilly
knickerbockered (par. 11)   dressed in short, loose trousers that
    are gathered below the knees

I was saved from sin when I was going on thirteen. But not really 1
saved. It happened like this. There was a big revival at my Auntie
Reed's church. Every night for weeks there had been much
preaching, singing, praying, and shouting, and some very hardened sinners had been brought to Christ, and the membership
of the church had grown by leaps and bounds. Then just before
the revival ended, they held a special meeting for children, "to
bring the young lambs to the fold." My aunt spoke of it for days
ahead. That night I was escorted to the front row and placed on the
mourners' bench with all the other young sinners, who had not yet
been brought to Jesus.

My aunt told me that when you were saved you saw a light, 2
and something happened to you inside! And Jesus came into your
life! And God was with you from then on! She said you could see
and hear and feel Jesus in your soul. I believed her. I had heard a
great many old people say the same thing and it seemed to me they
ought to know. So I sat there calmly in the hot, crowded church,
waiting for Jesus to come to me.

The preacher preached a wonderful rhythmical sermon, all 3
moans and shouts and lonely cries and dire pictures of hell, and
then he sang a song about the ninety and nine safe in the fold,
but one little lamb was left out in the cold. Then he said: "Won't
you come? Won't you come to Jesus? Young lambs, won't you
come?" And he held out his arms to all us young sinners there on
the mourners' bench. And the little girls cried. And some of them
jumped up and went to Jesus right away. But most of us just sat
there.

A great many old people came and knelt around us and prayed, 4
old women with jet-black faces and braided hair, old men with
work-gnarled hands. And the church sang a song about the lower

lights are burning, some poor sinners to be saved. And the whole building rocked with prayer and song.

5   Still I kept waiting to *see* Jesus.

6   Finally all the young people had gone to the altar and were saved, but one boy and me. He was a rounder's son named Westley. Westley and I were surrounded by sisters and deacons praying. It was very hot in the church, and getting late now. Finally Westley said to me in a whisper: "God damn! I'm tired o' sitting here. Let's get up and be saved." So he got up and was saved.

7   Then I was left all alone on the mourners' bench. My aunt came and knelt at my knees and cried, while prayers and songs swirled all around me in the little church. The whole congregation prayed for me alone, in a mighty wail of moans and voices. And I kept waiting serenely for Jesus, waiting, waiting—but he didn't come. I wanted to see him, but nothing happened to me. Nothing! I wanted something to happen to me, but nothing happened.

8   I heard the songs and the minister saying: "Why don't you come? My dear child, why don't you come to Jesus? Jesus is wait-ing for you. He wants you. Why don't you come? Sister Reed, what is this child's name?"

9   "Langston," my aunt sobbed.

10   "Langston, why don't you come? Why don't you come and be saved? Oh, Lamb of God! Why don't you come?"

11   Now it was really getting late. I began to be ashamed of myself, holding everything up so long. I began to wonder what God thought about Westley, who certainly hadn't seen Jesus either, but who was now sitting proudly on the platform, swinging his knickerbockered legs and grinning down at me, surrounded by deacons and old women on their knees praying. God had not struck Westley dead for taking his name in vain or for lying in the temple. So I decided that maybe to save further trouble, I'd better lie, too, and say that Jesus had come, and get up and be saved.

12   So I got up.

13   Suddenly the whole room broke into a sea of shouting, as they saw me rise. Waves of rejoicing swept the place. Women leaped in the air. My aunt threw her arms around me. The minister took me by the hand and led me to the platform.

14   When things quieted down, in a hushed silence, punctuated by a few ecstatic "Amens," all the new young lambs were blessed in the name of God. Then joyous singing filled the room.

That night, for the last time in my life but one—for I was a big 15
boy twelve years old—I cried. I cried, in bed alone, and couldn't
stop. I buried my head under the quilts, but my aunt heard me. She
woke up and told my uncle I was crying because the Holy Ghost
had come into my life, and because I had seen Jesus. But I was
really crying because I couldn't bear to tell her that I had lied, that
I had deceived everybody in the church, that I hadn't seen Jesus,
and that now I didn't believe there was a Jesus any more, since he
didn't come to help me.

BUILDING VOCABULARY

1. Throughout this essay, Hughes selects words dealing with
   religion to emphasize his ideas. Look up the following words
   in a dictionary. Then tell what *connotations* (see Glossary) the
   words have for you.
   a. sin (par. 1)
   b. mourner (par. 1)
   c. lamb (par. 3)
   d. salvation (title)
2. Locate additional words that deal with religion.
3. When Hughes talks about lambs in the fold—and lambs in
   general—he is using a figure of speech, a comparison (see
   Chapter 7). What is being compared? How does religion enter
   into the comparison? Why is it useful as a figure of speech?

THINKING CRITICALLY ABOUT THE ESSAY

Understanding the Writer's Ideas

1. According to Hughes's description, what is a revival meeting
   like? What is the effect of the "preaching, singing, praying,
   and shouting" on the "sinners" and the "young lambs"?
2. Why does Westley "see" Jesus? Why does Langston Hughes
   come to Jesus?
3. How does the author feel after his salvation? Does Hughes
   finally believe in Christ after his experience? How do you
   know?

Understanding the Writer's Techniques

1. Is there a thesis statement in the essay? Where is it located?
2. How does the first paragraph serve as an introduction to the narrative?
3. What is the value of description in this essay? List several instances of vivid description that contribute to the narrative.
4. Where does the main narration begin? How much time passes in the course of the action?
5. In narration, it is especially important to have effective *transitions*—or word bridges—from stage to stage in the action. Transitions help the reader shift easily from idea to idea, event to event. List several transition words that Hughes uses.
6. A piece of writing has *coherence* (see Glossary) if all its parts relate clearly and logically to one another. Each sentence grows naturally from the sentence before it; each paragraph grows naturally from the paragraph before it. Is Hughes's essay coherent? Which transitions help advance the action and relate the parts of a single paragraph to one another? Which transitions help connect paragraphs together? How does the way Hughes organized this essay help establish coherence?
7. A story (whether it is true or fiction) has to be told from the first-person ("I, we"), second-person ("you"), or third-person ("he, she, it, they") *point of view*. Point of view in narration sets up the author's position in regard to the action, making the author either a part of the action or an observer of it.
   a. What is the point of view in "Salvation"—is it first, second, or third person?
   b. Why has Hughes chosen this point of view instead of any other? Can you think of any advantages to this point of view?
8. What is your opinion about the last paragraph, the conclusion of this selection? What does it suggest about the mind of a twelve-year-old boy? What does it say about adults' misunderstanding of the activities of children?
9. What does the word *conversion* mean? What conversion really takes place in this piece? How does that compare with what people usually mean when they use *conversion* in a religious sense?

Exploring the Writer's Ideas

1. Hughes seems to suggest that we are forced to do things because of social pressures. Do you agree with his suggestion? Do people do things because their friends or families expect them to? To what extent are we part of the "herd"? Is it possible for a person to retain individuality under pressure from a group? When did you bow to group pressures? When did you resist?
2. Do you find the religious experience in Hughes's essay unusual or extreme? Why or why not? How do *you* define religion?
3. Under what circumstances might a person lie in order to satisfy others? Try to recall a specific episode in which you or someone you know was forced to lie in order to please others.

IDEAS FOR WRITING

Prewriting

Write a few sentences to define *group pressure*. Then give an example or two of a time when you gave in to group pressure or were forced to lie in order to impress others.

Guided Writing

Narrate an event in your life where you (or someone you know) gave in to group pressure or were forced to lie in order to please those around you.

1. Start with a thesis statement.
2. Set the stage for your narrative in the opening paragraph by telling where and when the incident took place. Use specific names for places.
3. Try to keep the action within as brief a time period as possible. If you can write about an event that took no more than a few minutes, so much the better.
4. Use description to sketch in the characters around you. Use colors, actions, sounds, smells, sensations of touch to fill in details of the scene.
5. Use effective transitions of time to link sentences and paragraphs.

6. Use the last paragraph to explain how you felt immediately after the incident.

Thinking and Writing Collaboratively

Exchange drafts of your Guided Writing essay with one other person in the class. Then, write out a brief outline of the events the writer has presented in the narrative. Is the sequence clear? Do the introduction and thesis set the stage appropriately for the sequence of events? Do the transitions link paragraphs and sentences effectively? Return the paper with your written response.

Writing About the Text

Write an essay that speculates about whether, as an adult, Hughes did—or didn't—discover a meaning in his life through religion. Use evidence from this essay, written, after all, when Hughes was an adult.

More Writing Projects

1. Explain in a journal entry an abstract word like *salvation, sin, love,* or *hatred* by narrating an event that reveals the meaning of the word to you.
2. Write an extended paragraph on an important event that affected your relationship with family, friends, or your community during your childhood.
3. Make a list of all the important details that you associate with some religious occasion in your life. Then write a narrative essay on the experience.

Let It Snow
David Sedaris

David Sedaris was born the day after Christmas in 1956. Before he found success as a writer and performer, he cleaned houses in New York City. He has made a career of writing about his life and then reading his work out loud, most notably on National Public Radio but also in theaters throughout the country. His collected essays appear in the books *Naked* (1997), *Me Talk Pretty One Day* (2000), *Dress Your Family in Corduroy and Denim* (2004), and *When You Are Engulfed in Flames* (2008). In this essay from *Dress Your Family in Corduroy and Denim*, Sedaris tells of having a white Christmas in North Carolina.

www.mhhe.com/
shortprose

To learn more about Sedaris, click on
**More Resources > Chapter 4 >
David Sedaris**

PREREADING: THINKING ABOUT THE ESSAY IN ADVANCE

Do you remember any incidents from your childhood in which you acted in a more adult manner than an adult? How did you respond to the situation? Why? In what ways did your upbringing prepare you for the situation?

Words to Watch

accumulated (par. 2)   collected, gathered together
disrupted (par. 2)   ended the pattern of
carport (par. 3)   garage connected to a house
goblet (par. 4)   a wine glass with a stem
dusk (par. 6)   sundown
mastodon (par. 6)   prehistoric species similar to elephants
canopy (par 10)   a covering set on posts

In Binghamton, New York, winter meant snow, and though I was   1
young when we left, I was able to recall great heaps of it, and use that memory as evidence that North Carolina was, at best, a third-rate institution. What little snow there was would usually melt an hour or two after hitting the ground, and there you'd be in your

windbreaker and unconvincing mittens, forming a lumpy figure made mostly of mud. Snow Negroes, we called them.

2   The winter I was in the fifth grade we got lucky. Snow fell, and for the first time in years, it accumulated. School was canceled and two days later we got lucky again. There were eight inches on the ground, and rather than melting, it froze. On the fifth day of our vacation my mother had a little breakdown. Our presence had disrupted the secret life she led while we were at school, and when she could no longer take it she threw us out. It wasn't a gentle request, but something closer to an eviction. "Get the hell out of my house," she said.

3   We reminded her that it was our house, too, and she opened the front door and shoved us into the carport. "And stay out!" she shouted.

4   My sisters and I went down the hill and sledded with other children from the neighborhood. A few hours later we returned home, surprised to find that the door was still locked. "Oh, come on," we said. I rang the bell and when no one answered we went to the window and saw our mother in the kitchen, watching television. Normally she waited until five o'clock to have a drink, but for the past few days she'd been making an exception. Drinking didn't count if you followed a glass of wine with a cup of coffee, and so she had both a goblet and a mug positioned before her on the countertop.

5   "Hey!" we yelled. "Open the door. It's us." We knocked on the pane, and without looking in our direction, she refilled her goblet and left the room.

6   "That bitch," my sister Lisa said. We pounded again and again, and when our mother failed to answer we went around back and threw snowballs at her bedroom window. "You are going to be in so much trouble when Dad gets home!" we shouted, and in response my mother pulled the drapes. Dusk approached, and as it grew colder it occurred to us that we could possibly die. It happened, surely. Selfish mothers wanted the house to themselves, and their children were discovered years later, frozen like mastodons in blocks of ice.

7   My sister Gretchen suggested that we call our father, but none of us knew his number, and he probably wouldn't have done anything anyway. He'd gone to work specifically to escape our mother, and between the weather and her mood, it could be hours or even days before he returned home.

"One of us should get hit by a car," I said. "That would teach 8
the both of them." I pictured Gretchen, her life hanging by a thread
as my parents paced the halls of Rex Hospital, wishing they had
been more attentive. It was really the perfect solution. With her out
of the way, the rest of us would be more valuable and have a bit
more room to spread out. "Gretchen, go lie in the street."

"Make Amy do it," she said.   9

Amy, in turn, pushed it off onto Tiffany, who was the young- 10
est and had no concept of death. "It's like sleeping," we told her.
"Only you get a canopy bed."

Poor Tiffany. She'd do just about anything in return for a little 11
affection. All you had to do was call her Tiff and whatever you
wanted was yours: her allowance money, her dinner, the contents
of her Easter basket. Her eagerness to please was absolute and
naked. When we asked her to lie in the middle of the street, her
only question was "Where?"

We chose a quiet dip between two hills, a spot where drivers 12
were almost required to skid out of control. She took her place,
this six-year-old in a butter-colored coat, and we gathered on the
curb to watch. The first car to happen by belonged to a neighbor, a fellow Yankee who had outfitted his tires with chains and
stopped a few feet from our sister's body. "Is that a person?" he
asked.

"Well, sort of," Lisa said. She explained that we'd been locked 13
out of our house and though the man appeared to accept it as a reasonable explanation, I'm pretty sure it was him who told on us.
Another car passed and then we saw our mother, this puffy figure
awkwardly negotiating the crest of the hill. She did not own a
pair of pants, and her legs were buried to the calves in snow. We
wanted to send her home, to kick her out of nature just as she had
kicked us out of the home, but it was hard to stay angry at someone
that pitiful-looking.

"Are you wearing your *loafers?*" Lisa asked, and in response 14
our mother raised her bare foot. "I *was* wearing loafers," she said.
"I mean, really, it was there a second ago."

This was how things went. One moment she was locking us 15
out of our own house and the next we were rooting around in the
snow, looking for her left shoe. "Oh, forget about it," she said. "It'll
turn up in a few days." Gretchen fitted her cap over my mother's
foot. Lisa secured it with her scarf, and surrounding her tightly on
all sides, we made our way back home.

BUILDING VOCABULARY

In this essay, Sedaris uses several common words in uncommon ways. Find the following words in a dictionary and identify which definition he is using. Write a sentence for each word using that definition.

a. pulled (par. 6)
b. naked (par. 11)
c. outfitted (par. 12)
d. negotiating (par. 13)
e. rooting (par. 15)

THINKING CRITICALLY ABOUT THE ESSAY

Understanding the Writer's Ideas

1. Where did Sedaris grow up?
2. Why does Sedaris say he "got lucky" when he was in fifth grade?
3. What does the writer mean when he says that he and his sisters "disrupted the secret life" their mother had while they were at school?
4. What did the writer's mother do while her children were sledding? What is Sedaris suggesting by his explanation of his mother's activities in paragraph 3?
5. How would you describe the different personalities of Sedaris's sisters?
6. What do Sedaris and his sisters decide to do, since they can't go home?
7. What does Amy mean when she tells Tiffany what death is like in paragraph 9?
8. How do they choose Tiffany to lie in the street?
9. Why does Sedaris's mother go outside in the snow without pants or proper shoes on?

Understanding the Writer's Techniques

1. Although this essay might not have a traditional thesis statement, you can readily infer its main idea. What is the main point that the essay sends to its readers? State it in your own words.

2. A narrative essay sometimes makes its points in a different way from an argumentative essay. Here, Sedaris uses humor to express the pain of his upbringing. Find at least three examples of this use of humor and explain them.

3. This essay uses *hyperbole* (see Glossary) to make its points. What examples can you find?

4. There is a shift in the tone of the essay after paragraph 7. What is that shift, and why is it effective?

5. Where does the action of the narrative pause so that the writer can explain something important to the story? Why does he do this?

6. What is the effect on the reader of Lisa's answer to the question about whether Tiffany was a person (paragraph 12)? How can one read this as more than a joke? Why does Sedaris use this technique?

7. What is your opinion of the last paragraph of the essay? What point is Sedaris trying to express, and, in your opinion, is he successful?

Exploring the Writer's Ideas

1. Sedaris seems to suggest that his mother's actions made his relations with his sisters closer. How do sibling closeness and, conversely, sibling rivalry, occur, do you think?

2. At the end of this essay, Sedaris and his sisters treat their mother almost as a child. How can children sometimes be more mature than their parents? What are the implications of such a situation?

3. Sedaris and his sisters come up with a foolish solution to being locked out of the house, but it isn't only children that act this way. Why do adults try to get attention, and how do they try to get it in self-destructive ways?

IDEAS FOR WRITING

Prewriting

Freewrite for fifteen minutes about a decision you made in childhood that led to a negative outcome about which you can laugh today. What was absurd or ridiculous about the situation, the decision, and the outcome? How has elapsed time reduced the pain of the memory?

Guided Writing

Write a narrative essay in which you relate a painful incident from your childhood that occurred as a result of a decision you made. Tell your story in a humorous manner, using *irony* (see Glossary).

1. Begin with an explanation of the situation and a description of the scene.
2. Introduce the characters who are involved in the story.
3. Using an ironic tone, introduce your decision and explain how you arrived at it.
4. Include references to opinions of other characters about what you should do.
5. Use *hyperbole* (see Glossary) to make sure your reader knows that you are being humorous.
6. Explain the results of your decision.
7. End on a note of solemnity or seriousness.

Thinking and Writing Collaboratively

In a small group of three or four, exchange your Guided Writing narrative essays. After each paper has been read once by each student, discuss each essay as a group, commenting on the effectiveness of the narrative, suggesting ideas for how to improve the description, and especially paying attention to the tone and level of humor.

Writing About the Text

Sedaris takes a fairly ambiguous view of his mother, her unhappiness, and her actions. Write an essay in which you discuss whether she was a bad mother or not. Offer examples and explain your points fully. Explain how you account for the essay's ending.

More Writing Projects

1. Write a journal entry about the effect of alcoholic parents on children.

2. Find a recording of Sedaris reading this or one of his other essays. Write an extended paragraph about the difference between listening to and reading an essay.
3. Think of an event in your childhood that you remember well. Interview members of your family about the event. Write a narrative essay about the event that takes into account all the facts you learned, using your memory as the basis for the structure.

✷ A Hanging
George Orwell

Mixing Patterns

George Orwell (the pen name of Eric Blair) was born in Bengal, India, in 1903. His parents were members of the British Civil Service in India, and Orwell followed in their footsteps when as a young man he joined the Imperial Police in Burma. But ironically Orwell's experience as a policeman in Burma turned him against British colonialism, as he recounts in a famous essay, "Shooting an Elephant." Indeed, he became a committed socialist but a fiercely antiautocratic one. In the mid-1930s, like many left-wing intellectuals and writers, he went to Spain to fight with the International Brigade in support of the recently elected Popular Front government, then under military attack by Fascist forces led by the ultimately victorious General Franco. Orwell was seriously wounded in the Spanish Civil War, and when the Spanish Communists, under orders from Moscow, attempted to wipe out their allies on the left, he fought against them, finally fleeing for his life.

Orwell became famous in the early years of the Cold War for two prophetic, satirical books fed by his experiences with Communism, books that brilliantly attack totalitarian forms of government. The first, *Animal Farm* (1945), tells the story of the terror tactics and deception that pigs use to take over a farm—but it is an allegorical fable aimed against Stalinism. The second, *Nineteen Eighty-Four* (1949), is a "dystopian" novel, a futuristic novel that portrays the future as dreadful rather than an amazing improvement on life as we have known it (as "utopian" works do). It is to *Nineteen Eighty-Four* that we owe the idea and the expression, "Big Brother is watching you." This selection is one of a group of enormously influential essays by Orwell that employ personal narrative to explore issues of broad concern, in particular social and political issues. In "Politics and the English Language," Orwell maintained that muddy writing, obscurity, inaccuracy, pretentiousness are closely related to a flawed political outlook, and that democracy and equality are strengthened by clear, honest, and direct writing. Saying things clearly, writing to be understood, were, for Orwell, *political* virtues. Orwell died of tuberculosis in 1950.

www.mhhe.com/
shortprose

To learn more about Orwell, click on
**More Resources > Chapter 4 >
George Orwell**

PREREADING: THINKING ABOUT
THE ESSAY IN ADVANCE

The number of people executed through the system of justice in the
United States has increased dramatically over the past few years.
How do you explain this increase in the number of executions by
lethal injection or the electric chair? Why does U.S. society continue to use capital punishment? Under what circumstances is a
person sentenced to capital punishment?

Words to Watch

sodden (par. 1)   heavy with water
absurdly (par. 2)   ridiculously
desolately (par. 3)   gloomily; lifelessly; cheerlessly
prodding (par. 3)   poking or thrusting at something
Dravidian (par. 4)   any member of a group of intermixed races
    of southern India and Burma
pariah (par. 6)   outcast; a member of a low caste of southern
    India and Burma
servile (par. 11)   slavelike; lacking spirit or independence
reiterated (par. 12)   repeated
abominable (par. 13)   hateful; disagreeable; unpleasant
timorously (par. 15)   fearfully
oscillated (par. 16)   moved back and forth between two points
garrulously (par. 20)   in a talkative manner
refractory (par. 22)   stubborn
amicably (par. 24)   in a friendly way; peaceably

It was in Burma, a sodden morning of the rains. A sickly light, like   1
yellow tinfoil, was slanting over the high walls into the jail yard.
We were waiting outside the condemned cells, a row of sheds
fronted with double bars, like small animal cages. Each cell measured about ten feet by ten and was quite bare within except for
a plank bed and a pot of drinking water. In some of them brown
silent men were squatting at the inner bars, with their blankets
draped round them. These were the condemned men, due to be
hanged within the next week or two.

One prisoner had been brought out of his cell. He was a   2
Hindu, a puny wisp of a man, with a shaven head and vague liquid
eyes. He had a thick, sprouting moustache, absurdly too big for

his body, rather like the moustache of a comic man on the films. Six tall Indian warders were guarding him and getting him ready for the gallows. Two of them stood by with rifles with fixed bayonets, while the others handcuffed him, passed a chain through his handcuffs and fixed it to their belts, and lashed his arms tight to his sides. They crowded very close about him, with their hands always on him in a careful, caressing grip, as though all the while feeling him to make sure he was there. It was like men handling a fish which is still alive and may jump back into the water. But he stood quite unresisting, yielding his arms limply to the ropes, as though he hardly noticed what was happening.

3   Eight o'clock struck and a bugle call, desolately thin in the wet air, floated from the distant barracks. The superintendent of the jail, who was standing apart from the rest of us, moodily prodding the gravel with his stick, raised his head at the sound. He was an army doctor, with a grey toothbrush moustache and a gruff voice. "For God's sake hurry up, Francis," he said irritably. "The man ought to have been dead by this time. Aren't you ready yet?"

4   Francis, the head jailer, a fat Dravidian in a white drill suit and gold spectacles, waved his black hand. "Yes sir, yes sir," he bubbled. "All iss satisfactorily prepared. The hangman iss waiting. We shall proceed."

5   "Well, quick march, then. The prisoners can't get their breakfast till this job's over."

6   We set out for the gallows. Two warders marched on either side of the prisoner, with their files at the slope; two others marched close against him, gripping him by arm and shoulder, as though at once pushing and supporting him. The rest of us, magistrates and the like, followed behind. Suddenly, when we had gone ten yards, the procession stopped short without any order or warning. A dreadful thing had happened—a dog, come goodness knows whence, had appeared in the yard. It came bounding among us with a loud volley of barks, and leapt round us wagging its whole body, wild with glee at finding so many human beings together. It was a large woolly dog, half Airedale, half pariah. For a moment it pranced round us, and then, before anyone could stop it, it had made a dash for the prisoner, and jumping up tried to lick his face. Everyone stood aghast, too taken aback even to grab at the dog.

7   "Who let that bloody brute in here?" said the superintendent angrily. "Catch it, someone!"

A warder, detached from the escort, charged clumsily after 8
the dog, but it danced and gambolled just out of his reach, taking
everything as part of the game. A young Eurasian jailer picked up
a handful of gravel and tried to stone the dog away, but it dodged
the stones and came after us again. Its yaps echoed from the jail
walls. The prisoner, in the grasp of the two warders, looked on
incuriously, as though this was another formality of the hanging.
It was several minutes before someone managed to catch the dog.
Then we put my handkerchief through its collar and moved off
once more, with the dog still straining and whimpering.

It was about forty yards to the gallows. I watched the bare 9
brown back of the prisoner marching in front of me. He walked
clumsily with his bound arms, but quite steadily, with that bobbing
gait of the Indian who never straightens his knees. At each step his
muscles slid neatly into place, the lock of hair on his scalp danced
up and down, his feet printed themselves on the wet gravel. And
once, in spite of the men who gripped him by each shoulder, he
stepped slightly aside to avoid a puddle on the path.

It is curious, but till that moment I had never realised what it 10
means to destroy a healthy, conscious man. When I saw the prisoner step aside to avoid the puddle, I saw the mystery, the unspeakable wrongness, of cutting a life short when it is in full tide. This
man was not dying, he was alive just as we were alive. All the
organs of his body were working—bowels digesting food, skin
renewing itself, nails growing, tissues forming—all toiling away
in solemn foolery. His nails would still be growing when he stood
on the drop, when he was falling through the air with a tenth of a
second to live. His eyes saw the yellow gravel and the grey walls,
and his brain still remembered, foresaw, reasoned—reasoned even
about puddles. He and we were a party of men walking together,
seeing, hearing, feeling, understanding the same world; and in two
minutes, with a sudden snap, one of us would be gone—one mind
less, one world less.

The gallows stood in a small yard, separate from the main 11
grounds of the prison, and overgrown with tall prickly weeds. It
was a brick erection like three sides of a shed, with planking on
top, and above that two beams and a crossbar with the rope dangling. The hangman, a grey-haired convict in the white uniform
of the prison, was waiting beside his machine. He greeted us with
a servile crouch as we entered. At a word from Francis the two
warders, gripping the prisoner more closely than ever, half led,

half pushed him to the gallows and helped him clumsily up the ladder. Then the hangman climbed up and fixed the rope round the prisoner's neck.

12   We stood waiting, five yards away. The warders had formed in a rough circle round the gallows. And then, when the noose was fixed, the prisoner began crying out on his god. It was a high, reiterated cry of "Ram! Ram! Ram! Ram!", not urgent and fearful like a prayer or a cry for help, but steady, rhythmical, almost like the tolling of a bell. The dog answered the sound with a whine. The hangman, still standing on the gallows, produced a small cotton bag like a flour bag and drew it down over the Prisoner's face. But the sound, muffled by the cloth, still persisted, over and over again: "Ram! Ram! Ram! Ram! Ram!"

13   The hangman climbed down and stood ready, holding the lever. Minutes seemed to pass. The steady, muffled crying from the prisoner went on and on, "Ram! Ram! Ram!" never faltering for an instant. The superintendent, his head on his chest, was slowly poking the ground with his stick; perhaps he was counting the cries, allowing the prisoner a fixed number—fifty, perhaps, or a hundred. Everyone had changed colour. The Indians had gone grey like bad coffee, and one or two of the bayonets were wavering. We looked at the lashed, hooded man on the drop, and listened to his cries—each cry another second of life; the same thought was in all our minds: oh, kill him quickly, get it over, stop that abominable noise!

14   Suddenly the superintendent made up his mind. Throwing up his head he made a swift motion with his stick. "Chalo!" he shouted almost fiercely.

15   There was a clanking noise, and then dead silence. The prisoner had vanished, and the rope was twisting on itself. I let go of the dog, and it galloped immediately to the back of the gallows; but when it got there it stopped short, barked, and then retreated into a corner of the yard, where it stood among the weeds, looking timorously out at us. We went round the gallows to inspect the prisoner's body. He was dangling with his toes pointed straight downwards, very slowly revolving, as dead as a stone.

16   The superintendent reached out with his stick and poked the bare body; it oscillated, slightly. "*He's* all right," said the superintendent. He backed out from under the gallows, and blew out a deep breath. The moody look had gone out of his face quite suddenly. He glanced at his wristwatch. "Eight minutes past eight. Well, that's all for this morning, thank God."

The warders unfixed bayonets and marched away. The dog, 17
sobered and conscious of having misbehaved itself, slipped after
them. We walked out of the gallows yard, past the condemned cells
with their waiting prisoners, into the big central yard of the prison.
The convicts, under the command of warders armed with lathis,
were already receiving their breakfast. They squatted in long rows,
each man holding a tin pannikin, while two warders with buckets
marched round ladling out rice; it seemed quite a homely, jolly
scene, after the hanging. An enormous relief had come upon us
now that the job was done. One felt an impulse to sing, to break
into a run, to snigger. All at once everyone began chattering gaily.

The Eurasian boy walking beside me nodded towards the way we 18
had come, with a knowing smile: "Do you know, sir, our friend (he
meant the dead man), when he heard his appeal had been dismissed,
he pissed on the floor of his cell. From fright—Kindly take one of my
cigarettes, sir. Do you not admire my new silver case, sir? From the
boxwallah, two rupees eight annas. Classy European style."

Several people laughed—at what, nobody seemed certain.   19

Francis was walking by the superintendent, talking garru- 20
lously: "Well, sir, all hass passed off with the utmost satisfac-
toriness. It wass all finished—flick! like that. It iss not always
so—oah, no! I have known cases where the doctor wass obliged
to go beneath the gallows and pull the prisoner's legs to ensure
decease. Most disagreeable!"

"Wriggling about, eh? That's bad," said the superintendent. 21

"Ach, sir, it iss worse when they become refractory! One man, 22
I recall, clung to the bars of hiss cage when we went to take him
out. You will scarcely credit, sir, that it took six warders to dislodge
him, three pulling at each leg. We reasoned with him. My dear fellow, we said, think of all the pain and trouble you are causing to
us! But no, he would not listen! Ach, he wass very troublesome!"

I found that I was laughing quite loudly. Everyone was laugh- 23
ing. Even the superintendent grinned in a tolerant way. "You'd
better all come out and have a drink," he said quite genially. "I've
got a bottle of whisky in the car. We could do with it."

We went through the big double gates of the prison, into the 24
road. "Pulling at his legs!" exclaimed a Burmese magistrate suddenly, and burst into a loud chuckling. We all began laughing
again. At that moment Francis's anecdote seemed extraordinarily
funny. We all had a drink together, native and European alike,
quite amicably. The dead man was a hundred yards away.

BUILDING VOCABULARY

1. Use *context clues* (see Glossary) to make an "educated guess" about the definitions of the following words in italics. Before you guess, look back to the paragraph for clues. Afterward, check your guess in a dictionary.
   a. *condemned* men (par. 1)
   b. puny *wisp* of a man (par. 2)
   c. Indian *warders* (par. 2)
   d. careful, *caressing* grip (par. 2)
   e. stood *aghast* (par. 6)
   f. it danced and *gambolled* (par. 8)
   g. *solemn* foolery (par. 10)
   h. armed with *lathis* (par. 17)
   i. a tin *pannikin* (par. 17)
   j. quite *genially* (par. 23)
2. What are definitions for the words below? Look at words within them, which you may be able to recognize.
   a. moodily
   b. dreadful
   c. Eurasian
   d. incuriously
   e. formality

THINKING CRITICALLY ABOUT THE ESSAY

Understanding the Writer's Ideas

1. The events in the essay occur in a country in Asia, Burma (also called Myanmar, since 1989). Describe in your own words the specific details of the action.
2. Who are the major characters in this essay? Why might you include the dog as a major character?
3. In a narrative essay the writer often tells the events in chronological order. Examine the following events from "A Hanging." Arrange them in the order in which they occurred.
   a. A large woolly dog tries to lick the prisoner's face.
   b. A Eurasian boy talks about his silver case.
   c. The superintendent signals "Chalo!" to the hangman.
   d. One prisoner, a Hindu, is brought from his cell.

    e. Francis discusses with the superintendent a prisoner who had to be pulled off the bars of his cage.

    f. The prisoner steps aside to avoid a puddle as he marches to the gallows.

4. What is the author's opinion of *capital punishment* (legally killing someone who has disobeyed the laws of society)? How does the incident with the puddle suggest that opinion, even indirectly?

Understanding the Writer's Techniques

1. What is the main point that the writer wishes to make in this essay? Which paragraph tells the author's thesis most clearly? Which sentence in that paragraph best states the main idea of the essay?

2. In the first paragraph of the essay, we see clear images such as "brown silent men were squatting at the inner bars, with their blankets draped around them." The use of color and action makes an instant appeal to our sense of sight.

    a. What images in the rest of the essay do you find most vivid?

    b. Which sentence gives the best details of sound?

    c. What word pictures suggest action and color?

    d. Where do you find words that describe a sensation of touch?

3. In order to make their images clearer, writers use *figurative language* (see Glossary). "A Hanging" is especially rich in *similes,* which are comparisons using the word *like* or *as.*

    a. What simile does Orwell use in the first paragraph in order to let us see how the light slants over the jail yard walls? How does the simile make the scene clearer?

    b. What other simile does Orwell use in the first paragraph?

    c. Discuss the similes in the paragraphs listed below. What are the things being compared? Are the similes, in your opinion, original? How do they contribute to the image the author intends to create?

        (1) It was like men handling a fish (par. 2)

        (2) a thick sprouting moustache . . . rather like the moustache of a comic man on the films (par. 2)

        (3) It was a high, reiterated cry . . . like the tolling of a bell. (par. 12)

      (4) The Indians had gone grey like bad coffee (par. 13)

      (5) He was dangling with his toes pointed straight downwards, very slowly revolving, as dead as a stone. (par. 15)

4. You know that an important feature of narration is the writer's ability to look at a brief span of time and to expand that moment with specific language.

  a. How has Orwell limited the events in "A Hanging" to a specific moment in time and place?

  b. How does the image "a sodden morning of the rains" in paragraph 1 set the mood for the main event portrayed in the essay? What is the effect of the image "brown silent men"? Why does Orwell describe the prisoner as "a puny wisp of a man, with a shaven head and vague liquid eyes" (par. 2)? Why does the author present him in almost a comic way?

  c. What is the effect of the image about the bugle call in paragraph 3? Why does Orwell create the image of the dog trying to lick the prisoner's face (par. 6)? How does it contribute to his main point? In paragraph 12, Orwell tells us that the dog whines. Why does he give that detail? Discuss the value of the images about the dog in paragraphs 15 and 17.

  d. Why does Orwell offer the image of the prisoner stepping aside "to avoid a puddle on the path"? How does it advance the point of the essay? What is the effect of the image of the superintendent poking the ground with his stick (par. 13)?

  e. What is the importance of the superintendent's words in paragraph 3? What is the value of the Eurasian boy's conversation in paragraph 18? How does the dialogue in paragraphs 20 to 24 contribute to Orwell's main point?

  f. Why has Orwell left out information about the crime the prisoner committed? How would you feel about the prisoner if you knew he were, say, a rapist, a murderer, a molester of children, or a heroin supplier?

5. Analyze the point of view in the essay. Is the "I" narrator an observer, a participant, or both? Is he neutral or involved? Support your opinion.

6. In "A Hanging," Orwell skillfully uses several forms of *irony* to support his main ideas. Irony, in general, is the use of language to suggest the opposite of what is said. First, there is *verbal irony,* which involves a contrast between what is said and what is actually meant. Second, there is *irony of situation,* where there is a contrast between what is expected or thought appropriate and what actually happens. Then, there is *dramatic irony,* in which there is a contrast between what a character says and what the reader (or the audience) actually knows or understands.

  a. In paragraph 2, why does Orwell describe the prisoner as a *comic* type? Why does he emphasize the prisoner's *smallness?* Why does Orwell write that the prisoner "hardly noticed what was happening"? Why might this be called ironic?

  b. When the dog appears in paragraph 6, how is its behavior described? How do the dog's actions contrast with the situation?

  c. What is the major irony that Orwell analyzes in paragraph 10?

  d. In paragraph 11, how does the fact that one prisoner is being used to execute another prisoner strike you?

  e. Why is the superintendent's remark in paragraph 16— "*He's* all right"—a good example of verbal irony?

  f. After the hanging, the men engage in seemingly normal actions. However, Orwell undercuts these actions through the use of irony. Find at least two examples of irony in paragraphs 17 to 24.

✳ MIXING PATTERNS

"Description," we say in the introduction to Chapter 3, "is frequently used to make abstract ideas more *concrete.*" In this essay, basically a narrative, how does Orwell use description to make an abstract idea—capital punishment is wrong—concrete? Identify three or four examples.

Exploring the Writer's Ideas

  1. Orwell is clearly against capital punishment. Why might you agree or disagree with him? Are there any crimes for which capital punishment is acceptable to you? If not, what should society do with those convicted of serious crimes?

2. Do you think the method used to perform capital punishment has anything to do with the way we view it? Is death by hanging or firing squad worse than death by gas or by the electric chair? Or are they all the same? Socrates—a Greek philosopher convicted of conspiracy—was forced to drink *hemlock,* a fast-acting poison. Can you accept that?

3. Orwell shows a variety of reactions people have to an act of execution. Can you believe the way the people behave here? Why? How do you explain the large crowds that gathered to watch public executions in Europe in the sixteenth and seventeenth centuries?

IDEAS FOR WRITING

Prewriting

Make two columns on a sheet of paper that you have headed "Capital Punishment." In one column, jot down all the reasons you can think of in favor of capital punishment. In the other column, indicate all the reasons you can think of against it.

Guided Writing

Write a narrative essay in which you tell about a punishment you either saw or received. Use sensory language, selecting your details carefully. At one point in your paper—as Orwell does in paragraph 10—state your opinion or interpretation of the punishment clearly.

1. Use a number of images that name colors, sounds, smells, and actions.
2. Try to write at least three original similes. Think through your comparisons carefully. Make sure they are logical. Avoid overused comparisons like "He was white as a ghost."
3. Set your narrative in time and place. Tell the season of the year and the place in which the event occurred.
4. Fill in details of the setting. Show what the surroundings look like.
5. Name people by name. Show details of their actions. Quote some of their spoken dialogue.
6. Use the first-person point of view.

Thinking and Writing Collaboratively

In small groups, read drafts of each other's essays for the Guided Writing activity. Look especially at the point at which the writer states an opinion about or interprets the punishment received. Does the writer adequately explain the event? What insights has the writer brought to the moment by analyzing it? How could either the narrative itself or the interpretation be made clearer or more powerful?

Writing About the Text

Write an essay in which you consider why Orwell chose to include the dog in this essay. How would the essay be different without the dog? Do you think the dog was *actually* present at the scene of the hanging, or do you suspect that Orwell made him up?

More Writing Projects

1. Narrate in your journal an event that turned out differently from what you expected—a blind date, a picnic, a holiday. Try to stress the irony of the situation.
2. Write a narrative paragraph that describes a vivid event in which you hid your true feelings about the event, such as a postelection party, the wedding of someone you disliked, a job interview, a visit to the doctor.
3. Write an editorial for your college newspaper supporting or attacking the idea of capital punishment. Communicate your position through the use of real or hypothetical narration of a relevant event.

SUMMING UP: CHAPTER 4

1. Orwell's essay has remained one of the outstanding essays of our age. It is widely anthologized and often read in English composition classes. How do you account for its popularity? Would you consider it the best essay in this chapter or in the four chapters you have read in this book so far? Why or why not? Write an essay in which you analyze and evaluate "A Hanging."

2. Both Langston Hughes and David Sedaris use humor to make serious points about their childhoods. Using their essays as a starting point, write a humorous essay about your childhood view of an adult decision.

3. What have you learned about writing strong narratives from the writers in this chapter? What generalizations can you draw? What "rules" can you derive? Write an essay called "How to Write Narratives" based on what you have learned from Wong, Hughes, Sedaris, and (or) Orwell. Make specific references to the writer(s) of your choice.

4. Hughes's essay highlights the role of religion in life. Write an essay in which you narrate an important religious experience that you remember.

5. Writers often use narrative to re-create a memory, as with the essays in this chapter. But our memories, especially of emotional moments from long ago, are notoriously unreliable. How do the writers in this chapter deal—or not deal—with the problem of the possible unreliability of memory? How much would it matter if some of the incidents narrated here were *in*-accurately recalled by the writer, or even altered to make a better essay?

6. Compare and contrast the attitudes toward language as reflected in the essays of Amy Tan (pp. 41–46) and Elizabeth Wong (pp. 143–145).

7. Hughes and Orwell explore the ambiguities involved in thinking or feeling things that distinguish them from most people around them—such as being a skeptic in an evangelical church or a colonial policeman opposed to colonialism. Compare and contrast how these writers treat the situation of a person who does not conform to society's values and beliefs.

✳ FROM SEEING TO WRITING

Write a narrative essay in which you tell what you think is the story of the award-winning photograph reprinted here. Develop your thesis, present lively details to hold your reader's attention, and introduce your details in a sequence that is easy to follow.

CHAPTER 5

Process Analysis

WHAT IS PROCESS ANALYSIS?

Process analysis explains to a reader how to do something, how something works, or how something occurs. Like narration, it is a form of sequencing or presentation of events in order, or taking apart a process in order better to understand how it functions. This kind of writing is often called *expository* because it *exposes* or shows us information. If you use cookbooks, you are encountering process analysis each time you read a recipe. If you are setting up a new DVD, you may wish the writer of the manual were more adept at writing process analysis when you find the steps hard to follow. "How to" writing can therefore give the reader steps for carrying out a process. The writer might also analyze the steps someone took already in completing a process, such as explaining how Harriet Tubman organized the Underground Railroad or how women won the right to vote.

Planning a good process analysis requires the writer to include all the essential steps. Be sure you have all the tools or ingredients needed. Arrange the steps in the correct sequence. Like all good writing, a good process essay requires a thesis to tell the reader the *significance* of the process. The writer can tell the reader how to do something, but also should inform the reader about the usefulness or importance of the endeavor.

In this chapter, Bill Bryson instructs readers—whimsically—on what to do with their new computers. Like Bryson, Nora Ephron also injects humor into her essay on how to foil a terrorist plot. From Ernest Hemingway, we learn how to make our next experience of camping a success. And Henry Louis Gates Jr. explains how to "de-kink" your hair. As you read about these processes, watch how each writer uses the same technique to achieve a different result.

HOW DO WE READ PROCESS ANALYSIS?

Identify what process the writer is going to analyze. As you read, make a quick outline of the steps the writer introduces.

Watch the use of transitions as the writer moves from one step to the next.

Assess the audience that the writer has aimed at. Is the writer addressing innocents or experts? If the writer's purpose was to explain how to prepare beef stew, he would give different directions to a college freshman who has never cooked before than he would give to a cooking class at the Culinary Institute of America, where everyone was familiar with the fundamentals of cooking. Ask yourself, then: Is there enough information in the analysis? too much?

How does the writer try to make the piece lively? Does it sound as dry as a technical manual, or is there an engaging tone?

HOW DO WE WRITE PROCESS ANALYSIS?

Decide to analyze a process with which you are very familiar. Unless you can do it well yourself, you won't be able to instruct or inform your readers.

Process begins with a good shopping list. Once you have your topic, make lists of ingredients or tools.

Arrange the essential steps in logical order. Don't assume your reader already knows how to do the process. As you know from those often incomprehensible instructions for putting together a child's toy, the reader should be given *every* step.

List the steps to *avoid* when carrying out the procedure.

If possible, actually try out the process, using your list as a guide, if you are presenting a method for a tangible product, like making an omelet. Or imagine that you are explaining the procedure over the telephone.

If your topic is abstract, like telling someone how to become an American citizen, read it aloud to a willing listener to see if he or she can follow the steps clearly.

Use *definition* to explain terms the reader may not know, especially if you are presenting a technical process. At the same time, avoid jargon. Make the language as plain as possible.

Describe the appearance of the product or *compare* an unfamiliar item with a familiar one.

Be sure to think about your audience. Link the audience to the purpose of the process.

Formulate a thesis statement that tells what the process is, and why it is a good process to know.

Sample thesis statement:

> Buying and renovating an old car is a time-consuming process, but the results are worthwhile.

Writing the Draft

Write a rough draft. Turn your list into an essay by developing the steps into sentences, using your thesis to add significance and coherence to the process you are presenting. Don't just list; analyze the procedure as you go along. Keep in mind the techniques of writers like Ernest Hemingway, who doesn't just cook a trout but uses the process to represent the whole morality of "doing things right," raising his process analysis beyond the ordinary.

Add transitions when necessary to alert the reader that a new step is coming. The most common transition words help a reader to follow steps: *first, second, third; first, next, after, last.*

Proofread, revise, and create a final draft.

A STUDENT PARAGRAPH: PROCESS ANALYSIS

Process analysis lends itself to a variety of approaches, ranging from a methodical step-by-step explanation of a task such as how to prepare a pie, to assessment of a series of related historical events. As you read the following one-paragraph composition, consider the student's success in providing the reader with a flexible approach to a typical problem.

Finding the right used car can be a real challenge. Unless you are totally open to possibilities, the first step in the process is to focus on one make and model that interests you. Next, you should consult the Blue Book, which lists car makes and models by year, and provides a rough guide to

Topic sentence

Phrase "the first step" starts the process.

"Next" signals
the second step.

Parenthetical
remark qualifies
earlier statement.

"At this point"
moves reader to
third step.

"Continue your
hunt by consult-
ing" advances
the process.

"Several other
promising routes"
adds to process.

Concluding step
cautions, adds
humor.

fair prices based on condition. It's a good idea to have the book handy before moving to the next stage in your search; you can probably disqualify a number of cars based on asking price alone. (If the asking price is significantly higher than the Blue Book suggests, the seller is not always trying to hoodwink you. There might be a good reason for the price—exceptionally good condition, or an unusual number of "add-ons," for example. Still, it makes sense to use caution in these cases.) At this point, you are ready to start the actual search, beginning with a scanning of these resources. Don't limit your search to these resources, however; continue your hunt by consulting more local venues, such as campus bulletin-board postings. There are several other promising routes to finding the wheels of your dreams: car rental companies usually sell off their rentals after they've reached a ripe old age—sometimes a venerable 3 to 5 years! Police auctions are another possibility, though the successful bidder is usually required to plunk down cash for the car right away, and the cars come with no warranty—you can find a real bargain here, but it's only really a safe bet if you can take along a mechanic. In fact, consulting a good mechanic should *always* be the last step in the process: after you have located the car of your dreams, get an inspection before you write that check, just to make sure that your dream machine doesn't explode.

www.mhhe.com/
shortprose

To learn more about using process analysis, click on

**Writing > Writing Tutor:
                      Process Analysis
Writing > Paragraph Patterns**

Your New Computer
Bill Bryson

In 1973, Bill Bryson, an Iowa native, moved to England to be with his wife. After a short time back in the United States in the late 1990s, Bryson and his family went back across the Atlantic. His travels underlie many of his books, including his first, 1989's *The Lost Continent,* about driving his mother's car around America; *Notes from a Small Island* (1996), about life as an American in England; and *A Walk in the Woods* (1998), a hilarious account of his attempt to hike the Appalachian Trail from Georgia to Maine. He has also written *The Life and Times of the Thunderbolt Kid* (2004) and *Bryson's Dictionary for Writers and Editors* (2008). In 1999 Bryson published *I'm a Stranger Here Myself,* the source for this selection, in which Bryson grapples with technology.

www.mhhe.com/
shortprose

To learn more about Bryson, click on
**More Resources > Chapter 5 >
Bill Bryson**

PREREADING: THINKING ABOUT THE ESSAY IN ADVANCE

Have the instructions included with a piece of electronics you've bought ever baffled you? What was most confusing about them—your ignorance? the bad writing? What can writers of instructions do to help consumers understand how to use the product?

Words to Watch

diversion (par. 1)   distraction
configured (par. 4)   set up for use
invalidate (par. 6)   cause to be canceled
warranty (par. 6)   written guarantee for repairs
vouchers (par. 7)   coupons for future purchases
auxiliary (par. 8)   extra
longhand (par. 20)   with a pen or pencil on paper

1 Congratulations. You have purchased an Anthrax/2000 Multimedia 615X Personal Computer with Digital Doo-Dah Enhancer. It will

give years of faithful service, if you ever get it up and running. Also included with your PC is a bonus pack of preinstalled software— Lawn Mowing Planner, Mr. Arty-Farty, Blank Screen Saver, and Antarctica Route Finder—which will provide hours of pointless diversion while using up most of your computer's spare memory.

So turn the page and let's get started!   2

Getting Ready

Congratulations. You have successfully turned the page and are 3 ready to proceed.

Important meaningless note: The Anthrax/2000 is configured 4 to use 80386, 214J10, or higher processors running at 2472 Herz on variable speed spin cycle. Check your electrical installations and insurance policies before proceeding. Do not machine wash.

To prevent internal heat build-up, select a cool, dry envi- 5 ronment for your computer. The bottom shelf of a refrigerator is ideal.

Unpack the box and examine its contents. (Warning: Do not 6 open box if contents are missing or faulty, as this will invalidate your warranty. Return all missing contents in their original packaging with a note explaining where they have gone and a replacement will be sent within twelve working months.)

The contents of the box should include some of the following: 7 monitor with mysterious De Gauss button; keyboard; computer unit; miscellaneous wires and cables not necessarily designed for this model; 2,000-page Owner's Manual; Short Guide to the Owner's Manual; Quick Guide to the Short Guide to the Owner's Manual; Laminated Super-Kwik Set-Up Guide for People Who Are Exceptionally Impatient or Stupid; 1,167 pages of warranties, vouchers, notices in Spanish, and other loose pieces of paper; 292 cubic feet of Styrofoam packing material.

Something They Didn't Tell You at the Store

Because of the additional power needs of the preinstalled bonus 8 software, you will need to acquire an Anthrax/2000 auxiliary software upgrade pack, a 900-volt memory capacitator for the auxiliary software pack, a 50-megaherz oscillator unit for the memory capacitator, 2,500 mega-gigabytes of additional memory for the oscillator, and an electrical substation.

Setting Up

9 Congratulations. You are ready to set up. If you have not yet acquired a degree in electrical engineering, now is the time to do so.

10   Connect the monitor cable (A) to the portside outlet unit (D); attach power offload unit suborbiter (Xii) to the coaxial AC/DC servo channel (G); plug three-pin mouse cable into keyboard housing unit (make extra hole if necessary); connect modem (B2) to offside parallel audio/video lineout jack. Alternatively, plug the cables into the most likely looking holes, switch on, and see what happens.

11   Additional important meaningless note: The wires in the ampule modulator unit are marked as follows according to international convention: blue = neutral or live; yellow = live or blue; blue and live = neutral and green; black = instant death. (Except where prohibited by law.)

12   Switch the computer on. Your hard drive will automatically download. (Allow three to five days.) When downloading is complete, your screen will say: "Yeah, what?"

13   Now it is time to install your software. Insert Disc A (marked "Disc D" or "Disc G") into Drive Slot B or J, and type: "Hello! Anybody home?" At the DOS command prompt, enter your License Verification Number. Your License Verification Number can be found by entering your Certified User Number, which can be found by entering your License Verification Number. If you are unable to find your License Verification or Certified User numbers, call the Software Support Line for assistance. (Please have your License Verification and Certified User numbers handy as the support staff cannot otherwise assist you.)

14   If you have not yet committed suicide, then insert Installation Diskette 1 in drive slot 2 (or vice versa) and follow the instructions on your screen. (Note: Owing to a software modification, some instructions will appear in Turkish.) At each prompt, reconfigure the specified file path, double-click on the button launch icon, select a single equation default file from the macro selection register, insert the VGA graphics card in the rear aerofoil, and type "C:\>" followed by the birthdates of all the people you have ever known.

        Your screen will now say: "Invalid file path. Whoa! Abort 15 or continue?" Warning: Selecting "Continue" may result in irreversible file compression and a default overload in the hard drive. Selecting "Abort," on the other hand, will require you to start the installation process all over again. Your choice.

When the smoke has cleared, insert disc A2 (marked "Disc A1")   16
and repeat as directed with each of the 187 other discs.

When installation is complete, return to file path, and type your   17
name, address, and credit card numbers and press "SEND." This will
automatically register you for our free software prize, "Blank Screen-
saver IV: Nighttime in Deep Space," and allow us to pass your name
to lots and lots of computer magazines, online services, and other
commercial enterprises, who will be getting in touch shortly.

Congratulations. You are now ready to use your computer.   18
Here are some simple exercises to get you off to a flying start.

Writing a Letter

Type "Dear _____" and follow it with a name of someone you   19
know. Write a few lines about yourself, and then write, "Sincerely
yours" followed by your own name. Congratulations.

Saving a File

To save your letter, select File Menu. Choose Retrieve from Sub-   20
Directory A, enter a backup file number, and place an insertion
point beside the macro dialogue button. Select secondary text box
from the merge menu, and double-click on the supplementary
cleared document window. Assign the tile cascade to a merge file
and insert in a text equation box. Alternatively, write the letter out
longhand and put it in a drawer.

Advice on Using the Spreadsheet Facility

Don't.   21

BUILDING VOCABULARY

Bryson employs many technical terms in his essay (although not
all of them are strictly computer terms). Look up the following
words and define them in your own words:

a. multimedia (par. 1)
b. processors (par. 4)
c. capacitator (par. 8)
d. oscillator (par. 8)

e. gigabytes (par. 8)
f. coaxial (par. 10)
g. servo (par. 10)
h. ampule (par. 11)
 i. aerofoil (par. 14)

THINKING CRITICALLY ABOUT THE ESSAY

Understanding the Writer's Ideas

1. What is Bryson suggesting by naming the preinstalled software "Lawn Mowing Planner," "Mr. Arty-Farty," and so on?
2. What is the joke in the warning in paragraph 6?
3. Why does Bryson write that "if you have not yet acquired a degree in electrical engineering, now is the time to do so" (par. 9)?
4. Explain the implication of the joke in paragraph 10.
5. What is absurd about paragraph 13?
6. What does Bryson imply will happen if one registers for the prize in paragraph 17?
7. Why does Bryson give an alternative solution to saving a letter in paragraph 20?

Understanding the Writer's Techniques

1. Why does Bryson present his essay as a set of instructions for a computer? What is the rhetorical effect?
2. Why does Bryson present the instructions in the order he does?
3. Who is the ideal reader of this essay? How does the tone reflect that?
4. For what purpose does Bryson repeat "Congratulations" five times?
5. Is there a thesis here? Explain your answer.
6. How effective is the last section as an ending for this humorous essay? Explain.

Exploring the Writer's Ideas

1. Computers today demand a certain level of technical knowledge, despite what computer manufacturers insist. What can the manufacturers do to make computers more user-friendly and accessible to everyone?

2. While many contend that computers in the home and office have improved our lives, some people argue that computers have actually caused productivity to slow down. Offer at least two examples of how computers have decreased productivity.

3. Why do you think manuals for computers and other machines are so poorly written? What rules could you provide to manual writers to help them produce clearer instructions?

IDEAS FOR WRITING

Prewriting

Freewrite for fifteen minutes about the fact that there are few rule books or manuals for human problems such as people's relations or responsibilities.

Guided Writing

Write an essay in the form of an instruction manual for something that normally doesn't receive one, for example, a new baby, a new marriage or relationship, a new dog or cat.

1. Look again at Bryson's first two paragraphs and write a similar introduction, starting your essay as well with the word *congratulations.*

2. Write your essay using as much humor as possible. Really push it.

3. Prepare headers, such as Bryson's "Getting Ready" and "Setting Up" to help organize your essay.

4. Move in chronological order. Write a paragraph for each major step in the process.

5. Continue to congratulate your reader often.

6. Develop a tone of ironic pessimism in your essay, suggesting that whatever your reader does, something will go wrong.

7. Conclude your essay with a pithy instruction based on Bryson's last tip.

Thinking and Writing Collaboratively

Divide the class into two groups. Each group should prepare a list of instructions for a student on how to write an essay, from prewriting to proofreading. Write the instructions out in your group and then cut the instructions up into individual steps. Mix up the slips and give them to the other group. Reassemble the other group's instructions. Then present the instructions to the entire class, reading them out loud.

Writing About the Text

Write an essay in which you analyze the humor in this essay. Is Bryson funny? Think about the audience for this essay. What is the effect of the years that have passed since this essay was published for the first time?

More Writing Projects

1. Each generation must face new technology. In your journal, write an entry about what technologies you think you or your children will struggle with in fifteen, thirty, and forty-five years.
2. Using process analysis, write a paragraph explaining how to decide what model computer to buy. What are the considerations? What kind of advice might you give to someone who is faced with that decision?
3. Write a process-analysis paper explaining how to become a successful college student.

How to Foil a Terrorist Plot in Seven Simple Steps

Nora Ephron

Nora Ephron has enjoyed a varied and successful career as a reporter, columnist, essayist, novelist, screenwriter, movie director, and producer. Born in New York City in 1941 but raised in Beverly Hills, where her parents were famous screenwriters, Ephron returned to the East Coast to attend Wellesley College (BA, 1962). Subsequently she was hired as a reporter for the *New York Post*, then did freelance work before joining the staff at *New York* and *Esquire*. She achieved notoriety with the publication of *Heartburn* (1983), a comic novel recounting Ephron's highly publicized breakup with her second husband, Watergate journalist Carl Bernstein. Ephron wrote the screenplay for *Heartburn* (1986), and wrote and/or produced the films *Silkwood* (1983), *When Harry Met Sally* (1989), *Sleepless in Seattle* (1993), *You've Got Mail* (1998), and *Bewitched* (2005). Known as one of the most powerful women in Hollywood, Ephron is also an acclaimed essayist whose collections include *Wallflower at the Orgy* (1970), *Crazy Salad* (1975), and *I Feel Bad About My Neck* (2006). The following selection, which appeared in the online *Huffington Post* on June 4, 2007, is typical of Ephron's witty, often quirky style.

PREREADING: THINKING ABOUT THE ESSAY IN ADVANCE

Writers tend to view terrorists (and terrorism) as a serious subject. What is the value or appropriateness of treating serious subjects in comic fashion?

Words to Watch

foil (par. 1)   to keep from being successful; frustrate
deter (par. 2)   to keep a person from doing something; prevent
impending (par. 4)   about to happen
remuneration (par. 6)   reward; pay; compensation
feasible (par. 7)   capable of being done or carried out; possible

1. In order to foil a terrorist plot, you must first find a terrorist plot. 1
This is not easy.

    2. Not just anyone can find and then foil a terrorist plot. You 2
must have an incentive. The best incentive is to be an accused

felon, looking at a long prison term. Under such circumstances, your lawyer will explain to you, you may be able to reduce your sentence by acting as an informant in a criminal case, preferably one involving terrorists.

3   3. The fact that you do not know any actual terrorists should not in any way deter you. Necessity is the mother of invention: if you can find the right raw material—a sad, sick, lonely, drunk, deranged, disgruntled or just plain anti-American Muslim somewhere in the United States—you can make your very own terrorist.

4   4. Now the good part begins. Money! The FBI will give you lots of money to take your very own terrorist out to lots of dinners where you, wearing a wire, can record yourself making recommendations to him about possible targets and weapons that might be used in the impending terrorist attack that your very own terrorist is going to mastermind, with your help. It will even buy you a computer so you can go to Google Earth in order to show your very own terrorist a "top secret" aerial image of the target you have suggested.

5   5. More money!! The FBI will give you even more money to travel to foreign countries with your very own terrorist, and it will make suggestions about terrorist groups you can meet while in said foreign countries.

6   6. Months and even years will pass in this fashion, while you essentially get the FBI to pay for everything you do. (Incidentally, be sure your lawyer negotiates your expense account well in advance, or you may be forced—as the informant was in the Buffalo terrorist case—to protest your inadequate remuneration by setting yourself on fire in front of the White House.)

7   7. At a certain point, something will go wrong. You may have trouble recruiting other people to collaborate with your very own terrorist, who is, as you yourself know, just an ordinary guy in a really bad mood. Or, alternatively, the terrorist cell you have carefully cobbled together may malfunction and fail to move forward—probably as a result of sheer incompetence or of simply not having been genuinely serious about the acts of terrorism you were urging it to commit. At this point, you may worry that the FBI is going to realize that there isn't much of a terrorist plot going on here at all, just a case of entrapment. Do not despair: the FBI is way ahead of you. The FBI knows perfectly well what's going on. The FBI has as much at stake as you do. So before it can be obvious to the world

that there's no case, the FBI will arrest your very own terrorist, hold a press conference and announce that a huge terrorist plot has been foiled. It will of course be forced to admit that this plot did not proceed beyond the pre-planning stage, that no actual weapons or money were involved, and that the plot itself was "not technically feasible," but that will not stop the story from becoming a front-page episode all over America and, within hours, boilerplate for all the Republican politicians who believe that you need to arrest a "homegrown" terrorist now and then to justify the continuing war in Iraq. Everyone will be happy, except for the schmuck you shmikeled into becoming a terrorist, and no one really cares about him anyway.

So congratulations. You have foiled a terrorist plot. Way to go.   8

BUILDING VOCABULARY

1. Examine the words and definitions in the Words to Watch section, and write an original sentence that uses each word correctly.
2. Consult a specialized dictionary of slang terms in order to explain the expression "the schmuck you shmikeled" (par. 7).

THINKING CRITICALLY ABOUT THE ESSAY

Understanding the Writer's Ideas

1. Briefly summarize Ephron's strategy for foiling a terrorist plot.
2. Why, according to Ephron, is a convicted felon the ideal informant?
3. What does Ephron mean when she writes "Necessity is the mother of invention" (par. 2)? Explain this expression in the context of the paragraph and essay.
4. Why should the informant have a lawyer?
5. What is Ephron's attitude toward the FBI? How do you know?
6. In the final analysis, according to Ephron, is it important that a terrorist or terrorist plot might not exist, despite what authorities and the media claim? Justify your response.

Understanding the Writer's Techniques

1. Why doesn't Ephron ever state a thesis directly in this essay? What *is* her main idea? How does she present and develop this idea?

2. For whom is Ephron writing this essay? How does her *tone* (see Glossary) reflect her audience?

3. What is Ephron's level of *diction?* (See Glossary.) Is her language formal or informal, and why? Cite specific examples to support your response.

4. Why do you suppose Ephron numbers all her paragraphs (except the last one)? In what way is this strategy part of her process analysis?

5. What are the steps in the process that Ephron presents? Are these steps mutually exclusive or do they overlap? Explain.

6. Many of Ephron's paragraphs are brief, no more than a sentence or two, including the introductory and concluding paragraphs. What is Ephron's purpose in designing such short paragraphs?

7. Would you say that Ephron is ironic in this essay? Is she ever *sarcastic* or *satiric?* (See Glossary.) Point to places in the essay that demonstrate these varieties of humor.

Exploring the Writer's Ideas

1. Although this essay is written in a humorous vein, there are certainly many serious implications to the subject and content. Discuss your position on such issues as terrorism, informants, the FBI, "anti-American Muslims," the media, and the war in Iraq.

2. Is it possible for anyone reading this essay to take it seriously? Is it possible for someone to be offended? Why or why not?

3. Has Ephron presented a balanced picture of the issues or is her claim or main argument one-sided? Support your opinion with specific references to the essay.

IDEAS FOR WRITING

Prewriting

Write a preliminary outline for a process essay dealing with some aspect of current events.

Guided Writing

Write a humorous essay on a serious subject drawn from politics, economics, or popular culture. As preparation for your essay of process analysis, provide a title beginning "How to_____," and fill in the blank.

1. In imitation of Ephron, begin with a numbered paragraph and continue this strategy throughout the essay.
2. In a brief introductory paragraph, explain your thesis and the basic purpose in presenting the process.
3. Introduce a new step or procedure for each successive paragraph. Provide at least five steps, procedures, or rules that will lead readers through the process.
4. Employ a colloquial style of writing.
5. Try using irony and satire to make your point. (Avoid any sarcasm, which generally is inappropriate in college writing.)
6. Conclude on a note that suggests you are highly critical of the process you have just analyzed.

Thinking and Writing Collaboratively

With one or two other classmates, log onto the *Huffington Post* to find out more about the site and its contributors (including Ephron). Take notes, and share your findings with the class.

Writing About the Text

Satire is one of the more difficult forms to master. Write an analysis of Ephron's satiric method in "How to Foil a Terrorist Plot in Seven Simple Steps," and evaluate her relative effectiveness in using this strategy.

More Writing Projects

1. In your journal, write an entry exploring your feelings about the issue of terrorism.
2. Compose a humorous paragraph in which you list the steps involved in managing an important activity—for instance, getting along with a roommate, doing the laundry, getting to class on time.
3. Write an essay giving directions and providing steps that should be taken in the event of a natural or "homegrown" disaster.

Camping Out
Ernest Hemingway

Through his life and his work, Ernest Hemingway influenced world culture more than any other American writer of his time. Born in Oak Park, Illinois, in 1899, Hemingway began his writing career as a reporter, and throughout his life he worked for newspapers, often on the front lines of armed conflicts such as the Spanish Civil War (1936–1939) and the Second World War (1939–1945). His adventures brought him close to death several times—in the Spanish Civil War when shells landed in his hotel room, in the Second World War when he was struck by a taxi during a blackout, and in 1954 when his plane crashed in Africa.

Writing in an unadorned, unemotional but taut style, Hemingway placed at the heart of his fiction the search for meaning in a world disenchanted with old ideals. In his life as in his writing he was drawn to individuals committed to the art of doing things well regardless of the larger world's lack of direction or faith; he especially admired those who achieved grace or beauty in the face of death, such as bullfighters, hunters, and soldiers. His best-known books are *The Sun Also Rises* (1926), the novel that established his reputation; *A Farewell to Arms* (1929); *For Whom the Bell Tolls* (1940); and *The Old Man and the Sea* (1953). For the last he was awarded a Pulitzer Prize, and in the following year he received the Nobel Prize in Literature. Hemingway committed suicide in Ketchum, Idaho, in 1961.

In this essay, Hemingway uses the pattern of process analysis to order his materials on the art of camping. He wrote this piece for the *Toronto Star* in the early 1920s, before he gained worldwide recognition as a major American writer. In it, we see his lifelong interest in the outdoors and his desire to do things well.

PREREADING: THINKING ABOUT THE ESSAY IN ADVANCE

As you prepare to read Hemingway's essay, take a minute or two to think about your own experiences in nature or any unknown place you once visited. If you have ever camped out or attended summer camp, for example, how did you prepare for, enter into, and survive the experience? What problems did you encounter, and how did you overcome them?

Words to Watch

relief map (par. 2)   a map that shows by lines and colors the various heights and forms of the land

Caucasus (par. 2)   a mountain range in southeastern Europe

proprietary (par. 7)   held under patent or trademark

rhapsodize (par. 9)   to speak enthusiastically

browse bed (par. 9)   a portable cot

tyro (par. 11)   an amateur; a beginner in learning something

dyspepsia (par. 13)   indigestion

mulligan (par. 18)   a stew made from odds and ends of meats and vegetables

Thousands of people will go into the bush this summer to cut the 1 high cost of living. A man who gets his two weeks' salary while he is on vacation should be able to put those two weeks in fishing and camping and be able to save one week's salary clear. He ought to be able to sleep comfortably every night, to eat well every day and to return to the city rested and in good condition.

But if he goes into the woods with a frying pan, an ignorance 2 of black flies and mosquitoes, and a great and abiding lack of knowledge about cookery the chances are that his return will be very different. He will come back with enough mosquito bites to make the back of his neck look like a relief map of the Caucasus. His digestion will be wrecked after a valiant battle to assimilate half-cooked or charred grub. And he won't have had a decent night's sleep while he has been gone.

He will solemnly raise his right hand and inform you that he 3 has joined the grand army of never-agains. The call of the wild may be all right, but it's a dog's life. He's heard the call of the tame with both ears. Waiter, bring him an order of milk toast.

In the first place he overlooked the insects. Black flies, no-see- 4 ums, deer flies, gnats and mosquitoes were instituted by the devil to force people to live in cities where he could get at them better. If it weren't for them everybody would live in the bush and he would be out of work. It was a rather successful invention.

But there are lots of dopes that will counteract the pests. The 5 simplest perhaps is oil of citronella. Two bits' worth of this purchased at any pharmacist's will be enough to last for two weeks in the worst fly and mosquito-ridden country.

Rub a little on the back of your neck, your forehead and your 6 wrists before you start fishing, and the blacks and skeeters will shun you. The odor of citronella is not offensive to people. It smells like gun oil. But the bugs do hate it.

7   Oil of pennyroyal and eucalyptol are also much hated by mosquitoes, and with citronella they form the basis for many proprietary preparations. But it is cheaper and better to buy the straight citronella. Put a little on the mosquito netting that covers the front of your pup tent or canoe tent at night, and you won't be bothered.

8   To be really rested and get any benefit out of a vacation a man must get a good night's sleep every night. The first requisite for this is to have plenty of cover. It is twice as cold as you expect it will be in the bush four nights out of five, and a good plan is to take just double the bedding that you think you will need. An old quilt that you can wrap up in is as warm as two blankets.

9   Nearly all outdoor writers rhapsodize over the browse bed. It is all right for the man who knows how to make one and has plenty of time. But in a succession of one-night camps on a canoe trip all you need is level ground for your tent floor and you will sleep all right if you have plenty of covers under you. Take twice as much cover as you think that you will need, and then put two-thirds of it under you. You will sleep warm and get your rest.

10   When it is clear weather you don't need to pitch your tent if you are only stopping for the night. Drive four stakes at the head of your made-up bed and drape your mosquito bar over that, then you can sleep like a log and laugh at the mosquitoes.

11   Outside of insects and bum sleeping the rock that wrecks most camping trips is cooking. The average tyro's idea of cooking is to fry everything and fry it good and plenty. Now, a frying pan is a most necessary thing to any trip, but you also need the old stew kettle and the folding reflector baker.

12   A pan of fried trout can't be bettered and they don't cost any more than ever. But there is a good and bad way of frying them.

13   The beginner puts his trout and his bacon in and over a brightly burning fire; the bacon curls up and dries into a dry tasteless cinder and the trout is burned outside while it is still raw inside. He eats them and it is all right if he is only out for the day and going home to a good meal at night. But if he is going to face more trout and bacon the next morning and other equally well-cooked dishes for the remainder of two weeks he is on the pathway to nervous dyspepsia.

14   The proper way is to cook over coals. Have several cans of Crisco or Cotosuet or one of the vegetable shortenings along that

are as good as lard and excellent for all kinds of shortening. Put the bacon in and when it is about half cooked lay the trout in the hot grease, dipping them in corn meal first. Then put the bacon on top of the trout and it will baste them as it slowly cooks.

The coffee can be boiling at the same time and in a smaller 15 skillet pancakes being made that are satisfying the other campers while they are waiting for the trout.

With the prepared pancake flours you take a cupful of pancake 16 flour and add a cup of water. Mix the water and flour and as soon as the lumps are out it is ready for cooking. Have the skillet hot and keep it well greased. Drop the batter in and as soon as it is done on one side loosen it in the skillet and flip it over. Apple butter, syrup or cinnamon and sugar go well with the cakes.

While the crowd have taken the edge from their appetites with 17 flapjacks the trout have been cooked and they and the bacon are ready to serve. The trout are crisp outside and firm and pink inside and the bacon is well done—but not too done. If there is anything better than that combination the writer has yet to taste it in a lifetime devoted largely and studiously to eating.

The stew kettle will cook you dried apricots when they have 18 resumed their predried plumpness after a night of soaking, it will serve to concoct a mulligan in, and it will cook macaroni. When you are not using it, it should be boiling water for the dishes.

In the baker, mere man comes into his own, for he can make 19 a pie that to his bush appetite will have it all over the product that mother used to make, like a tent. Men have always believed that there was something mysterious and difficult about making a pie. Here is a great secret. There is nothing to it. We've been kidded for years. Any man of average office intelligence can make at least as good a pie as his wife.

All there is to a pie is a cup and a half of flour, one-half teaspoon- 20 ful of salt, one-half cup of lard and cold water. That will make pie crust that will bring tears of joy into your camping partner's eyes.

Mix the salt with the flour, work the lard into the flour, make it 21 up into a good workmanlike dough with cold water. Spread some flour on the back of a box or something flat, and pat the dough around a while. Then roll it out with whatever kind of round bottle you prefer. Put a little more lard on the surface of the sheet of dough and then slosh a little flour on and roll it up and then roll it out again with the bottle.

Cut out a piece of the rolled out dough big enough to line a pie 22 tin. I like the kind with holes in the bottom. Then put in your dried apples that have soaked all night and been sweetened, or your apricots, or your blueberries, and then take another sheet of the dough and drape it gracefully over the top, soldering it down at the edges with your fingers. Cut a couple of slits in the top dough sheet and prick it a few times with a fork in an artistic manner.

23   Put it in the baker with a good slow fire for forty-five minutes and then take it out and if your pals are Frenchmen they will kiss you. The penalty for knowing how to cook is that the others will make you do all the cooking.

24   It is all right to talk about roughing it in the woods. But the real woodsman is the man who can be really comfortable in the bush.

BUILDING VOCABULARY

For each word below write your own definition, based on how the word is used in the selection. Check back to the appropriate paragraph in the essay for more help, if necessary.

a. abiding (par. 2)
b. valiant (par. 2)
c. assimilate (par. 2)
d. charred (par. 2)
e. solemnly (par. 3)
f. requisite (par. 8)
g. succession (par. 9)
h. studiously (par. 17)
i. concoct (par. 18)
j. soldering (par. 22)

THINKING CRITICALLY ABOUT THE ESSAY

Understanding the Writer's Ideas

1. What is Hemingway's main purpose in this essay? Does he simply want to explain how to set up camp and how to cook outdoors?
2. What, according to the writer, are the two possible results of camping out on your vacation?
3. Why is oil of citronella the one insecticide that Hemingway recommends over all others?
4. Is it always necessary to pitch a tent when camping out? What are alternatives to it? How can you sleep warmly and comfortably?

5. Explain the writer's process for cooking trout. Also explain his process for baking a pie.
6. Is it enough for Hemingway simply to enjoy "roughing it" while camping out?

Understanding the Writer's Techniques

1. Does Hemingway have a stated thesis? Explain.
2. Identify those paragraphs in the essay that involve process analysis, and explain how Hemingway develops his subject in each.
3. What is the main writing pattern in paragraphs 1 and 2? How does this method serve as an organizing principle throughout the essay?
4. How would you characterize Hemingway's style of writing? Is it appropriate to a newspaper audience? Is it more apt for professional fishermen?
5. In what way does Hemingway employ classification (see Chapter 9) in this essay?
6. Analyze the tone of the essay.
7. The concluding paragraph is short. Is it effective, nevertheless, and why? How does it reinforce the opening paragraph?

Exploring the Writer's Ideas

1. Camping out was popular in the 1920s, as it is today. What are some of the reasons that it remains so attractive today?
2. Hemingway's essay describes many basic strategies for successful camping. He does not rely on "gadgets" or modern inventions to make camping easier. Do such gadgets make camping more fun today than it might have been in the 1920s?
3. The writer suggests that there is a right way and a wrong way to do things. Does it matter if you perform a recreational activity correctly as long as you enjoy doing it? Why?

IDEAS FOR WRITING

Prewriting

Freewrite for fifteen minutes about your favorite pastime, activity, or hobby. How do you approach this activity? What steps must be observed in order to be successful at it? How might other people fail at it whereas you are successful?

Guided Writing

Write an essay on how to do something wrong, and how to do it right—going on vacation, looking for a job, fishing, or whatever.

1. Reexamine the author's first three paragraphs and imitate his method of introducing the right and wrong ways about the subject, and the possible results.
2. Adopt a simple, informal, "chatty" style. Feel free to use a few well-placed clichés and other forms of spoken English. Use several similes.
3. Divide your subject into useful categories. Just as Hemingway treated insects, sleeping, and cooking, try to cover the main aspects of your subject.
4. Explain the process involved for each aspect of your subject. Make certain that you compare and contrast the right and wrong ways of your activity.
5. Write a short, crisp conclusion that reinforces your longer introduction.

Thinking and Writing Collaboratively

As a class, choose a process—for example, applying to college—which clearly involves a "right way" and "wrong way" of accomplishing the activity. Then divide the class into two groups, with one group outlining the correct steps and the other the incorrect or incomplete steps to completing the process. List both approaches on the chalkboard for comparative discussion.

Writing About the Text

Write an essay discussing Hemingway's view of doing things "the proper way" (par. 14), looking at how his personal views are translated into authoritative instructions. Is Hemingway being overly judgmental? Or does "the proper way" mean everything in life?

More Writing Projects

1. How do you explain the fascination that camping out holds for many people? Reflect on this question in your journal.
2. In a paragraph, describe how to get to your favorite vacation spot, and what to do when you get there.
3. If you have ever camped out, write a process paper explaining one important feature of setting up camp.

In the Kitchen
Henry Louis Gates Jr.

Mixing Patterns

One of the nation's leading literary scholars, Henry Louis Gates Jr., was born in 1950 in Piedmont, West Virginia. Educated in the newly desegregated local public schools, Gates went on to receive his BA from Yale and his PhD from Clare College at the University of Cambridge (England). Having begun his career writing for *Time* magazine in London, Gates established his reputation as a major literary critic with his book *The Signifying Monkey: Toward a Theory of Afro-American Literary Criticism* (1989), which received the National Book Award. He is editor of the authoritative *Norton Anthology of African American Literature* and co-editor of *Transition* magazine. He is the author of *Wonders of the African World* (1999), the book companion to the public television series of the same name. Gates's many awards include the prestigious MacArthur Foundation "Genius Award." Gates is W. E. B. Du Bois Professor of Humanities and Chair of Afro-American Studies at Harvard University. In this selection, which first appeared in the *New Yorker* in 1994, Gates examines the politics of the hairdo by recalling his experiences as a child in his mother's home beauty parlor.

www.mhhe.com/
shortprose

To learn more about Gates, click on
**More Resources > Chapter 5 >
Henry Louis Gates Jr.**

PREREADING: THINKING ABOUT THE ESSAY IN ADVANCE

Michael Jackson, America's pop icon, was criticized by some in the African American community for altering his appearance to conform to Anglo features (such as straight hair). Do you think you should have the right to change your looks even if it means trying to conform to the standards of beauty of an ethnic or cultural group other than your own?

Words to Watch

transform (par. 4)   to change the appearance or form of
southpaw (par. 4)   a left-handed person, especially a left-handed baseball pitcher

refrain (par. 7)   repeated phrase or utterance
preposterous (par. 7)   absurd
tiara (par. 24)   a crown or fine headdress

We always had a gas stove in the kitchen, in our house in Pied- 1
mont, West Virginia, where I grew up. Never electric, though using
electric became fashionable in Piedmont in the sixties, like using
Crest toothpaste rather than Colgate, or watching Huntley and
Brinkley rather than Walter Cronkite. But not us: gas, Colgate, and
good ole Walter Cronkite, come what may. We used gas partly out
of loyalty to Big Mom, Mama's Mama, because she was mostly
blind and still loved to cook, and could feel her way more easily
with gas than with electric. But the most important thing about our
gas-equipped kitchen was that Mama used to do hair there. The
"hot comb" was a fine-toothed iron instrument with a long wooden
handle and a pair of iron curlers that opened and closed like scissors. Mama would put it in the gas fire until it glowed. You could
smell those prongs heating up.

I liked that smell. Not the smell so much, I guess, as what the 2
smell meant for the shape of my day. There was an intimate warmth
in the women's tones as they talked with my Mama, doing their hair.
I knew what the women had been through to get their hair ready to
be "done," because I would watch Mama do it to herself. How that
kink could be transformed through grease and fire into that magnificent head of wavy hair was a miracle to me, and still is.

Mama would wash her hair over the sink, a towel wrapped 3
around her shoulders, wearing just her slip and her white bra.
(We had no shower—just a galvanized tub that we stored in the
kitchen—until we moved down Rat Tail Road into Doc Wolverton's
house, in 1954.) After she dried it, she would grease her scalp thoroughly with blue Bergamot hair grease, which came in a short, fat
jar with a picture of a beautiful colored lady on it. It's important
to grease your scalp real good, my Mama would explain, to keep
from burning yourself. Of course, her hair would return to its natural kink almost as soon as the hot water and shampoo hit it. To me,
it was another miracle how hair so "straight" would so quickly
become kinky again the second it even approached some water.

My Mama had only a few "clients" whose heads she "did"— 4
did, I think, because she enjoyed it, rather than for the few pennies
it brought in. They would sit on one of our red plastic kitchen
chairs, the kind with the shiny metal legs, and brace themselves

for the process. Mama would stroke that red-hot iron—which by this time had been in the gas fire for half an hour or more—slowly but firmly through their hair, from scalp to strand's end. It made a scorching, crinkly sound, the hot iron did, as it burned its way through kink, leaving in its wake straight strands of hair, standing long and tall but drooping over at the ends, their shape like the top of a heavy willow tree. Slowly, steadily, Mama's hands would transform a round mound of Odetta kink into a darkened swamp of everglades. The Bergamot made the hair shiny; the heat of the hot iron gave it a brownish-red cast. Once all the hair was as straight as God allows kink to get, Mama would take the well-heated curling iron and twirl the straightened strands into more or less loosely wrapped curls. She claimed that she owed her skill as a hairdresser to the strength in her wrists, and as she worked her little finger would poke out, the way it did when she sipped tea. Mama was a southpaw, and wrote upside down and backward to produce the cleanest, roundest letters you've ever seen.

5   The "kitchen" she would all but remove from sight with a hand-held pair of shears, bought just for this purpose. Now, the kitchen was the room in which we were sitting—the room where Mama did hair and washed clothes, and where we all took a bath in that galvanized tub. But the word has another meaning, and the kitchen that I'm speaking of is the very kinky bit of hair at the back of your head, where your neck meets your shirt collar. If there was ever a part of our African past that resisted assimilation, it was the kitchen. No matter how hot the iron, no matter how powerful the chemical, no matter how stringent the mashed-potatoes-and-lye formula of a man's "process," neither God nor woman nor Sammy Davis, Jr., could straighten the kitchen. The kitchen was permanent, irredeemable, irresistible kink. Unassimilably African. No matter what you did, no matter how hard you tried, you couldn't de-kink a person's kitchen. So you trimmed it off as best you could.

6   When hair had begun to "turn," as they'd say—to return to its natural kinky glory—it was the kitchen that turned first (the kitchen around the back, and nappy edges at the temples). When the kitchen started creeping up the back of the neck, it was time to get your hair done again.

7 Sometimes, after dark, a man would come to have his hair done. It was Mr. Charlie Carroll. He was very light-complected and had a ruddy nose—it made me think of Edmund Gwenn, who played Kris

Kringle in "Miracle on 34th Street." At first, Mama did him after my brother, Rocky, and I had gone to sleep. It was only later that we found out that he had come to our house so Mama could iron his hair—not with a hot comb or a curling iron but with our very own Proctor-Silex steam iron. For some reason I never understood, Mr. Charlie would conceal his Frederick Douglass-like mane under a big white Stetson hat. I never saw him take it off except when he came to our house, at night, to have his hair pressed. (Later, Daddy would tell us about Mr. Charlie's most prized piece of knowledge, something that the man would only confide after his hair had been pressed, as a token of intimacy. "Not many people know this," he'd say, in a tone of circumspection, "but George Washington was Abraham Lincoln's daddy." Nodding solemnly, he'd add the clincher: "A white man told me." Though he was in dead earnest, this became a humorous refrain around our house—"a white man told me"—which we used to punctuate especially preposterous assertions.)

My mother examined my daughters' kitchens whenever we 8 went home to visit, in the early eighties. It became a game between us. I had told her not to do it, because I didn't like the politics it suggested—the notion of "good" and "bad" hair. "Good" hair was "straight," "bad" hair kinky. Even in the late sixties, at the height of Black Power, almost nobody could bring themselves to say "bad" for good and "good" for bad. People still said that hair like white people's hair was "good," even if they encapsulated it in a disclaimer, like "what we used to call 'good.'"

Maggie would be seated in her high chair, throwing food this 9 way and that, and Mama would be cooing about how cute it all was, how I used to do just like Maggie was doing, and wondering whether her flinging her food with her left hand meant that she was going to be left-handed like Mama. When my daughter was just about covered with Chef Boyardee Spaghetti-O's, Mama would seize the opportunity: wiping her clean, she would tilt Maggie's head to one side and reach down the back of her neck. Sometimes Mama would even rub a curl between her fingers, just to make sure that her bifocals had not deceived her. Then she'd sigh with satisfaction and relief: No kink . . . yet. Mama! I'd shout, pretending to be angry. Every once in a while, if no one was looking, I'd peek, too.

I say "yet" because most black babies are born with soft, 10 silken hair. But after a few months it begins to turn, as inevitably as do the seasons or the leaves on a tree. People once thought baby oil would stop it. They were wrong.

11   Everybody I knew as a child wanted to have good hair. You could be as ugly as homemade sin dipped in misery and still be thought attractive if you had good hair. "Jesus moss," the girls at Camp Lee, Virginia, had called Daddy's naturally "good" hair during the war. I know that he played that thick head of hair for all it was worth, too.

12   My own hair was "not a bad grade," as barbers would tell me when they cut it for the first time. It was like a doctor reporting the results of the first full physical he has given you. Like "You're in good shape" or "Blood pressure's kind of high—better cut down on salt."

13   I spent most of my childhood and adolescence messing with my hair. I definitely wanted straight hair. Like Pop's. When I was about three, I tried to stick a wad of Bazooka bubble gum to that straight hair of his. I suppose what fixed that memory for me is the spanking I got for doing so: he turned me upside down, holding me by my feet, the better to paddle my behind. Little *nigger,* he had shouted, walloping away. I started to laugh about it two days later, when my behind stopped hurting.

14   When black people say "straight," of course, they don't usually mean literally straight—they're not describing hair like, say, Peggy Lipton's (she was the white girl on "The Mod Squad"), or like Mary's of Peter, Paul & Mary fame; black people call that "stringy" hair. No, "straight" just means not kinky, no matter what contours the curl may take. I would have done *anything* to have straight hair—and I used to try everything, short of getting a process.

15   Of the wide variety of techniques and methods I came to master in the challenging prestidigitation of the follicle, almost all had two things in common: a heavy grease and the application of pressure. It's not an accident that some of the biggest black-owned companies in the fifties and sixties made hair products. And I tried them all, in search of that certain silken touch, the one that would leave neither the hand nor the pillow sullied by grease.

16   I always wondered what Frederick Douglass put on *his* hair, or what Phillis Wheatley put on hers. Or why Wheatley has that rag on her head in the little engraving in the frontispiece of her book. One thing is for sure: you can bet that when Phillis Wheatley went to England and saw the Countess of Huntingdon she did not stop by the Queen's coiffeur on her way there. So many black people still get their hair straightened that it's a wonder we don't have a national holiday for Madame C. J. Walker, the woman who invented the process of straightening kinky hair. Call it Jheri-Kurled or call it "relaxed," it's still fried hair.

I used all the greases, from sea-blue Bergamot and creamy 17
vanilla Duke (in its clear jar with the orange-white-and-green label)
to the godfather of grease, the formidable Murray's. Now, Murray's
was some *serious* grease. Whereas Bergamot was like oily jello,
and Duke was viscous and sickly sweet, Murray's was light brown
and *hard*. Hard as lard and twice as greasy, Daddy used to say.
Murray's came in an orange can with a press-on top. It was so hard
that some people would put a match to the can, just to soften the
stuff and make it more manageable. Then, in the late sixties, when
Afros came into style, I used Afro Sheen. From Murray's to Duke
to Afro Sheen: that was my progression in black consciousness.

We used to put hot towels or washrags over our Murray-coated 18
heads, in order to melt the wax into the scalp and the follicles.
Unfortunately, the wax also had the habit of running down your
neck, ears, and forehead. Not to mention your pillowcase. Another
problem was that if you put two palmfuls of Murray's on your
head your hair turned white. (Duke did the same thing.) The challenge was to get rid of that white color. Because if you got rid of
the white stuff you had a magnificent head of wavy hair. That was
the beauty of it: Murray's was so hard that it froze your hair into
the wavy style you brushed it into. It looked really good if you
wore a part. A lot of guys had parts *cut* into their hair by a barber,
either with the clippers or with a straightedge razor. Especially if
you had kinky hair—then you'd generally wear a short razor cut,
or what we called a Quo Vadis.

We tried to be as innovative as possible. Everyone knew about 19
using a stocking cap, because your father or your uncle wore one
whenever something really big was about to happen, whether
sacred or secular: a funeral or a dance, a wedding or a trip in which
you confronted official white people. Any time you were trying
to look really sharp, you wore a stocking cap in preparation. And
if the event was really a big one, you made a new cap. You asked
your mother for a pair of her hose, and cut it with scissors about
six inches or so from the open end—the end with the elastic that
goes up to the top of the thigh. Then you knotted the cut end,
and it became a beehive-shaped hat, with an elastic band that you
pulled down low on your forehead and down around your neck
in the back. To work well, the cap had to fit tightly and snugly,
like a press. And it had to fit that tightly because it *was* a press:
it pressed your hair with the force of the hose's elastic. If you
greased your hair down real good, and left the stocking cap on

long enough, voilá: you got a head of pressed-against-the-scalp waves. (You also got a ring around your forehead when you woke up, but it went away.) And then you could enjoy your concrete do. Swore we were bad, too, with all that grease and those flat heads. My brother and I would brush it out a bit in the mornings, so that it looked—well, "natural." Grown men still wear stocking caps—especially older men, who generally keep their stocking caps in their top drawers, along with their cufflinks and their see-through silk socks, their "Maverick" ties, their silk handkerchiefs, and whatever else they prize the most.

20   A Murrayed-down stocking cap was the respectable version of the process, which, by contrast, was most definitely not a cool thing to have unless you were an entertainer by trade. Zeke and Keith and Poochie and a few other stars of the high-school basketball team all used to get a process once or twice a year. It was expensive, and you had to go somewhere like Pittsburgh or D.C. or Uniontown—somewhere where there were enough colored people to support a trade. The guys would disappear, then reappear a day or two later, strutting like peacocks, their hair burned slightly red from the lye base. They'd also wear "rags"—cloths or handkerchiefs—around their heads when they slept or played basketball. Do-rags, they were called. But the result was straight hair, with just a hint of wave. No curl. Do-it-yourselfers took their chances at home with a concoction of mashed potatoes and lye.

21   The most famous process of all, however, outside of the process Malcolm X describes in his "Autobiography," and maybe the process of Sammy Davis, Jr., was Nat King Cole's process. Nat King Cole had patent-leather hair. That man's got the finest process money can buy, or so Daddy said the night we saw Cole's TV show on NBC. It was November 5, 1956. I remember the date because everyone came to our house to watch it and to celebrate one of Daddy's buddies' birthdays. Yeah, Uncle Joe chimed in, they can do shit to his hair that the average Negro can't even *think* about—secret shit.

22   Nat King Cole was *clean.* I've had an ongoing argument with a Nigerian friend about Nat King Cole for twenty years now. Not about whether he could sing—any fool knows that he could—but about whether or not he was a handkerchief head for wearing that patent-leather process.

23   Sammy Davis, Jr.'s process was the one I detested. It didn't look good on him. Worse still, he liked to have a fried strand

dangling down the middle of his forehead, so he could shake it out from the crown when he sang. But Nat King Cole's hair was a thing unto itself, a beautifully sculpted work of art that he and he alone had the right to wear. The only difference between a process and a stocking cap, really, was taste; but Nat King Cole, unlike, say, Michael Jackson, looked *good* in his. His head looked like Valentino's head in the twenties, and some say it was Valentino the process was imitating. But Nat King Cole wore a process because it suited his face, his demeanor, his name, his style. He was as clean as he wanted to be.

I had forgotten all about that patent-leather look until one day 24 in 1971, when I was sitting in an Arab restaurant on the island of Zanzibar surrounded by men in fezzes and white caftans, trying to learn how to eat curried goat and rice with the fingers of my right hand and feeling two million miles from home. All of a sudden, an old transistor radio sitting on top of a china cupboard stopped blaring out its Swahili music and started playing "Fly Me to the Moon," by Nat King Cole. The restaurant's din was not affected at all, but in my mind's eye I saw it: the King's magnificent sleek black tiara. I managed, barely, to blink back the tears.

BUILDING VOCABULARY

For each word below write your own definition based on how the word is used in the selection. Check back to the appropriate paragraph in the essay for more help, if necessary.

a. galvanized (par. 5)
b. assertions (par. 7)
c. prestidigitation (par. 15)
d. follicle (par. 15)
e. din (par. 24)

THINKING CRITICALLY ABOUT THE ESSAY

Understanding the Writer's Ideas

1. The word *kitchen* in the title takes on two meanings in the essay. What are they?
2. Gas was used in Gates's kitchen even though people had turned to electricity in the 1960s. Why?

3. What does the writer mean when he states that his mother "did hair"?

4. What does the word *turn* (par. 6) describe?

5. What is the history behind "good" and "bad" hair?

6. As a child, how did Gates worry about his hair? Explain.

7. Describe the two things all hair-straightening techniques have in common.

8. What was it about Nat King Cole's hair that impressed this writer so much?

9. How were the hot irons used to straighten hair?

10. Hearing a Nat King Cole song while in Zanzibar, the writer says he had to "blink back the tears." Why?

Understanding the Writer's Techniques

1. Find the thesis and paraphrase it.

2. What process does Gates describe in paragraph 3? Give examples of the process he describes there.

3. Given the detailed descriptions of de-kinking hair, what audience does this writer have in mind in employing this strategy?

4. Where in the essay does the writer make a transition to describe two of the most common processes of hair straightening? How are these processes detailed?

5. Though the other de-kinking processes mentioned in the essay are detailed, the most famous one (Nat King Cole's) is not described at all. What might this suggest about the writer's attitude toward this subject?

6. What makes Gates's concluding paragraph different from others more common in essays?

✴ MIXING PATTERNS

The essay's structure is not focused entirely on process. What other rhetorical pattern does the writer use? Identify the places where this pattern occurs.

Exploring the Writer's Ideas

1. Gates claims the "kitchen," those hairs on the back of the neck, are "unassimilably" African. Yet, his mother specialized

in getting rid of the kitchen. Do you think this writer approves or disapproves of his mother's activity? Explain.

2. Gates tells of jokes about the "white man." Gates says he found the jokes funny even though he also admits he wanted good hair, like that of whites. How would you explain this writer's contradictory feelings about white people?

3. How do you feel about this writer's claims that most everyone he knew thought kinky hair was "bad"? Do you think this is an exaggeration? Why or why not?

4. What examples exist today of people who remake themselves to look "white" or like those who are held up as role models, like Eminem or other rock stars? Is this impulse positive or negative? Why?

5. The author suggests that the de-kinking was physically painful. Does anything in the essay suggest all the pain was worth it? Explain.

6. By calling Nat King Cole's straightened hair a "black tiara" is this author concluding that straight hair (looking white) is indeed admirable? How do you feel?

IDEAS FOR WRITING

Prewriting

Use your journal to recall times when you felt good or bad about the way you look.

Guided Writing

Write an essay on how you once may have tried to make yourself look the "right" or "wrong" way. Remember the time you dressed for a date or to go to church or to get a job.

1. Examine Gates's first paragraph and imitate his method of introducing the thesis.

2. Divide your process into its important parts, like Gates who divides de-kinking into its steps: hot comb, the kitchen, the clients, the grease, and the pressure.

3. Make sure that your process is detailed in a way that keeps a general audience in mind (or people who don't know your process).

4. Try to use definition paragraphs to explain terms that describe your process which are unknown to your general audience.
5. Write a conclusion that tells a story, like Gates on Nat King Cole. Remember that this story should reflect an overall feeling you have about your topic.

Thinking and Writing Collaboratively

Your group is responsible for creating a behavior code pamphlet for your school. Use process technique to make clear how students should act in different situations. Explain what happens (the process) if someone's behavior challenges the guidelines.

Writing About the Text

This essay is a reminiscence, an essay about a dear memory. Yet the writer seems ambivalent about his mother's hairdressing. Write an essay that explores the relation between Gates's *tone* and his attitude toward his mother's activity.

More Writing Projects

1. In your journal, make notes on the ways that you have seen people change their looks to please others.
2. In a paragraph, describe the process by which people learn who looks the right way or the wrong way.
3. Write a process essay on something your parents or caregiver taught you as a child. Tell of learning to swim or to ride a bike.

SUMMING UP: CHAPTER 5

1. On the basis of the four essays in this chapter, write about the processes writers use and how they manage these processes. Make sure the main steps in those processes are clear.

2. Write a recipe for your favorite dish to include in a class cookbook. In addition to describing the step-by-step process for preparing the food, you should also tell something about the tradition behind the food, special occasions for eating it, the first time you ate it, and so forth. The goal should be to make the process clear and reassuring, to emphasize how following these simple steps will yield a delicious meal.

3. Two of the essays in this chapter tell us how to do things that can have direct and immediate effects on our lives—how to straighten hair and go camping. Try to write an essay that describes a process with much less immediate effect.

4. Interview a classmate about something that he or she does very well. Make sure the questions you ask don't omit any important steps or materials used in the process. Take careful notes during the interview, then try to replicate the process on your own. If you have difficulties in accomplishing the process, reinterview your classmate. After you are satisfied that no steps or materials have been left out, write up the procedure in such a way that someone else could easily follow it.

5. Both Ernest Hemingway and Henry Louis Gates Jr. show how to perform a process with great rigor and devotion, not to say enthusiasm; they also show how to perform a process less carefully and even, according to Hemingway, indifferently. Choose a process that you care about—playing an instrument, cooking a dish, playing a sport—and discuss how to do it either well or poorly, and what it means to you to see it done well or poorly.

6. Many essays in this book look back to the writer's childhood; frequently the writers remember vividly the process of doing something, or of watching something being done, that symbolizes or epitomizes childhood. Write an essay about your childhood that focuses on a process—either something that you did or that you watched being done—that stands out as especially evocative of your childhood in particular and childhood in general.

7. Bill Bryson's essay takes a whimsical look at instructions for setting up a new computer, and Nora Ephron writes comically about foiling a terrorist plot. Rewrite Hemingway's essay on camping using Bryson's or Ephron's style.

✳ FROM SEEING TO WRITING

Consider the standard legal process the judge in this cartoon ignored in arriving at his sentencing decision. Explain the precise steps he should have followed, the order of those steps, and the relation of the steps to the final decision. In your essay, help the reader understand the situation or circumstances under which a judge normally performs any legal process.

"In the interest of streamlining the judicial process, we'll skip the evidence and go directly to sentencing."

© *The New Yorker Collection 1995 J. B. Handelsman from cartoonbank.com. All rights reserved.*

CHAPTER 6

Illustration

WHAT IS ILLUSTRATION?

One convenient way for writers to present and to support a point is through *illustration*—that is, by means of several examples to back up an idea. Illustration (or *exemplification*) helps a writer put general or abstract thoughts into specific examples. As readers, we often find that we are able to understand a writer's point more effectively because we respond to the concrete examples. We are familiar with illustration in everyday life. If a police officer is called a racist, the review board will want *illustrations* of the racist behavior. The accuser will have to provide concrete examples of racist language, or present arrest statistics that show the officer was more likely to arrest Korean Americans, for instance, than white Americans.

Writing that uses illustration is most effective if it uses *several* examples to support the thesis. A single, isolated example might not convince anyone easily, but a series of examples builds up a stronger case. Writers can also use an *extended example,* which is one example that is developed at length.

For instance, you might want to illustrate your thesis that American patchwork quilts are an important record of women's history. Since your reader might not be familiar with quilts, you would have to illustrate your argument with examples such as these:

- Baltimore album quilts were given to Eastern women heading West in the nineteenth century and contain signatures and dates stitched in the squares to mark the event.
- Women used blue and white in quilt patterns to show their support for the temperance movement that opposed sale of alcohol.

- Women named patterns after geographic and historical events, creating such quilts as Rocky Road to Kansas and Abe Lincoln's Platform.
- African American quilters adapted techniques from West Africa to make blankets for slave quarters.
- One quilter from Kentucky recorded all the deaths in her family in her work. The unusual quilt contains a pattern of a cemetery and coffins with names for each family member!

If you visited a museum and there was only one painting on the wall, you would probably feel that you hadn't gotten your money's worth. You expect a museum to be a *collection* of paintings, so that you can study a variety of types of art or several paintings by the same painter. In the same way, through the accumulation of illustrations, the writer builds a case for the thesis.

In this chapter, writers use illustration forcefully to make their points. Brent Staples, an African American journalist, shows how some people perceive his mere presence on a street at night as a threat. Barbara Ehrenreich uses irony to illustrate, from a feminist perspective, what women can learn from men. Eleanor Bader offers profiles of homelessness on campus. Finally, Jared Diamond uses examples from history to demonstrate that globalization is nothing new. Each writer knows that one example is insufficient to create a case, but that multiple examples make a convincing case.

HOW DO WE READ ILLUSTRATION?

Reading illustration requires us to ask ourselves these questions:

- What is the writer's thesis? What is the *purpose* of the examples?
- What audience is the writer addressing? How do we know?
- What other techniques is the writer using? Is there narration? description? How are these used to help the illustration?
- In what order has the writer arranged the examples? Where is the most important example placed?
- How does the writer use *transitions*? Often, transitions in illustration essays enumerate: *first, second, third; one, another.*

HOW DO WE WRITE WITH ILLUSTRATIONS?

Read the selections critically to see the many ways in which writers can use illustrations to support an idea.

Select your topic and write a thesis that tells the reader what you are going to illustrate and what your main idea is about the subject. Sample thesis statement:

Many people have long cherished quilts for their beautiful colors and patterns, but few collectors recognize the history stitched into the squares.

Make a list of *examples* to support the thesis.

Examples by quilt types: Baltimore album quilts, political quilts, suffrage quilts, slave quilts, graveyard quilts

Examples by quilt pattern names: Radical Rose; Drunkard's Path; Memory Blocks; Old Maid's Puzzle; Wheel of Mystery; Log Cabin; Rocky Road to Kansas; Slave Chain; Underground Railroad; Delectable Mountains; Union Star; Jackson Star; Old Indian Trail; Trip around the World

Determine who the audience will be: a group of experienced quilters? museum curators? a PTA group? Each is a different audience with different interests and needs.

Plan an arrangement of the examples. Begin with the least important and build up to the most important. Or arrange the examples in chronological order.

Plan to use other techniques (such as description), especially if your audience is unfamiliar with your subject. If you are writing the quilt paper and using the example of the Baltimore album quilt, you would then have to *describe* it for readers who do not know what such a quilt looks like.

Be sure that the *purpose* of the illustrations is clearly stated, especially in the conclusion. In the quilt essay, for instance, different quilt patterns might be illustrated in order to encourage readers to preserve and study quilts.

Writing and Revising the Draft

Use the first paragraph to introduce the subject and to set up a clear thesis. You might introduce an *abstract* idea, such as forgotten history, that will be *illustrated* in the examples.

Plan the body to give the reader lots of examples, and to develop the examples if necessary. Use narration, description, and dialogue to enhance the illustrations. Write a conclusion that returns to the abstract idea you began with in the introduction.

Write a second draft for reading aloud.

Revise, based on your listener's comments. Proofread the essay carefully. Check spelling and grammar. Make a final copy.

A STUDENT PARAGRAPH: ILLUSTRATION

This paragraph from a student's illustration paper on quiltmaking shows how the use of examples advances the thesis of the essay. The thesis, which you examined on page 218, asserts that, the colors and patterns of quilts aside, "few collectors recognize the history stitched into the squares."

We can find a significant example of the historical, record-keeping function of quiltmaking in Mary Kinsale's needle-work. Kinsale lived in Kentucky in the mid-nineteenth century. Unlike the political quilts discussed earlier, and the various quilts that document "official" history, Kinsale's quilts deal only with the history of her family. Specifically, Kinsale set out to document the precise dates of death of all her family members, illustrating the squares with coffins, open graves, and other symbols of death. What we might call morbid or tasteless today probably struck members of Kinsale's community as natural and proper; the American culture had not yet restricted images of gaunt, grinning skulls, mossy tombstones, and other symbols of death to horror movies. In fact, Kinsale's images served an impor-tant religious and social purpose by reminding family and friends to reform their lives while there was still time. Kinsale decided to record the vital dates of her dearly departed, and remind the living of their duty in life, by stitching a quilt, rather than simply writing an entry in the family Bible, or leaving the task to the government. Her quiltmaking illus-trates nineteenth-century society's old-fashioned attitude towards death, as well as their understanding of the role ordinary individuals could play in recording history.

Reference to essay thesis, "history stitched into squares"

Transition ("a significant example") asserts order according to significance

Reference to other points in essay provides *unity*

Kinsale's work is main *illustration* developed in the paragraph

Supporting detail

Supporting detail

Closing sentence connects to essay's thesis

www.mhhe.com/
shortprose

To learn more about using illustration, click on
**Writing > Writing Tutor:
    Exemplification
Writing > Paragraph Patterns**

Night Walker

Brent Staples

Brent Staples is an editorial writer for the *New York Times* who holds
a PhD in psychology from the University of Chicago. Yet, since
his youth, he has instilled fear and suspicion in many just by taking nighttime walks to combat his insomnia. In this essay, which
appeared in the *Los Angeles Times* in 1986, Staples explains how
others perceive themselves as his potential victims simply because
he is a black man in "urban America."

www.mhhe.com/
shortprose

To learn more about Staples, click on
**More Resources > Chapter 6 >
Brent Staples**

PREREADING: THINKING ABOUT
THE ESSAY IN ADVANCE

Imagine this scene: you are walking alone at night in your own
neighborhood and you hear footsteps behind you that you believe
are the footsteps of someone of a different race from yours. How
do you feel? What do you do? Why?

Words to Watch

affluent (par. 1)   wealthy
discreet (par. 1)   showing good judgment; careful
quarry (par. 2)   prey; object of a hunt
dismayed (par. 2)   discouraged
taut (par. 4)   tight; tense
warrenlike (par. 5)   like a crowded tenement district
bandolier (par. 5)   gun belt worn across the chest
solace (par. 5)   relief; consolation; comfort
retrospect (par. 6)   review of past event
ad hoc (par. 7)   unplanned; for the particular case at hand
labyrinthine (par. 7)   like a maze
skittish (par. 9)   nervous; jumpy
constitutionals (par. 10)   regular walks

1   My first victim was a woman—white, well dressed, probably in her early 20s. I came upon her late one evening on a deserted street in Hyde Park, a relatively affluent neighborhood in an otherwise mean, impoverished section of Chicago. As I swung onto the avenue behind her, there seemed to be a discreet, uninflammatory distance between us. Not so. She cast back a worried glance. To her, the youngish black man—a broad six feet two inches with a beard and billowing hair, both hands shoved into the pockets of a bulky military jacket—seemed menacingly close. She picked up her pace and was soon running in earnest. Within seconds she disappeared into a cross street.

2   That was more than a decade ago. I was 22 years old, a graduate student newly arrived at the University of Chicago. It was in the echo of that terrified woman's footfalls that I first began to know the unwieldy inheritance I'd come into—the ability to alter public space in ugly ways. It was clear that she thought herself the quarry of a mugger, a rapist, or worse. Suffering a bout of insomnia, however, I was stalking sleep, not defenseless wayfarers. As a softy who is scarcely able to take a knife to a raw chicken—let alone hold one to a person's throat—I was surprised, embarrassed, and dismayed all at once. Her flight made me feel like an accomplice in tyranny. It also made it clear that I was indistinguishable from the muggers who occasionally seeped into the area from the surrounding ghetto. I soon gathered that being perceived as dangerous is a hazard in itself: Where fear and weapons meet—and they often do in urban America—there is always the possibility of death.

3   In that first year, my first away from my hometown, I was to become thoroughly familiar with the language of fear. At dark, shadowy intersections, I could cross in front of a car stopped at a traffic light and elicit the *thunk, thunk, thunk, thunk* of the driver—black, white, male, female—hammering down the door locks. On less traveled streets after dark, I grew accustomed to but never comfortable with people crossing to the other side of the street rather than pass me. Then there were the standard unpleasantries with policemen, doormen, bouncers, cabdrivers, and others whose business it is to screen out troublesome individuals *before* there is any nastiness.

4   I moved to New York nearly two years ago and I have remained an avid night walker. In central Manhattan, the near-constant crowd covers the tense one-on-one street encounters. Elsewhere, things can get very taut indeed.

After dark, on the warrenlike streets of Brooklyn where I live, 5 I often see women who fear the worst from me. They seem to have set their faces on neutral, and with their purse straps strung across their chests bandolier-style, they forge ahead as though bracing themselves against being tackled. I understand, of course, that the danger they perceive is not a hallucination. Women are particularly vulnerable to street violence, and young black males are drastically overrepresented among the perpetrators of that violence. Yet these truths are no solace against the alienation that comes of being ever the suspect, an entity with whom pedestrians avoid making eye contact.

It is not altogether clear to me how I reached the ripe old age 6 of 22 without being conscious of the lethality nighttime pedestrians attributed to me. Perhaps it was because in Chester, Pa., the small, angry industrial town where I came of age in the 1960s, I was scarcely noticeable against a backdrop of gang warfare, street knifings, and murders. I grew up one of the good boys, had perhaps a half-dozen fistfights. In retrospect, my shyness of combat has clear sources. As a boy, I saw countless tough guys locked away; I have since buried several, too. They were babies, really—a teen-age cousin, a brother of 22, a childhood friend in his mid-20s—all gone down in episodes of bravado played out in the streets. I chose, perhaps unconsciously, to remain a shadow— timid, but a survivor.

The fearsomeness mistakenly attributed to me in public places 7 often has a perilous flavor. The most frightening of these confusions occurred in the late 1970s and early 1980s, when I worked as a journalist in Chicago. One day, rushing into the office of a magazine I was writing for with a deadline story in hand, I was mistaken for a burglar. The office manager called security and, with an ad hoc posse, pursued me through the labyrinthine halls, nearly to my editor's door. I had no way of proving who I was. I could only move briskly toward the company of someone who knew me.

Relatively speaking, however, I never fared as badly as another 8 black male journalist. He went to nearby Waukegan, Ill., a couple of summers ago to work on a story about a murderer who was born there. Mistaking the reporter for the killer, police officers hauled him from his car at gunpoint and but for his press credentials would probably have tried to book him. Such episodes are not uncommon. Black men trade tales like this all the time.

9 Over the years, I learned to smother the rage I felt at so often being mistaken for a criminal. Not to do so would surely have led to madness. I now take precautions to make myself less threatening. I move about with care, particularly late in the evening. I give a wide berth to nervous people on subway platforms during the wee hours. If I happen to be entering a building behind some people who appear skittish, I may walk by, letting them clear the lobby before I return, so as not to seem to be following them. I have been calm and extremely congenial on those rare occasions when I've been pulled over by the police.

10 And on late-evening constitutionals I employ what has proved to be an excellent tension-reducing measure: I whistle melodies from Beethoven and Vivaldi and the more popular classical composers. Even steely New Yorkers hunching toward nighttime destinations seem to relax, and occasionally they even join in the tune. Virtually everybody seems to sense that a mugger wouldn't be warbling bright, sunny selections from Vivaldi's *Four Seasons*. It is my equivalent of the cowbell that hikers wear when they are in bear country.

BUILDING VOCABULARY

1. Use context clues to determine the meaning of each word in italics. Return to the appropriate paragraph in the essay for more clues. Then, if necessary, check your definitions in a dictionary and compare the dictionary meaning with the meaning you derived from the context.
    a. seemed *menacingly* close (par. 1)
    b. I was *indistinguishable* from the muggers who occasionally *seeped* into the area (par. 2)
    c. I have remained an *avid* night walker (par. 4)
    d. they *forge* ahead (par. 5)
    e. Women are particularly *vulnerable* to street violence (par. 5)
    f. the *lethality* nighttime pedestrians attributed to me (par. 6)
    g. episodes of *bravado* played out in the streets (par. 6)
    h. I learned to *smother* the rage I felt . . . so often (par. 9)
    i. I now take *precautions* to make myself less threatening (par. 9)

    j. Even *steely* New Yorkers *hunching* toward nighttime destinations (par. 10)

  2. Reread paragraph 1. List all the words suggesting action and all the words involving emotion. What is the cumulative effect?

THINKING CRITICALLY ABOUT THE ESSAY

Understanding the Writer's Ideas

1. How does Staples describe himself in paragraph 1? What point is he making by such a description?

2. Explain in your own words the incident Staples narrates in paragraph 1. Where does it take place? when? How old was the author at the time? What was he doing? During the incident, why did the woman "cast back a worried glance"? Was she really his "victim"? Explain. What was Staples's reaction to the incident?

3. What is the "unwieldy inheritance" mentioned in paragraph 2? What is Staples's definition of it? What is the implied meaning?

4. How would you describe Staples's personality? What does he mean when he describes himself as "a softy"? How does he illustrate the fact that he is "a softy"? Why did he develop this personality?

5. Explain the meaning of the statement, "I soon gathered that being perceived as dangerous is a hazard in itself" (par. 2).

6. What is "the language of fear" (par. 3)? What examples does Staples provide to illustrate this "language"?

7. Why did car drivers lock their doors when the author walked in front of their cars? How did Staples feel about that?

8. Where did Staples grow up? Did he experience the same reactions there to his nighttime walks as he did in Chicago? Why? How was Manhattan different from Chicago for the author? How was Brooklyn different from Manhattan?

9. What has been Staples's reaction to the numerous incidents of mistaken identity? How has he dealt with that reaction? What "precautions" does he take to make himself "less threatening"?

10. Summarize the example Staples narrates about the black journalist in Waukegan.

11. What have been the author's experiences with the police? Explain.
12. Does the author feel that all the danger people attribute to him when he takes night walks is unfair or unwarranted? Explain.
13. Why does his whistling selections from Beethoven and Vivaldi seem to make people less afraid of the author?

Understanding the Writer's Techniques

1. What is Staples's thesis in this essay?
2. How do the title and opening statement of this essay grasp and hold the reader's interest?
3. Reread the first paragraph. What *mood* or *tone* does Staples establish here? How? Does he sustain that mood? Is there a shift in tone? Explain.
4. How does the author use *narration* in paragraph 1 as a way to illustrate a point? What point is illustrated? Where else does he use narration?
5. What is the effect of the two-word sentence "Not so" in paragraph 1?
6. Staples uses *description* in this essay. Which descriptions serve as illustrations? Explain what ideas they support.
7. *Onomatopoeia* is the use of words whose sounds suggest their sense or action. Where in the essay does Staples use this technique? What action does the sound represent? Why does the author use this technique instead of simply describing the action?
8. What examples from Staples's childhood illustrate why he developed his particular adult personality?
9. Explain the meaning of the final sentence in the essay.
10. *Stereotypes* are oversimplified, uncritical judgments about people, races, issues, events, and so forth. Where in this essay does the author present stereotypes? For what purpose?
11. For whom was this article intended? Why do you think so? Is it written primarily for a white or black audience? Explain.

Exploring the Writer's Ideas

1. In this essay, Staples gives not only examples of his own experiences but also those of other black men. It is interesting, however, that he does not include examples of the experiences

of black women. Why do you think he omitted these references? How do you feel about the omission? Are there any recent news stories, either in your city or in others, that might be included as such illustrations?

2. What prejudices and stereotypes about different racial and cultural groups do people in your community hold? Where do these prejudices and stereotypes come from? Do you think any are justified?

3. What everyday situations do you perceive as most dangerous? Why do you perceive them as such? How do you react to protect yourself? Do you feel your perceptions and reactions are realistic? Explain.

IDEAS FOR WRITING

Prewriting

Write down a few of your personality traits, and then jot down ways in which people identify those traits. Also, indicate how people misperceive you—that is, how they reach wrong conclusions about your personality.

Guided Writing

Write an essay that illustrates how something about your personality has been incorrectly perceived at some time or over a period of time.

1. Begin your essay by narrating a single incident that vividly illustrates the misperception. Begin this illustration with a statement.

2. Explain the time context of this incident as it fits into your life or into a continuing misperception.

3. Describe and illustrate "who you really are" in relation to this misperception.

4. Explain how this misperception fits into a larger context outside your immediate, personal experience of it.

5. Write a series of descriptive illustrations to explain how this misperception has continued to affect you over time.

6. Explain how you first became aware of the misperception.

7. If possible, offer illustrations of others who have suffered the same or similar misperceptions of themselves.

8. Write about your emotional reaction to this overall situation.

9. Illustrate how you have learned to cope with the situation.

10. Give your essay a "catchy" title.

Thinking and Writing Collaboratively

Form groups of four or five, and recommend productive ways to solve the key problems raised by Staples in his essay. Take notes, and then as a group write down the problems and their possible solutions. Share the group's writing with the rest of the class.

Writing About the Text

To advance his thesis, Staples relies on language that suggests anger, fear, and violence. Write an essay in which you examine this language in "Night Walker." Which words seem to express those elements? How do they relate to Staples's thesis? In what ways, if at all, is Staples angry, fearful, or violent? the people around him?

More Writing Projects

1. Usually stereotypes are thought of as negative. Illustrate at least three *positive* stereotypes in your latest journal entry.

2. Write a paragraph in which you illustrate your family's or friends' misconceptions about your girlfriend/boyfriend, wife/husband, or best friend.

3. What tension-reducing measures do you use in situations that might frighten you or in which you might frighten others? Write an essay to address the issue.

What I've Learned from Men

Barbara Ehrenreich

In this essay from *Ms.* magazine, the feminist author and historian Barbara Ehrenreich illustrates the qualities that have made her one of our most-read voices of dissent. Among these qualities is a sense of humor—though she can use her humor to deadly effect, as readers of her regular contributions to *The Nation* magazine, a weekly devoted to left-liberal commentary, can attest. Her work has been characterized by the *New York Times* as "elegant, trenchant, savagely angry, morally outraged and outrageously funny." Ehrenreich is the author of numerous essays and books, including *Fear of Falling: The Inner Life of the Middle Class* (1989), *The Snarling Citizen* (1995), and *Nickel and Dimed: On (Not) Getting By in America* (2001). *Nickel and Dimed* recounts three month-long stints in different American cities where Ehrenreich lived entirely on earnings from jobs paying $7 or $8 per hour. A recent essay for *The Nation,* "The Faith Factor" (2004), takes on politicians who use faith to obscure important social and political issues. Ehrenreich is the recipient of a National Magazine Award for Excellence in Reporting and of a Guggenheim Fellowship. In this selection, Ehrenreich shows that sometimes you can learn the most important things from your enemies, in this case, men. Aside from being able to catch the eye of a waiter, a not inconsiderable attribute, men have one wrongly maligned quality that women would do well to learn, Ehrenreich argues: how to be tough.

www.mhhe.com/
shortprose

To learn more about Ehrenreich, click on
**More Resources > Chapter 6 >
Barbara Ehrenreich**

PREREADING: THINKING ABOUT THE ESSAY IN ADVANCE

What have you learned from the opposite sex? What expectations are raised by a woman saying she has learned something from men?

Words to Watch

euthanasia (par. 1)   mercy killing
lecherous (par. 3)   lewd

unconscionable (par. 3)   beyond reasonable bounds
servility (par. 4)   attitude appropriate to servants
AWOL (par. 4)   used in military for Absent Without Leave
veneer (par. 4)   mere outside show
rueful (par. 4)   regretful
aura (par. 6)   distinctive air
self-deprecation (par. 6)   putting oneself down
brazenly (par. 6)   shamelessly
taciturn (par. 9)   silent
purveyors (par. 10)   providers
emulating (par. 11)   imitating
basso profundo (par. 11)   deep bass voice
blandishments (par. 12)   allurements

1   For many years I believed that women had only one thing to learn from men: how to get the attention of a waiter by some means short of kicking over the table and shrieking. Never in my life have I gotten the attention of a waiter, unless it was an off-duty waiter whose car I'd accidentally scraped in a parking lot somewhere. Men, however, can summon a maître d' just by thinking the word "coffee," and this is a power women would be well advised to study. What else would we possibly want to learn from them? How to interrupt someone in mid-sentence as if you were performing an act of conversational euthanasia? How to drop a pair of socks three feet from an open hamper and keep right on walking? How to make those weird guttural gargling sounds in the bathroom?

2   But now, at mid-life, I am willing to admit that there are some real and useful things to learn from men. Not from all men—in fact, we may have the most to learn from some of the men we like the least. This realization does not mean that my feminist principles have gone soft with age: what I think women could learn from men is how to get *tough*. After more than a decade of consciousness-raising, assertiveness training, and hand-to-hand combat in the battle of the sexes, we're still too ladylike. Let me try that again— we're just too *damn* ladylike.

3   Here is an example from my own experience, a story that I blush to recount. A few years ago, at an international conference held in an exotic and luxurious setting, a prestigious professor invited me to his room for what he said would be an intellectual discussion on matters of theoretical importance. So far, so good.

I showed up promptly. But only minutes into the conversation—
held in all-too-adjacent chairs—it emerged that he was interested
in something more substantial than a meeting of minds. I was dis-
gusted, but not enough to overcome 30-odd years of programming
in ladylikeness. Every time his comments took a lecherous turn,
I chattered distractingly; every time his hand found its way to my
knee, I returned it as if it were something he had misplaced. This
went on for an unconscionable period (as much as 20 minutes);
then there was a minor scuffle, a dash for the door, and I was out—
with nothing violated but my self-esteem. I, a full-grown feminist,
conversant with such matters as rape crisis counseling and sexual
harassment at the workplace, had behaved like a ninny—or, as I
now understand it, like a lady.

The essence of ladylikeness is a persistent servility masked 4
as "niceness." For example, we (women) tend to assume that it is
our responsibility to keep everything "nice" even when the person
we are with is rude, aggressive, or emotionally AWOL. (In the
above example, I was so busy taking responsibility for preserv-
ing the veneer of "niceness" that I almost forgot to take responsibility for myself.) In conversations with men, we do almost all
the work: sociologists have observed that in male-female social
interactions it's the woman who throws out leading questions and
verbal encouragements ("So how did you *feel* about that?" and
so on) while the man, typically, says "Hmmmm." Wherever we
go, we're perpetually smiling—the on-cue smile, like the now-
outmoded curtsy, being one of our culture's little rituals of submis-
sion. We're trained to feel embarrassed if we're praised, but if we
see a criticism coming at us from miles down the road, we rush
to acknowledge it. And when we're feeling aggressive or angry
or resentful, we just tighten up our smiles or turn them into rueful
little moues. In short, we spend a great deal of time acting like
wimps.

For contrast, think of the macho stars we love to watch. Think, 5
for example, of Mel Gibson facing down punk marauders in "The
Road Warrior" . . . John Travolta swaggering his way through the
early scenes of "Saturday Night Fever" . . . or Marlon Brando
shrugging off the local law in "The Wild One." Would they simper their way through tight spots? Chatter aimlessly to keep the
conversation going? Get all clutched up whenever they think they
might—just might—have hurt someone's feelings? No, of course
not, and therein, I think, lies their fascination for us.

6   The attraction of the "tough guy" is that he has—or at least seems to have—what most of us lack, and that is an aura of power and control. In an article, feminist psychiatrist Jean Baker Miller writes that "a Woman's using self-determined power for herself is equivalent to selfishness [and] destructiveness"—an equation that makes us want to avoid even the appearance of power. Miller cites cases of women who get depressed just when they're on the verge of success—and of women who do succeed and then bury their achievement in self-deprecation. As an example, she describes one company's periodic meetings to recognize outstanding sales-people: when a woman is asked to say a few words about her achievement, she tends to say something like, "Well, I really don't know how it happened. I guess I was just lucky this time." In con-trast, the men will cheerfully own up to the hard work, intelligence, and so on, to which they owe their success. By putting herself down, a woman avoids feeling brazenly powerful and potentially "selfish"; she also does the traditional lady's work of trying to make everyone else feel better ("She's not really so smart, after all, just lucky").

7   So we might as well get a little tougher. And a good place to start is by cutting back on the small acts of deference that we've been programmed to perform since girlhood. Like unnecessary smiling. For many women—waitresses, flight attendants, recep-tionists—smiling is an occupational requirement, but there's no reason for anyone to go around grinning when she's not being paid for it. I'd suggest that we save our off-duty smiles for when we truly feel like sharing them, and if you're not sure what to do with your face in the meantime, study Clint Eastwood's expressions— both of them.

8   Along the same lines, I think women should stop taking responsibility for every human interaction we engage in. In a social encounter with a woman, the average man can go 25 min-utes saying nothing more than "You don't say?" "Izzat so?" and, of course, "Hmmmm." Why should we do all the work? By taking so much responsibility for making conversations go well, we act as if we had much more at stake in the encounter than the other party—and that gives him (or her) the power advantage. Every now and then, we deserve to get more out of a conversation than we put into it: I'd suggest not offering information you'd rather not share ("I'm really terrified that my sales plan won't work") and not, out of sheer politeness, soliciting information you don't

really want ("Wherever did you get that lovely tie?"). There will
be pauses, but they don't have to be awkward for *you*.

It is true that some, perhaps most, men will interpret any 9
decrease in female deference as a deliberate act of hostility. Omit
the free smiles and perky conversation-boosters and someone is
bound to ask, "Well, what's come over *you* today?" For most of us,
the first impulse is to stare at our feet and make vague references to
a terminally ill aunt in Atlanta, but we should have as much right to
be taciturn as the average (male) taxi driver. If you're taking a vacation from smiles and small talk and some fellow is moved to inquire
about what's "bothering" you, just stare back levelly and say, the
international debt crisis, the arms race, or the death of God.

There are all kinds of ways to toughen up—and potentially 10
move up—at work, and I leave the details to the purveyors of
assertiveness training. But Jean Baker Miller's study underscores
a fundamental principle that anyone can master on her own. We
can stop acting less capable than we actually are. For example, in
the matter of taking credit when credit is due, there's a key difference between saying "I was just lucky" and saying "I had a plan
and it worked." If you take the credit you deserve, you're letting
people know that you were confident you'd succeed all along, and
that you fully intend to do so again.

Finally, we may be able to learn something from men about 11
what to do with anger. As a general rule, women get irritated: men
get *mad*. We make tight little smiles of ladylike exasperation; they
pound on desks and roar. I wouldn't recommend emulating the full
basso profundo male tantrum, but women do need ways of expressing justified anger clearly, colorfully, and, when necessary, crudely.
If you're not just irritated, but *pissed off,* it might help to say so.

I, for example, have rerun the scene with the prestigious pro- 12
fessor many times in my mind. And in my mind, I play it like
Bogart. I start by moving my chair over to where I can look the
professor full in the face. I let him do the chattering, and when it
becomes evident that he has nothing serious to say, I lean back and
cross my arms, just to let him know that he's wasting my time. I
do not smile, neither do I nod encouragement. Nor, of course, do I
respond to his blandishments with apologetic shrugs and blushes.
Then, at the first flicker of lechery, I stand up and announce coolly,
"All right, I've had enough of this crap." Then I walk out—slowly,
deliberately, confidently. Just like a man.

Or—now that I think of it—just like a woman. 13

BUILDING VOCABULARY

1. The writer uses a number of words ascribed to "ladies" for ironic effect. Try the same in sentences of your own that use the following:
   a. curtsy
   b. simper
   c. chatter
2. The writer is comfortable using a mixture of formal and informal words, as the essay requires. Use the following combinations of words in sentences or paragraphs of your own:
   a. prestigious (par. 3) *and* hand-to-hand combat (par. 2)
   b. theoretical (par. 3) *and* clutched up (par. 5)
   c. deliberate (par. 9) *and* perky (par. 9)

THINKING CRITICALLY ABOUT THE ESSAY

Understanding the Writer's Ideas

1. What does Ehrenreich's opening paragraph tell us about her attitude toward men?
2. The writer contrasts "being tough" and "being ladylike." What are the attitudes and behaviors that she associates with these opposing ways of being?
3. Why does the writer risk embarrassing herself by telling the story of her encounter with the "prestigious professor" of paragraph 3?
4. According to Ehrenreich, why are women reluctant to exert power?
5. The writer advocates two alternative strategies women should pursue "to get tough." The first is to stop doing things that are subservient; the second is to begin to act differently. What does she recommend women should stop doing, and why? What does she recommend women should start doing, and why?

Understanding the Writer's Techniques

1. *Tone* (see Glossary) expresses a writer's attitude toward his or her subject. What is the tone of the opening paragraph? What

does the tone of this paragraph suggest we can expect in the rest of the essay?

2. Why does Ehrenreich delay her thesis statement until close to the end of the second paragraph?

3. One key to a smooth, graceful essay is effective use of transitions. Explain how the writer establishes effective transitions between paragraphs 3 and 4, 4 and 5, and 6 and 7.

4. Writers sometimes seek to strengthen their arguments by quoting supporting views from authorities. For what reasons does the writer quote Jean Baker Miller?

5. Why does Ehrenreich mix informal and formal diction in this essay? What does this choice of diction suggest about her intended audience?

6. Why does the writer "rerun" the scene with the "prestigious professor" to conclude her essay?

Exploring the Writer's Ideas

1. Perhaps it is in the nature of waiters—who are often busy and pestered by customers—to make it hard for you to catch their attention, regardless of your gender. In that case, was Ehrenreich's envy of "men's" sway over waiters another case of a feminine inferiority complex, or is Ehrenreich simply using a rhetorical ploy to grab your attention at the start of her essay? Explain.

2. Ehrenreich seems to want us to distinguish between the servile characteristics of what is ladylike and the more robust qualities of women. Do you believe her portrait of a lady is fair and accurate? Why?

3. Is it a moral failing of the essay that the writer acknowledges only one possible character for all men, and that is the unattractive character of the "macho" male? Ought the essay to have provided us with a positive example of male character too? Does the absence of positive male role models weaken the essay's argument about women? Why or why not?

4. Ehrenreich's argument proceeds by building one generalization on another. She quotes Jean Baker Miller, for example, to make the point that *for all women* the exercise of power is associated with selfishness and destructiveness. If you can think of exceptions to her main general statements, does this undermine her argument for you, or do you remain persuaded

of her generalizations despite the exceptions? Discuss this in relation to one or two examples.

5. You are likely to have heard someone described as "one tough lady." How are the attributes of such a person the same as or different from those that Ehrenreich advocates for all women?

IDEAS FOR WRITING

Prewriting

Make a list of character traits generally associated with men, and another of traits generally associated with women. Then make a second list of those traits men might wish to adapt from women, and women from men.

Guided Writing

Write an essay titled "What I've Learned from _____." Fill in the blank with a word of your choice. Your essay should illustrate how you came to realize you could learn something positive from those you had long ago given up on as sources of wisdom. Some possible titles might be "What I've Learned from Parents," "What I've Learned from Professional Wrestlers," or "What I've Learned from the Boss."

1. Begin your essay by indicating why you long ago abandoned the idea that you could learn anything from "_____."
2. But then explain why you have realized that the very thing that made "_____" so unattractive might be instructive after all.
3. Provide an example from your own behavior where having a little more of that something undesirable you always disliked in "_____" might have been a good thing.
4. Now explain how that nice quality of your own character that is just the opposite of the undesirable "_____" might actually reflect a weakness or flaw in your character.
5. If possible, quote an authoritative source to underscore how your apparently good quality masks a serious weakness (as in the flaws of being a lady).
6. Now illustrate how adopting some of "_____" behaviors would be a good thing.

7. Conclude by showing how this quality in "_____," when adopted by you and those like you, actually better brings out what you are truly like.

Thinking and Writing Collaboratively

In small groups, discuss the lists of attributes of men and women you drew up in your Prewriting exercise. Do the qualities listed compose stereotypes, or do they reflect abiding truths about the differences between the sexes? Compare the lists made up by the students in your group—what can you conclude from the similarities and differences among these lists?

Writing About the Text

Many words in this essay are "man" words, that is, words that our culture often uses to describe and identify males. Similarly, many "woman" words appear here too. How does Ehrenreich use "man" and "woman" language to advantage here? Identify several words that she uses in each gender category and explore their effect on the essay.

More Writing Projects

1. For a journal entry, write about a quality, usually associated with the opposite sex, that you secretly admire, or wish you could say was a quality of your own.

2. In an essay, explore a quality in yourself or in people more generally that is commonly viewed as good—such as kindness—for its possibly "weak" or self-defeating underside (in the case of kindness, for example, always doing for others and never thinking of yourself).

3. Write an essay on the dangers of stereotyping, that is, of thinking of individuals as necessarily having the characteristics of a group.

Homeless on Campus

Eleanor J. Bader

Eleanor J. Bader is a social worker, freelance writer, and adjunct college instructor who has reviewed books for *Library Journal*. She is the coauthor of *Targets of Hatred: Anti-Abortion Terrorism* (2001), a study analyzing attitudes toward abortion and tracing crimes against family-planning clinics and personnel from the time of *Roe v. Wade* through the 1990s. Bader begins the following essay, published in *The Progressive* in July 2004, by profiling a young college student named Aesha, whom she taught at a New York City community college in the fall 2003 semester.

PREREADING: THINKING ABOUT THE ESSAY IN ADVANCE

Imagine that you discover a student who, unknown to others, is homeless on campus. What could you do to help this individual?

Words to Watch

respite (par. 2)   an interval of temporary rest or relief
confide (par. 4)   share secrets or discuss private affairs
rendered (par. 7)   caused to be or become
temperate (par. 11)   mild

1   Aesha is a twenty-year-old at Kingsborough Community College in Brooklyn, New York. Until the fall of 2003, she lived with five people—her one-year-old son, her son's father, her sister, her mother, and her mother's boyfriend—in a three-bedroom South Bronx apartment. Things at home were fine until her child's father became physically abusive. Shortly thereafter, Aesha realized that she and her son had to leave the unit.

2   After spending thirty days in a temporary shelter, they landed at the city's emergency assistance unit (EAU). "It was horrible," Aesha says. "We slept on benches, and it was very crowded. I was so scared I sat on my bag and held onto the stroller day and night, from Friday to Monday." Aesha and her son spent several nights in the EAU before being sent to a hotel. Sadly, this proved to be a temporary respite. After a few days, they were returned to the EAU, where they remained until they were finally moved to a family shelter in Queens.

Although Aesha believes that she will be able to stay in this 3
facility until she completes her associate's degree, the ordeal of
being homeless has taken a toll on her and her studies. "I spend
almost eight hours a day on the trains," she says. "I have to leave
the shelter at 5:00 a.m. for the Bronx where my girlfriend watches
my son for me. I get to her house around 7:00. Then I have to
travel to school in Brooklyn—the last stop on the train followed
by a bus ride—another two hours away."

Reluctantly, Aesha felt that she had no choice but to confide in 4
teachers and explain her periodic absences. "They've all said that
as long as I keep up with the work I'll be OK," she says. But that
is not easy for Aesha or other homeless students.

Adriana Broadway lived in ten places, with ten different fam- 5
ilies, during high school. A native of Sparks, Nevada, Broadway
told the LeTendre Education Fund for Homeless Children, a
scholarship program administered by the National Association
for the Education of Homeless Children and Youth, that she left
home when she was thirteen. "For five years, I stayed here and
there with friends," she wrote on her funding application. "I'd
stay with whoever would take me in and allow me to live under
their roof."

Johnny Montgomery also became homeless in his early teens. 6
He told LeTendre staffers that his mother threw him out because
he did not get along with her boyfriend. "She chose him over me,"
he wrote. "Hard days and hard nights have shaped me." Much of
that time was spent on the streets.

Asad Dahir has also spent time on the streets. "I've been 7
homeless more than one time and in more than one country," Dahir
wrote on his scholarship application. Originally from Somalia, he
and his family fled their homeland due to civil war and ended up
in a refugee camp in neighboring Kenya. After more than a year in
the camp, he and his thirteen-year-old brother were resettled, first
in Atlanta and later in Ohio. There, high housing costs once again
rendered the pair homeless.

Broadway, Montgomery, and Dahir are three of the forty-four 8
homeless students from across the country who have been awarded
LeTendre grants since 1999. Thanks, in part, to these funds, all
three have been attending college and doing well.

But few homeless students are so lucky. "Each year at our nation- 9
al conference, homeless students come forward to share their

stories," says Jenn Hecker, the organizing director of the National Student Campaign Against Hunger and Homelessness. "What often comes through is shame. Most feel as though they should be able to cover their costs." Such students usually try to blend in and are reluctant to disclose either their poverty or homelessness to others on campus, she says. Hecker blames rising housing costs for the problem and cites a 2003 survey that found the median wage needed to pay for a two-bedroom apartment in the United States to be $15.21, nearly three times the federal minimum.

10 Even when doubled up, students in the most expensive states—Massachusetts, California, New Jersey, New York, and Maryland—are scrambling. "In any given semester, there are four or five families where the head of household is in college," says Beth Kelly, a family service counselor at the Clinton Family Inn, a New York City transitional housing program run by Homes for the Homeless.

11 Advocates for the homeless report countless examples of students sleeping in their cars and sneaking into a school gym to shower and change clothes. They speak of students who couch surf or camp in the woods—bicycling or walking to classes—during temperate weather. Yet, for all the anecdotes, details about homeless college students are hazy.

12 "I wish statistics existed on the number of homeless college students," says Barbara Duffield, executive director of the National Association for the Education of Homeless Children and Youth. "Once state and federal responsibility to homeless kids stops—at the end of high school—it's as if they cease to exist. They fall off the map."

13 Worse, they are neither counted nor attended to.

14 "Nobody has ever thought about this population or collected data on them because nobody thinks they are a priority to study," says Martha Burt, principal research associate at the Urban Institute.

15 Critics say colleges are not doing enough to meet—or even recognize—the needs of this group.

16 "The school should do more," says Aesha. "They have a child care center on my campus, but they only accept children two and up. It would have helped if I could've brought my son to day care at school." She also believes that the college should maintain emergency housing for homeless students.

"As an urban community college, our students are commut- 17
ers," responds Uda Bradford, interim dean of student affairs at
Kingsborough Community College. "Therefore, our student support services are developed within that framework."

"As far as I know, no college has ever asked for help in 18
reaching homeless students," says Mary Jean LeTendre, a
retired Department of Education administrator and creator of
the LeTendre Education Fund. "Individual colleges have come
forward to help specific people, but there is nothing systematic
like there is for students in elementary and high school."

"There is a very low awareness level amongst colleges," 19
Duffield adds. "People have this 'you can pull yourself up by
your bootstraps' myth about college. There is a real gap between
the myth and the reality for those who are trying to overcome
poverty by getting an education."

Part of the problem is that the demographics of college atten- 20
dance have changed. "Most educational institutions were set up to
serve fewer, less diverse, more privileged students," says Andrea
Leskes, a vice president with the Association of American Colleges and Universities. "As a result, we are not successfully educating all the students who come to college today. This means that
nontraditional students—the older, returning ones as well as those
from low income or other disenfranchised communities—often
receive inadequate support services."

"It's not that colleges are not concerned, but attention today is 21
not on serving the poor," says Susan O'Malley, chair of the faculty
senate at the City University of New York. "It's not in fashion.
During the 1960s, people from all over the country were going to
Washington and making a lot of noise. The War on Poverty was
influenced by this noise. Now the poor are less visible."

Mary Gesing, a counselor at Kirkwood Community College 22
in Cedar Rapids, Iowa, agrees. "Nothing formal exists for this
population, and the number of homeless students on campus is not
tracked," she says. Because of this statistical gap, programs are not
devised to accommodate homeless students or address their needs.

Despite these programmatic shortfalls, Gesing encounters two 23
to three homeless students—often single parents—each semester.
Some became homeless when they left an abuser. Others lost their
housing because they could no longer pay for it due to a lost job,
the termination of unemployment benefits, illness, the cessation of
child support, or drug or alcohol abuse.

24   Kirkwood's approach is a "patchwork system," Gesing explains, and homeless students often drop out or fail classes because no one knows of their plight. "When people don't know who to come to for help they just fade away," she says.

25   "Without housing, access to a work space, or access to a shower, students' lives suffer, their grades suffer, and they are more likely to drop classes, if not withdraw entirely from school. I've seen it happen," says Amit Rai, an English professor at a large, public university in Florida. "If seen from the perspective of students, administrators would place affordable housing and full access to health care at the top of what a university should provide."

26   Yet for all this, individual teachers—as well as administrators and counselors—can sometimes make an enormous difference.

27   B.R., a faculty member who asked that neither her name nor school be disclosed, has allowed several homeless students to sleep in her office during the past decade. "Although there is no institutional interest or involvement in keeping these students enrolled, a few faculty members really care about the whole student and don't shy away from helping," she says.

28   One of the students she sheltered lived in the space for three months, whenever she couldn't stay with friends. Like Aesha, this student was fleeing a partner who beat her. Another student had been kicked out of the dorm because her stepfather never paid the bill. She applied for financial assistance to cover the cost, but processing took months. "This student stayed in my office for an entire semester," B.R. says.

29   A sympathetic cleaning woman knew what was going on and turned a blind eye to the arrangement. "Both students showered in the dorms and kept their toothbrushes and cosmetics in one of the two department bathrooms which I gave them keys to," B.R. adds. "The administration never knew a thing. Both of the students finished school and went on to become social workers. They knew that school would be their saving grace, that knowledge was the only thing that couldn't be snatched."

BUILDING VOCABULARY

1. Bader uses a number of words and phrases connected with the social sciences, including sociology, economics, and public

policy. Consider the following words and phrases in context, and then write definitions for them:

   a. emergency assistance unit (par. 2)
   b. median (par. 9)
   c. federal minimum (par. 9)
   d. transitional housing program (par. 10)
   e. principal research associate (par. 14)
   f. demographics (par. 20)
   g. nontraditional students (par. 20)

2. The key word in this essay is *homeless*. List some of the connotations that you associate with this word.

THINKING CRITICALLY ABOUT THE ESSAY

Understanding the Writer's Ideas

1. Identify the students whom Bader discusses in this essay. Where do they live? What are their backgrounds? How do they cope with their problems?
2. According to Bader, do college administrations acknowledge that they have homeless students on their campus? Explain.
3. What is a LeTendre grant? Do you think that such grants are an answer to the problem of homelessness on campus? Why or why not?
4. What do you think of Bader's observation that "for all the anecdotes, details about homeless college students are hazy"? Does such an admission undercut or compromise her article? Why or why not?
5. Why do you think the faculty member that Bader presents in the last section of the essay doesn't want her name or college disclosed? How does this fact temper your overall response to the problem that Bader presents?

Understanding the Writer's Techniques

1. Bader wrote this essay for a progressive magazine. Why would this magazine's audience be interested in Bader's subject? How do you think the readership would respond? Would readers accept the writer as an authority on the subject? Why or why not?

2. How does the opening paragraph of Bader's essay color the rest of what she writes about students who are homeless on campus? Does this opening paragraph have a thesis? More broadly, what *is* the thesis of the essay?

3. Bader's essay is made up largely of extended examples. What are they, and what do they have in common? What do they contribute to the essay? How successful would the essay be without them?

4. What other types of illustration does Bader use, and where? What is her specific purpose in each instance?

5. Why does Bader divide her essay into four sections? How does she maintain *unity* and *coherence* (see Glossary for these terms) from section to section?

Exploring the Writer's Ideas

1. Colleges and universities confront numerous problems that seem larger and more consequential than the possibility of homelessness. Do you think that colleges should devote time, attention, and money to a small group of students who might lack proper housing?

2. If, as Bader admits, it is hard to quantify the issue that she discusses, is it truly an issue? Why or why not? Can you think of another campus issue that might be hard to quantify completely?

3. According to Bader, certain cultural and demographic differences separate "ordinary" college students from those among their peers who are homeless. Discuss some of these differences, and how they might color campus life.

IDEAS FOR WRITING

Prewriting

Look around your classroom, and jot down several examples that serve to create a demographic profile of the students registered for the course.

Guided Writing

Write an essay titled "_____ on Campus." Fill in the blank with a problem or issue that you consider significant.

1. Begin with a profile, actual or imaginary, of a typical student who exemplifies the problem.
2. Provide a clearly stated thesis rather than an implied one.
3. Write, as Bader does, with an objective or calm tone.
4. Do some research or interview subjects, and incorporate your findings into the essay.
5. Present both extended and specific examples, making sure you have a variety of illustrative facts that illuminate your thesis.
6. End your paper with one final extended example that reinforces the main idea of the essay.

Thinking and Writing Collaboratively

In a group of four or five students, discuss the issue of homelessness on campus. Does anyone know of a homeless student or suspect that someone might be homeless? Are there forms of dress or behavior that might serve to "profile" a homeless student? Alternately, is your student body so homogenous and affluent, and the university so famous, that campus homelessness could never occur or be a problem?

Writing About the Text

Bader, as you already have discovered, makes use of several types of illustration. Write an essay in which you analyze these varieties of exemplification and the ways in which examples provide a center of gravity and unity for Bader's article.

More Writing Projects

1. Imagine that you are suddenly homeless on campus. In your journal, recount a typical day in your life.
2. Write a 150-word paragraph that gives an extended example of one type of student common to your campus.
3. Write an essay illustrating what you consider the inadequacy of your college to address a specific problem—for example, parking facilities, cafeteria cuisine, or campus violence.

Globalization Rocked the Ancient World Too

Jared Diamond

Mixing Patterns

Jared Diamond has published several well-received books and hundreds of articles spanning the fields of geography, ecology, evolutionary biology, physiology, history, and economics. Born in Boston in 1937, Diamond received his BA from Harvard University (1958) and a PhD from Cambridge University (1961). Currently a professor of geography at UCLA, he has conducted notable field research in New Guinea and other Pacific islands, and has served as director of the World Wildlife Fund. He received a Pulitzer Prize for *Guns, Germs, and Steel: The Fates of Human Societies* (1997) and also wrote the best-selling *Collapse: How Societies Choose to Fail or Succeed* (2004). Diamond brings his wide-ranging expertise and knowledge to bear in an inquiry into globalization that appeared in the *Los Angeles Times* on September 14, 2003.

PREREADING: THINKING ABOUT THE ESSAY IN ADVANCE

There are few words more controversial or provocative today than *globalization*. What does this term mean to you? Why do people, organizations, and nations argue about it? Do you think that this argument is new—the result of recent trends or phenomena, or has globalization been a feature of political, economic, and social life for a long time?

Words to Watch

dispersal (par. 1)   a distribution or scattering in all directions
domesticated (par. 3)   tamed; to cause plants or animals to be no longer wild
pods (par. 5)   the seedcase of peas, beans, etc.
nomadic (par. 7)   characteristic of peoples who move about constantly in search of food, pasture, or conditions favorable to survival
conferred (par. 8)   gave; bestowed on

intrinsic (par. 13)   essential; inherent; not dependent on external circumstances

paradox (par. 16)   a statement that seems contradictory or unbelievable but that may actually be true in fact

We tend to think of globalization as uniquely modern, a product 1 of 20th century advances in transportation, technology, agriculture and communications. But widespread dispersal, from a few centers, of culture, language, political ideas and economic systems— even genetically modified foods—is actually quite an ancient phenomenon.

The first wave of globalization began around 8500 BC, driven 2 primarily by genetically modified foods created in the Mideast and China, and to a lesser extent Mexico, the Andes and Nigeria. As those foods spread to the rest of the world, so did the cultures that created them, a process that reshaped the ancient world in much the same way the U.S., Europe and Japan are reshaping today's world.

Our ancient ancestors' method of genetically modifying food 3 was of course much different from the way it is done today. When humans lived as hunters and gatherers, they had to make do with whatever wild plants and animals they found. It turned out, though, that some of the wild species upon which humans relied for food could be domesticated. Early farmers soon learned not only how to cultivate the resulting crops and raise livestock but also how to select the traits they valued, thereby genetically modifying foods.

In choosing to sow seeds from wild plants with particularly 4 desirable traits—often the result of mutations—early farmers changed genetically, albeit unconsciously, the foods they raised.

Take the case of peas. Most wild pea plants carry a gene that 5 makes their pods pop open on the stalk, causing the peas to spill onto the ground. It is no surprise that early farmers sought out mutant plants with a gene for pods that stayed closed, which made for an easier harvest. As a consequence of their preference, by selecting, over many generations, seeds from the plants that best served them, they ended up with a genetically modified variety of peas.

Would-be farmers in some regions had a huge advantage. 6 It turned out that only a few species of wild plants and animals could be domesticated, most of them native to the Mideast, China, Mexico, the Andes or Nigeria—precisely those places that became ancient centers of power. The crops and livestock of those five restricted homelands of agriculture still dominate our foods today.

Many of the lands most productive for modern agriculture—including California, Europe, Japan and Java—contributed no species that were domesticated.

7   Ancient people lucky enough to live in one of the few areas with wild plants that could be domesticated radically altered their societies. Hunters and gatherers traded their nomadic lifestyles for safer, more settled lives in villages near their gardens, orchards and pastures. Agricultural surpluses, like wheat and cheese, could be stored for winter or used to feed inventors and bureaucrats. For the first time in history, societies could support individuals who weren't directly involved in producing food and who therefore had time to govern or to figure out how to smelt iron and steel. As a result of all the extra food and stability, farming societies increased in population density a thousandfold over neighboring hunter-gatherers.

8   Ultimately, ancient genetically modified foods conferred military and economic might on the societies that possessed them. It was easy for armies of 1,000 farmers, brandishing steel swords and led by a general, to kill or drive out small bands of nomads armed only with wooden spears. The result was globalization, as early farmers spread out from those first five homelands, carrying their genes, foods, technologies, cultures, scripts and languages around the world.

9   It is because of this first wave of globalization that almost every literate person alive today uses one of only two writing systems: an alphabet derived from the first Mideastern alphabet or a character-based language that grew out of Chinese. This is also why more than 90% of people alive today speak languages belonging to just a half-dozen language families, derived thousands of years ago from a half-dozen languages of the five ancient homelands. The Indo-European family that includes English, for example, originated in the Mideast. But then as now, there was also a cost: Countless other ancient languages and cultures were eliminated as the early farmers and their languages spread.

10   The first wave of globalization moved faster along east-west axes than along north-south axes. The explanation is simple: Regions lying due east or west of one another share the same latitude, and therefore the same day length and seasonality. They are also likely to share similar climates, habitats and diseases, all of which means that crops, livestock and humans can spread east and west more easily, since the conditions to which they have adapted

are similar. Conversely, crops, animals and technologies adapted to one latitude spread only with difficulty north or south to another latitude with a different seasonality and climate.

There are certainly differences between modern globalization 11 and that first ancient wave. Today, crops are deliberately engineered in the laboratory rather than unconsciously in the field. And globalizing influences spread much more quickly by plane, phone and Internet than they did on foot and horseback. But the basic similarity remains: Now, as then, a few centers of innovation and power end up dominating the world.

Even in our modern wave of globalization, genetically modi- 12 fied crops tend to spread along an east-west rather than a north-south axis. That's because crops still remain as tied to particular climates as in ancient times. Plant breeders at U.S. firms like Monsanto concentrate on genetically modifying wheat, corn and other temperate-zone crops rather than coconuts, oil palms and other plants that grow in the tropics. That makes good business sense for American plant breeders, because the rich farmers who can afford their products live in the temperate zone, not in the tropics. But it also contributes to the widening gap between rich and poor countries.

Does this mean that tropical Paraguay and Zambia are eter- 13 nally cursed, and that their citizens should accept poverty as fate? Of course not. Europeans and Americans themselves enjoy no intrinsic biological advantages: They just had the good luck to acquire useful technologies and institutions through accidents of geography. Anyone else who now acquires those same things can reap the same benefits. Japan, Malaysia, Singapore, South Korea and Taiwan already have; China and others are trying and will probably succeed. In addition, some poor countries that don't acquire enough technology to become rich can still acquire enough technology (like a few nukes, missiles, chemical weapons, germs or box-cutters) to cause a lot of trouble.

The biggest problem with today's wave of globalization 14 involves differences between the First and Third worlds. Today, citizens in North America, Europe and Japan consume, on average, 32 times more resources (and produce 32 times more waste) than the billions of citizens of the Third World. Thanks to TV, tourism and other aspects of globalization, though, people in less affluent societies know about our lifestyle, and of course they aspire to it.

15   Vigorous debates are going on today about whether our world could sustain double its present population (along with its consumption and waste), or even whether our world's economy is sustainable at its present level. Yet those aren't the biggest risks. If, through globalization, everyone living on Earth today were to achieve the standard of living of an average American, the effect on the planet would be some 10 times what it is today, and it would certainly be unsustainable.

16   We can't prevent people around the world from aspiring to match our way of life any more than the exporters of culture during the first wave of globalization could expect other cultures not to embrace the farming way of life. But since the world couldn't sustain even its present population if all people lived the way that those in the First World do now, we are left with a paradox. Globalization, most analysts feel, is unstoppable. But its consequences may overtax the Earth's ability to support us. That's a paradox that needs resolving.

BUILDING VOCABULARY

1. Write sentences using the following words. Consult a dictionary if you are uncertain of a word's meaning.
   a. genetically modified foods (par. 2)
   b. species (par. 3)
   c. mutations (par. 4)
   d. Indo-European (par. 9)
   e. temperate zone (par. 12)
2. The word *globalization* appears often in this essay, but Diamond never defines it. Nevertheless, by examining the word in context, you can arrive at an understanding of what the writer means by the term. Write your own definition of globalization based on the evidence that Diamond offers.

THINKING CRITICALLY ABOUT THE ESSAY

Understanding the Writer's Ideas

1. What is the "first wave" of globalization as Diamond presents it? What are some of this first wave's features?
2. Identify the paragraph or paragraphs that focus on genetically modified foods. What effect do they have?

3. Where does Diamond discuss language, and why?
4. According to Diamond, what are the differences between ancient and modern globalization?
5. Explain the "paradox" that Diamond presents in paragraph 16. Does this paradox make him optimistic or pessimistic about the future, in your opinion?

Understanding the Writer's Techniques

1. What paragraphs mark Diamond's introduction and conclusion? How are the two connected?
2. How does Diamond establish his authority in this essay? Does he use his extensive knowledge to convince his audience? Is he objective or subjective in the presentation of facts? How do you know?
3. Which paragraphs constitute the first and second halves of the essay? What paragraph functions as a transitional unit?
4. Diamond supports his thesis with examples drawn from numerous fields of knowledge. What are some of the areas that he taps for facts and information? Which examples are the most effective and why?
5. What types of illustration does Diamond use, and where do they appear in the essay?
6 Explain whether you find Diamond's examples sufficient evidence for his thesis.

✳ MIXING PATTERNS

Illustration is a major rhetorical strategy that Diamond uses here, but comparison and contrast (see Chapter 7) is also a key organizing method. How do these two writing strategies interact? How do illustration and comparison and contrast, working together, help to advance Diamond's thesis?

Exploring the Writer's Ideas

1. Diamond concludes his essay with the statement, "Globalization, most analysts feel, is unstoppable. But its consequences may overtax the Earth's ability to support us. That's a paradox

that needs resolving." Do you think that this paradox can be resolved? Why or why not?

2. Why does Diamond focus so much on genetically modified foods? Is his concentration on this subject justified? Justify your response.

3. Does Diamond persuade you to his point of view that globalization seems to be as old as civilization itself? Explain.

IDEAS FOR WRITING

Prewriting

What might history—ancient or more modern—tell us about today's global problems? Can we learn anything from history? For five or ten minutes, brainstorm in response to these questions.

Guided Writing

Write an essay responding to Diamond's claim that globalization contributes to the widening gap between rich and poor nations.

1. Write an introduction that clearly states your thesis or opinion on the subject.

2. Begin the body of your essay by limiting your scope and time frame. Will you focus exclusively on the present, provide historical background (which might require research on your part), concentrate on one country, region, or continent, or what?

3. Offer vivid examples designed to illustrate how globalization affects rich and poor, developed and underdeveloped nations and regions.

4. Draw at least two examples from Diamond's essay, being certain to cite him for this information.

5. Write with an objective tone—as if you are trying to lay out a problem (or paradox) in a calm, balanced way.

6. Offer a conclusion in which you state your opinion as to whether the issues raised by globalization can be resolved.

Thinking and Writing Collaboratively

Exchange your Guided Writing essay with another student and write a one-paragraph response to it in which you focus on the nature and effectiveness of the examples. Does your classmate provide sufficient examples to support the thesis? What types of examples—for instance, facts, statistics, expert testimony—appear in the essay? Which types work best? For those essays where you find insufficient evidence, explain how your fellow student could strengthen the paper with new examples.

Writing About the Text

Diamond makes many references to peoples, nations, and regions in order to make his point. Write an essay in which you identify and analyze the use of these examples. How do they advance Diamond's thesis?

More Writing Projects

1. Write a journal entry about your own experience with the forces of globalization.
2. Compose a paragraph outlining your opinion of genetically modified foods.
3. Assume that you have been asked by the editor of your college newspaper to write an article on globalization and its effect on your campus. Prepare a 750-word response to this request.

SUMMING UP: CHAPTER 6

1. Staples's essay is about problems between ethnic and racial groups. Ehrenreich's essay is about gender problems. How do both selections deal with the way these problems affect society today? Write your own essay about this issue. Draw on examples from both of these essays to help illustrate your argument.

2. From this chapter select the essay that you think best uses the mode of illustration. Write an essay entitled "How to Write an Exemplification Essay" in which you analyze the writer's techniques and strategies and explain how to make use of them. Make sure you use specific references to the text.

3. The world of the night, the environment of Staples's "Night Walker," challenges our senses and our perceptions, simply because it is so different from the typical daytime worlds we usually inhabit. What unusual nighttime experiences have you had? How do you feel about the nighttime? Write an essay of illustration to address these questions.

4. Both Staples and Bader write about how stereotypes can prevent us from seeing a more diverse truth. What ideas and examples from Bader's essay would support Staples's thesis? What ideas and examples from Staples's essay would support Bader's thesis?

5. All the writers in this chapter use illustration to challenge a widely held view. The view, these essays suggest, is held by many people, maybe by most people. For example, many white women feel nervous about black men walking behind them on dark deserted streets; many people don't think about how globalization affects the wider environment; and so forth. How is illustration an effective method for writers to use in order to achieve this purpose? What other rhetorical means could these writers have used? Write an essay that argues for or against the view that illustration is an extremely effective tool for poking holes in a commonly held point of view.

6. You could easily overhear the following comment in a casual conversation: "I don't know about that—give me an example." The comment implies that the speaker has heard something she's skeptical about; she wants an example to support the contention. A social scientist might say skeptically to Diamond, "Globalization isn't new? I don't believe it. Give me an example."

Or one of us might ask Bader, "What do you mean by saying homelessness on campus is a problem? I don't get it. Give me an example." Do the examples provided in "Homelessness on Campus" and "Globalization Rocked the Ancient World Too" persuade you to agree with the thesis of the essays? Explain your answer in an essay.

✳ FROM SEEING TO WRITING

Look at the photograph of the destruction caused by Hurricane Katrina when it swept through Mississippi and Louisiana. Develop a thesis about the picture that you can support through the strategies of illustration explored in this chapter. Then, write an essay in which you draw on features of the photographic image to support your thesis. Make specific references to what you see in the picture.

CHAPTER 7

Comparison and Contrast

WHAT IS COMPARISON AND CONTRAST?

When we compare two things, we look for similarities. When we contrast, we look for differences. The comparison-contrast writing strategy, then, is a way of analyzing likenesses and differences between two or more subjects. Usually, the purpose is to evaluate or judge which is superior. Thus we might appreciate soccer if we compare it with football; we understand Roman Catholicism better if we see it in light of Buddhism.

Writers who use the comparison-contrast technique know that careful planning is required to *organize* the likenesses and differences into logical patterns. Some authors might use only *comparison* to look at the similarities between subjects. Others might use only *contrast*. Often, writers combine the two in a carefully structured essay that balances one with the other.

Like many of the writing and reading strategies you have learned, comparison and contrast is familiar from everyday life. If you were about to buy a new car, for instance, you would look at several models before you made a choice. You might consider price, size, horsepower, options, safety features, status, and dependability before you spent such a large amount of money. If you were deciding whether to send your daughter to a public school or a private school, you would compare and contrast the features of each type of institution: cost, teacher quality, class size, location, curriculum, and composition of the student body might all be considered. If you were an art historian, you might compare and contrast an early picture by Matisse with one he completed late in life in order to understand his development as an artist.

Writing a comparison-contrast essay requires more careful planning, however, than the everyday life application technique. Both call for common sense. You wouldn't compare parochial schools with an Oldsmobile, for instance; they simply don't relate. But you would compare The Dalton School with Public School 34, or a Cutlass Supreme with a Volvo, a Matisse with a Cézanne. Clearly, any strong pattern of comparison and contrast treats items that are in the same category or class. Moreover, there always has to be a basis for comparison; in other words, you compare or contrast two items in order to try to deal with all-important aspects of the objects being compared before arriving at a final determination. These commonsense characteristics of comparison and contrast apply to our pattern of thought as well as our pattern of writing.

Author Rachel Carson, for instance, contrasts two visions of the future for planet Earth: a flourishing environment or a devastated landscape. Thus she has a common category: the condition of the global ecology. She can use *contrast* because she has a common ground for her analysis. Dave Barry looks at social behaviors among men and women, Michele Ingrassia discusses the different body images of black girls and white girls, and Erica Goode examines two "dueling theories" about racial and ethnic diversity. Each author sets up a formal pattern for contrasting and comparing subjects within a related class. One side of the pattern helps us understand the other. Finally, we may establish a preference for one or the other subject.

HOW DO WE READ COMPARISON AND CONTRAST?

Reading comparison and contrast requires us to ask ourselves these questions:

- What subjects has the author selected? Are they from a similar class or category?
- What is the basis for the comparison or contrast? What is the writer's *thesis*?
- What is the arrangement of topics? How has the writer organized each paragraph? Notice where transitional expressions (*on the one hand, on the other hand, similarly, in contrast*) help the reader follow the writer's train of thought.
- Is the writer fair to each subject, devoting an equal amount of space to each side? Make an outline of one of the reading selections to see how the writer has balanced the two subjects.

- Has the writer used narration, description, or illustration to develop the comparison? What other techniques has the author used?
- Does the conclusion show a preference for one subject over the other? Is the conclusion justified by the evidence in the body?

HOW DO WE WRITE COMPARISON AND CONTRAST?

After reading the professional writers in this chapter, you will be better prepared to organize your own essay. Begin by clearly identifying the subjects of your comparison and by establishing the basis for it. The thesis sentence performs this important function for you.

Sample thesis statement:

> Living in a small town is better than living in a big city because life is safer, friendlier, and cheaper.

Plan a strategy for the comparison and contrast. Writers can use one of three main techniques: block, alternating, or combination. The *block method* requires that the writer put all the points about one side (the small town in this case) in one part of the essay, and all the points about the other side (big-city life) together in another part of the essay. In the *alternating method,* the writer explains one point about small-town life and then immediately gives the contrasting point about big-city life. The *combination* pattern allows the writer to use both alternating and block techniques.

Make a careful outline. For each point about one side, try to find a balancing point about the other. If, for instance, you write about the housing available in a small town, write about housing in the big city. Although it may be impossible to manage exact matches, try to be as fair as possible to each side.

Writing and Revising the Draft

Set up a purpose for the comparison and contrast in the thesis sentence.

Write an outline using paragraph blocks to indicate subject A and subject B. For instance, if you were going to write in the block form, your outline would look like this:

Introduction (with thesis)
Block A: Small Town
    1. housing
    2. jobs
    3. social life
Block B: Big City
    1. housing
    2. jobs
    3. social life
Conclusion

If you were going to use the alternating form, the outline would look as follows:

Introduction (with thesis)
Block A: Housing
    1. big city
    2. small town
Block B: Jobs
    1. big city
    2. small town
Block C: Social Life
    1. big city
    2. small town
Conclusion

Use transitional devices, especially with the alternating form. Each time you shift from one subject to the other, use a transition as needed: *like, unlike, on the one hand, on the other hand, in contrast, similarly.*

In the conclusion, offer your view of the two subjects.

Proofread carefully. Check the draft for clarity and correctness and make a final copy.

A STUDENT PARAGRAPH: COMPARISON AND CONTRAST

Here is a body paragraph from a student essay comparing small-town life and city life. Using the alternating method described above, the student concentrates here on housing, presenting the efforts she made first to find an apartment in her home town and then to find a place to live in Chicago.

DESCRIPTION AND NARRATION

1. What story do you think this photograph tells? What sensory elements, such as action and colors, does the photograph present? What sensory images, such as sound, touch, and smell, does the photograph imply?
2. Write a few paragraphs in which you tell the story of this photograph. Use clear sensory images to bring the scene to life. Or, if you prefer, write a lively narrative about an athletic contest based on your own experience.

PROCESS

1. It looks as if the figure in the illustration is reaching up to pluck a piece of fruit—a pear perhaps—from a tree, but the object is actually a light bulb. What is the usual significance of the light bulb in visual representations? (Think of a cartoon in which you see a light bulb over the head of one of the human figures.) Why is there only one light bulb on the tree? What do you think the artist is trying to show about getting an idea or about the creative process in general?
2. Write a few paragraphs about the creative process as you see it. Identify the various steps: remember that the steps do not have to be linear, that is, they need not follow each other in an exact sequence.

ILLUSTRATION

1. What point do you think this series of ads is attempting to make? What similarities and differences do you note among them? How do you account for the differences?
2. Write a brief illustrative essay about how these advertisements for Coca-Cola use women to sell the product. Or select a series of advertisements for some other product or products, and write an essay about how they use women to improve sales.

COMPARISON AND CONTRAST

1. Describe the three characters portrayed in this magazine cover. What does their clothing tell you about them? How are they different? In what ways are they similar?
2. Write a brief paper in which you compare and contrast the basic values implied by the three figures in this illustration. What point is the illustrator making about the generations and about systems of belief?

CAUSE AND EFFECT

1. What scene does the photograph represent? Why are the two figures releasing doves?
2. Write a few paragraphs in which you identify the causes that led to the scene portrayed here. Or write about the effects of the action shown here.

CLASSIFICATION

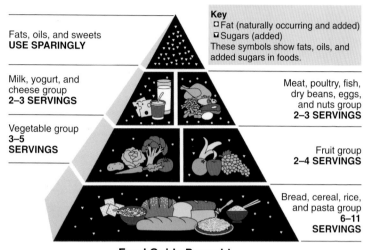

Fats, oils, and sweets
USE SPARINGLY

Key
□ Fat (naturally occurring and added)
◙ Sugars (added)
These symbols show fats, oils, and
added sugars in foods.

Milk, yogurt, and
cheese group
2–3 SERVINGS

Meat, poultry, fish,
dry beans, eggs,
and nuts group
2–3 SERVINGS

Vegetable group
**3–5
SERVINGS**

Fruit group
2–4 SERVINGS

Bread, cereal, rice,
and pasta group
**6–11
SERVINGS**

Food Guide Pyramid

1. What is the main point of the classification scheme shown here? What categories appear, and how are they organized? Why was a pyramid selected as the key design element?
2. Write a brief essay in which you classify the types of food that you enjoy and those that you tend to avoid. How well does your diet reflect the recommendations contained in the U.S. Department of Agriculture's Food Guide Pyramid?

DEFINITION

1. What does this ad imply about the nature of work in today's marketplace? What exactly is a workaholic? Do you think the ad is legitimate or just a humorous attempt to make us think about work in a new light?
2. Write a brief paper defining the word *workaholic*. Draw on your own experience or readings, and use the ad above as a springboard for your paper.

ARGUMENT

1. Why did the milk promotion board select tennis stars Venus and Serena Williams for this advertisement? What elements in this ad stand out? How does the image of the Williams sisters reinforce the ad's slogan "Got Milk"?
2. Write an essay on the power of celebrities from the worlds of sports, music, and film to sell a product or promote a cause. Refer to specific stars to support your main idea or claim.

Finding an apartment back home in Quincy was easy, but Chicago was a whole different ball game. In Quincy, I found an affordable one-bedroom place with the help of a friendly local real estate agent. The apartment consisted of three huge, sunny, high-ceilinged rooms that looked out over a stretch of velvety green lawn—and it was all just for me, no roommates, since I could easily pay the rent out of my weekly paycheck. When I moved to the big city, however, my luck ran out. The phonebook's long list of realtors looked too intimidating, so I first scoured the classified ads in the Chicago Tribune. After visiting all the places I could afford, I realized that in the language of the classifieds, "cozy" meant the size of a Quincy closet, and "fixer-upper" meant that slamming a door would bring the place tumbling down over my ears. I decided to try an apartment-finding service instead. When I admitted how little I had to spend on rent, a grim-faced woman who worked there offered me a list of apartments to share. The first potential roomie I met this way opened the door flushed, sweating, and dressed in blue Spandex from head to toe. Bad 1980s dance music blared from the living room. She looked put out that I had interrupted her aerobics routine and handed me a list of rules that specified, among other things, that I could bring only fat-free food into the kitchen. Another required an oath to engage only in "healthy thoughts" while on the premises. I excused myself as politely as I could and called home to Quincy to see if I could get my old place back.

Topic statement

Alternating method of contrast: Quincy first

Supporting detail

Transition reminds reader of previous point and flows smoothly into next point to produce *coherence*

Alternating method: Chicago second

Supporting detail

"Quincy closet" connects to previous point

Supporting detail

Supporting detail

Closing sentence clinches paragraph's main point

www.mhhe.com/
shortprose

To learn more about using comparison and contrast, click on

Writing > Writing Tutor:
              Comparison/Contrast
Writing > Paragraph Patterns

A Fable for Tomorrow

Rachel Carson

Rachel Carson (1907–1964), "the mother of the modern environmental movement," was raised in a simple farmhouse outside the
river town of Springdale in western Pennsylvania. The first woman
to take and pass the civil service exam, Carson worked for the
Bureau of Fisheries from 1936 to 1952, rising to be the editor-in-
chief of publications for the U.S. Fish and Wildlife Service. In 1951
she published *The Sea Around Us,* a ground-breaking book on life
under the sea based on her years of work as a marine biologist. Her
most famous book, *Silent Spring* (1962), raised the alarm about the
use of pesticides and other chemicals in the production of food. The
book was one of the earliest popular works alerting Americans to
the dangers facing our natural environment. *Silent Spring* impressed
President Kennedy, who ordered testing of and research into the substances Carson brought under scrutiny in the book. In this selection
from *Silent Spring,* Carson establishes contrasts for an imaginary
town as part of a literary strategy to call attention to the implications of today's practices for tomorrow. A concerned citizen and an
informed advocate for a clean environment, Carson here makes her
argument not through statistics or other facts, but through a *fable.* A
fable is a story, usually fictitious, intended to point to a moral. Why
does Carson choose to make her argument through a fable?

www.mhhe.com/
shortprose

To learn more about Carson, click on
**More Resources > Chapter 7 >
Rachel Carson**

PREREADING: THINKING ABOUT
THE ESSAY IN ADVANCE

What dangers do you see affecting our environment over the next
decades? How can we as a society address these environmental
problems?

Words to Watch

migrants (par. 2)   people, animals, or birds that move from one
place to another
blight (par. 3)   a disease or condition that kills or checks growth

maladies (par. 3)   illnesses
moribund (par. 4)   dying
pollination (par. 5)   the transfer of pollen (male sex cells) from
    one part of the flower to another
granular (par. 7)   consisting of grains
specter (par. 9)   a ghost; an object of fear or dread
stark (par. 9)   bleak; barren; standing out in sharp outline

1   There was once a town in the heart of America where all life seemed to live in harmony with its surroundings. The town lay in the midst of a checkerboard of prosperous farms, with fields of grain and hillsides of orchards where, in spring, white clouds of bloom drifted above the green fields. In autumn, oak and maple and birch set up a blaze of color that flamed and flickered across a backdrop of pines. Then foxes barked in the hills and deer silently crossed the fields, half hidden in the mists of the fall mornings.

2   Along the roads, laurel, viburnum and alder, great ferns and wildflowers delighted the traveler's eye through much of the year. Even in winter the roadsides were places of beauty, where count-less birds came to feed on the berries and on the seed heads of the dried weeds rising above the snow. The countryside was, in fact, famous for the abundance and variety of its bird life, and when the flood of migrants was pouring through in spring and fall people traveled from great distances to observe them. Others came to fish the streams, which flowed clear and cold out of the hills and contained shady pools where trout lay. So it had been from the days many years ago when the first settlers raised their houses, sank their wells, and built their barns.

3   Then a strange blight crept over the area and everything began to change. Some evil spell had settled on the community: mysterious maladies swept the flocks of chickens; the cattle and sheep sickened and died. Everywhere was a shadow of death. The farmers spoke of much illness among their families. In the town the doctors had become more and more puzzled by new kinds of sickness appearing among their patients. There had been several sudden and unexplained deaths not only among adults but even among children, who would be stricken suddenly while at play and die within a few hours.

4   There was a strange stillness. The birds, for example—where had they gone? Many people spoke of them, puzzled and disturbed. The feeding stations in the backyards were deserted.

The few birds seen anywhere were moribund; they trembled violently and could not fly. It was a spring without voices. On the mornings that had once throbbed with the dawn chorus of robins, catbirds, doves, jays, wrens, and scores of other bird voices there was now no sound; only silence lay over the fields and woods and marsh.

On the farms the hens brooded, but no chicks hatched. The 5 farmers complained that they were unable to raise any pigs— the litters were small and the young survived only a few days. The apple trees were coming into bloom but no bees droned among the blossoms, so there was no pollination and there would be no fruit.

The roadsides, once so attractive, were now lined with browned 6 and withered vegetation as though swept by fire. These, too, were silent, deserted by all living things. Even the streams were now lifeless. Anglers no longer visited them, for all the fish had died.

In the gutters under the eaves and between the shingles of the 7 roofs, a white granular powder still showed a few patches; some weeks before it had fallen like snow upon the roofs and the lawns, the fields and streams.

No witchcraft, no enemy action had silenced the rebirth of new 8 life in this stricken world. The people had done it themselves.

This town does not actually exist, but it might easily have 9 a thousand counterparts in America or elsewhere in the world. I know of no community that has experienced all the misfortunes I describe. Yet every one of these disasters has actually happened somewhere, and many real communities have already suffered a substantial number of them. A grim specter has crept upon us almost unnoticed, and this imagined tragedy may easily become a stark reality we all shall know.

BUILDING VOCABULARY

1. In the second paragraph, find at least five concrete words that relate to trees, birds, and vegetation. How many of these objects could you identify? Look in a dictionary for the meanings of those words you do not know.
2. Try to identify the italicized words through the *context clues* (see Glossary) provided by the complete sentence.

a. half-hidden in the *mists* (par. 1)
b. when the first settlers *raised* their houses (par. 2)
c. *stricken* suddenly while at play (par. 3)
d. the hens *brooded,* but no chicks hatched (par. 5)
e. *Anglers* no longer visited them, for all the fish had died. (par. 6)

THINKING CRITICALLY ABOUT THE ESSAY

Understanding the Writer's Ideas

1. What is the quality of the world that Carson describes in her opening paragraph? If you had to describe it in just one or two words, which would you use?
2. What are some of the natural objects that Carson describes in her first two paragraphs? Why does she not focus on simply one aspect of nature—like animals, trees, or flowers?
3. How does Carson describe the "evil spell" that settles over the countryside?
4. What does Carson mean when she declares, "It was a spring without voices" (par. 4)? Why does she show that the critical action takes place in the springtime?
5. What do you think is the "white granular powder" that Carson refers to in paragraph 7? Why does she not explain what it is or where it came from?
6. In paragraph 9, the writer states her basic point. What is it? Does she offer a solution to the problem that she poses?

Understanding the Writer's Techniques

1. A *fable* is a story with a moral; in other words, a fable is a form of teaching narrative. How does Carson structure her narrative in this essay? What is the "moral" or thesis?
2. What is the purpose of the description in this essay? Why does the writer use such vivid and precise words?
3. Where in this essay does the writer begin to shift from an essentially positive tone to a negative one?
4. Does Carson rely on comparison or contrast in this essay? Defend your choice with references to the text.

5. In the *block method* of comparison and contrast, the writer presents all information about one subject, and then all information about a second subject, as in the following:

   a. How does Carson use this pattern in her essay?
   b. Are there actually two subjects in this essay, or two different aspects of one subject? How does chronology relate to the block structure?
   c. Are the two major parts of Carson's essay equally weighted? Why or why not?
   d. In the second part of the essay, does Carson ever lose sight of the objects introduced in the first part? What new terms does she introduce?

6. How can you explain paragraphs 8 and 9—which do not involve narration, description, or comparison and contrast—in relation to the rest of the essay? What is the nature of Carson's conclusion?

Exploring the Writer's Ideas

1. Today we use chemicals to destroy crop insects, to color and preserve food, and to purify our water, among other things. Would Carson term this "progress"? Would you? Do you think that there are inadequate safeguards and controls in the use of chemicals? What recent examples of chemical use have made the news?

2. Why would you agree or disagree that factories and corporations should protect the environment that they use? Should a company, for example, be forced to clean up an entire river that it polluted? What about oil spills?

3. What problems with the use of chemicals and the environment can you identify in your own area? How do local citizens feel about these problems?

4. Do you think that it will be possible in the future for Americans to "live in harmony" with their natural surroundings? Why do you believe what you do?

IDEAS FOR WRITING

Prewriting

Define the word *fable*. List the various elements that you think contribute to successful fables.

Guided Writing

Write a fable (an imaginary story with a moral) in which you contrast one aspect of the life of a person, community, or nation with another.

1. Begin with a phrase similar to Carson's "There was once. . . ." so that the reader knows you are writing a narrative fable.
2. Relate your story to an American problem.
3. Use the block method in order to establish your contrast. Write first about one aspect of the topic and then about the other.
4. Use sensory detail in order to make your narrative clear and interesting.
5. Make certain that you establish an effective transition as you move into the contrast.
6. In the second part of your essay, be sure to refer to the same points you raised in the first part.
7. Use the conclusion to establish the "moral" of your fable.

Thinking and Writing Collaboratively

Exchange Guided Writing essays with another member of the class. Has the writer produced a successful fable? Why or why not? Is the moral clear? Is the American problem well defined? Finally, discuss the structure of the essay. Has the writer used the block method of development appropriately? Does an effective transition link the contrast with the stated problem?

Writing About the Text

Write an essay arguing *either* that Carson's fable changed your view of the responsibility of corporations to protect the environment *or* that Carson's fable was too imaginary to influence your thinking one way or another.

More Writing Projects

1. In a journal entry, describe a place you know well, one that has changed for better or worse. Contrast the place as it once was with the way it is now. Use concrete images that appeal to color, action, sound, smell, taste, and touch.

2. Examine in two block paragraphs the two sides of a specific ecological issue today—for instance, acid rain, the global warming trend, or the use of nuclear energy.

3. Using the block method, compare and contrast Carson's fable with the fable you wrote in Guided Writing.

Punch and Judy
Dave Barry

Dave Barry, a syndicated columnist for *The Miami Herald,* has a reputation as one of the funniest writers in the country. He started his career as a reporter but found his great success in writing his regular column, for which he won the Pulitzer Prize for commentary in 1988. Barry is the author of *Dave Barry Is Not Taking This Sitting Down!* (2000), *Dave Barry's Money Secrets* (2006), and *Dave Barry's History of the Millennium, So Far* (2007), among many others. Network television turned his life into a sitcom called *Dave's World,* which ran from 1993 to 1997. In this selection, Barry explains the difference between how men and women play.

PREREADING: THINKING ABOUT THE ESSAY IN ADVANCE

Think about jobs you've held or classes you've been in. Have you noticed any differences between how men and women approach work? What are some of those differences, and why do you think they exist?

Words to Watch

snag (par. 2)   problem
deadlock (par. 2)   seemingly unsolvable problem
compromise (par. 2)   agreement to resolve a matter
syndrome (par. 5)   combinations of symptoms that point to a particular problem
subatomic (par. 7)   relating to particles smaller than an atom
puncturing (par. 8)   damaging by making a hole

1 Are you a male, or a female? To find out, take this scientific quiz:

2 **1.** Your department is on a tight deadline for developing a big sales proposal, but you've hit a snag on a key point. You want to go one way; a co-worker named Bob strongly disagrees. To break the deadlock, you:

   a. Present your position, listen to the other side, then fashion a workable compromise.
   b. Punch Bob.

2. Your favorite team is about to win the championship, but at   3
   the last second the victory is stolen away by a terrible referee's
   call. You:

   a. Remind yourself that it's just a game, and that there are
      far more important things in your life.

   b. Punch Bob again.

   How to score: If you answered "b" to both questions, then you   4
are a male. I base this statement on a recent article in the *New York
Times* about the way animals, including humans, respond to stress.
According to the article, a group of psychology researchers have
made the breakthrough discovery that—prepare to be astounded—
males and females are different.

   The researchers discovered this by studying both humans and   5
rats, which are very similar to humans except that they are not
stupid enough to purchase lottery tickets. The studies show that
when males are under stress, they respond by either fighting or
running away (the so-called "fight or flight" syndrome); whereas
females respond by nurturing others and making friends (the so-
called "tend and befriend" syndrome).

   This finding is big news in the psychology community, which   6
apparently is located on a distant planet. Here on Earth, we have
been aware for some time that males and females respond differently to stress. We know that if two males bump into each other,
they will respond like this:

FIRST MALE: Hey, watch it!
SECOND MALE: No, *you* watch it!
FIRST MALE: Oh yeah?
(They deliberately bump into each other again.)

Two females, in the identical situation, will respond like this:

FIRST FEMALE: I'm sorry!
SECOND FEMALE: No, it's my fault!
FIRST FEMALE: Say, those are cute shoes!
(They go shopping.)

   If the psychology community needs further proof of the dif-   7
ference between genders, I invite it to attend the party held in my
neighborhood each Halloween. This party is attended by several hundred small children, who are experiencing stress because
their bloodstreams—as a result of the so-called "trick or treat"

syndrome—contain roughly the same sugar content as Cuba. Here's how the various genders respond:

— The females, 97 percent of whom are dressed as either a ballerina or a princess, sit in little social groups and exchange candy.
— The males, 97 percent of whom are dressed as either Batman or a Power Ranger, run around making martial-arts noises and bouncing violently off one another like crazed subatomic particles.

8   Here are some other gender-based syndromes that the psychology community might want to look into:

— The "laundry refolding" syndrome: This has been widely noted by both me and a friend of mine named Jeff. What happens is, the male will attempt to fold a piece of laundry, and when he is done, the female, with a look of disapproval, will immediately pick it up and refold it so that it is much neater and smaller. "My wife can make an entire bed-sheet virtually disappear," reports Jeff.
— The "inflatable pool toy" syndrome: From the dawn of human civilization, the task of inflating the inflatable pool toy has always fallen to the male. It is often the female who comes home with an inflatable pool toy the size of the Hindenburg, causing the youngsters to become very excited. But it is inevitably the male who spends two hours blowing the toy up, after which he keels over with skin the color of a Smurf, while the kids, who have been helping out by whining impatiently, leap joyfully onto the toy, puncturing it immediately.

9   I think psychology researchers should find out if these syndromes exist in other species. They could put some rats into a cage with tiny pool toys and miniature pieces of laundry, then watch to see what happens. My guess is that there would be fighting. Among the male researchers, I mean. It's a shame, this male tendency toward aggression, which has caused so many horrible problems, such as war and ice hockey. It frankly makes me ashamed of my gender. I'm going to punch Bob.

BUILDING VOCABULARY

In this essay, Barry makes several cultural references. It is important for his jokes that you understand the references. Identify the following and explain why Barry uses them in the essay:

a. Punch and Judy (title)
b. "the same sugar content as Cuba" (par. 7)
c. Power Ranger (par. 7)
d. Hindenburg (par. 8)
e. Smurf (par. 8)
f. ice hockey (par. 9)

THINKING CRITICALLY ABOUT THE ESSAY

Understanding the Writer's Ideas

1. What point does Barry make with his "scientific quiz" at the beginning of the essay?
2. Why does Barry write "prepare to be astounded" in paragraph 4?
3. According to Barry, how do males and females respond differently to stress?
4. What purpose do the dialogues serve in paragraph 6?
5. According to Barry, how do boys and girls react differently during Halloween?
6. Barry makes a slightly different point in paragraph 8 than he does in the rest of the essay. What is the point, and why does he make it?
7. What does Barry's friend Jeff mean when he says, "My wife can make an entire bed-sheet virtually disappear" (par. 8)?
8. Why does Barry say that he's going to "punch Bob" at the end? What serious point does he make?

Understanding the Writer's Techniques

1. How is Barry's first sentence an example of *irony* (see Glossary)? Explain the irony.
2. Does Barry have a *thesis* statement in his essay? If so, where is it? If not, where does he best express his main point?
3. Who is Barry's audience for this essay? How can you tell?
4. In what ways is the "scientific quiz" at the beginning of the essay effective?
5. How does Barry transition from the quiz to the point he's trying to make in the essay?
6. Why does Barry keep referring to researchers and psychology in his essay?

7. How would you describe the *tone* of Barry's essay? Cite at least three examples to support your answer.
8. What is the central comparison and contrast that appears in this essay? How does it support the writer's thesis?
9. Does this essay use one of the traditional methods of writing comparison essays—*block* or *alternating*—or does he use a combination? Explain your answer.
10. Where in the essay does Barry use *hyperbole* (see Glossary)?
11. There are four jokes in the last paragraph. What are they, and why are they funny? Does the humor help make Barry's point, or does it weaken it? Explain fully.

Exploring the Writer's Ideas

1. Are Barry's conclusions about male aggression generally true? Explain your answer. Have you seen men or boys act in a different way? When?
2. Why does Barry stick to stereotypes of men and women instead of showing exceptions? How do the stereotypes strengthen or weaken his essay?
3. Where in popular culture do we see stereotypes of men and women?
4. When women are stereotyped, people often get upset, but when men are stereotyped, there usually isn't a problem. Why?

IDEAS FOR WRITING

Prewriting

In two columns, marked "Men" and "Women," list the ways the two sexes react differently to the pressures of college life. Be specific. For each item in one column, write a contrasting item in the other column.

Guided Writing

Write a humorous essay that contrasts the ways in which men and women deal differently with the stresses of college life. Narrow your topic down to one aspect of college life: writing papers, social life, staying in the dorms, commuting, and so on.

1. Begin with a "quiz" that highlights the difference you are going to discuss.
2. Next, phrase your thesis statement in an ironic fashion, as in the last two lines of Barry's essay.
3. Develop your contrast by offering at least three differences.
4. Illustrate your contrast by providing examples in quick succession.
5. Emphasize the differences by using *hyperbole* (see Glossary).
6. Conclude your essay with a paragraph that sums up the major points you have made.
7. End with a sentence that recalls a joke from the beginning of your essay.

Thinking and Writing Collaboratively

Working in groups of three or four, read each other's Guided Writing essays. Focus on the tone of the essay. Which of the ironic, humorous statements is most effective? Which is least effective? Why? Where in the essay is the writer's *tone* clearest?

Writing About the Text

Write an essay in which you discuss at least two strengths and two weaknesses in Barry's use of comparison and contrast. Refer to the opening material of this chapter and the questions that appear in Understanding the Writer's Techniques on pages 270–271.

More Writing Projects

1. Make a journal entry in which you compare how gender differences have changed since you were a child.
2. Write an extended paragraph in which you compare how men and women approach the idea of war differently.
3. Watch some television commercials and then write an essay explaining how the commercials portray men and women differently. Identify specific categories of difference (such as self-confidence, body image, and so forth), and organize your essay according to these categories.

The Body of the Beholder

Michele Ingrassia

Michele Ingrassia has worked as a writer, reporter, and features editor for several publications, including *Newsday, Newsweek*, and the *New York Times*. In an essay that originally appeared in *Newsweek,* Ingrassia takes a look at a study that shows why white girls dislike their bodies, but black girls are proud of theirs. Why do some find that being fat can also mean being fit?

PREREADING: THINKING ABOUT THE ESSAY IN ADVANCE

Look in the mirror. What do you see? How do you feel about your body? Why do you feel that way?

Words to Watch

dissect (par. 1)   to cut apart or separate (tissue), especially for anatomical study

anthropologist (par. 3)   a scientist who studies the origin, behavior, and physical, social, and cultural development of human beings

superwaif (par. 4)   a slang phrase meaning a model who makes a lot of money because she looks gaunt, like an orphaned child (waif)

magnetism   (par. 5) unusual power to attract, fascinate, or influence

1   When you're a teenage girl, there's no place to hide. Certainly not in gym class, where the shorts are short, the T shirts revealing and the adolescent critics eager to dissect every flaw. Yet out on the hardwood gym floors at Morgan Park High, a largely African-American school on Chicago's Southwest Side, the girls aren't talking about how bad their bodies are, but how good. Sure, all of them compete to see how many sit-ups they can do—Janet Jackson's washboard stomach is their model. But ask Diane Howard about weight, and the African-American senior, who carries 133 pounds on her 5-foot 7½-inch frame, says she'd happily add 15 pounds—if she could ensure they'd land on her hips. Or La'Taria Stokes, a stoutly built junior who takes it as high praise when boys remark, "Your hips are screaming for twins!" "I know I'm fat," La'Taria says. "I don't care."

In a society that worships at the altar of supermodels like 2
Claudia, Christy and Kate, white teenagers are obsessed with
staying thin. But there's growing evidence that black and white
girls view their bodies in dramatically different ways. The latest
findings come in a study to be published in the journal *Human
Organization* this spring by a team of black and white researchers
at the University of Arizona. While 90 percent of the white junior-
high and high-school girls studied voiced dissatisfaction with their
weight, 70 percent of African-American teens were satisfied with
their bodies.

In fact, even significantly overweight black teens described 3
themselves as happy. That confidence may not carry over to other
areas of black teens' lives, but the study suggests that, at least here,
it's a lifelong source of pride. Asked to describe women as they
age, two thirds of the black teens said they get more beautiful,
and many cited their mothers as examples. White girls responded
that their mothers may have been beautiful—back in their youth.
Says anthropologist Mimi Nichter, one of the study's coauthors,
"In white culture, the window of beauty is so small."

What is beauty? White teens defined perfection as 5 feet 4
7 and 100 to 110 pounds—superwaif Kate Moss's vital stats.
African-American girls described the perfect size in more attainable terms—full hips, thick thighs, the sort of proportions about
which Hammer ("Pumps and a Bump") and Sir Mix-Alot ("Baby
Got Back") rap poetic. But they said that true beauty—"looking
good"—is about more than size. Almost two thirds of the black
teens defined beauty as "the right attitude."

The disparity in body images isn't just in kids' heads. It's 5
reflected in fashion magazines, in ads, and it's out there, on TV, every
Thursday night. On NBC, the sitcom "Friends" stars Courteney Cox,
Jennifer Aniston and Lisa Kudrow, all of them white and twentysomething, classically beautiful and reed thin. Meanwhile, Fox Television's "Living Single," aimed at an African-American audience,
projects a less Hollywood ideal—its stars are four twentysomething
black women whose bodies are, well, *real*. Especially the big-boned,
bronze-haired rapper Queen Latifah, whose size only adds to her
magnetism. During a break at the Lite Nites program at the Harlem
YMCA, over the squeal of sneakers on the basketball court, Brandy
Wood, 14, describes Queen Latifah's appeal: "What I like about
her is the way she wears her hair and the color in it and the clothes
she wears."

6   Underlying the beauty gap are 200 years of cultural differences. "In white, middle-class America, part of the great American Dream of making it is to be able to make yourself over," says Nichter. "In the black community, there is the reality that you might not move up the ladder as easily. As one girl put it, you have to be realistic—if you think negatively about yourself, you won't get anywhere." It's no accident that Barbie has long embodied a white-adolescent ideal—in the early days, she came with her own scale (set at 110) and her own diet guide ("How to Lose Weight: Don't Eat"). Even in this postfeminist era, Barbie's tight-is-right message is stronger than ever. Before kindergarten, researchers say, white girls know that Daddy eats and Mommy diets. By high school, many have split the world into physical haves and have-nots, rivals across the beauty line. "It's not that you hate them [perfect girls]," says Sarah Immel, a junior at Evanston Township High School north of Chicago. "It's that you're kind of jealous that they have it so easy, that they're so perfect-looking."

7   In the black community, size isn't debated, it's taken for granted—a sign, some say, that after decades of preaching black-is-beautiful, black parents and educators have gotten across the message of self-respect. Indeed, black teens grow up equating a full figure with health and fertility. Black women's magazines tend to tout NOT TRYING TO BE SIZE 8, not TEN TIPS FOR THIN THIGHS. And even girls who fit the white ideal aren't necessarily comfortable there. Supermodel Tyra Banks recalls how, in high school in Los Angeles, she was the envy of her white girlfriends. "They would tell me, 'Oh, Tyra, you look so good,'" says Banks. "But I was like, 'I want a booty and thighs like my black girlfriends.'"

8   Men send some of the strongest signals. What's fat? "You got to be *real* fat for me to notice," says Muhammad Latif, a Harlem 15-year-old. White girls follow what they *think* guys want, whether guys want it or not. Sprawled across the well-worn sofas and hard-back chairs of the student lounge, boys at Evanston High scoff at the girls' idealization of Kate Moss. "Sickly," they say, "gross." Sixteen-year-old Trevis Milton, a blond swimmer, has no interest in dating Kate wanna-bes. "I don't want to feel like I'm going to break them." Here, perfection is a hardbody, like Linda Hamilton in "Terminator II." "It's not so much about eating broccoli and water as running," says senior Kevin Mack.

And if hardbodies are hot, girls often need to diet to achieve 9
them, too. According to the Arizona study, which was funded by
the National Institute of Child Health and Human Development,
62 percent of the white girls reported dieting at least once in the
past year. Even those who say they'd rather be fit than thin get
caught up. Sarah Martin, 16, a junior at Evanston, confesses she's
tried forcing herself to throw up but couldn't. She's still frustrated:
". . . have a big appetite, and I feel so guilty when I eat."

Black teens don't usually go to such extremes. Anorexia and 10
bulimia are relatively minor problems among African-American
girls. And though 51 percent of the black teens in the study said
they'd dieted in the last year, follow-up interviews showed that far
fewer were on sustained weight-and-exercise programs. Indeed,
64 percent of the black girls thought it was better to be "a little"
overweight than underweight. And while they agreed that "very
overweight" girls should diet, they defined that as someone who
"takes up two seats on the bus."

The black image of beauty may seem saner, but it's not neces- 11
sarily healthy. Black women don't obsess on size, but they do worry
about other white cultural ideals that black men value. "We look at
Heather Locklear and see the long hair and the fair, pure skin," says
Essence magazine senior editor Pamela Johnson. More troubling,
the acceptance of fat means many girls ignore the real dangers of
obesity. Dieting costs money—even if it's not a fancy commercial
program; fruits, vegetables and lean meats are pricier than high-fat
foods. Exercise? Only one state—Illinois—requires daily physical
education for every kid. Anyway, as black teenagers complain, exercise can ruin your hair—and, if you're plunking down $35 a week
at the hairdresser, you don't want to sweat out your 'do in the gym.
"I don't think we should obsess about weight and fitness, but there
is a middle ground," says the well-toned black actress Jada Pinkett.
Maybe that's where Queen Latifah meets Kate Moss.

BUILDING VOCABULARY

These words have medical denotations. What are they? Check a
medical dictionary.

a. anorexia (par. 10)
b. bulimia (par. 10)
c. obsess (par. 11)

THINKING CRITICALLY ABOUT THE ESSAY

Understanding the Writer's Ideas

1. What does the writer mean when she says that teenage girls generally have "no place to hide" (par. 1)?
2. What did the findings of a study by the journal *Human Organization* reveal about the way young girls see their bodies?
3. How did black and white teens view the bodies of their mothers?
4. How does superwaif Kate Moss serve as a model for teenage girls?
5. Television seems to reflect the different attitudes about body image of black and white teenage girls. How?
6. What may account for the differing views of beauty for black and white girls?
7. How are full-figured black women viewed in their community? Why?
8. Dieting is an American obsession. But is this true for black teens? Explain.
9. Are attitudes about black women's bodies potentially harmful, leading to an increase in obesity in black girls?

Understanding the Writer's Techniques

1. Where does Ingrassia state her thesis? How does the statement make the essay's plan clear?
2. How are the essay's paragraphs ordered around the comparison-contrast structure?
3. How does the writer use statistics to support the comparison-contrast paragraph technique?
4. What audience does Ingrassia have in mind? Do you think this essay is written for men or women? Explain.
5. What makes the transition sentences in paragraph 4 different from the others?
6. Do all the paragraphs (including par. 4) have a topic sentence? Give examples.
7. In the concluding paragraph of the comparison-contrast essay, it is common to bring the two subjects together for a final observation. How does Ingrassia follow that strategy?

Exploring the Writer's Ideas

1. Do you agree with the writer's premise that white girls are mostly obsessed with being thin? Why or why not?

2. Given the reported differences in the way black and white girls see their bodies, whose view do you prefer and why?

3. Do you believe, as the essay suggests, that there is a connection between how girls see their mothers' bodies and how they see their own? Why or why not?

4. Critics blame television for many of society's ills. Should television be more responsible for the body types it chooses if it influences the way young girls see their own bodies? Why or why not?

5. In the black community, "there is the reality that you might not move up the ladder as easily." How do you feel about this statement? What does it mean, and how does it relate to body image?

6. If the "black-is-beautiful" movement helped black women avoid negative body images, do white women need a similar movement? Why or why not?

7. How do men in your community communicate what they think constitutes a beautiful body? What is a beautiful man's body?

8. Despite the positive aspects of liking yourself (even if you are heavy), can an acceptance of weight lead to ill health? Why or why not? What do you propose?

IDEAS FOR WRITING

Prewriting

Make a list of your body features or those of someone you know, and explain what you like or dislike about them.

Guided Writing

Compare your attitudes about body shape to those examined in Ingrassia's essay.

1. Begin with a description that shows whether your community shares (or does not share) your attitudes about body shapes.

2. Make sure your thesis reflects the comparison your essay plans to make between your views of body image and those discussed in Ingrassia's essay.

3. Focus on how your ideas of beauty differ from (or are the same as) the ideas in the essay. Try to make at least three comparisons (paragraphs).

4. Tell how your culture has historically looked at beauty.

5. How (and what) do men make clear about feminine (or masculine) beauty in your community?

6. Conclude by evaluating what you think the ideal body type should be.

Thinking and Writing Collaboratively

Working in a group of four, use what you know about body image and the ways it can hurt some people, and do research into ways society can change to make people of all body types feel more comfortable with themselves. Then write an essay using what the group has gathered to compare ways society can change to help all people develop a positive body image.

Writing About the Text

Write an essay that probes Ingrassia's analysis by looking at how white and black women think of their bodies in similar ways. What instances can you find in Ingrassia's essay in which gender may be more important than (or at least as important as) race?

More Writing Projects

1. Watch television commercials for women's and men's products. Reflect in your journal on what beauty messages the television commercials are communicating.

2. Look at the body images of men and women in magazine ads. Then write a paragraph that compares the beauty messages you find in television commercials and magazine ads.

3. Write an essay that compares the images of men and women in television commercials and magazine ads. Take a position on which ones are acceptable or not acceptable. Consider which ones have the most harmful effects on young people or society in general.

Home Alone

Erica Goode

Erica Goode is science editor at the *New York Times*. Previously she worked as a staff writer for the *San Francisco Chronicle* and senior writer and managing editor for *U.S. News and World Report*. Goode has contributed essays to several magazines, including *Scientific American* and *Psychology Today*. She also has published *Letters for Our Children: Fifty Americans Share Lessons in Living* (1996). With a background in psychology and sociology (she earned a master's degree in social psychology from the University of California), Goode often uses studies and statistics to investigate people's attitudes and the state of American society. Goode's essay on diversity appeared in the *New York Times Magazine* on June 17, 2007.

Mixing Patterns (sidebar)

PREREADING: THINKING ABOUT THE ESSAY IN ADVANCE

What comes to mind when you encounter the word *diversity*? Are your friends diverse? your hometown? your campus? What do you see as the risks and benefits of diversity?

Words to Watch

trumps (par. 1)   surpasses, beats
insularity (par. 1)   the state of being set apart; hence detached, isolated
pervasive (par. 2)   tending to be spread throughout
precipitous (par. 6)   very sudden, unexpected, or abrupt
misanthropic (par. 7)   having the nature of someone who distrusts or hates all people
nuanced (par. 10)   varied slightly in tone, color, meaning
disconcerting (par. 10)   upsetting
intractable (par. 12)   hard to manage, cure, or treat; stubborn

For decades, students of American society have offered dueling 1
theories about how encountering racial and ethnic diversity affects
the way we live. One says that simple contact—being tossed into a
stew of different cultures, values, languages and styles of dress—
is likely to nourish tolerance and trust. Familiarity, in this view,

trumps insularity. Others argue that just throwing people together is rarely enough to breed solidarity: when diversity increases, they assert, people tend to stick to their own groups and distrust those who are different from them.

2   But what if diversity had an even more complex and pervasive effect? What if, at least in the short term, living in a highly diverse city or town led residents to distrust pretty much everybody, even people who looked like them? What if it made people withdraw into themselves, form fewer close friendships, feel unhappy and powerless and stay home watching television in the evening instead of attending a neighborhood barbecue or joining a community project?

3   This is the unsettling picture that emerges from a huge nationwide telephone survey by the famed Harvard political scientist Robert Putnam and his colleagues. "Diversity seems to trigger *not* in-group/out-group division, but anomie or social isolation," Putnam writes in the June issue of the journal Scandinavian Political Studies. "In colloquial language, people living in ethnically diverse settings appear to 'hunker down'—that is, to pull in like a turtle."

4   In highly diverse cities and towns like Los Angeles, Houston and Yakima, Wash., the survey found, the residents were about half as likely to trust people of other races as in homogenous places like Fremont, Mich., or rural South Dakota, where, Putnam noted, "diversity means inviting a few Norwegians to the annual Swedish picnic."

5   More significant, they were also half as likely to trust people of their own race. They claimed fewer close friends. They were more apt to agree that "television is my most important form of entertainment." They had less confidence in local government and less confidence in their own ability to exert political influence. They were more likely to join protest marches but less likely to register to vote. They rated their happiness as generally lower. And this diversity effect continued to show up even when a community's population density, average income, crime levels, rates of home ownership and a host of other factors were taken into account.

6   It was not a result that Putnam, the author of the much-discussed 2000 book "Bowling Alone," was looking for when he sat down six years ago to examine the mass of data he had collected. He was hoping to build on his earlier work, which described a precipitous decline in the nation's "social capital," the formal and informal networks—bowling leagues, parent-teacher associations,

fraternal organizations, pick-up basketball games, youth service groups—that tie people together, shore up civic engagement and forge bonds of trust and reciprocity. Now he wanted to find out more about how social capital varied regionally and over time.

But the diversity finding was so surprising that Putnam said 7 his first thought was that maybe something was wrong with the data. He and his research team spent five years testing other explanations. Maybe people in more diverse areas had less political clout and thus fewer amenities, like playgrounds and pothole-free streets, putting them in a misanthropic mood; or maybe diversity caused "hunkering down" only in people who were older or richer or white or female. But the effect did not go away. When colleagues who heard about the results protested, "I bet you haven't thought about X"—a frequent occurrence, Putnam said—the researchers went back and looked at X.

The idea that it is diversity (the researchers used the census's 8 standard racial categories to define diversity) that drives social capital down has its critics. Among them is Steven Durlauf, an economist at the University of Wisconsin and a critic of Putnam's past work, who said he thinks some other characteristic, as yet unidentified, explains the lowered trust and social withdrawal of people living in diverse areas. But without clear evidence to the contrary, Putnam says, he has to believe the conclusion is solid.

Few would question that it is provocative. The public discourse 9 on diversity runs at a high temperature. Told by one side, the narrative of how different ethnic and racial groups come together in schools, workplaces, churches and shopping centers can sound as if it was lifted from "Sesame Street." Told by the other, it often carries the shrill tones of a recent caller to a radio talk show on immigration reform: "The school my kid goes to is 45 percent Mexican," he said, "and I don't see this as being a good thing for this country. Do we want to turn into a Latin American country?"

Putnam's argument is more nuanced. Diversity has clear 10 benefits, he says, among them economic growth and enhanced creativity—more top-flight scientists, more entrepreneurs, more artists. But difference is also disconcerting, he maintains, "and people like me, who are in favor of diversity, don't do ourselves any favors by denying that it takes time to become comfortable," Putnam says.

Why that discomfort seems to translate into social isolation 11 and a weakening of civic bonds remains anyone's guess. Studies by Wendy Berry Mendes, a social psychologist at Harvard, and her colleagues find that when research subjects play a cooperative game with someone of another race, they can show physiological signs of distress—reduced cardiac efficiency and arterial constriction, for example. On a daily basis, this alarmed reaction might make people pull inward. Putnam himself speculates that, with kaleidoscopic changes going on around them, people in diverse communities might experience a kind of system overload, shutting down "in the presence of confusing or multiple messages from the environment."

12   Still, in Putnam's view, the findings are neither cause for despair nor a brief against diversity. If this country's history is any guide, what people perceive as unfamiliar and disturbing—what they see as "other"—can and does change over time. Seemingly intractable group divisions can give way to a larger, overarching identity. When he was in high school in the 1950s, Putnam notes, he knew the religion of almost every one of the 150 students in his class. At the time, religious intermarriage was uncommon, and knowing whether a potential mate was a Methodist, a Catholic or a Jew was crucial information. Half a century later, for most Americans, the importance of religion as a mating test has dwindled to near irrelevance, "hardly more important than left- or right-handedness to romance."

13   The rising marriage rates across racial and ethnic lines in a younger generation, raised in a more diverse world, suggest the current markers of difference can also fade in salience. In some places, they already have: soldiers have more interracial friendships than civilians, Putnam's research finds, and evangelical churches in the South show high rates of racial integration. "If you're asking me if, in the long run, I'm optimistic," Putnam says, "the answer is yes."

BUILDING VOCABULARY

1. List the connotations that you associate with the word *diversity*.
2. Define the following words and phrases, all of which draw on social science concepts:
    a. racial and ethnic diversity (par. 1)
    b. anomie or social isolation (par. 3)
    c. homogenous places (par. 4)

   d. social capital (par. 6)
   e. public discourse (par. 9)
   f. civic bonds (par. 11)

THINKING CRITICALLY ABOUT THE ESSAY

Understanding the Writer's Ideas

1. According to Goode, what are the "dueling theories" of racial and ethnic diversity?
2. Goode alludes to several studies in this essay. Summarize the survey by Robert Putnam and the earlier book by him (*Bowling Alone*) and the studies by Wendy Berry Mendes.
3. What is the "nuanced" picture of diversity that emerges from the findings that Goode presents?
4. How do cities, towns, and rural areas all confirm the "unsettling picture" of diversity that Goode analyzes?
5. What does Goode conclude about diversity in the United States?

Understanding the Writer's Techniques

1. Which paragraph or paragraphs constitute Goode's introduction? Does she state her thesis or imply it? Explain.
2. Why does Goode pose a series of questions in paragraph 2? What is the effect?
3. How does Goode use comparison and contrast to organize certain paragraphs and ultimately the entire essay? Would you say that she uses the block or alternating method of comparative development, a combination, or some other strategy of comparative development? Justify your response.
4. Examine and evaluate the transitional techniques that Goode uses to move from paragraph to paragraph. Why are her topic sentences at the outset of each paragraph especially effective in unifying the essay? Cite specific examples to support your analysis.
5. What is the level of diction in this essay? Would Goode's primary audience—readers of the *New York Times Magazine*—find her style to be accessible? Justify your response.
6. How does Goode's conclusion confirm the ideas and information that she presents in the body of the essay?

> ## ✳ MIXING PATTERNS
>
> What forms of illustration (Chapter 6) and strategies for definition (Chapter 10) does Goode use, and why? How does she employ causal analysis (Chapter 8) to develop her thesis? What causes and effects does she examine?

Exploring the Writer's Ideas

1. According to Goode, one optimistic sign for diversity in the United States is "rising marriage rates across racial and ethnic lines in a younger generation." Do you have any experience of this phenomenon, either personal or by observation? Might the younger generation have a more open approach to diversity than older generations? Why or why not?

2. Do you believe that "familiarity . . . trumps diversity," or are you of the opinion that people tend to stick to their own groups and mistrust others? In other words, which "dueling theory" of diversity do you support? Or do you reject both theories in favor of a more "nuanced" approach? Explain.

3. How can you arrive at the truth of a situation or phenomenon like diversity when research studies seemingly draw contradictory conclusions? Refer to Goode's essay in responding to this question.

IDEAS FOR WRITING

Prewriting

Goode states that there are two basic ways to view diversity. (For now, ignore a possible third way that she suggests in her conclusion.) Create two lists that describe the features associated with each viewpoint.

Guided Writing

Write a comparative essay in which you examine a social problem from two different perspectives or viewpoints. For example, you might want to focus on immigration, poverty, religion and politics, homeschooling, abortion rights, or any other topic that interests you.

1. Begin by presenting and explaining the two viewpoints or "theories."
2. In your second paragraph, pose a series of questions that lead the reader deeper into the topic.
3. Conduct online research to locate studies supporting each of the viewpoints or perspectives that you present. Cite these studies. Incorporate the evidence you've uncovered into your paper. Make certain that you have sufficient illustration to support your thesis.
4. In presenting your materials, try to adhere to either the block or alternating comparative method. Maintain a balanced perspective and weight as you present the two competing perspectives.
5. Feel free to consult other chapters in this book in order to incorporate definition and analysis of causes and effects into your essay.
6. Develop a concluding paragraph in which you suggest a way of reconciling the two competing approaches to your subject.

Thinking and Writing Collaboratively

In groups of four, discuss the issue of diversity on your campus. Focus on the connection or contrast between diversity on the one hand and pluralism on the other. (First arrive at a consensus about what these two terms mean.) Assign one member of the group to take notes and another to present a summary to the class.

Writing About the Text

Write an essay analyzing the comparative organizational methods Goode uses.

More Writing Projects

1. In your journal, write about your personal response to Goode's essay—whether you liked it or not, and why.
2. Compose an extended paragraph in which you tell about diversity (or the lack of it) in your hometown.
3. Write an essay comparing and contrasting two places that you know well, focusing on the people, classes and ethnicities, environment, and other demographic details.

SUMMING UP: CHAPTER 7

1. In the essays you have read thus far in this book, you have learned much about the personal lives of many of the authors. Select two who seem very different, and write an essay in which you contrast their lives. In your essay, use only illustrations you can cite or derive from the selections; that is, don't do any research.

2. In her essay in this chapter, Rachel Carson uses a very old fictional form: the fable. Check the Glossary for a definition of *fable* and read some fables—most are very short. Then, write an essay in which you explore Carson's use of the word.

3. Write an essay called "How to Write a Comparison-Contrast Essay" in which you analyze the reading selection you think best represents the comparison-contrast form. Indicate the techniques and strategies the writer uses. Make specific references to the essay that you have chosen as a model.

4. In the manner of Rachel Carson, write your own "Fable for Tomorrow," in which you show how today's indifference to the environment will affect the future. Remember: *Silent Spring* was written in 1962, and many scholars believe that the way people abuse the environment today is even more serious than it was then.

5. Examine the essays by Dave Barry ("Punch and Judy," pp. 267–269), and Michele Ingrassia ("The Body of the Beholder," pp. 273–276). Compare and contrast the ways in which they discuss boys and girls, men and women, and white and black Americans, respectively.

6. Michele Ingrassia and Erica Goode examine issues of race and diversity. Write an essay that analyzes their approach to this topic.

7. Compare and contrast Elizabeth Wong's (pp. 143–145) and Dave Barry's ideas about the differences between men and women. Include in your comparison and contrast a consideration of the *tone* each writer takes in the essay.

✷ FROM SEEING TO WRITING

Write a comparative essay that focuses, as this cartoon suggests, on differences between cats and dogs—and the owners who prefer one species to the other. What do dog lovers like about their pets, and what do they dislike about cats? Similarly, what do cat fans find so appealing about felines, and why might they reject dogs as pets? Could both warring parties be in need of a psychiatrist? Use a humorous tone to develop these contrasts.

"'Bad dog, bad dog,' she said. 'We should have gotten a cat.'"

CHAPTER 8

Cause-and-Effect Analysis

WHAT IS CAUSE-AND-EFFECT ANALYSIS?

Cause-and-effect analysis answers the basic human question: *Why?* Why do events occur, such as hurricanes or the election of a new president? Why does one student do better in math than another? In addition, this form of analysis looks at the *expected* consequences of a chain of happenings. If we raise the minimum wage, what will the likely consequences be?

Basically, cause-and-effect analysis (also called causal analysis) looks for *causes* or conditions, and suggests or examines *results* or consequences (the effects).

Like most of the writing strategies you have been studying, causal analysis parallels a kind of thinking we do in everyday life. If you are a student who has returned to school after being away for several years, someone might ask you why you decided to come back. In answering, you would give causes: you needed a better job to support your children; you wanted to learn a new skill; your intellectual curiosity drove you back; and so on. These would be *causes*. Once you were attending school, a classmate might ask you what changes coming back to school have made in your life. You might consider the pride your children feel in your achievement, or the fact that you have less time to prepare meals, or that you sleep only four hours a night. Those are the *consequences* or results of your decision. In a few years' time, after graduation, the effects might be very different: a better job or a scholarship to graduate school might be one of the long-term results.

Thinking about causes can go beyond everyday life to help us understand social and political change: What were the causes of the American Civil War? What were the consequences for the nation? What caused the Great Depression? Why were women denied the vote until 1920? Why did so many Irish immigrants come to America around 1900, and what were the consequences for the growth of American industry?

In looking at such large questions, you will realize that there are different kinds of causes. First, there is the *immediate* cause that gives rise to a situation. This is the cause (or causes) most directly related, the one closest at hand. But as you can see from the historical questions in the previous paragraph, we also need to go beyond the immediate cause to the *ultimate* cause, the basic conditions that stimulated the more obvious or immediate ones.

For example, although we might identify the immediate cause of the 9/11 World Trade Center disaster of 2001 as the crashing of commercial airlines by suicide bombers, the ultimate causes for terrorism against the United States grew from long fomenting hatred and envy directed at our country by fanatics. To find the "real" causes, we have to think critically, to examine the situation deeply.

Often, a writer has to consider many causes and rank them in order of importance. Depending on the length of the essay, a writer may have to select from among many causes. If a small town begins to lose businesses to a large mall, the chamber of commerce may ask why businesses and customers prefer the mall to shopping in town. Convenience, parking, competitive pricing, and entertainment may be identified as causes: Since the town cannot solve all these problems at once, it may focus on one, and try to lure shoppers back downtown by building a larger municipal parking lot. The result, perhaps, will be that shoppers will return to Main Street.

One difficulty in working with causal analysis is that we cannot always prove that a cause or an effect is absolute. We can only do our best to offer as much evidence as possible to help the reader see the relation we wish to establish. Therefore, we have to support our causes and effects with specific details and evidence drawn from personal experience, from statistics, or from experts' statements in newspapers or books. A writer can interview people, for instance, and collect data from an online government Web site or visit the library to read articles on the post-traumatic stress syndrome among Iraq War veterans.

In the essays in this chapter, you will find a variety of uses for causal analysis. Stephen King analyzes why we crave horror movies. Elie Wiesel explains the reasons for his great love for his adopted country. Harry Crews explains how he has come to settle in one particular place. Finally, Steve Olson examines the unintended consequences of genetic screening for disease. As you read each piece, keep in mind the kinds of causes the writers present and the ways in which they add support to their analysis.

HOW DO WE READ CAUSAL ANALYSIS?

Reading causal analysis requires us to ask ourselves these questions:

- What are the writer's topic and the main cause? Make an outline of the causes as you read.
- Are immediate causes or ultimate causes presented? How do you know?
- Does the author show the consequences of the event? Why or why not?
- How does the author develop the analysis? Identify the writing strategies used: narrative, description, illustration, process analysis, and so on. Which is most effective in supporting the causal analysis and why?
- What is the tone of the essay?

HOW DO WE WRITE CAUSAL ANALYSIS?

Select a topic you can manage. If you try to find the causes of psychological depression, you may need to study a great deal of Freud before you can write the essay. If, on the other hand, you decide to write about causes of suicide among college freshmen, you would narrow the scope of the essay and thus control it more easily.

Write a working thesis that tells the cause and effect you are analyzing. Why is it important?

Sample thesis statement:

> Many causes lie behind Americans' return to more healthful eating habits, but the most important are fear of disease, desire to lose weight, and curiosity about new types of food.

Make a list of the major causes and under each cause, add at least one specific example to support it.

Plan whether you want to concentrate on either causes or effects, or on a balance of the two.

Be sure that you have included all the necessary links in the chain of reasoning that you began in the thesis.

Avoid oversimplification.

Include both major and minor causes and effects.

Writing the Draft

Write an introduction that presents the thesis and your statement of the significance of the thesis.

Use transitions as you move from one cause to the next.

Use narrative, description, process analysis, and other techniques to support your causes.

Conclude by reminding your reader of the importance of understanding this chain of events.

Proofread your draft carefully. Ask a classmate to read it to see if your causes seem logical.

Make corrections and prepare a final copy.

A STUDENT PARAGRAPH: CAUSE-AND-EFFECT ANALYSIS

To focus her causal analysis, the student who wrote the following paragraph concentrated on one aspect of the thesis sentence provided earlier in this chapter's introduction. Examine the way she weaves examples as her support for an analysis of Americans' changing eating habits.

Topic sentence	The arrival of ethnic restaurants and groceries in what used to be called "white-bread" neighborhoods has
Contrasting examples	transformed the eating habits of mainstream American culture—in most cases, for the better. While *chicharron de pollo* (fried chicken cracklings) and jerk pork might not be
Supporting examples, with definitions	much better for you nutritionally than what you can get at McDonald's, much of the newly arrived "exotic" food is far less fatty than typical fast-food fare. Pô (a Vietnamese noodle soup), rice and beans, hummus, *chana saag* (Indian chickpeas and spinach), and similar dishes

provide leaner, more healthful fuel for the body than a
Philly cheese steak and fries. Many people are beginning
to think they taste better, too. The positive influence of
these cuisines doesn't stop at the restaurant door, either.
Many Americans are beginning to bring the culinary
habits of other cultures into their own kitchens, imitating
their techniques (stir frying, for example), adopting their
principles (using meat as a flavoring, instead of the cen-
terpiece of the meal), and borrowing their more healthful
ingredients (yogurt instead of sour cream, olive oil instead
of butter, a wider range of fresh vegetables and spices).
In the process, the traditions of newly arrived immigrants
receive appropriate recognition, and native habits evolve
in a positive direction: the effect is not only better eating,
but a broadening of the American cultural horizon.

Transition "too"
signals shift to
related topic;
examples follow

Concluding sen-
tence establishes
main effect of
altered eating
habits

www.mhhe.com/
shortprose

To learn more about using cause-and-effect
analysis, click on
Writing > Writing Tutor:
                    Causal Analysis
Writing > Paragraph Patterns

Why We Crave Horror Movies

Stephen King

Stephen King, America's best-known writer of horror fiction, was born in 1947 in Portland, Maine. He graduated from the University of Maine at Orono. King's masterly plots and prolific output reestablished horror as a hugely popular contemporary genre. Among his widely read novels are *The Shining* (1976), which was adapted into a classic of modern horror films; *The Girl Who Loved Tom Gordon* (1999); and *Dama Key* (2008). King also writes science fiction and has published a series that features Roman Gilead, entitled *The Dark Tower*. His most recent volume in that series is *The Dark Tower VII* (2004). His short story collection *Everything's Eventual* appeared in 2002. In 2000 King became the first major author to publish his work, the story "Riding the Bullet," exclusively as an e-book. Because he is an acknowledged master of this genre, his thoughts on why people love horror movies offer an unusual insight into this question. King also gives us a unique glimpse into why he himself creates horror. This selection originally appeared in *Playboy* in January 1982.

www.mhhe.com/
shortprose

To learn more about King, click on
**More Resources > Chapter 8 >
Stephen King**

PREREADING: THINKING ABOUT THE ESSAY IN ADVANCE

Do you think that we all have a dark side to our personalities that we rarely reveal? Explain.

Words to Watch

innately (par. 4)   by essential characteristic; by birth
voyeur (par. 6)   a person who derives gratification from observing the acts of others
penchant (par. 7)   a definite liking; a strong inclination
remonstrance (par. 10)   an expression of protest
anarchistic (par. 11)   active resistance and terrorism against the state
subterranean (par. 12)   hidden; secret

1   I think that we're all mentally ill; those of us outside the asylums only hide it a little better—and maybe not all that much better, after all. We've all known people who talk to themselves, people who sometimes squinch their faces into horrible grimaces when they believe no one is watching, people who have some hysterical fear—of snakes, the dark, the tight place, the long drop . . . and, of course, those final worms and grubs that are waiting so patiently underground.

2   When we pay our four or five bucks and seat ourselves at tenth-row center in a theater showing a horror movie, we are daring the nightmare.

3   Why? Some of the reasons are simple and obvious. To show that we can, that we are not afraid, that we can ride this roller coaster. Which is not to say that a really good horror movie may not surprise a scream out of us at some point, the way we may scream when the roller coaster twists through a complete 360 or plows through a lake at the bottom of the drop. And horror movies, like roller coasters, have always been the special province of the young; by the time one turns 40 or 50, one's appetite for double twists or 360-degree loops may be considerably depleted.

4   We also go to re-establish our feelings of essential normality; the horror movie is innately conservative, even reactionary. Freda Jackson as the horrible melting woman in *Die, Monster, Die!* confirms for us that no matter how far we may be removed from the beauty of a Robert Redford or a Diana Ross, we are still light-years from true ugliness.

5   And we go to have fun.

6   Ah, but this is where the ground starts to slope away, isn't it? Because this is a very peculiar sort of fun indeed. The fun comes from seeing others menaced—sometimes killed. One critic has suggested that if pro football has become the voyeur's version of combat, then the horror film has become the modern version of the public lynching.

7   It is true that the mythic, "fairytale" horror film intends to take away the shades of gray. . . . It urges us to put away our more civilized and adult penchant for analysis and to become children again, seeing things in pure blacks and whites. It may be that horror movies provide psychic relief on this level because this invitation to lapse into simplicity, irrationality and even outright madness is extended so rarely. We are told we may allow our emotions a free rein . . . or no rein at all.

If we are all insane, then sanity becomes a matter of degree. 8
If your insanity leads you to carve up women like Jack the Ripper
or the Cleveland Torso Murderer, we clap you away in the funny
farm (but neither of those two amateur-night surgeons was ever
caught, heh-heh-heh); if, on the other hand your insanity leads you
only to talk to yourself when you're under stress or to pick your
nose on the morning bus, then you are left alone to go about your
business . . . though it is doubtful that you will ever be invited to
the best parties.

The potential lyncher is in almost all of us (excluding saints, 9
past and present; but then, most saints have been crazy in their own
ways), and every now and then, he has to be let loose to scream
and roll around in the grass. Our emotions and our fears form their
own body, and we recognize that it demands its own exercise to
maintain proper muscle tone. Certain of these emotional muscles
are accepted—even exalted—in civilized society; they are, of
course, the emotions that tend to maintain the status quo of civilization itself. Love, friendship, loyalty, kindness—these are all the
emotions that we applaud, emotions that have been immortalized
in the couplets of Hallmark cards and in the verses (I don't dare
call it poetry) of Leonard Nimoy.

When we exhibit these emotions, society showers us with 10
positive reinforcement; we learn this even before we get out of
diapers. When, as children, we hug our rotten little puke of a
sister and give her a kiss, all the aunts and uncles smile and twit
and cry, "Isn't he the sweetest little thing?" Such coveted treats
as chocolate-covered graham crackers often follow. But if we
deliberately slam the rotten little puke of a sister's fingers in the
door, sanctions follow—angry remonstrance from parents, aunts
and uncles; instead of a chocolate-covered graham cracker, a
spanking.

But anticivilization emotions don't go away, and they demand 11
periodic exercise. We have such "sick" jokes as, "What's the difference between a truckload of bowling balls and a truckload of
dead babies?" (You can't unload a truckload of bowling balls with
a pitchfork . . . a joke, by the way, that I heard originally from a
ten-year-old.) Such a joke may surprise a laugh or a grin out of
us even as we recoil, a possibility that confirms the thesis: If we
share a brotherhood of man, then we also share an insanity of man.
None of which is intended as a defense of either the sick joke or
insanity but merely as an explanation of why the best horror films,

like the best fairy tales, manage to be reactionary, anarchistic, and revolutionary all at the same time.

12   The mythic horror movie, like the sick joke, has a dirty job to do. It deliberately appeals to all that is worst in us. It is morbidity unchained, our most base instincts let free, our nastiest fantasies realized . . . and it all happens, fittingly enough, in the dark. For those reasons, good liberals often shy away from horror films. For myself, I like to see the most aggressive of them—*Dawn of the Dead,* for instance—as lifting a trap door in the civilized forebrain and throwing a basket of raw meat to the hungry alligators swimming around in that subterranean river beneath.

13   Why bother? Because it keeps them from getting out, man. It keeps them down there and me up here. It was Lennon and McCartney who said that all you need is love, and I would agree with that.

14   As long as you keep the gators fed.

BUILDING VOCABULARY

King uses descriptive language in this essay to re-create some of the scary images from horror stories, such as snakes and grubs (par. 1). Make a list of his scary words (at least five). Then find a synonym for each word and use each in a sentence.

THINKING CRITICALLY ABOUT THE ESSAY

Understanding the Writer's Ideas

1. King uses the cause-and-effect method to explore why people crave horror. He says we share an "insanity of man" (par. 11). What does he mean by *insanity*?
2. For what three reasons does the writer think we dare the nightmare?
3. What does King mean when he says the "'fairytale'" horror films "take away the shades of gray" (par. 7)?
4. How does King explain his view on anticivilization emotions?
5. King uses the image of alligators (the gator) to make a final point. How do you interpret this?

Understanding the Writer's Techniques

1. What is the thesis? Where is it? How does the essay's title reflect the writer's thesis?
2. King uses first person narration in this essay. What other rhetorical modes does he use to develop his essay?
3. In this cause-and-effect essay, what is the cause and what is the effect?
4. King says we are all insane. What tone does this create for the reader? Is he accusing? humorous? serious?
5. King uses both specific and broad generalizations to develop his thesis. Give an example of something specific and something generalized. Which better supports the thesis and why?
6. Notice how the last and concluding sentence of the essay suddenly addresses the reader ("you"). Why? What purpose does this shift to the second person serve in this essay's conclusion?

Exploring the Writer's Ideas

1. How do you feel about the writer's bold opening statement that we are all mentally ill? Does this statement make you want to stop reading? How do you feel about his assumption?
2. Do you go to horror movies or do you avoid them? Why do you or don't you go? Explain.
3. Why do you think King chose to write out his ideas rather than discuss them with a friend? In what way is the process of writing out our ideas different from the process of thinking out loud in conversation?
4. This writer claims he isn't defending anticivilization emotions (par. 11), but he tells us that we need to "scream and roll around in the grass" (par. 9). Which side is this writer on? Which side are you on? Why?
5. Is it true that in horror tales the villains are always destroyed and good always triumphs? Should this be the case? Why or why not?

IDEAS FOR WRITING

Prewriting

Make a scratch outline of your strongest feelings for or against horror stories.

Guided Writing

Write an essay in which you analyze your reactions to horror books or movies.

1. Begin the essay by stating your feelings on why you personally like or dislike horror. Use some examples to bring to life for the reader your experience with horror.
2. Describe two or more causes for the way you react to horror.
3. Analyze some of the effects you think horror movies may have on you or others who crave them.
4. Respond to the issue of horror allowing anticivilization emotions to be exercised so they don't "get out," as King says.
5. Conclude by addressing readers, telling them why they should embrace or avoid the horror genre.

Thinking and Writing Collaboratively

Working in a group of four to five students, research what experts say about the causes and effects of television violence on children. Then write an essay that makes these causes and effects clear to an audience of parents.

Writing About the Text

If King's opening statement contains little truth, his argument in effect falls apart. Write an essay that explores the validity of his opening and then analyzes the essay's argument based on your conclusions about its opening.

More Writing Projects

1. In your journal, write about something that scares you.
2. Write a paragraph that explains what causes you to fear something.
3. In an essay, examine the causes and effects of something in your life that frightens you (for example, stage fright, test anxiety, fear of flying, and so forth).

The America I Love

Elie Wiesel

In 1943, the Nazis took fifteen-year-old Elie Wiesel and his family from their home in Romania and sent them to a concentration camp. His mother, father, and sister all died, but Elie Wiesel survived to be liberated by the Americans at Buchenwald in 1945. In 1963 he became an American citizen. His first book, *Night* (1960), told the story of his experience at Buchenwald. Since that book, he has written forty others, most recently, *The Time of the Uprooted* (2005). For his work as a defender of victims of war and violence around the world, he was awarded the Nobel Peace Prize in 1986. In this essay, published on the Fourth of July in 2004, Wiesel answers critics of American foreign policy by taking the long view of America's record overseas.

www.mhhe.com/
shortprose

To learn more about Wiesel, click on
More Resources > Chapter 8 >
Elie Wiesel

PREREADING: THINKING ABOUT THE ESSAY IN ADVANCE

Do you think that the United States should police the world? Many people say that America has a responsibility to fight tyranny and oppressive regimes throughout the world, while others say that our own national security is our most important objective. What is your opinion?

Words to Watch

gratitude (par. 1)   thankfulness
privileged (par. 2)   favored, lucky
grandiloquent (par. 4)   pompous
introspection (par. 4)   self-examination, reflection
throes (par. 5)   struggles
sanctified (par. 6)   made holy
intonation (par. 6)   the way something is said
loftier (par. 10)   higher in status or better
credo (par. 10)   motto, statement of belief
expediency (par. 13)   the way that will bring fastest results

1 The day I received American citizenship was a turning point in my life. I had ceased to be stateless. Until then, unprotected by any government and unwanted by any society, the Jew in me was overcome by a feeling of pride mixed with gratitude.

2   From that day on, I felt privileged to belong to a country which, for two centuries, has stood as a living symbol of all that is charitable and decent to victims of injustice everywhere—a country in which every person is entitled to dream of happiness, peace and liberty; where those who have are taught to give back.

3   In America, compassion for the refugee and respect for the other still have biblical connotations.

4   Grandiloquent words used for public oratory? Even now, as America is in the midst of puzzling uncertainty and understandable introspection because of tragic events in Iraq, these words reflect my personal belief. For I cannot forget another day that remains alive in my memory: April 11, 1945.

5   That day I encountered the first American soldiers in the Buchenwald concentration camp. I remember them well. Bewildered, disbelieving, they walked around the place, hell on earth, where our destiny had been played out. They looked at us, just liberated, and did not know what to do or say. Survivors snatched from the dark throes of death, we were empty of all hope—too weak, too emaciated to hug them or even speak to them. Like lost children, the American soldiers wept and wept with rage and sadness. And we received their tears as if they were heartrending offerings from a wounded and generous humanity.

6   Ever since that encounter, I cannot repress my emotion before the flag and the uniform—anything that represents American heroism in battle. That is especially true on July Fourth. I reread the Declaration of Independence, a document sanctified by the passion of a nation's thirst for justice and sovereignty, forever admiring both its moral content and majestic intonation. Opposition to oppression in all its forms, defense of all human liberties, celebration of what is right in social intercourse: All this and much more is in that text, which today has special meaning.

7   Granted, U.S. history has gone through severe trials, of which anti-black racism was the most scandalous and depressing. I happened to witness it in the late fifties, as I traveled through the South. What did I feel? Shame. Yes, shame for being white. What made it worse was the realization that, at that time, racism was the law, thus making the law itself immoral and unjust.

Still, my generation was lucky to see the downfall of prejudice 8 in many of its forms. True, it took much pain and protest for that law to be changed, but it was. Today, while fanatically stubborn racists are still around, some of them vocal, racism as such has vanished from the American scene. That is true of anti-Semitism too. Jew-haters still exist here and there, but organized anti-Semitism does not—unlike in Europe, where it has been growing with disturbing speed.

As a great power, America has always seemed concerned with 9 other people's welfare, especially in Europe. Twice in the 20th century, it saved the "Old World" from dictatorship and tyranny.

America understands that a nation is great not because its 10 economy is flourishing or its army invincible but because its ideals are loftier. Hence America's desire to help those who have lost their freedom to conquer it again. America's credo might read as follows: For an individual, as for a nation, to be free is an admirable duty—but to help others become free is even more admirable.

Some skeptics may object: But what about Vietnam? And 11 Cambodia? And the support some administrations gave to corrupt regimes in Africa or the Middle East? And the occupation of Iraq? Did we go wrong—and if so, where?

And what are we to make of the despicable, abominable 12 "interrogation methods" used on Iraqi prisoners of war by a few soldiers (but even a few are too many) in Iraqi military prisons?

Well, one could say that no nation is composed of saints alone. 13 None is sheltered from mistakes or misdeeds. All have their Cain and Abel. It takes vision and courage to undergo serious soul-searching and to favor moral conscience over political expediency. And America, in extreme situations, is endowed with both. America is always ready to learn from its mishaps. Self-criticism remains its second nature.

Not surprising, some Europeans do not share such views. 14 In extreme left-wing political and intellectual circles, suspicion and distrust toward America is the order of the day. They deride America's motives for its military interventions, particularly in Iraq. They say: It's just money. As if America went to war only to please the oil-rich capitalists.

They are wrong. America went to war to liberate a population 15 too long subjected to terror and death.

We see in newspapers and magazines and on television 16 screens the mass graves and torture chambers imposed by Saddam

Hussein and his accomplices. One cannot but feel grateful to the young Americans who leave their families, some to lose their lives, in order to bring to Iraq the first rays of hope—without which no people can imagine the happiness of welcoming freedom.

17   Hope is a key word in the vocabulary of men and women like myself and so many others who discovered in America the strength to overcome cynicism and despair. Remember the legendary Pandora's box? It is filled with implacable, terrifying curses. But underneath, at the very bottom, there is hope. Now as before, now more than ever, it is waiting for us.

BUILDING VOCABULARY

1. In this essay, Wiesel uses literary and historical references that you might not know. Identify the following:
    a. Buchenwald (par. 5)
    b. Old World (par. 9)
    c. Cambodia (par. 11)
    d. Cain and Abel (par. 13)
    e. Pandora's box (par. 17)
2. For each of the following words, write a definition and use it in a sentence of your own:
    a. connotations (par. 3)
    b. bewildered (par. 5)
    c. emaciated (par. 5)
    d. scandalous (par. 7)
    e. abominable (par. 12)
    f. implacable (par. 17)

THINKING CRITICALLY ABOUT THE ESSAY

Understanding the Writer's Ideas

1. Why was getting American citizenship a "turning point" in Wiesel's life?
2. What does Wiesel mean when he writes that he was proud and grateful because of "the Jew in me"?
3. What is it about being an American that makes Wiesel proud?
4. What has caused the "puzzling uncertainty" Wiesel refers to?

5. What happened to Wiesel on April 11, 1945?

6. What was the experience of American soldiers who discovered the Nazi concentration camps in eastern Europe, according to Wiesel?

7. What was the result for Wiesel of his liberation from Buchenwald?

8. What answer does Wiesel have for those who criticize the United States' involvement in questionable wars?

9. Why does Wiesel use the image of Pandora's box at the end of the essay?

Understanding the Writer's Techniques

1. Where is the writer's thesis statement? Is it in an effective location? Explain.

2. How does the title of the essay suggest an argument?

3. Why does Wiesel begin his essay with the emotions he felt on becoming a U.S. citizen? How does this relate to the thesis?

4. What is the effect on the reader of Wiesel's description of April 11, 1945?

5. Why does Wiesel mention the Declaration of Independence? Explain his motives, in your opinion.

6. This essay appeared in *Parade* magazine, which is included with Sunday newspapers all across the country. Who is the intended audience for this essay, and how can you tell?

7. What does Wiesel say were the causes of the war in Iraq? Is his analysis of the causes effective? Explain.

8. What do you think of Wiesel's conclusion? Is it effective or not, and why?

Exploring the Writer's Ideas

1. Wiesel provides reasons why the United States should be admired as a nation. Come up with at least three that Wiesel does not mention. Explain why these are admirable traits for a country.

2. Wiesel writes that Americans "are taught to give back." What does he mean by this, and do you agree with him? Explain your answer.

3. Wiesel contrasts his patriotic feeling about the United States with those of "skeptics." What are your own feelings about the United States as a moral force in the world?
4. What is patriotism? What are its causes?
5. Excessive patriotism is called *jingoism*. What could be some negative effects of jingoism? Do you believe that Wiesel is guilty of jingoism? Why or why not?
6. Some people say that questioning the motives of the leaders of the United States is the same as hating the country. Do you think someone can love a country and still, as Wiesel says in paragraph 14, "deride America's motives for its military interventions"?

IDEAS FOR WRITING

Prewriting

Freewrite for fifteen minutes about why you love the town or city where you grew up or where you've visited. What has led to the positive feelings you have?

Guided Writing

Using cause-and-effect analysis, write an essay titled "The _____ I Love," filling in the blank with the name of the town or city where you grew up.

1. In your introduction, recall how your positive feelings began.
2. Next, explain the origins or causes of your affection.
3. Continue by tracing how those origins led to further or more complicated admiration.
4. Emphasize why you are qualified to write about the place. What about your background lends you authority?
5. Write using emotional and/or manipulative language.
6. Mention any detractors from your town. What do they say?
7. Make it clear why the detractors are wrong, why their hearts are not in the right place.
8. Write a conclusion that points to why all people should love your town or city.

Thinking and Writing Collaboratively

Working in groups of three or four, have group members read their essays out loud. Decide as a group which essay is the strongest, and then discuss the reasons why you feel this way. Present your group's findings to the rest of the class.

Writing About the Text

Write an essay that explores whether Wiesel's own experiences influence the essay excessively. Do you think his argument remains valid despite his emotional standpoint?

More Writing Projects

1. Wiesel writes that he admires "American heroism in battle" and appreciates those American soldiers who wept over the plight of the Jewish prisoners. Still, some soldiers are sent to be heroic in the name of unheroic ideals. Is it possible to separate the soldier from the commander or from his country, to admire the soldier but not what he is doing? Write a journal entry about this topic.

2. Wiesel won the Nobel Peace Prize and several other prestigious awards. Write a paragraph or two on the influence an author's credentials have on you as a reader. Do they affect you? Why or why not?

3. Do some research on a dark part of U.S. history, such as moving Native Americans to reservations, interning Japanese Americans during World War II, oppressing blacks under Jim Crow laws, fighting what some consider an unjust war in Vietnam, and so on. Write an essay in which you argue that the action was either warranted or unwarranted, taking into account the historical context.

Why I Live Where I Live

Harry Crews

Harry Crews was born to a poor farming family in Alma, Georgia, in 1935. When he was twenty-one months old, his father died. At seventeen, Crews joined the Marines; he enrolled in the University of Florida at Gainesville upon his discharge and eventually received his BA. Since 1968, when his novel *The Gospel Singer* was published, Crews has published eighteen novels, most recently *An American Family* (2006). A frequent contributor to *Playboy* and *Esquire,* where this selection first appeared, Crews has collected his nonfiction in *Blood and Grits* (1979), *Florida Frenzy* (1982), and *Madonna at Ringside* (1991). He has also published a memoir, *A Childhood: The Biography of a Place* (1978). In 1998 he published *Where Does One Go When There's No Place Left to Go,* a sequel to *The Gospel Singer,* in a limited edition. Crews writes in the Southern gothic tradition of literature, often, as in this selection, immersing his characters in a richly detailed and powerfully evocative Southern landscape.

PREREADING: THINKING ABOUT THE ESSAY IN ADVANCE

Why *do* people live where they live? Is it a matter of choice? Do certain climates, certain kinds of neighborhoods, certain styles of houses, certain views agree with certain people and not with others? Or is it something that happens by accident—because of family or where the person was brought up or happens to have a job?

Words to Watch

pall (par. 1)   to lose its attraction
indices (par. 2)   plural of *index*
circuitous (par. 4)   roundabout
skiff (par. 5)   small boat, sometimes a rowboat but also a powerboat
slough (par. 5)   creek in a marsh or swamp
precious (par. 7)   affected
pretentious (par. 7)   showy
symptomatic (par. 8)   indicative
malaise (par. 8)   moral illness

I can leave the place where I live a couple of hours before daylight 1
and be on a deserted little strip of sand called Crescent Beach in
time to throw a piece of meat on a fire and then, in a few minutes, lie back sucking on a vodka bottle and chewing on a hunk of
bloody beef while the sun lifts out of the Atlantic Ocean (somewhat
unnerving but also mystically beautiful to a man who never saw a
body of water bigger than a pond until he was grown) and while the
sun rises lie on a blanket, brain singing from vodka and a bellyful
of beef, while the beautiful bikinied children from the University of
Florida drift down the beach, their smooth bodies sweating baby oil
and the purest kind of innocent lust (which of course is the rankest
sort) into the bright air. If all that starts to pall—and what *doesn't*
start to pall?—I can leave the beach and be out on the end of a
dock, sitting in the Captain's Table eating hearts-of-palm salad and
hot boiled shrimp and sipping on a tall, icy glass of beer while the
sun I saw lift out of the Atlantic that morning sinks into the warm,
waveless Gulf of Mexico. It makes for a hell of a day. But that isn't
really why I live in the north-central Florida town of Gainesville.

　　Nor do I live in Gainesville because seven blocks from my house 2
there are two enormous libraries filled with the most courteous, helpful
people you can imagine, people who, after explaining some of the more
intricate mysteries of how the place works, including the purposes of
numerous indices, will go ahead and cheerfully find what I cannot: for
example, the car capacity of drive-in theaters in Bakersfield, California,
in 1950. A man never knows when he may need a bit of information
like that, but it isn't enough to keep him living in a little town in Florida
as opposed to, say, Ann Arbor, Michigan.

　　I love the size of Gainesville. I can walk anywhere I want 3
to go, and consequently I have very little to do with that abomi-
nation before the Lord, the car. It's a twenty-minute stroll to my
two favorite bars, Lillian's Music Store and the Winnjammer; ten
minutes to a lovely square of grass and trees called the Plaza of
the Americas; less than ten minutes to the house of a young lady
who has been hypnotizing me for six years. Some people get analyzed; I get hypnotized. It leaves me with the most astonishing and
pleasurable memories. But there must be ten thousand towns like
Gainesville in this country, and surely several hundred of them
would have good places to drink and talk and at least one house
where a young lady lived who would consent to hypnotize me into
astonishing and pleasurable memories. So I cannot lean too heavily on walking and memories to justify being where I am.

4   The reason I live where I do is more complicated than the sorts of things I've been talking about thus far—more complicated and, I expect, ultimately inexplicable. Or, said another way: anyone other than I may find that the explanation does not satisfy. To start, I live right in the middle of town on three acres of land, land thick with pines a hundred feet tall, oak, wild plum trees, and all manner of tangled, unidentifiable underbrush. The only cleared space is the very narrow road leading down to the house. No lawn. (There are many things I absolutely refuse to do in this world, but the three things leading the list are: wash my car, shine my shoes, and mow a lawn.) The back wall of the room I work in at the rear of the house is glass, and when I raise my eyes from the typewriter I look past an enormous bull bay tree through a thin stand of reeds into a tiny creek, the banks of which are thick with the greenest fern God ever made. In my imagination I can follow that little creek upstream to the place where, after a long, circuitous passage, it joins the Suwannee River, and then follow the dark waters of the Suwannee upriver to the place where it rises in the nearly impenetrable fastness of the Okefenokee Swamp. Okefenokee: Creek Indian word for Land of the Trembling Earth, because most of the islands in the swamp—some of them holding hundreds of huge trees growing so thick that their roots are matted and woven as closely as a blanket—actually float on the water, and when a black bear crashes across one of them, the whole thing trembles.

5   I saw the Okefenokee Swamp long before I saw the Suwannee River, and the Suwannee River long before I saw the little creek I'm looking at as I write this. When I was a boy, I was in the swamp a lot, on the edges of it practically all the time that I was not in the fields working. I went deep into the Okefenokee with T. J., the husband of one of my first cousins. His left leg was cut off at the knee and he wore a peg, but he got along fine with it because we were usually in a flat skiff casting nets for crawfish, which he sold for fish bait at a penny apiece. I did not know enough then and do not know enough now to go into the deep middle swamp, but T. J. did; he knew the twisting maze of sloughs like his back yard, could read every sign of every living thing in the swamp, and made a good living with the crawfish nets and his string of traps and his gun. He sold alligator, wore alligator, and ate alligator. This was long before the federal government made the place a national wildlife refuge.

6   T. J. made his living out of the swamp, and I make mine now out of how the swamp shaped me, how the rhythms and patterns of

speech in that time and place are still alive in my mouth today and, more important, alive in my ear. I feed off now and hope always to feed off the stories I heard told in the early dark around fires where coffee boiled while our clothes, still wet from stringing traps all day, slowly dried to our bodies. Even when I write stories not set in Georgia and not at all about anything in the South, that writing is of necessity still informed by my notions of the world and of what it is to be caught in it. Those notions obviously come out of South Georgia and out of everything that happened to me there, or so I believe.

Living here in North Florida, I am a little more than a hundred 7 miles from where I was born and raised to manhood. I am just far enough away from the only place that was ever mine to still see it, close enough to the only people to whom I was ever kin in ways deeper than blood to still hear them. I know that what I have just written will sound precious and pretentious to many people. So be it. Let them do their work as they will, and I'll do mine.

I've tried to work—that is, to write—in Georgia, but I could 8 not. Even under the best of circumstances, at my mama's farm, for instance, it was all too much for me. I was too deep in it, too close to it to use it, to make anything out of it. My memory doesn't even seem to work when I'm writing in Georgia. I can't seem to hold a story in my head. I write a page, and five pages later what I wrote earlier has begun to slide out of focus. If this is all symptomatic of some more profound malaise, I don't want to know about it and I certainly don't want to understand it.

Living here in Gainesville seems to give me a kind of geo- 9 graphic and emotional distance I need to write. I can't write if I get too far away. I tried to work on a novel in Tennessee once and after a ruined two months gave it up in despair. I once spent four months near Lake Placid in a beautiful house lent to me by a friend—perfect place to write—and I didn't do a damn thing but eat my guts and look out the window at the mountains.

And that, all of it, precious, pretentious, or whatever, is why 10 I live where I live. And unless something happens that I cannot control, I plan to die here.

BUILDING VOCABULARY

Central to the essay is the evocation of a certain place. One way that Crews achieves his evocative effects is through diction, that is, through his choice of words. Rewrite the sentences below, finding new words for those in italics.

   a. "... and while the sun *rises lie* on a blanket, brain *singing* from vodka and a *bellyful* of beef, while the *beautiful* bikinied *children* from the University of Florida *drift* down the beach, their *smooth* bodies *sweating* baby oil and the *purest* kind of innocent *lust* (which of course is the *rankest* sort) into the *bright* air" (par. 1).

   b. "The *back* wall of the room *I work in* at the rear of the house is glass, and when I *raise my eyes* from the typewriter I *look past an enormous* bull bay tree *through a thin stand* of reeds into a *tiny* creek, the *banks* of which are *thick with the greenest* fern *God ever made*" (par. 4).

THINKING CRITICALLY ABOUT THE ESSAY

Understanding the Writer's Ideas

1. What do we learn about the writer from his opening paragraph?
2. Why does the writer bother to write his opening paragraph only to end it by saying "that isn't really why" he lives in Gainesville?
3. What do we learn about the writer from the second and third paragraphs? Why does he write these paragraphs if they, too, fail to explain why he lives in Gainesville?
4. In what ways is his reason for living in Gainesville "more complicated" (par. 4) than "the sorts of things" he writes about in paragraphs 1, 2, and 3?
5. Why is the Okefenokee Swamp important to the writer?
6. Why doesn't the writer live in South Georgia?

Understanding the Writer's Techniques

1. How does the writer introduce the *topic* of his essay?
2. In this cause-and-effect essay, what is the cause? Where in the essay is the cause identified?
3. The writer approaches his subject obliquely rather than head-on. Why do you think he takes this approach? What does he gain, and what does he lose as a consequence of this approach?

4. The writer provides a great deal of detail to explain why he lives in Gainesville but little by way of generalizations or "abstract" reasons. His argument, in effect, is made by means of details. What do the details "say"?

5. Why does the writer describe what he sees outside his window (par. 4)?

6. Does this essay have a thesis statement? If so, where is it located in the essay? If not, how does the essay succeed without one?

7. In what ways could what the writer says be interpreted as being "precious and pretentious" (par. 7)?

8. What is the *tone* of this essay? Quote two examples to illustrate the tone.

9. Do you find the essay's conclusion effective? Why or why not? How does it connect with the tone of the rest of the essay?

Exploring the Writer's Ideas

1. The writer paints a fairly full portrait of himself. Do you like the man portrayed? Offer the details that lead you to like or dislike him, and explain why.

2. Does the writer want to be "liked" or does he want to be "understood"? Explain your answer.

3. Are Crews's reasons for living where he does "precious and pretentious"? Say why you think they are or are not.

4. The concluding sentences in paragraphs 7, 8, and 9 seem insistent or aggressive. Do you think that the writer is overdoing it, pushing away too hard at things he does not want to hear? Or is he just being in character, and explaining himself honestly? Support your answer.

IDEAS FOR WRITING

Prewriting

What sort of place would you *like* to live in? List some of the characteristics of such a place. Think about how that place compares and contrasts with the place where you live now.

Guided Writing

Write an essay titled "Why My Room Is the Way It Is."

1. Begin with an attractive or interesting detail about your room either at home or at college—but a detail that doesn't answer the question, Why is my room the way it is?
2. Continue with another feature of your room that does go some way toward answering the question—but that doesn't get to the heart of the matter.
3. Finally, get at the main reason, which should try to mimic Crews in being fairly philosophical, or tending toward the existentially revealing. ("I fear the disorder of life and therefore keep my room especially neat.")
4. Offer examples of your having tried to live in your room when it was quite different from the way it is today—and say why that didn't work.
5. End by reaffirming why your room is as it is and saying how you hope always to have a room like the one you have now.

Thinking and Writing Collaboratively

In small groups compare ideas about places people have lived in that they especially liked or disliked. Make a list of outstanding positive and negative qualities that advertisers for towns or cities could promote by claiming the town or city has—or doesn't have—them.

Writing About the Text

Write an essay with one of the following two titles: "Harry Crews: When Do I Get to Meet Him?" or "Harry Crews: A Man I Never Want to Meet." Support your perspective with evidence from the selection.

More Writing Projects

1. In your journal, write one or two real estate ads based on the collaborative project above, aimed at enticing residents to a particular town or city.

2. Choose an activity that you find especially satisfying—fishing, staying in bed till afternoon, collecting buttons—and write a paragraph or two about it as a way of drawing a portrait of yourself that highlights some of your essential qualities.

3. Read a work by Harry Crews—fiction or nonfiction—and write an essay comparing the "persona" that emerges from that work with the one found in this selection.

Who's Your Daddy?

Steve Olson

Steve Olson is a freelance writer whose work focuses on math, science, and science education. Born in 1956 in a small cattle-ranching, wheat-growing town in Washington state, Olson went east to study science at Yale University (BA, 1978), where he wrote articles for campus publications. Since then, Olson has published *Biotechnology: An Industry Comes of Age* (1986), *Shaping the Future: Biology and Human Values* (1989), and *Mapping Human History: Discovering the Past through Our Genes* (2002), which was nominated for a National Book Award. His most recent book is *Countdown: Six Kids Vie for Glory at the World's Toughest Math Competition* (2004), Olson's account of the annual International Math Olympiad, an event that he has followed for years. In the essay that follows, published in the July/August 2007 issue of the *Atlantic Monthly,* Olson explores the unintended consequences of genetic screening for disease.

Mixing Patterns

PREREADING: THINKING ABOUT THE ESSAY IN ADVANCE

How much do you know about your ancestry? If you could have a free genetic test to find out more about your family background, would you do it? Why or why not?

Words to Watch

doughty (par. 2)   brave, bold, strong
cuckold (par. 5)   a man whose wife has committed adultery
canonical (par. 6)   authoritative, accepted
inordinate (par. 8)   excessive
unadulterated (par. 9)   pure, genuine
shunning (par. 12)   avoiding, keeping away from
stringent (par. 16)   strict, severe

1   A few months ago, I sat down at my desk to open a letter that could tell me whether my father was really my father. In fact, that letter could tell me whether the men going back 10 generations on my paternal side were the biological fathers of their children.

I wasn't caught up in some bizarre multigenerational paternity 2
suit. A scientific officer at a genetic testing company knew that I
was interested in genealogy, and he had offered to run my DNA
through a sequencer. A few weeks earlier, I'd swished mouthwash
inside my cheeks, sealed the mouthwash in a tube, and mailed the
tube to the company.

My doughty Scandinavian ancestors passed the test. My DNA 3
revealed no obvious instances where the man named on a birth
certificate differed from the man who was my biological ancestor. But I was lucky. Many efforts to trace male ancestry using
DNA terminate at what geneticists delicately call a "non-paternity
event." According to Bennett Greenspan, whose company, Family
Tree DNA, sponsors projects that attempt to link different families to common ancestors, "Any project that has more than 20 or
30 people in it is likely to have an *oops* in it."

The law of unintended consequences is about to catch up with 4
the genetic-testing industry. Geneticists and physicians would like
us all to have our DNA sequenced. That way we'll know about
our genetic flaws, and this knowledge could let us take steps to
prevent future health problems. But genetic tests can also identify
the individuals from whom we got our DNA. Widespread genetic
testing could reveal many uncomfortable details about what went
on in our parents' and grandparents' bedrooms.

The problem would not loom so large if non-paternity were 5
rare. But it isn't. When geneticists do large-scale studies of populations, they sometimes can't help but learn about the paternity of
the research subjects. They rarely publish their findings, but the
numbers are common knowledge within the genetics community.
In graduate school, genetics students typically are taught that 5 to
15 percent of the men on birth certificates are not the biological
fathers of their children. In other words, as many as one of every
seven men who proudly carry their newborn children out of a hospital could be a cuckold.

Non-paternity rates appear to be substantially lower in some 6
populations. The Sorenson Molecular Genealogy Foundation,
which is based in Salt Lake City, now has a genetic and genealogical
database covering almost 100,000 volunteers, with an overrepresen-
tation of people interested in genealogy. The non-paternity rate for
a representative sample of its father-son pairs is less than 2 percent.
But other reputed non-paternity rates are higher than the canonical numbers. One unpublished study of blood groups in a town in

southeastern England indicated that 30 percent of the town's husbands could not have been the biological fathers of their children.

7   Even with a low non-paternity rate, the odds increase with each successive generation. Given an average non-paternity rate of 5 percent, the chance of such an event occurring over 10 generations exceeds 40 percent.

8   Most people can't look that far back on their family trees, but I can. Someone on the Olson side of my family once spent an inordinate amount of time tracing the family's male lineage. My relative's genealogical research indicated that my father's father's father's father's father's father's father's father's father migrated from Finland to Norway in the middle of the 17th century. If that is the case, I have a particular connection to that man.

9   Men pass most of their Y chromosomes down to their sons intact and unadulterated. I therefore have the same Y chromosome as my father, and his father, and so on. (In fact, all men living today have inherited the Y chromosome of a single man who lived about 50,000 years ago, probably in eastern Africa. But mutations have slowly changed the Y chromosome over many generations, which is why the Y chromosomes of Finns generally differ from those of Greeks. Nevertheless, over the course of 10 or even 100 generations, the changes typically are small and the heritage is clear.) The continuity of the Y chromosome is how we know that Thomas Jefferson almost certainly had children with his slave Sally Hemings: Her direct male descendants have the same Y chromosome as Jefferson's paternal uncle, who presumably had the same Y chromosome as Jefferson. (Similar tests can reveal whether sons and daughters are really descended from their mothers and grandmothers, though non-maternity is much rarer than non-paternity.)

10   My Y chromosome turned out to be as Finnish as sautéed reindeer—I almost certainly inherited it from that 17th-century Finnish émigré. But even if my Y chromosome had turned out to be suspiciously un-Finnish, I probably could have come up with a story to protect my legitimacy. I could have said that my Finnish ancestor was the descendant of a Mongolian invader, or the son of a trader from Istanbul, or even a Spanish diplomat fallen on hard times (though in fact I know that he was a peasant farmer). I could have said that one of the men in my paternal lineage was adopted after his mother and father died. The imagination is a wonderful balm for bruised expectations.

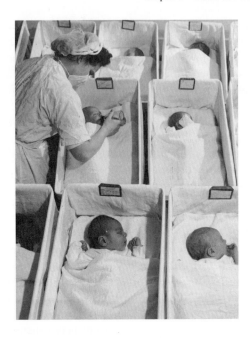

But genetic tests don't lie, which means that our imagina- 11
tions may be in for a workout. For example, groups of people in
many parts of the world trace their lineage to particularly promi-
nent male ancestors. In some cases, genetic tests reveal a kernel of
truth behind these stories. Genghis Khan's Y chromosome really is
widely distributed in Asia, for instance. Still, many of these stories
have social rather than genealogical roots. "Many times we romanticize about the different groups that we have ancestry with," says
Rick Kittles, a geneticist at the University of Chicago who founded
the company African Ancestry. When Kittles has told clients that
their genetic tests don't coincide with what they believe, a few, he
says, have been shattered.

Frankly, I hadn't thought much about these issues before sitting 12
down to open that letter from the genetic testing company. If I
had, I doubt I would have agreed to the test. If my Y chromosome
was not what I expected, would I tell other family members about
it—including my teenaged son? Would I have been tempted to
encourage my brother, then my male cousins through my father's
brothers, then my male second cousins through my grandfather's
brothers, and so on to be tested so that I could determine where

the non-paternity occurred? I think we'd all have been better off assuming the best and shunning the test.

13   But the pressure to undergo genetic testing is about to increase. New technologies are reducing the cost of sequencing DNA. Researchers are now establishing extensive databases of DNA sequences combined with health information so they can link specific genes to diseases. And once the contributions of our genes to common diseases are discovered, everyone could benefit from DNA testing. Already, the Personal Genome Project at Harvard University is seeking volunteers who are willing to have their DNA sequences and medical information posted on the Web for biomedical purposes, even though the project warns that a person's DNA could be used to "infer paternity or other features of the volunteer's genealogy."

14   Two of the men most responsible for the sequencing of the human genome—James Watson and Craig Venter—are making most of their genomes available on the Web. But if their sons ever decide to have their DNA tested, they could face the same situation I did in opening that letter. Watson has kept part of his genome private because he doesn't want his sons and the public to know whether he has a genetic variant predisposing him to Alzheimer's disease; he seems unconcerned about what the rest might reveal.

15   Genetic counselors have been struggling with the issue of non-paternity for years. When a child is born with a genetic disorder, the parents may go to a counselor to learn whether they should try to have more children. If tests reveal that the presumed father of the child is not the biological father, most counselors will tell only the mother. But a vocal minority insists that paternity should be known to all.

16   So far, the expense of these tests has limited their use to cases like the one above, where a serious genetic disorder is already apparent. But what will happen when people begin sequencing large parts of their DNA routinely, to see whether they are vulnerable to specific diseases? If you discovered a predisposition to heart attacks or prostate cancer, and medications could reduce your vulnerability, wouldn't you want to tell your siblings and cousins? And shouldn't they be tested, too? Yet in the absence of stringent and possibly unattainable privacy protections, widespread testing will lead to many unpleasant surprises.

17   Geneticists have only begun to think about how to protect people from knowing themselves too well. But they probably

should have seen this problem coming a long time ago. An oft-quoted definition of their field is: "Genetics explains why you look like your father—and if you don't, why you should."

BUILDING VOCABULARY

First write definitions for the following terms relating to the field of genetics, and then use each word in a sentence:

  a. paternal side (par. 1)
  b. DNA (par. 2)
  c. sequencer (par. 2)
  d. Y chromosomes (par. 9)
  e. mutations (par. 9)
  f. human genome (par. 14)
  g. genetic variant (par. 14)

THINKING CRITICALLY ABOUT THE ESSAY

Understanding the Writer's Ideas

  1. What do we learn about Olson from this article? What caused him to engage in genetic testing? What is the effect—in other words, what does he learn about his ancestry?
  2. Explain Olson's attitude toward genetic testing. What benefits and problems does he raise? Where does he discuss genetic testing for disease? What surprises might await someone who submits to genetic testing?
  3. What does Olson say in paragraph 9 and elsewhere about our common lineage?
  4. Why does Olson declare that "genetic tests don't lie" (par. 11)? What is his purpose in making this claim?
  5. According to Olson, will genetic testing become common-place in the future? Why or why not?

Understanding the Writer's Techniques

  1. Why does Olson pose a question in his title? How does the title capture the essence of the essay?
  2. How does Olson introduce his subject? Which paragraph or paragraphs constitute the introduction? Within the introductory section, where does Olson state his thesis?

3. Why does Olson personalize, or inject himself, into his essay? How does this personal element affect the essay's tone as well as the reader's relationship to the subject?

4. Olson divides his essay into three sections. Carefully examine each section, concentrating on the strategies for causal analysis that he relies on. What are the primary causes and effects that he discusses in each part?

5. Explain the irony that Olson employs, and cite specific examples. What are the ironic effects that Olson draws?

6. Where and why does Olson give examples based on the Sorenson Molecular Genealogy Foundation, Thomas Jefferson, Genghis Khan, and the Personal Genome Project?

7. How does Olson construct his conclusion? What is the relevance of the quotation to the thesis of the essay?

✴ MIXING PATTERNS

Analyze Olson's use of narration as a rhetorical device in the essay. How does narration aid in your understanding of the complex subject of genetic testing?

Exploring the Writer's Ideas

1. Olson writes, "Geneticists and physicians would like us all to have our DNA sequenced" (par. 4). Do you think this is a good idea? Justify your response.

2. Imagine that you do have your DNA sequenced and learn that you are not your father's child? Would you be shattered? Would the testing have been worth it?

3. Outline some of the ethical issues raised by genetic testing, and formulate your position on them.

IDEAS FOR WRITING

Prewriting

Olson writes that "widespread [genetic] testing will lead to many unpleasant surprises" (par. 16). Spend five minutes freewriting about these potentially shocking surprises.

Guided Writing

Imagine that you have had a genetic test. Write an essay in which you analyze the causes and effects associated with the procedure.

1. Begin by narrating and describing the arrival of a letter from the genetic testing service that you used.
2. Provide details about your family's background and history, especially any history of illness. Use this information to establish the reasons why you wanted to have a genetic test. The reasons should help you to formulate your thesis.
3. Provide evidence, paraphrased from Olson's essay or from your own research, confirming that "genetic tests don't lie."
4. Discuss the "unintended consequences" that you are prepared for.
5. Describe the results of the test and the effect of the procedure on you and your family.
6. Conclude the essay by telling whether you think the test was worth it.

Thinking and Writing Collaboratively

In small groups, discuss the pros and cons of genetic testing. Discuss your list with the class, comparing and contrasting each group's notes.

Writing About the Text

Write an essay in which you analyze the strategies Olson uses to create a balanced presentation of genetic testing.

More Writing Projects

1. In a journal entry, explain something you would like to know about your ancestry.
2. Compose an extended paragraph in which you explain how a medical test other than DNA sequencing would influence your life.
3. In an essay, analyze a pervasive health problem—for example, obesity, AIDS, high blood pressure, or anorexia—in terms of its causes and effects.

SUMMING UP: CHAPTER 8

1. Working in small groups, develop a questionnaire that focuses on men's and women's roles in our society. Then have each group member get at least three people outside the group to complete it. When all the questionnaires have been completed, analyze the results and present them to the class.

2. For the next week, keep a journal about something that is currently causing you to have mixed emotions. (Note: This should not be the same issue you wrote about in the Guided Writing assignment following the Stephen King essay; this should be a *current* issue.) Try to write five reasons for the emotions each day (or expand upon previous ones). At the end of the week, write an essay that analyzes how the issue is affecting your life or how you plan to deal with it in the future.

3. Some of the essays in this chapter identify inner drives that seem to function as compulsions—as things that have to be, that arise from us no matter what we would like. King writes about our anticivilizational emotions, Crews about being driven to live where he does, Wiesel about patriotism, Olson about preoccupation with our ancestry. Write an essay that analyzes these writers' responses to the compulsions they describe.

4. Compare and contrast Elie Wiesel's view of how cause-and-effect analysis works in feelings of patriotism with Brent Staples's view of how it operates in race relations ("Night Walker," pp. 221–223).

5. What do you think Elie Wiesel, a Holocaust survivor, would say to Stephen King's assertion that people need some insanity in their lives to stay sane? Write an essay about how Wiesel would respond to King's essay.

6. Do you think Wiesel's cause-and-effect analysis of why he loves America is right for all immigrants? Why or why not?

✳ FROM SEEING TO WRITING

Why has the person in this photograph been stopped by a police officer? Analyze some of the possible causal relationships, moving from the obvious (the driver was speeding) to more subtle and complex causes. Offer a complete analysis in which you consider a range of possible main and secondary causes as well as possible effects.

CHAPTER 9

Classification

WHAT IS CLASSIFICATION?

Classification is the arrangement of information into groups or categories in order to make clear the relations among members of the group. In a supermarket, the soups are together in one aisle, the frozen foods in another. In a music store, all the jazz selections are in one section while rap is in another section. You wouldn't expect to find a can of tomato soup next to the butter pecan ice cream any more than you'd look for a CD of John Coltrane's *Giant Steps* in the same section as Eminem's *Slim Shady*.

Writers need to classify because it helps them present a mass of material by means of some orderly system. Related bits of information seem clearer when presented together as parts of a group. Unlike writing narrative, for example, developing classification requires a different level of analysis and planning. The writer not only presents a single topic or event, but also places the subject into a complex network of relations. In a narrative, we can tell the story of a single event from start to finish, such as the time we saw a Van Gogh painting in an art museum. In classification, we have to think beyond the personal experience to try to place that Van Gogh painting in a wider context. Where does Van Gogh "fit" in the history of painting? Why is he different from other painters? How does his style relate to other work of the same period? In pursuing these questions, we seek not only to *record* our experience in looking at the painting but to *understand* it more fully.

Classification, then, begins by thinking about a body of material and trying to break it down into distinct parts, or categories. Called *division* (see Glossary) or *analysis,* this first task helps split an idea or object into usable components. Then, some of the parts can serve as categories into which the writer can fit individual pieces that share some common qualities.

For example, if the writer wanted to *analyze* the Van Gogh painting, she might begin with the large subject of painting. Then she could *divide,* or break the subject down, into two groups:

traditional painting
modern painting

Then, she could further *divide* the types of modern painting:

impressionist
postimpressionist
fauvist
art nouveau
cubist
art deco
abstract expressionist
op art
minimalist art

The purpose is to determine what the parts of the whole are. If we know what the components of *modern painting* are, then we can place or locate the Van Gogh painting in relation to other paintings. We would know whether it belonged in the soup aisle or the freezer section, so to speak. In this case, we would decide that it is *not* traditional painting, so that we would separate it from that group. We would place it in the modern group. Now we know which aisle it belongs in. But is it tomato or chicken soup? Now we relate it to the other modern types of painting, and place it in the postimpressionist group. Our decision is based on an analysis of the painter's use of color, his style, and the ways he differs from painters in the other groups.

Our analysis does not mean that the Van Gogh has nothing in common with traditional painting. Van Gogh, for instance, shares an interest in landscape and self-portraits with Rembrandt. But the bright, bold colors of his *Starry Night* are so dramatically different from the somber colors of the older Dutch painter's *Nightwatch* that we are inclined to emphasize their *division.* We could, for instance, set up a supermarket on the basis of what color the food labels were: all the red labels in one aisle, all the yellow labels together. But such a system would make it much harder to find what we wanted unless we were experts in package design. Similarly, our classification of painting is based on the most sensible method of division.

In this chapter, Judith Viorst classifies friends into eight groups, and she even numbers them to make it easy to follow her divisions. Jedediah Purdy explores basic types of environmentalism. Amy Rashap chronicles the changing stereotypes American magazines have used to portray ethnicity. And James T. Baker brings together a variety of writing techniques to analyze the world of education with some humor. Each writer has a different purpose for classification, but each uses the same basic system of organization.

HOW DO WE READ CLASSIFICATION?

Reading classification involves the following steps:

- Identify what the author is classifying. Find the thesis to determine what the purpose or basis of the classification is.
- Make an outline of the essay. Find the divisions and the classifications into which the author has sorted the subject.
- Determine whether the categories are clearly defined. Do they overlap?
- Be alert for stereotypes. Has the author used them in order to build the groups? If so, see if the groups are oversimplified and thus unreliable.
- Identify the intended audience. How do we know who the audience is?

HOW DO WE WRITE CLASSIFICATION?

The four essayists in this chapter should provide you with enough examples of how to classify to make your writing task easy. Classification resembles outlining. Whether the subject is personal, technical, simple, complex, or abstract, the writer can organize material into categories, and can move carefully from one category to another in developing an essay.

Select your topic and begin to separate it into categories. Try drawing a tree with branches or use a model from a biology book that shows the division of life into genus, species, phyla, and so on. Or make lists. Think about how your library classifies books. Arranging books by the color of the covers might look attractive, but it would presume that all library users already knew what a book looked like before they came to the library. Instead, libraries divide books by type. They generally begin with two large groups: fiction and nonfiction. Within these categories, they create small ones: English fiction, Mexican fiction, Australian fiction. Within nonfiction, they divide books into history, religion, geography, mathematics, and so on. In this way, a reader can find a book based on need, and not prior knowledge. Keeping the library in mind, make a list of categories for your topic.

Make an outline and arrange the groups to avoid overlap from one group to the next.

Decide on a system of classification. Don't force objects into arbitrary slots, though. Don't ignore differences that violate your categories. Try to create a legitimate system that avoids stereotyping or oversimplification; don't classify invalidly. Be sure your categories are legitimate.

Write a thesis that identifies the purpose of your system of classification. Think of the ways in which your system can broaden a reader's understanding of the subject rather than narrow it.

Sample thesis statement:

> At least three groups of immigrants reach the United States today— political refugees seeking asylum, economic refugees looking for a better life, and religious dissidents looking for freedom to practice their chosen beliefs.

Writing the Draft

Write a rough draft. Be sure that you explain the categories and give examples for each one.

For each category, use definition, description, illustration, or narrative to help the reader see the distinct nature of the division you have created. Use transitions between each category or group.

Proofread for correctness. Make a final copy.

A STUDENT PARAGRAPH: CLASSIFICATION

The student who wrote the following paragraph considered the sample thesis statement on immigration appearing earlier, and then modified it to suit her approach to the topic. Observe her various strategies for paragraph development, especially the way she subdivides the last of her categories.

Americans have mixed feelings about immigrants; they tend to judge different categories of immigrants—illegal aliens, poor immigrants, and political or religious refugees—very differently. Illegal aliens encounter the greatest degree of hostility, despite the fact that U.S. citizens often benefit from their work as maids, gardeners, and street vendors. The second category of immigrants, poor people who are here legally but who are looking to improve their standards of living, also tend to encounter some hostility from Americans. These immigrants, according to some Americans, compete for low-level jobs, go on welfare, and strain such social services as schools and hospitals. By contrast, Americans are usually more welcoming to political and religious refugees. For one thing, political refugees and religious dissidents are fewer in number, which automatically makes them less threatening. In addition, whether from Cuba, Iran, or the former Soviet Union, they are often better educated and wealthier than the illegal aliens and economic refugees, so they are perceived as less of a drain on resources. Undoubtedly, too, they receive a warmer welcome from many Americans because of the belief that their aims are "nobler" than those of illegal aliens or economic refugees, because they flee their homelands to maintain political and religious ideals, rather than simply to make more money.

Thesis statement announces classification scheme

First category with brief examples

Second category with greater detail

Transition "By contrast," introduces third category, further subdivided into two subcategories

Evidence supports position

www.mhhe.com/
shortprose

To learn more about using classification, click on
**Writing > Writing Tutor:
            Classification
Writing > Paragraph Patterns**

Friends, Good Friends—and Such Good Friends

Judith Viorst

Judith Viorst, author of eight collections of poetry and five books
of prose for adults, as well as twelve children's books, was born in
Newark, New Jersey, on February 2, 1931. She graduated from Rutgers
University with a degree in history, and went on to study at the Wash-
ington Psychoanalytical Institute. Her bestseller *Necessary Losses*
(1986) explores the profound impact of loss on our lives. In *Imperfect
Control* (1998), she writes about the struggle for control within human
relations. Viorst's children's books include the popular "Alexander"
stories, such as the classic *Alexander and the Terrible, Horrible, No
Good Very Bad Day* (1972). Among her other works are a comic novel,
Murdering Mr. Monti (1994), and, most recently, *Grown-up Marriage:
What We Know, Wish We Had Known, and Still Need to Know About
Being Married* (2003). In this essay, Viorst examines types of friends
in her life. As you read this essay, try to keep in mind the similarities
and distinctions that Viorst makes among types of friends, as well as
the principles of classification that she uses.

www.mhhe.com/
shortprose

To learn more about Viorst, click on
**More Resources > Chapter 9 >
Judith Viorst**

PREREADING: THINKING ABOUT
THE ESSAY IN ADVANCE

Take a few moments to think about the types of friends that play
various roles in your life. How many distinct varieties of friends
can you identify? Do you act differently with each type or have different expectations? How does each type of friend make you feel?

Words to Watch

nonchalant (par. 3)   showing an easy unconcern or disinterest
endodontist (par. 14)   a dentist specializing in diseases of dental
    pulp and root canals
sibling (par. 16)   brother or sister
dormant (par. 19)   as if asleep; inactive
self-revelation (par. 22)   self-discovery; self-disclosure
calibrated (par. 29)   measured; fixed; checked carefully

1 Women are friends, I once would have said, when they totally love and support and trust each other, and bare to each other the secrets of their souls, and run—no questions asked—to help each other, and tell harsh truths to each other (no, you can't wear that dress unless you lose ten pounds first) when harsh truths must be told.

2 Women are friends, I once would have said, when they share the same affection for Ingmar Bergman, plus train rides, cats, warm rain, charades, Camus, and hate with equal ardor Newark and Brussels sprouts and Lawrence Welk and camping.

3 In other words, I once would have said that a friend is a friend all the way, but now I believe that's a narrow point of view. For the friendships I have and the friendships I see are conducted at many levels of intensity, serve many different functions, meet different needs and range from those as all-the-way as the friendship of the soul sisters mentioned above to that of the most nonchalant and casual playmates.

4 Consider these varieties of friendship:

5 1. Convenience friends. These are the women with whom, if our paths weren't crossing all the time, we'd have no particular reason to be friends: a next-door neighbor, a woman in our car pool, the mother of one of our children's closest friends or maybe some mommy with whom we serve juice and cookies each week at the Glenwood Co-op Nursery.

6 Convenience friends are convenient indeed. They'll lend us their cups and silverware for a party. They'll drive our kids to soccer when we're sick. They'll take us to pick up our car when we need a lift to the garage. They'll even take our cats when we go on vacation. As we will for them.

7 But we don't, with convenience friends, ever come too close or tell too much; we maintain our public face and emotional distance. "Which means," says Elaine, "that I'll talk about being overweight but not about being depressed. Which means I'll admit being mad but not blind with rage. Which means I might say that we're pinched this month but never that I'm worried sick over money."

8 But which doesn't mean that there isn't sufficient value to be found in these friendships of mutual aid, in convenience friends.

9 2. Special-interest friends. These friendships aren't intimate, and they needn't involve kids or silverware or cats. Their value lies in some interest jointly shared. And so we may have an office friend or a yoga friend or a tennis friend or a friend from the Women's Democratic Club.

"I've got one woman friend," says Joyce, "who likes, as I do, 10
to take psychology courses. Which makes it nice for me—and nice
for her. It's fun to go with someone you know and it's fun to discuss what you've learned, driving back from the classes." And for
the most part, she says, that's all they discuss.

"I'd say that what we're doing is *doing* together, not being 11
together," Suzanne says of her Tuesday-doubles friends. "It's
mainly a tennis relationship, but we play together well. And I
guess we all need to have a couple of playmates."

I agree.   12

My playmate is a shopping friend, a woman of marvelous 13
taste, a woman who knows exactly *where* to buy *what,* and furthermore is a woman who always knows beyond a doubt what one
ought to be buying. I don't have the time to keep up with what's
new in eyeshadow, hemlines and shoes and whether the smock
look is in or finished already. But since (oh, shame!) I care a lot
about eyeshadow, hemlines and shoes, and since I don't *want to*
wear smocks if the smock look is finished, I'm very glad to have
a shopping friend.

3. Historical friends. We all have a friend who knew us 14
when . . . maybe way back in Miss Meltzer's second grade,
when our family lived in that three-room flat in Brooklyn, when
our dad was out of work for seven months, when our brother
Allie got in that fight where they had to call the police, when
our sister married the endodontist from Yonkers and when, the
morning after we lost our virginity, she was the first, the only,
friend we told.

The years have gone by and we've gone separate ways and 15
we've little in common now, but we're still an intimate part of
each other's past. And so whenever we go to Detroit we always
go to visit this friend of our girlhood. Who knows how we looked
before our teeth were straightened. Who knows how we talked
before our voice got unBrooklyned. Who knows what we ate before
we learned about artichokes. And who, by her presence, puts us in
touch with an earlier part of ourself, a part of ourself it's important
never to lose.

"What this friend means to me and what I mean to her," says 16
Grace, "is having a sister without sibling rivalry. We know the
texture of each other's lives. She remembers my grandmother's
cabbage soup. I remember the way her uncle played the piano.
There's simply no other friend who remembers those things."

17   4. Crossroads friends. Like historical friends, our crossroads friends are important for *what was*—for the friendship we shared at a crucial, now past, time of life. A time, perhaps, when we roomed in college together; or worked as eager young singles in the Big City together; or went together, as my friend Elizabeth and I did through pregnancy, birth and that scary first year of new motherhood.

18   Crossroads friends forge powerful links, links strong enough to endure with not much more contact than once-a-year letters at Christmas. And out of respect for those crossroads years, for those dramas and dreams we once shared, we will always be friends.

19   5. Cross-generational friends. Historical friends and crossroads friends seem to maintain a special kind of intimacy—dormant but always ready to be revived—and though we may rarely meet, whenever we do connect, it's personal and intense. Another kind of intimacy exists in the friendships that form across generations in what one woman calls her daughter-mother and her mother-daughter relationships.

20   Evelyn's friend is her mother's age—"but I share so much more than I ever could with my mother"—a woman she talks to of music, of books and of life. "What I get from her is the benefit of her experience. What she gets—and enjoys—from me is a youthful perspective. It's a pleasure for both of us."

21   I have in my own life a precious friend, a woman of 65 who has lived very hard, who is wise, who listens well; who has been where I am and can help me understand it; and who represents not only an ultimate ideal mother to me but also the person I'd like to be when I grow up.

22   In our daughter role we tend to do more than our share of self-revelation; in our mother role we tend to receive what's revealed. It's another kind of pleasure—playing wise mother to a questing younger person. It's another very lovely kind of friendship.

23   6. Part-of-a-couple friends. Some of the women we call our friends we never see alone—we see them as part of a couple at couples' parties. And though we share interests in many things and respect each other's views, we aren't moved to deepen the relationship. Whatever the reason, a lack of time or—and this is more likely—a lack of chemistry, our friendship remains in the context of a group. But the fact that our feeling on seeing each other is always, "I'm *so* glad she's here" and the fact that we spend half the

evening talking together says that this too, in its own way, counts as a friendship.

(Other part-of-a-couple friends are the friends that came with 24 the marriage, and some of these are friends we could live without. But sometimes, alas, she married our husband's best friend; and sometimes, alas, she *is* our husband's best friend. And so we find ourself dealing with her, somewhat against our will, in a spirit of what I'll call *reluctant* friendship.)

7. Men who are friends. I wanted to write just of women 25 friends, but the women I've talked to won't let me—they say I must mention man-woman friendships too. For these friendships can be just as close and as dear as those that we form with women. Listen to Lucy's description of one such friendship:

"We've found we have things to talk about that are different 26 from what he talks about with my husband and different from what I talk about with his wife. So sometimes we call on the phone or meet for lunch. There are similar intellectual interests—we always pass on to each other the books that we love—but there's also something tender and caring too."

In a couple of crises, Lucy says, "he offered himself, for talk- 27 ing and for helping. And when someone died in his family he wanted me there. The sexual, flirty part of our friendship is very small, but *some*—just enough to make it fun and different." She thinks—and I agree—that the sexual part, though small, is always *some*, is always there when a man and a woman are friends.

It's only in the past few years that I've made friends with 28 men, in the sense of a friendship that's *mine*, not just part of two couples. And achieving with them the ease and the trust I've found with women friends has value indeed. Under the dryer at home last week, putting on mascara and rouge, I comfortably sat and talked with a fellow named Peter. Peter, I finally decided, could handle the shock of me minus mascara under the dryer. Because we care for each other. Because we're friends.

8. There are medium friends, and pretty good friends, and very 29 good friends indeed, and these friendships are defined by their level of intimacy. And what we'll reveal at each of these levels of intimacy is calibrated with care. We might tell a medium friend, for example, that yesterday we had a fight with our husband. And we might tell a pretty good friend that this fight with our husband made us so mad that we slept on the couch. And we might tell a very good friend that the reason we got so mad in that fight that we

slept on the couch had something to do with that girl who works in his office. But it's only to our very best friends that we're willing to tell all, to tell what's going on with that girl in his office.

30   The best of friends, I still believe, totally love and support and trust each other, and bare to each other the secrets of their souls, and run—no questions asked—to help each other, and tell harsh truths to each other when they must be told.

31   But we needn't agree about everything (only 12-year-old girl friends agree about *everything*) to tolerate each other's point of view. To accept without judgment. To give and to take without ever keeping score. And to *be* there, as I am for them and as they are for me, to comfort our sorrows, to celebrate our joys.

BUILDING VOCABULARY

1. Find *antonyms* (words that mean the opposite of given words) for the following entries.
    a. harsh (par. 1)
    b. mutual (par. 8)
    c. crucial (par. 17)
    d. intimacy (par. 29)
    e. tolerate (par. 31)
2. The *derivation* of a word—how it originated and where it came from—can make you more aware of meanings. Your dictionary normally lists abbreviations (for instance, L. for Latin, Fr. for French) for word origins, and sometimes explains fully the way a word came into use. Look up the following words to determine their origins.
    a. psychology (par. 10)
    b. historical (par. 14)
    c. sibling (par. 16)
    d. Christmas (par. 18)
    e. sexual (par. 27)

THINKING CRITICALLY ABOUT THE ESSAY

Understanding the Writer's Ideas

1. In the first two paragraphs what is Viorst's definition of friendship? Does she accept this definition? Why or why not?

2. Name and describe in your own words the types of friends that Viorst mentions in her essay.
3. In what way are "convenience friends" and "special-interest friends" alike? How are "historical friends" and "crossroads friends" alike?
4. What does Viorst mean when she writes, "In our daughter role we tend to do more than our share of self-revelation; in our mother role we tend to receive what's revealed" (par. 22)?
5. How do part-of-a-couple friends who came with the marriage differ from primary part-of-a-couple friends?
6. Does Viorst think that men can be friends for women? Why or why not? What complicates such friendships?
7. For Viorst, who are the best friends?

Understanding the Writer's Techniques

1. Which paragraphs make up the introduction in this essay? How does Viorst organize these paragraphs? Where does she place her thesis sentence?
2. How does the thesis sentence reveal the principles of classification (the questions Viorst asks to produce the various categories) that the author uses in the essay?
3. Does Viorst seem to emphasize each of her categories equally? Is she effective in handling each category? Why or why not? Do you think that men belong in the article as a category? for what reasons?
4. Analyze the importance of illustration in this essay. From what sources does Viorst tend to draw her examples?
5. How do definition and comparison and contrast operate in the essay? Cite specific examples of these techniques.
6. The level of language in this essay is informal at times, reflecting patterns that are as close to conversation as to formal writing. Identify some sentences that seem to resemble informal speech. Why does Viorst try to achieve a conversational style?
7. Which main group in the essay is further broken down into categories?
8. Analyze Viorst's conclusion. How many paragraphs are involved? What strategies does she use? How does she achieve balanced sentence structure (parallelism) in her last lines?

Exploring the Writer's Ideas

1. Do you accept all of Viorst's categories of friendship? Why or why not? Which categories seem the most meaningful to you?
2. Try to think of people you know who fit into the various categories established by Viorst. Do you know people who might exist in more than one category? How do you explain this fact? What are the dangers in trying to stereotype people in terms of categories, roles, backgrounds, or functions?
3. Viorst maintains that you can define friends in terms of functions and needs (see paragraph 3 and paragraphs 29 to 31). Would you agree? Why or why not? What principle or principles do you use to classify friends? In fact, *do* you classify friends? for what reasons?

IDEAS FOR WRITING

Prewriting

Select a specific category of people—for example, teachers, friends, or family members—and freewrite for fifteen minutes about the characteristics of each type within the group.

Guided Writing

Using the classification method, write an essay on a specific group of individuals—for instance, types of friends, types of enemies, types of students, types of teachers, types of politicians, types of dates.

1. Establish your subject in the first paragraph. Also indicate to the reader the principle(s) of classification that you plan to use. (For guidelines look again at the second sentence in paragraph 3 of Viorst's essay.)
2. Start the body of the essay with a single short sentence that introduces categories, as Viorst does in paragraph 4. In the body, use numbers and category headings ("Convenience friends" . . . "Special-interest friends") to separate groups.
3. Try to achieve a balance in the presentation of information on each category. Define each type and provide appropriate examples.

4. If helpful, use comparison and contrast to indicate from time to time the similarities and differences among groups. Try to avoid too much overlapping of groups, because this is harmful to the classification process.

5. Employ the personal "I" and other conversational techniques to achieve an informal style.

6. Return to your principle(s) of classification and amplify this feature in your conclusion. If you want, make a value judgment, as Viorst does, about which type of person in your classification scheme is the most significant.

Thinking and Writing Collaboratively

Form groups of three or four, and have each group member draw a diagram showing the types of teachers they have encountered in school and college. Then, discuss the various divisions and try to develop one combined diagram. Finally, present your findings to the class.

Writing About the Text

Are you persuaded by Viorst's opening sentence in paragraph 3? If so, explain your position in an essay. If not, write an essay showing that thinking in terms of the "types" of friends Viorst enumerates may in fact undermine friendship.

More Writing Projects

1. As journal practice, classify varieties of show-business comedians, singers, talk-show hosts, star athletes, or the like.

2. In a paragraph, use division and (or) classification to explain the various roles that you must play as a friend.

3. Ask each student in your class to explain what he or she means by the term *friendship*. List all responses and then divide the list into at least three categories. Using your notes, write a classification essay reporting your findings.

Shades of Green
Jedediah Purdy

Jedediah Purdy, who was born in 1975 and homeschooled until he was fourteen at his parents' farm in West Virginia, teaches law at Duke University. He has degrees from Harvard University and Yale Law School. Purdy published his first book, *For Common Things: Irony, Trust, and Commitment in America Today* (1999), when he was just twenty-four years old. His next book was *Being America: Liberty, Commerce, and Violence in an American World* (2003). Purdy has also published articles in legal journals on ethics and international law, and contributed essays about American culture to periodicals such as the *Atlantic Monthly* and the *American Prospect,* where this essay appeared in the latter journal on June 3, 2000.

PREREADING: THINKING ABOUT THE ESSAY IN ADVANCE

How do you perceive and use *nature*? Do you consider yourself an environmentalist? Why or why not?

Words to Watch

consensus (par. 1)   general agreement
divergent (par. 2)   varying from the norm; different
pragmatic (par. 4)   practical
carnivores (par. 4)   meat-eaters
populist (par. 7)   one who supports the people
pristine (par. 7)   untouched, unspoiled
acrimony (par. 8)   bitterness or harshness of temper, speech, or manner
visceral (par. 11)   affecting or felt by the internal organs of the body

1   More than two-thirds of Americans call themselves environmentalists. Their rank includes every serious presidential candidate, a growing list of corporate executives, some of the country's most extreme radicals, and ordinary people from just about every region, class, and ethnic group. Even allowing for some hypocrisy, finding consensus so tightly overlaid on division is reason for a closer look.

In fact, there are several environmentalisms in this country, 2 and there have been for a long time. They are extensions of some of the most persistent strands of American thought and political culture. They stand for different and sometimes conflicting policy agendas, and their guiding concerns are often quite widely divergent. Recently, though, they have begun to contemplate a set of issues that promises to transform each of them—and to expand environmental politics from its traditional concern with a limited number of wild places and species to a broader commitment to the environment as the place where we all live, all the time.

The oldest and most familiar version of environmental con- 3 cern might be called romantic environmentalism. Still a guiding spirit of the Sierra Club and the soul of the Wilderness Society and many regional groups, this environmentalism arises from love of beautiful landscapes: the highest mountains, deepest canyons, and most ancient forests. As a movement, it began in the late nineteenth century when America's wealthy discovered outdoor recreation and, inspired by writers like Sierra Club founder John Muir, developed a reverence for untamed places. For these American romantics, encounters with the wild promised to restore bodies and spirits worn down by civilized life. Today's romantic environmentalists blend this ambition with a delight in whales, wolves, and distant rain forests. More than any other environmentalists, they—still disproportionately white and prosperous—feel a spiritual attachment to natural places.

Muir's environmentalism contains the idea that our true 4 selves await us in the wild. Another type, managerial environmentalism, puts the wild at our service. This approach is a direct descendant of the Progressive era's hopeful reformism, specifically of Teddy Roosevelt's forestry policies; it makes its basic task the fitting together of ecology and economy to advance human ends. Pragmatic, market oriented, but respectful of public institutions, managerial environmentalists design trading schemes for pollution permits at the Natural Resources Defense Council, head up programs at the Environmental Protection Agency (EPA) to collaborate with businesses in developing clean technologies, and envision global environmental standards advancing alongside free trade accords. In their wild-eyed moments, they imagine a high-tech economy that follows nature in producing no waste or, like *The New Republic*'s senior editor Gregg Easterbrook, genetic engineering that will turn carnivores into grass eaters and bring lion and lamb together at last. Although it began among policy makers, this managerial attitude is gaining ground in the optimistic culture of Silicon Valley and has many adherents younger than 35.

5   The environmental justice movement is another thing entirely. Only an idea a decade ago, this effort to address the relationships among race, poverty, and environmental harm has come to rapid prominence. Grassroots projects in inner cities and industrial areas around the country have drawn attention to urban air pollution, lead paint, transfer stations for municipal garbage and hazardous waste, and other environmental dangers that cluster in poor and minority neighborhoods. Eight years ago, romantic environmentalism was virtually the only movement that engaged students on college campuses; now young activists are equally likely to talk about connections between the environment and social justice or, on an international scale, the environment and human rights.

6   Environmental justice follows the tradition of social inclusion and concern for equity that had its last great triumphs during the civil rights movement and the War on Poverty. Some of its landmark moments are court cases ruling that federal projects can be challenged when they concentrate environmental harm in minority areas, which have begun to extend the principles of civil rights to environmental policy.

7   The environmental justice movement also reflects the populist streak that emerges in American politics wherever an isolated community finds itself up against big and anonymous institutions. Activists and community members tend to mistrust big business and government alike. The constituency of the environmental justice movement often perceives the gap between the prosperous and the poor, between whites and minorities, between mainstream culture and their own communities, as much more basic than the difference between the EPA and Monsanto. All outsiders are on the other side of that gap—an impression that has been reinforced where some local Sierra Club chapters have ignored community health issues and have endorsed proposals to put waste dumps in poor neighborhoods rather than in pristine valleys.

8   Environmental justice advocates have little patience for romantic environmentalism, and their culture of perpetual embattlement is worlds away from managerial optimism. When "environmentalists" of such different experiences and sensibilities address the same issue, it is no surprise that misunderstanding and acrimony

sometimes result. This tension was evident two years ago when the Sierra Club came close to endorsing strict controls on immigration to slow development and resource use in this country. The organization's justice-oriented members were outraged, as they had been over the waste-siting disputes a few years earlier. For the pure romantics, the concerns about poor communities and international equity didn't seem "environmental" at all. Meanwhile, the impassioned dispute was all rather alien to the measured rationality of the managerial environmentalists' plans for efficient resource use.

But our several environmentalisms are learning from their 9 interactions, and it is possible that the lessons will be good for them all. Romantic environmentalism has long withheld itself from cities, suburbs, and factories, sometimes following Muir in treating these as fallen places where nothing beautiful will grow. The other environmentalisms have challenged this idea by insisting that "the environment" means the space where we live and work, that the built environment of Manhattan and the industrial environment of the lower Mississippi matter as much as the ecosystem of Yellowstone.

The change brings environmental concern home to cities and 10 neighborhoods, where people live. This domesticated environmentalism is crystallized in the debates about sprawl, "smart growth," and the design of communities. It is powered by the recognition that the way we now pursue the things we seem to want—space, light, some trees, a little peace and quiet—can leave us feeling overcrowded and isolated, spending too much time in our cars, living and working in spaces that do not inspire our affection. Communities that decide to make walking or bicycling easy, develop dense housing in return for set-asides of open space, and foster neighborhoods where living, working, and shopping all happen on the same block, are addressing an environmental problem with an environmental solution. This is an environmentalism that urges not just setting aside a piece of wilderness for occasional visits but changing the way we live every day—the way we spend our money, build our homes, and move from place to place.

Attention to these domesticated environmental concerns thus 11 corrects a huge blind spot in romantic environmentalism's sometimes exclusive commitment to wilderness. It can also help to bridge a basic gap in the policy proposals of managerial environmentalism. Those proposals concentrate on technological innovation: taxing greenhouse gases, devising permit systems for pollution, and otherwise inventing better devices for living as we already do. The paradox that dogs the managers is that because their policy proposals generally cost money to ordinary people, big industry, or both, they stand little chance without a ground swell of popular support; yet they are just the thing to induce a fit of napping in the average citizen, whose visceral concern for the environment does not carry over into an interest in the tax code. Policies that foster, say, responsible logging, farming for stewardship, or sustainable grazing on public lands have more appeal when they come not as insights of microeconomic analysis and resource management but as part of a proposal that the work we do in nature is more appealing and honorable when it respects nature's requirements. Most of us care little about supply and demand curves, but a fair amount about where we live and how we work. Because it is close to the grain of everyday experience, the language of livable communities and environmentally responsible work can make environmental policy-designers more politically effective.

12   As for the environmental justice movement, it fits here as the Alabama bus boycotts fit into the 1964 Civil Rights Act. It fights against particular, sometimes quite outrageous, injustices. Its work is right and necessary but not usually connected with a broader agenda for sustaining dignified communities. Yet such an agenda needs not just constituents who are suburbanites upset by sprawl, but the people who suffer most from poor policies on toxics, land use, and transportation: the urban and rural poor. Moreover, a systematic response to the systematic problems those communities face is the only just way to end their thousands of brushfire struggles.

13   So one possible result of the present trends in environmental politics is a broader, more effective environmental movement. Such a movement might propose that we should need neither to withdraw our innermost selves to the woods nor to experience our neighborhoods as a species of oppression. It would make the human environment a complete and honored portion of environmental politics. Pursuing such goals would require romantics to bring some of their aspirations home from the wilderness, policy specialists to get their hands dirty in a political culture that does not yield to economists' graphs, and environmental justice activists to find reason to turn their populist anger to projects on common ground. None of our several environmentalisms will go away, and none should, but they are all better off with the recognition that the environment is very much a political, cultural, and human affair.

BUILDING VOCABULARY

1. Define the following terms—all relevant to Purdy's main subject—in the context of the essay:
   a. environmentalism (par. 1)
   b. policy agendas (par. 2)
   c. environmental politics (par. 2)
   d. free trade accords (par. 4)
   e. social justice (par. 5)
   f. tradition of social inclusion (par. 6)
   g. culture of perpetual embattlement (par. 8)
   h. ecosystem (par. 9)
   i. smart growth (par. 12)
2. Explain the following allusions (see Glossary) in Purdy's essay:
   a. Sierra Club (par. 3)
   b. John Muir (par. 3)
   c. Progressive era (par. 4)
   d. Teddy Roosevelt (par. 4)
   e. Silicon Valley (par. 4)
   f. War on Poverty (par. 6)
   g. Civil Rights Act (par. 12)

THINKING CRITICALLY ABOUT THE ESSAY

Understanding the Writer's Ideas

1. Explain in your own words the "several environmentalisms" that Purdy discusses in this essay.
2. Why, according to Purdy, must we be prepared to reexamine or look more closely at the environmental movement?
3. What forms of environmentalism engage students on college campuses, and why?
4. Purdy refers to the "populist streak . . . in American politics" (par. 7). What does he mean by this expression, and how does he expand the concept in the essay?
5. Why does Purdy refer not only to rural or wilderness areas but also to urban and suburban environments?
6. How do the current trends in environmentalism coincide? What advantages does Purdy see in this convergence?
7. What possible outcomes does Purdy predict for the various strands of environmentalism in the United States?

Understanding the Writer's Techniques

1. Why is "Shades of Green" an apt title for Purdy's essay?
2. Purdy's essay appeared in the *American Prospect,* a liberal magazine. Explain how you think Purdy tailors his content to his primary audience. How does Purdy's attention to his audience influence the tone that he adopts?
3. Where does Purdy's thesis statement appear? Why does he place his thesis where he does?
4. List the main categories in Purdy's essay. How does he introduce each category? What topics does he develop? Does he maintain a balance in his treatment of each category? Why or why not?
5. Where does Purdy use comparison and contrast as a rhetorical strategy? What is his purpose?
6. Purdy introduces "domesticated environmentalism" in paragraph 10. Does he set this unit up as a separate category, or do you think he violates the basic principles of division-and-classification? Justify your answer.
7. How does Purdy develop his conclusion? Do you find his conclusion optimistic or pessimistic? Explain.

Exploring the Writer's Ideas

1. Purdy grew up in rural West Virginia, where his parents were active in the "back-to-the-land" movement. How do you think Purdy's childhood tempers his approach to environmentalism as he presents it in this essay?
2. What are the values that Purdy associates with each of his several environmentalisms? Where do these values coincide, and where do they conflict? Do you think that these environmentalisms can be fully reconciled? Why or why not?
3. Does Purdy ever express a preference for one type of environmentalism over all other forms? Justify your response.

IDEAS FOR WRITING

Prewriting

Freewrite for fifteen minutes about the kinds of experiences you had with nature when you were growing up. How did these experiences influence your understanding of the natural world today?

Guided Writing

Write a classification-and-division essay entitled "Shades of _____." If you wish, you may compose your own paper on an environmental issue, but feel free to select other topics such as "shades of politics," "shades of men" or "women," "shades of pizza" or another favorite food that lends itself to classification, and so forth.

1. Begin by writing a paragraph providing an overview of the subject and the types or "shades" of meaning that you plan to develop.
2. State your thesis at the start of the second paragraph. Establish three or four categories, and clearly explain the principle of classification governing them.
3. Present each of your categories sequentially, offering equal amounts of information for each unit.
4. If you want, use comparison and contrast to distinguish between and among categories.
5. Conclude by offering an optimistic or pessimistic assessment of your subject.

Thinking and Writing Collaboratively

Go online with one or two other class members and find out more about John Muir. Then write a brief collaborative biography of Muir and present it to your instructor for evaluation.

Writing Critically About the Text

Write an analysis of Purdy's use of classification-and-division to organize his essay. Explain the benefits Purdy derives from his use of this rhetorical strategy, and evaluate his relative success in conveying information to his audience.

More Writing Projects

1. In your journal, write about the one form of environmentalism that most appeals to you.
2. Compose an extended paragraph describing the state of the environment in your hometown.
3. Use your extended paragraph as the foundation for an essay on what your town or city could do to improve its environment.

The American Dream for Sale: Ethnic Images in Magazines

Amy Rashap

Amy Rashap (b. 1955) holds a PhD from the University of Pennsylvania in cultural studies, and she has written about American popular culture, focusing on food, dieting, and images of the body in American society. Rashap currently teaches conversational English at the Center for American Education in Singapore. This selection appeared in the catalog published in conjunction with an exhibition mounted in 1984 at the Balch Institute for Ethnic Studies, a museum and research library in Philadelphia. Rashap classifies evolving ethnic images in U.S. popular magazines, noting how they have reflected the views and the assumed biases of readers and the society at large over the last century.

PREREADING: THINKING ABOUT THE ESSAY IN ADVANCE

One version of the American Dream conjures up the picture of boatfuls of immigrants floating by the Statue of Liberty onto the shores of the land of opportunity. How does the essay's title make use of this notion of America? What does the title imply about the role of advertising in relation to traditional notions of the American Dream?

Words to Watch

dictum (par. 1)   an authoritative saying
plethora (par. 2)   overabundance
subservience (par. 5)   submissiveness
protagonists (par. 9)   the main characters in a story
nominally (par. 9)   in name only but not in fact
superficial (par. 10)   shallow
impetus (par. 12)   incentive, stimulus
indigenous (par. 13)   from a particular region, ethnic

1   "Promise—large promise—is the soul of advertising," wrote Dr. Samuel Johnson in the eighteenth century. His dictum has remained remarkably accurate during the last two hundred and fifty years. Advertisements tell the viewer much more than the

merits of a particular product. From the glossy and colorful pages of magazines, catalogues, and newspaper supplements the reader can extract images of how to live the perfect American life. This exhibit shows how the depiction of ethnic groups has changed radically in the advertisements of nationally distributed magazines over the last century. The pictures tell a complex tale of economic power and mobility; of conflicting attitudes towards one's ethnic heritage and towards Anglo-American culture.

The development of modern advertising, with its sophisti- 2 cated use of imagery and catchy phrases, grew hand-in-hand with the advent of the affordable monthly and weekly magazines. By the 1880's factories were churning out a plethora of ready-made goods, and the expanded system of railways and roads linked producer and consumer into a national network. During this period magazine production rose apace. Due to a variety of factors, ranging from improved typesetting techniques and low postal rates to the utilization of increasingly sophisticated photoengraving processes, publishers began to produce low-priced, profusely illustrated magazines fashioned to appeal to a national audience. The contents of the magazines, such as *Collier's, The Saturday Evening Post* and *The Ladies Home Journal*, covered a wide variety of topics: from homemaking to current events, new inventions to briskly paced fiction. By 1905 twenty general monthlies, each with a circulation of over 100,000, were in existence. Ranging in price from 10 to 15¢, easily within the budget of tens of thousands of Americans, they were an ideal vehicle for carrying the manufacturer's messages to a national audience.

What were the implications of advertising for the masses? As 3 advertisers targeted their products towards a mass audience, the need arose to create an "average person," a type who embodied the qualities and attitudes of many others. Advertisers devised images that tapped into deeply held beliefs and myths of an "all-American" lifestyle—one that didn't just sell a product, but a way of life that people could buy.

The very nature of the advertising medium itself necessitates 4 the use of symbols and character types that could be understood at a glance. If the advertisement was to be effective, its message had to be quickly absorbed and understood. Thus, in their depiction of ethnic groups, advertisers often used commonly held stereotypes. Within these stock images, however, one can observe various levels of complexity.

5   When the N.H.M. Hotels ad in figure 1 appeared in 1936, the
nation was still in the midst of the Great Depression. The black
railroad porter, with his knowledge of the rails and reputation for
prompt and courteous service, was an effective spokesman for
a hotel chain dependent for its livelihood upon Americans getting back on the move. The portrayal of the porter is interesting
in this ad, for, beyond the obvious fact that the only blacks present are in service roles, the spokesman's subservience is visually
reinforced by his deferential smile, slight stoop, and bent knees.
As porters, blacks could assist in the resurgence of the American
economy, but not fully participate in its benefits.

6   An advertisement for the Milwaukee Railroad from a 1945
National Geographic (figure 2) reveals another way in which
ethnic groups are shown as outsiders—at the service of American culture while not actively participating in it. Here is the Noble
Savage, not as the representative of any particular group of Native
Americans, but as the symbol for the railroad itself, barely visible in
the advertisement. In both the visuals and the copy the sale is made
through stock images and associations. He is as familiar as a dime
store Indian; a reassuring and time-honored part of the American
landscape. However, while the Indian shown here still brandishes

Figure 1

Magazine advertisement,
1936

his bow and arrow, he has been tamed. He gazes mutely over the
changed landscape, another symbol of technological domination.

In a 1949 ad in *American Home*, Chiquita Banana entices us   7
to buy her goods. Wearing a traditional ruffled skirt and fruit-laden
hat, she embodies the stereotypical, fun-loving, gay Hispanic
woman. While she occasionally doffs the more demure chef's
hat, her smile and pert manner never waver. Her basic message is
one of festivity, tempered with the American housewife's concern
for nutrition: while bananas are good for you, they can be fun,
too! They make mealtimes a party. In the later television ads of
the 1960s, Chiquita Banana was transformed into a more overtly
sexual figure doing the rumba. Singing her famous "I'm Chiquita
Banana . . ." song in a Spanish accent, the advertisement's emphasis was more on festivity than wholesomeness.

The use of simple external attributes to symbolize ethnic iden-   8
tification has long been a favorite technique of advertisers. In a
Royal Crown Cola advertisement of 1938 (figure 3), the reader was

Figure 2

National Geographic
advertisement, July 1945

urged to be like the thrifty "Scotchman" and buy the economical refreshment. Presenting its Scotsman with a broad grin and conspiratorial, chummy wink, the ad pokes gentle fun at the Scottish reputation for miserliness. Whether the character in Scottish garb is Scottish or not is incidental, for the white American can easily put on this ethnic persona without compromising or jeopardizing his identity. The Scottish stereotype can be invoked by using a few external character traits; the image does not extend beyond that initial statement. The black stereotype represented in the N.H.M. Hotel ad, however, reflects more deeply-held attitudes toward cultural differences. Compare the closeness of the two men in the RC Cola ad with the black porter and the white traveler in figure 1. Even the spacing between the characters in both ads is significant: while the men in the RC Cola ad display an easy intimacy, the black porter stands deferentially apart from the white traveler.

9   Advertisements were not the only medium that reflected the subservient role certain ethnic groups occupied within mainstream

Figure 3

Good Housekeeping
advertisement, 1938

American culture. Magazine fiction too depicted a world in which white, Anglo-Americans were getting most of the world's material goods and occupying the more powerful roles in most human relationships. In story after story the heroes and heroines were of northern European stock, and in many cases when the protagonists were nominally foreign, their visual portrayal and characterization would belie the differences. This tendency is illustrated in a 1913 cover of the *Sunday Magazine of the Philadelphia Press,* which shows a pretty young Serbian dancer smiling languidly out at the viewer (figure 4). In her colorful native costume and dance pose, she plays her role of "old country" ethnic. But while her dress presents an image of quaint and wholesome rusticity, her features bear a reassuringly western European stamp. She satisfied an American need for foreign experience and armchair travel without really challenging any assumptions about significant cultural variation.

Figure 4
Magazine cover, November 9, 1913

10   Until the advent of the civil rights movement of the 1950's and 60's, American businessmen and advertisers assumed, on the whole, that the best way to sell their products was to address their advertisements to the white Anglo-American. Hence magazine stories and ads were geared towards appealing to this constituency through the use of images and symbols that were familiar and appealing to them. In recent years, however, though advertisers have become increasingly concerned with the purchasing power of the different ethnic groups, the images they use continue to reassure the consumer that the group's "foreignness" is carefully controlled. Their cultural identity is often reduced to a few superficial symbols.

11   A Sprite ad (figure 5) reveals a group of smiling Americans of all different lineages brandishing their favorite brand of soda. Yet while different ethnic groups are shown, they are all of the wholesome "all-American" type. The advertisement's point is that the "you"—the American youth, who chose Sprite, now includes Asians, Hispanics and blacks.

12   Advertisements that have appeared in nationally distributed magazines targeted at specific ethnic groups also need mentioning.

Figure 5

Newsweek
advertisement, 1983

Figure 6

Ebony *advertisement,*
January 1955

Until the Civil Rights movement gave many groups the impetus to speak out in their own voices, many of the advertisements in such magazines showed them displaying all the accoutrements and mannerisms of white, middle-class Americans. Thus the Ballantine Beer ad (figure 6) in a 1955 issue of *Ebony* portrays a group of thoroughly Anglicized and fair-complexioned black people. In black society light skin often gave a person enhanced prestige and eased acceptance into white American culture.

Today agencies have been formed to deal exclusively with 13 advertisements targeted towards specific minority groups. Many of these more recent ads reveal the complex negotiations involved in attempting to reconcile indigenous cultural needs with societal acceptance: a crucial issue facing many ethnic Americans today.

BUILDING VOCABULARY

1. Advertisers necessarily work with commonly held views, powerful social myths, and broad social categories. Explain the meaning of and the common associations implied by these terms:

a. mobility (par. 1)
b. homemaking (par. 2)
c. stock images (par. 4)
d. dime store Indian (par. 6)
e. "all-American" (par. 11)

THINKING CRITICALLY ABOUT THE ESSAY

Understanding the Writer's Ideas

1. According to Rashap, what can we learn from advertisements besides information on particular products?
2. What main features of ethnic life in America do magazine ads of the last century display?
3. What factors accounted for the growth of modern advertising?
4. How did the availability of a mass audience affect the nature of magazine advertisements in general? Of advertisements that depicted members of ethnic groups?
5. How do the ads the writer has selected as illustrative examples distinguish between white Americans and others?
6. In addition to advertisements, what else "reflected the subservient role" of certain ethnic groups?
7. How did the civil rights movement affect the nature of magazine advertising?
8. How do contemporary magazine ads reflect changes in American culture?

Understanding the Writer's Techniques

1. What is Rashap's thesis, and where does she state it?
2. Why does the writer provide a short history of advertising before showing the changing nature of images of ethnic groups in magazine ads?
3. Rashap notes that ethnic images in advertisements are often stereotypes, but there are "various levels of complexity" within the stereotypes. What types, or categories, of stereotypes does the author present? Which examples in each category do you find most convincing?

4. How does the writer organize her material to show "how the depiction of ethnic groups has changed"? How do her transitions help to move her essay forward in an orderly fashion?

5. The images of ethnic groups Rashap discusses are visual images. Do you think the essay would have been as effective without the illustrations, the reproductions of actual ads? If yes, why do you think the illustrations are unnecessary? If no, what do you think the illustrations add to the essay?

6. What would Rashap have had to do differently to write about images in literature? Provide some illustrative examples to support your point.

7. How does the conclusion draw the essay to an appropriate close?

Exploring the Writer's Ideas

1. Do you agree that advertising sells not just a product but a way of life (par. 3)? Support your answer with a few illustrative examples drawn from today's advertisements.

2. Could advertising, aimed naturally at large audiences, avoid stereotypes? Are the stereotypes used in advertising always "bad"—that is, somehow a distortion of the complex truth about the person or persons being depicted? Again, support your answer with illustrative examples.

3. Do you find the writer's interpretation of the ads she discusses to be fair? Look at the ads and the descriptions. On which points, if any, do you disagree? How, if at all, would your descriptions of the ads differ?

4. The essay's title implies that advertising has turned something noble—the American dream—into something for sale. Has the essay persuaded you that the advertising discussed does in fact turn something noble into a product? Why or why not?

IDEAS FOR WRITING

Prewriting

Look through a few magazines that you usually read—this time for the ads. Jot down a few of the most obvious ways in which these ads use stereotypes—ethnic or otherwise.

Guided Writing

Write an essay titled "The Image of _____ in Popular Magazine Advertising."

1. Begin with a clear statement about what you are going to classify—the image of women athletes, children, or home-makers, for example.
2. Classify the ads you have studied into at least three categories, illustrating the way magazines draw on current social stereotypes to sell their products.
3. Choose one especially useful advertisement to illustrate each of the three categories. In each case, examine the stereotype in some detail.
4. Write a paragraph that reflects on the contemporary image that you are presenting as it may differ from images ads portrayed in the past.
5. Consider whether these differences reflect a significant social shift (for example, greater equality for women) or simply a superficial change masking a persistence of an old stereotype.
6. Draw an appropriate conclusion, restating the main points of step 2.

Thinking and Writing Collaboratively

Work in small groups of four or five. Choose a well-known magazine (preferably one that none of the other groups is working on), and look through several issues, scrutinizing the advertising representations of ethnic groups. After discussing the ads as a group, report to the class on your findings, using sample ads to support your conclusions.

Writing About the Text

The writer presents several advertisements as illustrative of her theme. Do you find her analysis, ad by ad, to be impartial and persuasive? In an essay, say why. If you do not, offer a different reading of the ads. In a second part of the essay, look at the ads from a different perspective, the perspective of the advertiser. Which of these ads do you find to be especially effective? Which do you find to be least effective? What features of these ads make them effective or ineffective?

More Writing Projects

1. Choose one or two of your favorite ads—in print, on billboards, on television—and explain in your journal what you especially like about these ads.

2. Write two or three paragraphs examining one of your favorite advertisements that you feel effectively avoids stereotyping. Tell why you like the ad, and analyze what makes it work well—both text and visual elements—and how it avoids stereotyping.

3. Interview an executive at an advertising company in your community. Question the executive about the things she or he looks for in creating an ad to make it most effective. Write up your interview in an article of around 1,000 words.

✶How Do We Find the Student in a World of Academic Gymnasts and Worker Ants?

James T. Baker

James T. Baker is general editor of the Creators of the American Mind series, published by Wadsworth. He has contributed several books to the series, including volumes on Nat Turner, Eleanor Roosevelt, and Abraham Lincoln. Baker received his PhD in 1968 from Florida State University and is currently University Distinguished Professor at Western Kentucky University. In this witty selection from the *Chronicle of Higher Education,* Baker classifies student types that you may well recognize as you look around your classrooms, school cafeteria, lecture halls, or gymnasium. The writer enhances his unique categories by using description, definition, and colloquial language, which help make his deliberate stereotypes come alive.

PREREADING: THINKING ABOUT THE ESSAY IN ADVANCE

Before reading this essay, think about the different types of students you have encountered and the forms of behavior distinguishing one from the other. Does each type behave in a predictable way? Which category would you place yourself in? Which types do you prefer or associate with, and why?

Words to Watch

musings (par. 3)   dreamy, abstract thoughts

sabbatical (par. 3)   a paid leave from a job earned after a certain period of time

malaise (par. 3)   uneasiness; feelings of restlessness

impaired (par. 3)   made less effective

clones (par. 4)   exact biological replicas, asexually produced

recuperate (par. 5)   to undergo recovery from an illness

esoteric (par. 7)   understood by a limited group with special knowledge

primeval (par. 7)   primitive; relating to the earliest ages

mundane (par. 8)   ordinary
jaded (par. 20)   exhausted; bored by something from overexposure to it

Anatole France once wrote that "the whole art of teaching is only 1 the art of awakening the natural curiosity of young minds." I fully agree, except I have to wonder if, by using the word "only," he thought that the art of awakening such natural curiosity was an easy job. For me, it never has been—sometimes exciting, always challenging, but definitely not easy.

Robert M. Hutchins used to say that a good education pre- 2 pares students to go on educating themselves throughout their lives. A fine definition, to be sure, but it has at times made me doubt that my own students, who seem only too eager to graduate so they can lay down their books forever, are receiving a good education.

But then maybe these are merely the pessimistic musings of 3 someone suffering from battle fatigue. I have almost qualified for my second sabbatical leave, and I am scratching a severe case of the seven-year itch. About the only power my malaise has not impaired is my eye for spotting certain "types" of students. In fact, as the rest of me declines, my eye seems to grow more acute.

Has anyone else noticed that the very same students people 4 college classrooms year after year? Has anyone else found the same bodies, faces, personalities returning semester after semester? Forgive me for violating my students' individual "personhoods," but reality makes it so tempting to see them as types. Doubtless you will recognize at least some of them. They have twins, or perhaps clones, on your campus, too.

There is the eternal Good Time Charlie (or Charlene), who 5 makes every party on and off the campus, who by November of his freshman year has worked his face into a case of terminal acne, who misses every set of examinations because of "mono," who finally burns himself out physically and mentally by the age of 19 and drops out to go home and recuperate, and who returns at 20 after a long talk with Dad to major in accounting.

There is the Young General Patton, the one who comes to col- 6 lege on an R.O.T.C. scholarship and for a year twirls his rifle at basketball games while loudly sniffing out pinko professors, who at midpoint takes a sudden but predictable, radical swing from far right to far left, who grows a beard and moves in with a girl who refuses to shave her legs, who then makes the just as predictable, radical swing back to the right and ends up preaching fundamentalist sermons on the steps of the student union while the Good Time Charlies and Charlenes jeer.

7   There is the Egghead, the campus intellectual who shakes up his fellow students—and even a professor or two—with references to esoteric formulas and obscure Bulgarian poets, who is recognized by friend and foe alike as a promising young academic, someday to be a professional scholar, who disappears every summer for six weeks ostensibly to search for primeval human remains in Colorado caves, and who at 37 is shot dead by Arab terrorists while on a mission for the C.I.A.

8   There is the Performer—the music or theater major, the rock or folk singer—who spends all of his or her time working up an act, who gives barely a nod to mundane subjects like history, sociology, or physics, who dreams only of the day he or she will be on stage full time, praised by critics, cheered by audiences, who ends up either pregnant or responsible for a pregnancy and at 30 is either an insurance salesman or a housewife with a very lush garden.

9   There is the Jock, of course—the every-afternoon intramural champ, smelling of liniment and Brut, with bulging calves and a blue-eyed twinkle, the subject of untold numbers of female fantasies, the walking personification of he-manism—who upon graduation is granted managerial rank by a California bank because of his golden tan and low golf score, who is seen five years later buying the drinks at a San Francisco gay bar.

10   There is the Academic Gymnast—the guy or gal who sees college as an obstacle course, as so many stumbling blocks in the way of a great career or a perfect marriage—who strains every moment to finish and be done with "this place" forever, who toward the end of the junior year begins to slow down, to grow quieter and less eager to leave, who attends summer school, but never quite finishes those last six hours, who never leaves "this place," and who at 40 is still working at the campus laundry, still here, still a student.

11   There is the Medal Hound, the student who comes to college not to learn or expand any intellectual horizons but simply to win honors—medals, cups, plates, ribbons, scrolls—who is here because this is the best place to win the most the fastest, who plasticizes and mounts on his wall every certificate of excellence he wins, who at 39 will be a colonel in the U.S. Army and at

55 Secretary of something or other in a conservative Administration in Washington.

There is the Worker Ant, the student (loosely rendered) who 12
takes 21 hours a semester and works 49 hours a week at the local
car wash, who sleeps only on Sundays and during classes, who
will somehow graduate on time and be the owner of his own
vending-machine company at 30 and be dead of a heart attack at
40, and who will be remembered for the words chiseled on his
tombstone:

All This Was Accomplished Without Ever Having So Much 13
As Darkened The Door Of A Library

There is the Lost Soul, the sad kid who is in college only 14
because teachers, parents, and society at large said so, who hasn't
a career in mind or a dream to follow, who hasn't a clue, who
heads home every Friday afternoon to spend the weekend cruising
the local Dairee-Freeze, who at 50 will have done all his teachers,
parents, and society said to do, still without a career in mind or a
dream to follow or a clue.

There is also the Saved Soul—the young woman who has 15
received, through the ministry of one Gospel freak or another, a
Holy Calling to save the world, or at least some special part of
it—who majors in Russian studies so that she can be caught smuggling
Bibles into the Soviet Union and be sent to Siberia where
she can preach to souls imprisoned by the Agents of Satan in the
Gulag Archipelago.

Then, finally, there is the Happy Child, who comes to college 16
to find a husband or wife—and finds one—and there is the Determined
Child, who comes to get a degree—and gets one.

Enough said.   17

All of which, I suppose, should make me throw up my hands 18
in despair and say that education, like youth and love, is wasted on
the young. Not quite.

For there does come along, on occasion, that one of a hundred 19
or so who is maybe at first a bit lost, certainly puzzled; who may
well start out a Good Timer, an Egghead, a Performer, a Jock, a
Medal Hound, a Gymnast, a Worker Ant; who may indeed have
trouble settling on a major, who will be distressed by what sometimes
passes for education, who might even be a temporary dropout;
but who has a vital capacity for growth and is able to fall in
love with learning, who acquires a taste for intellectual pleasure,
who becomes in the finest sense of the word a Student.

20   This is the one who keeps the most jaded of us going back to class after class, and he or she must be oh-so-carefully cultivated. He or she must be artfully awakened, given the tools needed to continue learning for a lifetime, and let grow at whatever pace and in whatever direction nature dictates.

21   For I try always to remember that this student is me, my continuing self, my immortality. This person is my only hope that my own search for Truth will continue after me, on and on, forever.

BUILDING VOCABULARY

1. Explain these *colloquialisms* (see Glossary) in Baker's essay.
   a. someone suffering from battle fatigue (par. 3)
   b. I am scratching a severe case of the seven-year itch (par. 3)
   c. worked his face into a case of terminal acne (par. 5)
   d. burns himself out physically and mentally (par. 5)
   e. loudly sniffing out pinko professors (par. 6)
   f. working up an act (par. 8)
   g. gives barely a nod (par. 8)
   h. the walking personification of he-manism (par. 9)
   i. to spend the weekend cruising the local Dairee-Freeze (par. 14)
   j. he or she must be oh-so-carefully cultivated (par. 20)
2. Identify these references.
   a. R.O.T.C. (par. 6)
   b. C.I.A. (par. 7)
   c. Brut (par. 9)
   d. Dairee-Freeze (par. 14)
   e. Gospel freak (par. 15)
   f. Agents of Satan (par. 15)
   g. Gulag Archipelago (par. 15)

THINKING CRITICALLY ABOUT THE ESSAY

Understanding the Writer's Ideas

1. In common language, describe the various categories of college students that Baker names.

2. Who is Anatole France? What process is described in the quotation from him? Why does Baker cite it at the beginning of the essay? What is his attitude toward France's idea?

3. For how long has Baker been teaching? What is his attitude toward his work?

4. About what age do you think Baker is? Why? Explain the meaning of the sentence: "In fact, as the rest of me declines, my eye seems to grow more acute" (par. 3).

5. Choose three of Baker's categories and paraphrase each description and meaning in a serious way.

6. What does Baker feel, overall, is the contemporary college student's attitude toward studying and receiving an education? How does it differ from Baker's own attitude toward these things?

7. Although Baker's classification may seem a bit pessimistic, he refuses to "throw up . . . [his] hands in despair" (par. 18). Why?

8. Describe the characteristics that are embodied in the category of *Student*. To whom does Baker compare the "true" Student? Why?

Understanding the Writer's Techniques

1. What is Baker's thesis? Does he state it directly or not? What, in your own words, is his purpose?

2. In this essay Baker deliberately creates, rather than avoids, stereotypes. He does so to establish exaggerated representatives of types. Why?

    For paragraphs 5 to 16, prepare a paragraph-by-paragraph outline of the main groups of students classified. For each, include the following information:

    a. type represented by the stereotype
    b. motivation of type for being a student
    c. main activity as a student
    d. condition in which the type ends up

3. This article appeared in the *Chronicle of Higher Education*, a weekly newspaper for college and university teachers and administrators. How do you think this audience influenced Baker's analysis of types of students? his tone and language? How do you think his audience reacted to this essay?

4. What is Baker's tone in the essay? Give specific examples. In general, how would you characterize his attitude toward the contemporary college student? Why? Does his attitude or tone undergo any shifts in the essay? Explain.

5. Why does Baker use the term "personhoods" in paragraph 4? What attitude, about what subject, does he convey in his use of that word?

6. Why does the author capitalize the names he gives to the various categories of students? Why does he capitalize the word *Truth* in the last sentence?

7. What is the purpose of the one-sentence paragraph 13? Why does Baker set it aside from paragraph 12, since it is a logical conclusion to that paragraph? Why does he use a two-word sentence as the complete paragraph 17? In what ways do these words signal the beginning of the essay's conclusion?

✳ MIXING PATTERNS

How does Baker use description to enhance his analysis in this essay? Which descriptive details do you find most convincing? What purpose does description serve?

What is the role of *process analysis*? (Process analysis, discussed in Chapter 5, is telling how something is done or proceeds; see pages 179–182). Look especially at Baker's descriptions of each type of student. How does process analysis figure into the title of the essay?

Exploring the Writer's Ideas

1. Do you think Baker's classifications in this essay are fair? Are they representative of the whole spectrum of students? How closely do they mirror the student population at your school? The article was written in 1982: How well have Baker's classifications held up to the present conditions?

2. Into which category (or categories) would you place yourself? Why?

3. Based on your reaction to and understanding of this article, would you like to have Baker as your professor? Why or why not?

IDEAS FOR WRITING

Prewriting

Freewrite for fifteen minutes about the different types of students who are common to your campus. What are the traits or characteristics of each group? What do representatives of each group do? Where do they congregate? How many of these types can you recognize in this classroom?

Guided Writing

Write a classification of at least three "types" in a situation with which you are familiar, other than school—a certain job, social event, sport, or some such situation.

1. Begin your essay with a reference, direct or indirect, to what some well-known writer or expert said about this situation.
2. Identify your role in relation to the situation described.
3. Write about your attitude toward the particular situation and why you are less than thrilled about it at present.
4. Make sure you involve the reader as someone who would be familiar with the situation and activities described.
5. Divide your essay into exaggerated or stereotyped categories which you feel represent almost the complete range of types in these situations. In your categorization, be sure to include motivations, activities, and results for each type.
6. Use description to make your categories vivid.
7. Use satire and a bit of gentle cynicism as part of your description.
8. Select a lively title.
9. In the conclusion, identify another type that you consider the "purest" or "most truthful" representative of persons in this situation. Either by comparison with yourself or by some other means, explain why you like this type best.

Thinking and Writing Collaboratively

In groups of four to five class members, draft an article for your college newspaper in which you outline the types of students on the campus. Try to maintain a consistently lighthearted or humorous tone or point of view as you move from discussion to the drafting of the letter. Revise your paper, paying careful attention to the flow from one category to the next, before submitting the article for possible publication.

Writing About the Text

Much of the humor and energy of this essay comes from Baker's use of figurative language—from the title on. Write an essay in which you analyze the figurative language here. How does it contribute to the thesis? the tone?

More Writing Projects

1. In your journal, write your own classification of three college "types." Your entry can be serious or humorous.
2. In a 250-word paragraph, classify types of college dates.
3. Look in current magazines for advertisements directed at men or women, or both. Write an essay in which you classify current advertisements according to some logical scheme. Limit your essay to three to five categories.

SUMMING UP: CHAPTER 9

1. Reread Judith Viorst's "Friends, Good Friends—and Such Good Friends" in this chapter. Then, write down the names of several of your closest friends. Keep a journal for one week in which you list what you did with, how you felt about, and what you talked about with each of those friends. Then write an essay that classifies these friends into three categories. Use entries from your journal to support your method of classification.

2. In groups of four, using Amy Rashap's essay on ethnic images in magazines as a model, find advertisements from today's magazines that reflect popular stereotypes. Using your work, decide what the advertisements say or imply about societal ideas about race, gender, or class. Then, write your own essay.

3. Although Viorst's, Baker's, and Rashap's essays are classifications, they also present new ways of looking at a group of people. Viorst has an underlying message about how to choose friends, Baker has a warning about how not to be stereotyped, and Rashap shows how easily stereotyping can dominate portrayals of people. Write a classification essay entitled "How Not to Think About_____." Fill in the blank with a group of people that you believe is often misunderstood.

4. Many of the essays in this book deal with crucial experiences in the various writers' lives. Among others, Hughes and Wong tell us of coming-of-age experiences; Orwell tells of his growing dissatisfaction with his government's decisions; and Dillard and Ackerman explore their experiences with nature. Try writing an essay that classifies the personal essays that you have read in this anthology into sensible categories.

5. Several essays in this book explore childhood and the family. (See Thematic Contents for a list of those essays.) Compose a classification scheme for these essays, fitting them into three key categories.

6. Write an essay classifying views of the American Dream using the essays by Elizabeth Wong, Elie Wiesel, Amy Rashap, and Martin Luther King Jr. that appear in this book.

✱ FROM SEEING TO WRITING

The person in this cartoon obviously has an unwieldy "family" of chairs that he needs to classify or sort into categories. Write your own humorous classification essay in which you put the chairs into categories and make clear the relations among members of each group. As an alternative, write a humorous classification essay about a "family" that might be real—for example, your own extended family—or more fanciful, such as the "family" of toys in a child's room. Choose an illustration to support your classification, and organize your essay around at least three categories depicted there.

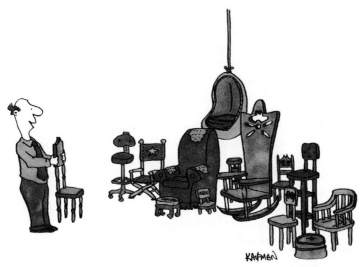

"Attention, everyone! I'd like to introduce the newest member of our family."

© *The New Yorker Collection 1977 Jeff Kaufman from cartoonbank.com. All rights reserved.*

CHAPTER 10

Definition

WHAT IS DEFINITION?

We know that we should open a dictionary when we want to *define* a word. Often, however, the dictionary definition is brief and does not fully explain the meaning of a word as an individual writer sees it. An *extended definition* is necessary when a writer wishes to convey the full meaning of a word that is central to the writer's or a culture's thought.

When an entire essay focuses on the meaning of a key word or group of related words, extended definition becomes the primary method of organization. However, formal extended definitions typically make use of other patterns of development. Among the most useful strategies for organizing an essay of extended definition are narration, description, illustration, comparison and contrast, process analysis, and classification.

Definition can look at the *denotation* of a word, which is its literal meaning, or at the *connotations,* which are the variety of meanings associated with the word through common use (see Glossary). Denotation is generally available in the dictionary. Connotation, on the other hand, requires the writer to examine not only the denotation but also the way that a particular writer uses the word. In defining, a writer can also explore levels of *diction* (see Glossary), such as standard English, colloquial expressions, and slang. The word *red,* for example, denotes a primary color. The connotations, however, are varied: In the early twentieth century Communists were called "Reds" because of the color of the Russian flag. We also associate red with the color of Valentine's cards, with passion and romance. "Redneck" derives from the sunburned skin of a white person who works outdoors and connotes a lifestyle associated with outdoor living and conservative political views. "Redskin" was a pejorative term used by European settlers to describe Native Americans.

We need extended definition to help us fully understand the complexity of our language. Most often, we use definition when words are abstract, controversial, or complex. Terms like *freedom, pornography, affirmative action, bisexual,* and *feminism* demand extended definition because they are often confused with some other word or term; because they are so easily misunderstood; or because they are of special importance to the writer, who chooses to redefine the term for his or her own purposes.

Although writers can, of course, offer an extended definition just for the sake of definition, they usually go through the trouble of defining because they have strong opinions about complex and controversial words; consequently, they try to provide an extended definition for the purpose of illuminating a thesis for readers. Writer Alice Walker, for instance, once wrote an essay about feminism and African American women. In her extended definition, she said that the meaning of *feminism* was restricted to white, upper- and middle-class women. As a result, the word did not apply to black women. She created the term *womanist,* and wrote her essay to define it. Because of the controversial nature of her definition of *feminist,* Walker relied on extended definition to support her thesis that the women's movement needed to pay more attention to women of color.

It *is* possible to give an objective definition of *feminism,* with the writer tracing its history, explaining its historic applications, and describing its various subdivisions, such as *radical feminism.* However, most of the time, writers have strong opinions. They would want to develop a thesis about the term, perhaps covering much of the same ground as the objective account but taking care that the reader understands the word as they do. It is normal for us to have our own opinions about any word, but in all instances writers must make the reader understand fully what they mean by it.

In this chapter, Nicholas Handler, a college student, coins a new word, *posteverything,* to define his generation. Fiction writer Dagoberto Gilb takes an unorthodox look at what the word *pride* means. Thomas Friedman praises today's young people, whom he terms "Generation Q." Gloria Naylor, an African American woman, uses extended definition to confront the hate word *nigger.* Her many *illustrations* of how and where the word is used show how definition is often determined by context.

372

HOW DO WE READ DEFINITION?

Reading definition requires us to ask ourselves these questions:

- What is the writer's thesis? Determine if the definition is *objective* or *subjective* (see Glossary).
- Does the writer state the definition directly, or expect the reader to understand it from the information the writer gives? When you finish reading the essay, write out a one-sentence definition of the term the writer has defined.
- What are the various techniques the writer uses, such as illustration with examples, description, narration, comparison and contrast? The writer may also use *negation,* a technique of defining a word by what it does *not* mean. In addition, a writer may use a strategy of defining some general group to which the subject belongs (for instance, an orange is a member of the larger group of citrus), and to show how the word differs from all other words in the general group (by its color, acid content, size, and so forth).
- What is the writer's tone? Is the definition comic or serious? Does it rely on *irony* (see Glossary)?

HOW DO WE WRITE A DEFINITION?

Reading the variety of *definitions* in this chapter will prepare you to write your own. The skill required in good definition writing is to make abstract ideas concrete. Writing good definitions allows you to practice many of the other writing strategies you already know, including narration, description, and illustration.

The thesis for your definition does not have to appear in the introduction, but it is helpful to write it out for yourself before you begin.

- Select the word: for example, *multiculturalism.*
- Place it in a class: multiculturalism is a *belief,* or *system of values,* or *philosophy.*
- Distinguish it from other members of that class: multiculturalists favor recognition and celebration of differences among various social groups instead of seeking similarities.
- Use negation: multiculturalism is not the "melting pot" metaphor of how American society is constituted.

By arranging these pieces, and revising the language, you can create a working thesis.

Sample thesis statement:

Multiculturalism supports the preservation and celebration of differences among people of diverse cultures rather than urging them to replace their ethnic identities with one single "American" identity.

Select supporting detail as evidence to illustrate, narrate, and describe the term. The selection of evidence can demonstrate the writer's *point of view* on the term. Is multiculturalism splitting the nation into separate groups, or is it affirming the identity of both minority and majority citizens? Look at how the term is used in a variety of settings, such as education, government, social services agencies, and religious institutions.

You might want to visit the library to see how a reference book's definition compares with your own. Libraries have a variety of dictionaries. Depending on the kind of word you are researching, you might want to look at a dictionary of slang, or even a dictionary of quotations to read some famous opinions about abstract words like *love, hope,* and *truth.*

What is the *purpose* of the definition? Decide whether you want to show support for the policy or argue against its effectiveness.

Who is the audience? The writer would choose different language for addressing a PTA meeting than for writing to Congress.

Plan an arrangement of the supporting evidence. Unlike comparison and contrast, for instance, definition does not require a formal method of outlining. Examples can be arranged to suit the kind of word being defined and the mood of the writer. Because so many methods can be applied effectively in an essay of extended definition, you should be able to organize and develop this type of composition easily.

Review the *transitions* you have used in other essays and see which ones apply here. You might want to focus on transitions that show addition: *another, in addition, furthermore.*

Writing and Revising the Draft

Think about where to put the thesis. What is the effect of placing it at the end rather than at the beginning?

Plan your strategy. Arrange the examples so that they most effectively create the extended definition you want. Your essay should have *coherence.* Avoid an unrelated collection of definitions.

Read your essay to a classmate who has defined a similar word. Decide whose definition is more successful, and why.

Revise. Revision may require that you reorganize, moving the examples and other supporting evidence to different sentences and paragraphs to make your argument more effective for a reader.

Proofread for correctness and make a final copy of your work.

A STUDENT PARAGRAPH: DEFINITION

Look at this introductory paragraph of a student's definition essay on multiculturalism and examine the comments in the margin to help you see the various elements of writing definitions.

Introduction of word to be defined	Some people these days use the term "multiculturalism" as a kind of insult, as if the idea of the American "melting pot" is the only valid way to define a culture of different
Comparison-contrast to aid definition: melting pot and multiculturalism	peoples. The *American Heritage Dictionary* defines "melting pot" as "a place where immigrants of different cultures or races form an integrated society." "Melting pot," of course is a metaphor. The image suggests that different cultures are like different kinds of metals that meld to form
Supporting detail: dictionary citation	a new alloy—an alloy that is stronger and more versatile than the original metals. This "alloy," of course, is the integrated society, in which everybody gives up his or her
Detail helps reader see "melting pot" metaphor	own distinctive cultural heritage to make a new (and, by implication, "better," "stronger") culture. "Multiculturalism," on the other hand, makes a very different point. Without rejecting the idea of an integrated society, it rejects the
Transition "on the other hand" signals shift to topic of multiculturalism	idea of a homogenous one. The idea is more along the lines of different vegetables in a big cauldron, imparting their various flavors to make the perfect soup, while still retaining much of their distinctive shape and color. Those who criticize the term "multicultural" are actually criticizing
Essay thesis; body paragraphs will offer support	the diversity that enriches our American culture. Multi-culturalism celebrates the differences among people of diverse cultures rather than urging them to replace their ethnic identities with an "American" identity.

www.mhhe.com/
shortprose

To learn more about using definition, click on

Writing > Writing Tutor:
              Definition

Writing > Paragraph Patterns

The Posteverything Generation
Nicholas Handler

In July 2007, the *New York Times Magazine* published an essay online called "What's the Matter with College," by the historian Rick Perlstein, and invited college students to respond in an essay contest. Some 600 did. The winning essay by Nicholas Handler appears below. When he wrote this, Handler, who comes from Glen Ridge, New Jersey, was a junior majoring in history at Yale University (class of 2009). He is active in social justice organizations and hopes to become a human rights lawyer. In "The Posteverything Generation," he points out how his generation "speaks in a language that makes sense."

PREREADING: THINKING ABOUT THE ESSAY IN ADVANCE

Handler made up the word *posteverything,* putting together the prefix *post,* meaning "after," with the noun *everything.* What do you think the word means? In what ways can it apply to a generation?

Words to Watch

jaded (par. 1)   world-weary; tired; bored
blasé (par. 1)   laid back; unconcerned
parodic (par. 2)   an amusing or poor imitation
reticent (par. 2)   shy
repressive (par. 3)   cruel; unfair
carnage (par. 4)   slaughter
pastiche (par. 6)   a piece of creative work that is a mixture of things borrowed from other works
perfunctory (par. 6)   unthinking; automatic; mechanical
agitate (par. 6)   stir up; disturb
defunct (par. 7)   out of use; obsolete

1   I never expected to gain any new insight into the nature of my generation, or the changing landscape of American colleges, in lit theory. Lit theory is supposed to be the class where you sit at the back of the room with every other jaded sophomore wearing skinny jeans, thick-framed glasses, an ironic T-shirt and oversize retro headphones, just waiting for the lecture to be over so you

can light up a Turkish Gold and walk to lunch while listening to Wilco. That's pretty much the way I spent the course, too; through structuralism, formalism, gender theory and postcolonialism, I was far too busy shuffling through my iPod to see what the patriarchal world order of capitalist oppression had to do with "Ethan Frome." But when we began to study postmodernism, something struck a chord with me and made me sit up and look anew at the seemingly blasé college-age literati of which I was so self-consciously one.

According to my textbook, the problem with defining post-   2 modernism is that it's impossible to. The difficulty is that it is so . . . *post*. It defines itself so negatively against what came before it—naturalism, romanticism and the wild revolution of modernism—that it's sometimes hard to see what it actually is. It denies that anything can be explained neatly or even at all. It is parodic, detached, strange and sometimes menacing to traditionalists who do not understand it. Although it arose in the postwar West, the generation that has witnessed its rise has yet to come up with an explanation of what postmodern attitudes mean for the future of culture or society. The subject intrigued me because, in a class otherwise consumed by dead-letter theories, postmodernism remained an open book, tempting to the young and curious. But it also intrigued me because the question of what postmodernism—what a movement so posteverything, so reticent to define itself—is spoke to a larger question about the political and popular culture of today, of the other jaded sophomores sitting around me who grew up in a postmodern world.

In many ways, my generation is also extremely post: post-   3 cold war, postindustrial, post-baby boom, post-9/11. At one point in his famous text "Postmodernism, or the Cultural Logic of Late Capitalism," the literary critic Fredric Jameson even calls us postliterate. We are a generation that is riding on the tail end of a century of war and revolution that toppled civilizations, overturned repressive social orders and left us with more privilege and opportunity than any other society in history. Ours could be an era to accomplish anything.

And yet do we take to the streets and the airwaves and say,   4 "Here we are, and this is what we demand"? Do we plant our flag of youthful rebellion on the Mall in Washington and say: "We are not leaving until we see change! Our eyes have been opened by our education, and our conception of what is possible has been expanded by our privilege and we demand a better world because it is our right"? It would seem that we do the opposite. We go to war without so much as questioning the rationale; we sign away our civil liberties; we say nothing when the Supreme Court cites Brown v. Board of Education in restricting efforts to combat segregation; and we sit back to watch the carnage on the evening news.

5   On campus, we sign petitions, join organizations, put our names on mailing lists, make small-money contributions, volunteer a spare hour to tutor and sport an entire wardrobe's worth of LiveStrong-like bracelets advertising our moderately priced opposition to everything from breast cancer to global warming. But what do we really stand for? A true postmodern generation, we refuse to weave together an overarching narrative to our own political consciousness, to present a cast of inspirational or revolutionary characters on our public stage or to define a specific philosophy. We are a story seemingly without direction or theme, structure or meaning—a generation defined negatively against what came before us. When Al Gore once said, "It's the combination of narcissism and nihilism that really defines postmodernism," he might as well have been echoing his entire generation's critique of our own. We are a generation for whom even revolution seems trite, and therefore as fair a target for bland imitation as anything else. We are the generation of the Che Guevara T-shirt.

6   Jameson calls it "pastiche": "the wearing of a linguistic mask, speech in a dead language." In literature, this means an author speaking in a style that is not his own—borrowing a voice and continuing to use it until the words lose all meaning and the chaos that is real life sets in. It is an imitation of an imitation, something that has been re-envisioned so many times that the original model is no longer relevant or recognizable. It is mass-produced individualism, anticipated revolution. It is why postmodernism lacks cohesion, why it seems to lack purpose or direction. For us, the posteverything generation, pastiche is the use and reuse of the old clichés of social change and moral outrage—a perfunctory rebelliousness that has culminated in the age of rapidly multiplying nonprofits and relief funds. We live our lives in masks and speak our minds in a dead language—the language of a society that expects us to agitate because that's what young people do.

7   But how do we rebel against a generation that is expecting, anticipating, nostalgic for revolution? How do we rebel against parents who sometimes seem to want revolution more than we

do? We don't. We rebel by not rebelling. We wear the defunct masks of protest and moral outrage, but the real energy in campus activism is on the Internet, with Web sites like MoveOn.org. It is in the rapidly developing ability to communicate ideas and frustration in chat rooms instead of on the streets, and to channel them into nationwide projects striving earnestly for moderate and peaceful change. We are the generation of Students Taking Action Now Darfur. We are the Rock the Vote generation, the generation of letter-writing campaigns and public-interest lobbies, the alternative-energy generation.

College as America once knew it—as an incubator of radical 8 social change—is coming to an end. To our generation the word "radicalism" evokes images of Al Qaeda, not the Weathermen. "Campus takeover" sounds more like Virginia Tech in 2007 than Columbia University in 1968. Such phrases are from a dead language to us. They are words from another era that do not reflect the realities of today. The technological revolution, however—the MoveOn.org revolution, the revolution of the Organization Kid—is just as real and just as profound as the revolution of the 1960s; it is just not as visible. It is a work in progress, but it is there. Perhaps when our parents finally stop pointing out the things that we are not, the stories that we do not write, they will see the threads of our narrative begin to come together. They will see that behind our pastiche, the postgeneration speaks in a language that does make sense. We are writing a revolution. We are just putting it in our own words.

BUILDING VOCABULARY

Define the following *isms* that Handler uses to identify philosophical concepts that he learned about in literary theory class. You might want to check some of the terms in a specialized dictionary of philosophy in your school library.

1. structuralism (par. 1)
2. formalism (par. 1)
3. postcolonialism (par. 1)
4. postmodernism (par. 1)
5. naturalism (par. 2)
6. romanticism (par. 2)
7. modernism (par. 2)
8. narcissism (par. 5)

9. nihilism (par. 5)
10. individualism (par. 6)
11. activism (par. 7)
12. radicalism (par. 8)

THINKING CRITICALLY ABOUT THE ESSAY

Understanding the Writer's Ideas

1. Where does Handler say he gained insights into the nature of his generation? Why does the location at which he came to his new awareness surprise him?
2. Why did the notion of postmodernism intrigue Handler?
3. What is the problem with defining postmodernism, according to the writer? Why did he sit up and take notice when he studied the concept?
4. What, according to Handler, does his generation *not* do? What does he indicate as steps his generation actually takes that are opposite to what one might expect?
5. What do members of Handler's generation do on campus, according to the writer?
6. What Web sites does the writer identify?

Understanding the Writer's Techniques

1. What is Handler's main point? Obviously he builds to it, stating it most clearly in the final paragraph. What is your reaction to the thesis finally declared near the end of the essay instead of near the beginning, which is the more conventional place for stating a thesis?
2. How would you characterize the writer's introduction? In what ways does it lay the groundwork for the thesis?
3. At first Handler indicates that *postmodernism* is impossible to define. Then he goes about trying to define it. What is your opinion of this strategy as a rhetorical device—saying that something can't be defined and then trying to define it?
4. Which elements of Handler's definition of postmodernism do you find most compelling? most clearly stated? most difficult to understand? most original?
5. Why does the writer choose not to define the long string of *isms* that he names in the essay? How does his lack of definitions reflect his sense of the audience for the piece?

6. What descriptive details does Handler provide to identify his fellow classmates? In what ways is the description accurate? In what ways is it ironic?
7. Handler asks questions in the essay: look at paragraphs 4 and 7 in this regard. Why does he ask them? Which questions seem most relevant in building his definition?
8. Handler quotes Frederic Jameson and Al Gore. Who are they? What is the value of citing them? In what ways does the testimony from each of them support the thesis?
9. How does the writer define the word *pastiche*?
10. Why does Handler identify Web sites? How do the citations support the thesis?
11. How does Handler ultimately define *posteverything*? What elements does he present for the reader to consider as part of that definition?
12. The writer refers to *Brown v. Board of Education,* Che Guevara, Al Qaeda, the Weathermen, Virginia Tech in 2007, and Columbia University in 1968. Identify these historical references. Why does Handler include them in the essay?
13. Handler uses the prefix *post* in many places. Identify at least three of them and explain what they mean. Why do you think the writer used so many of these *post* words?
14. The last two sentences of the essay are very short. What is your reaction to them? Do you find them powerful, weak, oversimplified, untrue—or something else? Explain your response.

✳ MIXING PATTERNS

To build his definition, Handler draws on a number of other patterns. Which can you identify? How effective are they in contributing to the essay?

Exploring the Writer's Ideas

1. How does the description of college students in paragraph 1 compare and contrast with the students in your college? Handler uses the word *jaded* twice (pars. 1 and 2) to describe students. Do you find that your fellow students are jaded? Why or why not?

2. Handler says about his generation, "Ours could be an era to accomplish anything." Do you agree? Why or why not? What in fact do you think your generation has or has not accomplished?

3. The writer asks in paragraph 5, "But what do we really stand for?" after providing a list of potentially damaging observations about what his generation does and does not do. How would you answer the question he poses?

4. What does Handler mean when he writes "We are a generation of the Che-Guevara T-shirt"? Does this observation appropriately characterize the current generation? Why or why not?

5. Handler calls the preceding generation one that is "expecting, anticipating, nostalgic for revolution." Why might you agree or disagree with him? How do your parents and relatives—and other members of the previous generation—feel about revolution? Do you believe that the previous generation really expects the current generation to "agitate because that's what young people do"? Explain your response.

6. Check online for the Web sites that Handler names. How would you characterize them? Do you agree with their intent? Why or why not?

7. Do you agree that "college as America once knew it—as an incubator of radical social change—is coming to an end"? Why or why not?

8. Go online to <www.nytimes.com/magazine> to read the runner-up essays in the contest. What were some of these essays about?

IDEAS FOR WRITING

Prewriting

Make a list of the defining qualities of your generation as you see them.

Guided Writing

Write your own essay called "The _____ Generation." Fill in the blank with a word that you think best defines your generation, and then attempt to define the phrase in your essay. You might use a word like *progressive, lucky, distressed, joyous, inactive*—the possibilities are almost limitless. If you can invent your own word, so much the better.

1. Write an introductory paragraph that explains how you came to choose the word.
2. Build to your thesis and try to state it toward the end of your essay.
3. Show why the word is a difficult word to define when used to identify a generation.
4. Make a reference to something you have read.
5. In order to support the word you have chosen, indicate the actions that your generation does not take as well as actions that it does take.
6. Show briefly how your generation compares with a previous generation in regard to the word you have chosen.
7. Ask relevant questions in your paper.
8. Identify Web sites that can support your definition.
9. Write a conclusion that ends with a single brief sentence or two to capture the essence of your point.

Thinking and Writing Collaboratively

Form groups to discuss the qualities of thought and writing that you believe made "The Posteverything Generation" the winning essay in the *New York Times* contest. What do you think the judges found outstanding about it?

Writing About the Text

Write an analysis of Handler's use of transitional elements between sentences and paragraphs. How effective is he in linking thoughts in the essay?

More Writing Projects

1. Write a journal entry about the attitudes and appearance of the students who sit in your college courses with you.
2. Go online and read the essay "What's the Matter with College," by the historian Rick Perlstein (*New York Times Magazine,* September 30, 2007). This is the essay that stimulated the contest Handler won. In an extended paragraph, write your own response to Perlstein's essay.
3. Write an essay in which you define the technological revolution and its importance in characterizing your generation.

Pride

Dagoberto Gilb

Dagoberto Gilb is a writer, teacher, and carpenter. Born in Los Angeles, he has lived in Arizona and Wyoming, and now lives in Texas. His book *The Magic of Blood* won the 1994 PEN/Hemingway Award and was a finalist for the PEN/Faulkner Award. Gilb's most recent work of fiction, a novel, is *The Flowers* (2008). His work has also appeared in the *New Yorker,* the *Threepenny Review,* and *Harper's.* A nonfiction collection, *Gritos,* appeared in 2003 and is the source of this essay, which offers an elaborately lyrical definition of a common human emotion. As you read the essay, think about why Gilb attempts to define this particular word, *pride.*

PREREADING: THINKING ABOUT THE ESSAY IN ADVANCE

What are you proud of? Think about your hometown, your job, your family. What do you take the most pride in? Is your pride always justified? From your thoughts, develop a preliminary definition of pride.

Words to Watch

asphalt (par. 1)   black material used for paving roads
watts (par. 2)   units of electrical power
hemline (par. 3)   line formed by the bottom of a skirt
agave (par. 8)   a plant native to the southwestern United States and Mexico
heritage (par. 8)   culture that is passed on from generation to generation
ancestors (par. 10)   earlier generations in one's family or race

1   It's almost time to close at the northwest corner of Altura and Copia in El Paso. That means it is so dark that it is as restful as the deepest unremembering sleep, dark as the empty space around this spinning planet, as a black star. Headlights that beam a little cross-eyed from a fatso American car are feeling around the asphalt road up the hill toward the Good Time Store, its yellow plastic smiley face bright like a sugary suck candy. The loose muffler holds only half the misfires, and, dry springs squeaking, the automobile curves slowly

into the establishment's lot, swerving to avoid the new self-serve
gas pump island. Behind it, across the street, a Texas flag—out too
late this and all the nights—pops and slaps in a summer wind that
finally is cool.

A good man, gray on the edges, an assistant manager in a 2
brown starched and ironed uniform, is washing the glass windows
of the store, lit up by as many watts as Venus, with a roll of paper
towels and the blue liquid from a spray bottle. Good night, m'ijo!
he tells a young boy coming out after playing the video game, a
Grande Guzzler the size of a wastebasket balanced in one hand,
an open bag of Flaming Hot Cheetos, its red dye already smearing
his mouth and the hand not carrying the weight of the soda, his
white T-shirt, its short sleeves reaching halfway down his wrists,
the whole XXL of it billowing and puffing in the outdoor gust.

A plump young woman steps out of that car. She's wearing a 3
party dress, wide scoops out of the top, front, and back, its hemline
way above the knees.

Did you get a water pump? the assistant manager asks her. Are 4
you going to make it to Horizon City? He's still washing the glass
of the storefront, his hand sweeping in small hard circles.

The young woman is patient and calm like a loving mother. I 5
don't know yet, she tells him as she stops close to him, thinking. I
guess I should make a call, she says, and her thick-soled shoes, the
latest fashion, slap against her heels to one of the pay phones at the
front of the store.

Pride is working a job like it's as important as art or war, is the 6
happiness of a new high score on a video arcade game, of a pretty
new black dress and shoes. Pride is the dear and blind confidence
of the good people who are too poor but don't notice.

A son is a long time sitting on the front porch where he played 7
all those years with the squirmy dog who still licks his face, both
puppies then, even before he played on the winning teams of Little
League baseball and City League basketball. They spring down
the sidewalk and across streets, side by side, until they stop to
rest on the park grass, where a red ant, or a spider, bites the son's
calf. It swells, but he no longer thinks to complain to his mom
about it—he's too old now—when he comes home. He gets ready,
putting on the shirt and pants his mom would have ironed but he
wanted to iron himself. He takes the ride with his best friend since
first grade. The hundreds of moms and dads, abuelos y abuelitas,
the tios and primos, baby brothers and older married sisters, all

are at the Special Events Center for the son's high school graduation. His dad is a man bigger than most, and when he walks in
his dress eel-skin boots down the cement stairs to get as close
to the hardwood basketball-court floor and ceremony to see—
m'ijo!—he feels an embarrassing sob bursting from his eyes and
mouth. He holds it back, and with his hands, hides the tears that
do escape, wipes them with his fingers, because the chavalitos in
his aisle are playing and laughing and they are so small and he is
so big next to them. And when his son walks to the stage to get
his high school diploma and his dad wants to scream his name,
he hears how many others, from the floor in caps and gowns and
from around the arena, are already screaming it—could be any
name, it could be any son's or daughter's: Alex! Vanessa! Carlos!
Veronica! Ricky! Tony! Estella! Isa!—and sees his boy waving
back to all of them.

8   Pride hears gritty dirt blowing against an agave whose stiff
fertile stalk, so tall, will not bend—the love of land, rugged like
the people who live on it. Pride sees the sunlight on the Franklin
Mountains in the first light of morning and listens to a neighbor's
gallo—the love of culture and history. Pride smells a sweet, musky
drizzle of rain and eats huevos con chile in corn tortillas heated on
a cast-iron pan—the love of heritage.

9   Pride is the fearless reaction to disrespect and disregard. It is
knowing the future will prove that wrong.

10 Seeing the beauty: look out there from a height of the mountain
and on the north and south of the Rio Grande, to the far away and
close, the so many miles more of fuzz on the wide horizon, knowing how many years the people have passed and have stayed, the
ancestors, the ones who have medaled, limped back on crutches or
died or were heroes from wars in the Pacific or Europe or Korea or
Vietnam or the Persian Gulf, the ones who have raised the fist and
dared to defy, the ones who wash the clothes and cook and serve
the meals, who stitch the factory shoes and the factory slacks, who
assemble and sort, the ones who laugh and the ones who weep, the
ones who care, the ones who want more, the ones who try, the ones
who love, those ones with shameless courage and hardened wisdom, and the old ones still so alive, holding their grandchildren,
and the young ones in their glowing prime, strong and gorgeous,
holding each other, the ones who will be born from them. The desert land is rock-dry and ungreen. It is brown. Brown like the skin
is brown. Beautiful brown.

BUILDING VOCABULARY

1. In this essay, Gilb uses several Spanish words without giving definitions. Locate the Spanish and look up their definitions, writing them out on a piece of paper.
2. Gilb uses some intriguing and intelligent diction to enliven his prose. Explain the meaning of the italicized words:
   a. *unremembering* sleep (par. 1)
   b. *billowing* (par. 2)
   c. *deaf and blind* confidence (par. 6)
   d. *squirmy* dog (par. 7)
   e. *stiff fertile* stalk (par. 8)
   f. *hardened* wisdom (par. 10)
   g. *rock-dry and ungreen* (par. 10)

THINKING CRITICALLY ABOUT THE ESSAY

Understanding the Writer's Ideas

1. Where is El Paso? What is at the corner of Altura and Copia?
2. What languages do the people described in this essay speak?
3. Explain the statement, "pride is working a job like it's as important as art or war."
4. What does Gilb mean by "both puppies then" (par. 7)?
5. Why does the father cry in paragraph 7?
6. Why does Gilb write, "could be any name, it could be any son's or daughter's"? What is he referring to?
7. What does the definition of pride in paragraph 8 have to do with the story of the son and father in paragraph 7?
8. Paraphrase the two sentences in paragraph 9.
9. What is "the beauty" Gilb refers to at the beginning of paragraph 10?
10. In the conclusion of his essay, how does Gilb compare the land to the people?

Understanding the Writer's Techniques

1. Does Gilb have a thesis? If so, what is it? If not, where is his main idea most clearly expressed?
2. Why does the writer begin his essay with a descriptive scene that shows what happens on a corner in El Paso?

3. What are the two most effective *images* (see Glossary) in the first two paragraphs? Why are they so effective?
4. Gilb changes strategies after paragraph 5. Describe the shift, and explain why you think he makes it.
5. What is the purpose of Gilb's offering multiple definitions of *pride*? Is this an effective technique? Explain your answer.
6. Why do you think the writer uses the present tense in paragraphs 1 to 5 and 7?
7. What example of pride in this essay do you find most effective? Explain why.
8. What is the *tone* of the essay? Cite at least three words that convey this tone.
9. Gilb disposes almost completely with *transitions* (see Glossary). Why? Explain how the essay still has *coherence* (see Glossary) without transitions.
10. Do you find Gilb's conclusion moving? Why or why not? Do you think it is his intention to move you? How can you tell?

Exploring the Writer's Ideas

1. Gilb writes about pride in the Latino community in the southwestern United States and how people's lives there connect to the land. Is the same true in all communities? in your community? Explain.
2. "Pride is working a job like it's as important as art or war" (par. 6). What is your reaction to this statement? Why? Should people take their jobs so seriously? Why or why not?
3. Have you ever felt as proud as the father who watches his son graduate? What or whom were you proud of? What does that kind of pride feel like?

IDEAS FOR WRITING

Prewriting

Freewrite for five minutes about the word *greed*. Think about the *connotations* of the word, from the physical to the emotional. Consider both positive and negative connotations of the word.

Guided Writing

Write an extended definition of the word *greed,* focusing on whichever *connotations* you think are most important but without ignoring the positive.

1. Begin with a scene in which you illustrate greed. Be as descriptive as possible, using vivid auditory, visual, and other imagery.
2. Define greed in a paragraph that includes several sentences that begin with "Greed is . . ."
3. Write another scene in which you illustrate another, conflicting aspect of greed.
4. Balance the earlier scene by being just as descriptive as before.
5. Write another paragraph in which you define greed (as shown in this second scene in step 2).
6. Conclude your essay with an extended paragraph that attempts to reconcile these two definitions of greed. Try to make your writing as lyrical and moving as possible.

Thinking and Writing Collaboratively

In groups of three, share your Guided Writing essays. Then discuss the definitions in each essay. Focus on the imagery—how well have you and the other writers in your group succeeded in bringing the illustrations to life?

Writing About the Text

Pride, traditionally one of the seven deadly sins, is often seen as the opposite of humility. Frequently, however, people are advised to take pride in their work or family. Write an essay discussing how Gilb's essay includes both connotations of pride.

More Writing Projects

1. In your journal, reflect on other human emotions that can be both constructive and destructive.
2. Write a paragraph that defines the word *desire.*
3. Consider what ties you have to the land where you live. Write an essay in which you examine what the land where you live means to you. If it means little to you, explore the reasons why.

Generation Q
Thomas L. Friedman

Thomas Lauren Friedman was born on July 20, 1953, in St. Louis Park, Minnesota, a suburb of Minneapolis. He graduated summa cum laude from Brandeis University with a degree in Mediterranean studies and received a master's degree in modern Middle East studies from Oxford University. A Pulitzer Prize–winning journalist, Friedman writes a regular column on international affairs for the *New York Times.* He has served as a visiting professor at Harvard University and has been awarded honorary degrees from several universities in the United States. He is the author of *From Beirut to Jerusalem* (1989), *The Lexus and the Olive Tree* (1999), *Longitudes and Attitudes: Exploring the World After September 11* (2002), *The World Is Flat: A Brief History of the Twenty-first Century* (2005), and *Flat, Hot, and Crowded: Why We Need a Green Revolution— and How It Can Renew America* (2008). In this essay he attempts to characterize some of the strengths and weaknesses of the current generation of college students.

PREREADING: THINKING ABOUT THE ESSAY IN ADVANCE

What world issues are most relevant on your campus today? Is it the environment, local elections, poverty—or some other important concern?

Words to Watch

impulses (par. 5)   whims; sudden desires
deficit (par. 8)   shortfall; shortage
subsidies (par. 11)   financial support or assistance
mitigating (par. 12)   making an offense seem less serious
neutrality (par. 13)   impartiality; objectivity; detachment

1 I just spent the past week visiting several colleges—Auburn, the University of Mississippi, Lake Forest and Williams—and I can report that the more I am around this generation of college students, the more I am both baffled and impressed.

2   I am impressed because they are so much more optimistic and idealistic than they should be. I am baffled because they are so much less radical and politically engaged than they need to be.

One of the things I feared most after 9/11—that my daughters 3 would not be able to travel the world with the same carefree attitude my wife and I did at their age—has not come to pass.

Whether it was at Ole Miss or Williams or my alma mater, 4 Brandeis, college students today are not only going abroad to study in record numbers, but they are also going abroad to build homes for the poor in El Salvador in record numbers or volunteering at AIDS clinics in record numbers. Not only has terrorism not deterred them from traveling, they are rolling up their sleeves and diving in deeper than ever.

The Iraq war may be a mess, but I noticed at Auburn and Old 5 Miss more than a few young men and women proudly wearing their R.O.T.C. uniforms. Many of those not going abroad have channeled their national service impulses into increasingly popular programs at home like "Teach for America," which has become to this generation what the Peace Corps was to mine.

It's for all these reasons that I've been calling them "Gen- 6 eration Q"—the Quiet Americans, in the best sense of that term, quietly pursuing their idealism, at home and abroad.

But Generation Q may be too quiet, too online, for its own 7 good, and for the country's own good. When I think of the huge budget deficit, Social Security deficit and ecological deficit that our generation is leaving this generation, if they are not spitting mad, well, then they're just not paying attention. And we'll just keep piling it on them.

There is a good chance that members of Generation Q will 8 spend their entire adult lives digging out from the deficits that we—the "Greediest Generation," epitomized by George W. Bush—are leaving them.

When I was visiting my daughter at her college, she asked me 9 about a terrifying story that ran in this newspaper on Oct. 2, reporting that the Arctic ice cap was melting "to an extent unparalleled in a century or more"—and that the entire Arctic system appears to be "heading toward a new, more watery state" likely triggered by "human-caused global warming."

"What happened to that Arctic story, Dad?" my daughter asked 10 me. How could the news media just report one day that the Arctic ice was melting far faster than any models predicted "and then the story just disappeared?" Why weren't any of the candidates talking about it? Didn't they understand: this has become the big issue on campuses?

11   No, they don't seem to understand. They seem to be too busy raising money or buying votes with subsidies for ethanol farmers in Iowa. The candidates could actually use a good kick in the pants on this point. But where is it going to come from?

12   Generation Q would be doing itself a favor, and America a favor, if it demanded from every candidate who comes on campus answers to three questions: What is your plan for mitigating climate change? What is your plan for reforming Social Security? What is your plan for dealing with the deficit—so we all won't be working for China in 20 years?

13   America needs a jolt of the idealism, activism and outrage (it must be in there) of Generation Q. That's what twentysomethings are for—to light a fire under the country. But they can't e-mail it in, and an online petition or a mouse click for carbon neutrality won't cut it. They have to get organized in a way that will force politicians to pay attention rather than just patronize them.

14   Martin Luther King and Bobby Kennedy didn't change the world by asking people to join their Facebook crusades or to download their platforms. Activism can only be uploaded, the old-fashioned way—by young voters speaking truth to power, face to face, in big numbers, on campuses or the Washington Mall. Virtual politics is just that—virtual.

15   Maybe that's why what impressed me most on my brief college swing was actually a statue—the life-size statue of James Meredith at the University of Mississippi. Meredith was the first African-American to be admitted to Ole Miss in 1962. The Meredith bronze is posed as if he is striding toward a tall limestone archway, re-enacting his fateful step onto the then-segregated campus—defying a violent, angry mob and protected by the National Guard.

16   Above the archway, carved into the stone, is the word "Courage." That is what real activism looks like. There is no substitute.

BUILDING VOCABULARY

Write definitions for these verbs, which Friedman uses in "Generation Q." Sometimes the verbs appear in the past tense. Use a dictionary to check on meanings.

1. baffle (par. 1)
2. deter (par. 4)
3. channel (par. 4)

4. epitomize (par. 8)
5. trigger (par. 9)
6. patronize (par. 13)

THINKING CRITICALLY ABOUT THE ESSAY

Understanding the Writer's Ideas

1. What is it about the current generation that baffles Friedman? What impresses him? What event led him to those conclusions?
2. Which fear that Friedman had "never came to pass"?
3. Why are students today going abroad, according to the writer?
4. What are those not going abroad doing to "channel their service impulses"?
5. Why does Friedman call the generation "Generation Q"? What does the Q stand for?
6. What issues, according to Friedman, should make Generation Q "spitting mad"? How do these issues inform the questions Friedman says Generation Q should ask candidates?
7. What questions did the writer's daughter ask him when he visited her college?
8. Why, according to Friedman, are candidates not paying attention to the big issues on campus?
9. What does Friedman believe motivates twentysomethings?
10. What impressed Friedman most on his "brief college swing"?

Understanding the Writer's Techniques

1. What is Friedman's thesis? Where does he come closest to stating it in the essay?
2. How does the title draw readers into Friedman's essay? What definition would a reader expect to find here?
3. Why does the writer tell about his visit to college campuses in the introduction? How effective a strategy is this bit of narrative detail at the start of the essay?
4. How effective is the writer's use of direct quotations from his daughter? Why would her statements matter here?
5. Friedman's paragraphs are consistently brief, usually no more than three sentences. Why has he chosen this kind of

length for his essay? How does it reflect his knowledge of his audience?

6. What would you say is the writer's tone? Is he harsh, judgmental, respectful, disappointed, gentle, or a combination of these? Or perhaps you would use some other word to characterize the tone. Explain your response.

7. What is your reaction to the label "Generation Q" that Friedman uses for today's college students? Is it just journalistic razzle-dazzle? He could have used the term the "Quiet Generation" just as well. Or is there a deeper issue at play here? Explain your response.

8. Why does Friedman name Martin Luther King and Bobby Kennedy? How do they contribute to the definition the writer is evolving?

9. How is the statue of James Meredith a *symbol* (see Glossary) of what Friedman hopes Generation Q will be like?

10. What is your reaction to the conclusion of the essay? The last paragraph has three short sentences. Why has Friedman chosen such an ending? Is he merely meeting the demands of journalistic style, or is he attempting to achieve something?

Exploring the Writer's Ideas

1. What is your view of the label "Quiet Generation" for your cohort of college students?

2. Friedman implies in paragraphs 13 and 14 that activism is absent from this generation's pursuits because of its attention to technology. Is this a valid criticism? Why or why not? What evidence could you propose to support Friedman's view? What evidence could you propose to challenge it?

3. Friedman lodges tough criticism against today's politicians, especially in paragraph 11. Is his assessment fair? Why or why not? Do you think that politicians deserve "a good kick in the pants on this point"?

4. Why does Friedman label his own generation the "Greediest Generation"? Is this a fair assessment? What acts of greed did his generation perform?

5. The last paragraph defines activism as *courage*. Is that an accurate definition? Are the two words synonyms? Can a person show courage without being an activist? Can a person be an activist without showing courage? Explain your answer.

IDEAS FOR WRITING

Prewriting

Write nonstop about how you would define a generation other than your own.

Guided Writing

Write your own essay called "Generation _____." Fill in the blank with a letter from the alphabet that is the first letter of a word you would use to highlight some generation other than your own. Choose any period in history that interests you, and, if necessary, do some research in your library. To follow Friedman's example, if you used the word *greediest* for his own generation, you'd call your essay "Generation G." Other options might be "Generation B" (for bravest), "Generation A" (for aggressive), "Generation W" (for weakest), "Generation H" (for happiest). You have many options. Then write an essay in which you define that generation—that is, identify the qualities that led you to choose the word you did.

1. Use two adjectives—other than the word you've chosen for your title—to identify how you feel about that generation. Friedman uses *baffled* and *impressed* to indicate his feelings about his daughter's generation.
2. Tell what experience led to your selection—a conversation with someone from that generation; Web sites you've examined; a book or article you have read; a film you've seen; a report you've heard on the radio or seen on TV.
3. Identify the strengths of the generation as well as the weaknesses.
4. Ultimately, tell why you chose the descriptive word that you did.
5. Make sure your thesis is clear.
6. Use a direct quote from a spoken or written resource.
7. Highlight one or two people in that generation who you think help to characterize the word you've chosen.
8. End your essay with a brief conclusion.

Thinking and Writing Collaboratively

Form groups to discuss the way your campus is reacting to the issue that Friedman's daughter finds so important: the melting of

Arctic ice in particular and global warming in general. Is this a major issue for students on your campus?

Writing About the Text

Write an analysis of Friedman's journalistic style. You might want to examine one of his books, some of which are compilations of his newspaper columns.

More Writing Projects

1. Write a journal entry about a statue on campus or in your neighborhood, a statue that represents something important for your community.
2. Write an extended paragraph in which you define the word *courage*.
3. Write an essay in which you define *twentysomethings*. Use descriptive detail, and identify the aspirations of the group as well as the problems and challenges facing twentysomethings.

A Word's Meaning
Gloria Naylor

(left margin, vertical text) **Mixing Patterns**

Gloria Naylor was born in New York City on January 25, 1950. When she was thirteen, her mother joined Jehovah's Witnesses; Naylor herself was baptized and became a Jehovah's Witnesses minister in 1968. She proselytized for Jehovah's Witnesses in New York, North Carolina, and Florida over a period of years, supporting herself as a switchboard operator. In 1975 she left Jehovah's Witnesses, suffered a nervous breakdown, and entered Medgar Evers College to study nursing. After reading Toni Morrison's *The Bluest Eye,* Naylor began to think of writing herself. In 1981 she graduated from Brooklyn College with a BA in English. The following year she published *The Women of Brewster Place,* still her best-known novel. She has also published *Mama Day* (1986), *Bailey's Cafe* (1992), and *The Men of Brewster Place* (1998). In 1990 Naylor established One Way Productions, her own multimedia production company. As an African American woman and a writer, Naylor has found that words can change their meaning, depending on who defines them. Telling of a confrontation with an angry classmate who called her a "nigger" in the third grade, Naylor develops an extended definition of the word and its multiple meanings. As you read, what other words can you identify that depend on context for their meaning?

www.mhhe.com/ **shortprose**

To learn more about Naylor, click on
More Resources > Chapter 10 > Gloria Naylor

PREREADING: THINKING ABOUT THE ESSAY IN ADVANCE

Naylor suggests that even offensive words mean different things to different people. Would you agree? Can you think of a word that you find offensive but that others might find acceptable?

Words to Watch

transcendent (par. 1)   rising above
fleeting (par. 1)   moving quickly
intermittent (par. 2)   alternate; repeated
consensus (par. 2)   agreement

verified (par. 3)   confirmed
gravitated (par. 4)   moved toward
inflections (par. 5)   pitch or tone of voice
endearment (par. 9)   expression of affection
disembodied (par. 9)   separated from the body
unkempt (par. 10)   messy
social stratum (par. 14)   status

1   Language is the subject. It is the written form with which I've managed to keep the wolf away from the door and, in diaries, to keep my sanity. In spite of this, I consider the written word inferior to the spoken, and much of the frustration experienced by novelists is the awareness that whatever we manage to capture in even the most transcendent passages falls far short of the richness of life. Dialogue achieves its power in the dynamics of a fleeting moment of sight, sound, smell and touch.

2   I'm not going to enter the debate here about whether it is language that shapes reality or vice versa. That battle is doomed to be waged whenever we seek intermittent reprieve from the chicken and egg dispute. I will simply take the position that the spoken word, like the written word, amounts to a nonsensical arrangement of sounds or letters without a consensus that assigns "meaning." And building from the meanings of what we hear, we order reality. Words themselves are innocuous; it is the consensus that gives them true power.

3   I remember the first time I heard the word nigger. In my third-grade class, our math tests were being passed down the rows, and as I handed the papers to a little boy in back of me, I remarked that once again he had received a much lower mark than I did. He snatched his test from me and spit out that word. Had he called me a nymphomaniac or a necrophiliac, I couldn't have been more puzzled. I didn't know what a nigger was, but I knew that whatever it meant, it was something he shouldn't have called me. This was verified when I raised my hand, and in a loud voice repeated what he had said and watched the teacher scold him for using a "bad" word. I was later to go home and ask the inevitable questions that every black parent must face—"Mommy, what does 'nigger' mean?"

4   And what exactly did it mean? Thinking back, I realize that this could not have been the first time the word was used in my presence. I was part of a large extended family that had migrated from the rural South after World War II and formed a close-knit

network that gravitated around my maternal grandparents. Their ground-floor apartment in one of the buildings they owned in Harlem was a weekend mecca for my immediate family, along with countless aunts, uncles and cousins who brought along assorted friends. It was a bustling and open house with assorted neighbors and tenants popping in and out to exchange bits of gossip, pick up an old quarrel or referee the ongoing checkers game in which my grandmother cheated shamelessly. They were all there to let down their hair and put up their feet after a week of labor in the factories, laundries and shipyards of New York.

Amid the clamor, which could reach deafening proportions— two or three conversations going on simultaneously, punctuated by the sound of a baby's crying somewhere in the back rooms or out on the street—there was still a rigid set of rules about what was said and how. Older children were sent out of the living room when it was time to get into the juicy details about "you-know-who" up on the third floor who had gone and gotten herself "p-r-e-g-n-a-n-t!" But my parents, knowing that I could spell well beyond my years, always demanded that I follow the others out to play. Beyond sexual misconduct and death, everything else was considered harmless for our young ears. And so among the anecdotes of the triumphs and disappointments in the various workings of their lives, the word nigger was used in my presence, but it was set within contexts and inflections that caused it to register in my mind as something else. 5

In the singular, the word was always applied to a man who had distinguished himself in some situation that brought their approval for his strength, intelligence or drive: 6

"Did Johnny *really* do that?" 7

"I'm telling you, that nigger pulled in $6,000 of overtime last year. Said he got enough for a down payment on a house." 8

When used with a possessive adjective by a woman—"my nigger"—it became a term of endearment for husband or boyfriend. But it could be more than just a term applied to a man. In their mouths it became the pure essence of manhood—a disembodied force that channeled their past history of struggle and present survival against the odds into a victorious statement of being: "Yeah, that old foreman found out quick enough—you don't mess with a nigger." 9

In the plural, it became a description of some group within the community that had overstepped the bounds of decency as my 10 family defined it: Parents who neglected their children, a drunken couple who fought in public, people who simply refused to look for work, those with excessively dirty mouths or unkempt households were all "trifling niggers." This particular circle could forgive hard times, unemployment, the occasional bout of depression—they had gone through all of that themselves—but the unforgivable sin was a lack of self-respect.

11   A woman could never be a "nigger" in the singular, with its connotation of confirming worth. The noun "girl" was its closest equivalent in that sense, but only when used in direct address and regardless of the gender doing the addressing. "Girl" was a token of respect for a woman. The one-syllable word was drawn out to sound like three in recognition of the extra ounce of wit, nerve or daring that the woman had shown in the situation under discussion.

12   "G-i-r-l, stop. You mean you said that to his face?"

13   But if the word was used in a third-person reference or shortened so that it almost snapped out of the mouth, it always involved some element of communal disapproval. And age became an important factor in these exchanges. It was only between individuals of the same generation, or from an older person to a younger (but never the other way around), that "girl" would be considered a compliment.

14   I don't agree with the argument that use of the word nigger at this social stratum of the black community was an internalization of racism. The dynamics were the exact opposite: the people in my grandmother's living room took a word that whites used to signify worthlessness or degradation and rendered it impotent. Gathering there together, they transformed "nigger" to signify the varied and complex human beings they knew themselves to be. If the word was to disappear totally from the mouths of even the most liberal of white society, no one in that room was naïve enough to believe it would disappear from white minds. Meeting the word head-on, they proved it had absolutely nothing to do with the way they were determined to live their lives.

15   So there must have been dozens of times that the "nigger" was spoken in front of me before I reached the third grade. But I didn't "hear" it until it was said by a small pair of lips that had already learned it could be a way to humiliate me. That was the word I went home and asked my mother about. And since she knew that I had to grow up in America, she took me in her lap and explained.

BUILDING VOCABULARY

1. In paragraph 3, Naylor says the word *nigger* is as puzzling to her as *nymphomaniac* and *necrophiliac*. Using a dictionary, find both meanings of these two terms and their etymology, or roots.

2. In paragraph 14, Naylor writes, "I don't agree with the argument that use of the word nigger at this social stratum of the black community was an internalization of racism." Put Naylor's idea into your own words. Use the context of the sentence to understand key terms such as "social stratum" and "internalization."

THINKING CRITICALLY ABOUT THE ESSAY

Understanding the Writer's Ideas

1. What is the original situation in which Naylor recognizes that *nigger* can be a hate word? What clues from outside the dictionary meaning of the word help her to recognize this meaning? What confirms her suspicion that the word is "bad"?

2. In paragraph 4, Naylor gives us information about her family and background. In your own words, what kind of family did Naylor come from? Where did she grow up? What economic and social class did her family come from? How do you know?

3. In paragraph 5, Naylor explains the values of her group. What was considered appropriate and what was inappropriate for children to hear? What kind of behavior did the group condemn?

4. Naylor defines at least five contexts in which the word *nigger* might be used. Make a list giving the five contexts, and write a sentence putting the use of the word into your own definition.

5. Explain one context in which Naylor says *nigger* was never used (par. 11). How are age and gender important in determining how the word was used?

6. When Naylor says in paragraph 14 that blacks' use of the word *nigger* about themselves rendered the word "impotent," what does she mean? How do they "transform" the meaning of the word?

7. In the last paragraph, Naylor recalls her mother's reaction to the experience of hearing a third-grade classmate use the word to humiliate her. What do you think the mother explained?

Understanding the Writer's Techniques

1. Where is the thesis statement of Naylor's essay? How do you know?

2. Why does Naylor begin with two paragraphs about language, in a very general or theoretical way? Explain what these two paragraphs tell us about the writer's authority to define words. How does she use her introduction to make herself sound like an expert on the problem of defining words?

3. In paragraph 3, the writer shifts tone. She moves from the formal language of the introduction to the personal voice as she retells her childhood experience. What is the effect of this transition on the reader? Why?

4. Look closely at the examples of usage Naylor provides in paragraphs 8, 9, 10, and 11. Why does she provide dialogue to illustrate the various contexts in which she heard the word *nigger* used? In what way is this variety of speakers related to her thesis statement?

5. Naylor uses grammatical terms to clarify differences in meaning, such as "in the singular" (par. 6), "possessive adjective" (par. 9), "plural" (par. 10), and "third-person reference" (par. 13). Why does she use these technical terms? What does it reveal about the audience for whom she is writing? What does it reveal about Naylor's understanding of that audience?

6. What do you think about the last sentence of the essay? Why does the writer return to the simple and direct language of her childhood experience in order to conclude rather than using the theoretical and technical language of other parts of the essay?

✳ MIXING PATTERNS

Why does Naylor use narration to organize her extended definition? What other rhetorical strategies does she rely on, and why?

Exploring the Writer's Ideas

1. Naylor chooses to define a difficult and controversial word in her essay. How does the way that she defines it make you think again about the meaning of the word *nigger*? Have you used the word in any of the ways she defines? How have contemporary rap musicians used the word in ways to suggest that Naylor's definition is accurate?

2. Naylor argues that the definition of words emerges from consensus. So, if the third-grader used *nigger* to humiliate his classmate, we must draw the conclusion that that little boy's society consented to the racism he intended by using the word. How does Naylor reinforce this idea in the last paragraph of the essay? What attitude toward racism does the mother seem to reveal when she picks up her daughter? Does Naylor's definition essay offer any solutions to the negative meaning the word carries? in what ways?

3. The classic American novel *The Adventures of Huckleberry Finn,* by Mark Twain, uses the word *nigger* almost 200 times. For this reason, some school libraries want to ban the book. In what ways does Naylor's definition essay engage in this censorship debate?

IDEAS FOR WRITING

Prewriting

Select an objectionable or offensive word, and for five minutes freewrite on the subject, trying to cover as many ways in which the word is used as possible.

Guided Writing

Choose a word that you have recently heard used that offended you because it was sexist, racist, anti-Semitic, homophobic, or otherwise objectionable. Write a definition essay in which you define the word, show examples of its power to offend, and conclude by offering alternate words.

1. Use an anecdote to show whom you heard using the word, where it was used, and how you felt when you heard it used.

In your introduction, explain who you are and who the other speaker was.

2. In your thesis, give the word and give an expanded definition of what the word means to you.

3. Explain the background of the word's negative use. Who uses it? What is the dictionary meaning of the word? How do you think the word got corrupted?

4. Give examples to expand your thesis that the word has negative meanings. Show who uses it and for what purpose. Draw your examples from people at work, the media, or historical figures.

5. Use another example to show how the word can change meaning if the speaker deliberately uses it in order to mock its usual meaning or "render it impotent" as Naylor says.

6. If possible, try to define the word by negation—that is, by what it does not mean.

7. Connect your paragraphs with transitions that relate one idea thoughtfully to the next.

8. In your conclusion, place the term in a broader perspective, one that goes beyond the specific word to the power of language to shape reality or control behavior.

Thinking and Writing Collaboratively

Many colleges and universities are trying to find ways to discourage or prevent hate speech by writing codes of conduct. In groups of five or six, discuss possible approaches to this issue, and then draft a policy statement that defines what unacceptable language is and how your campus will respond to it.

Writing About the Text

In what way does Naylor's discussion of language raise issues similar to those discussed by Amy Tan in "Mother Tongue" (pages 40–46)? Although Tan is dealing with language among immigrants and Naylor is addressing the varieties of meaning of words to native speakers of English, both writers deal with the politics of language. How does each writer define the relationship between language and power?

More Writing Projects

1. In your journal, record an incident in which someone addressed you or someone you know with an offensive word. Explain how you reacted and why.

2. Write a one-paragraph definition of a word or phrase by which you would feel comfortable being labeled. Are you a single parent? an Italian American? an honor student? Write a sharp thesis to define the term, and then expand the definition with examples.

3. Read the following poem by Countee Cullen (1903–1946). Then write an essay in which you compare and contrast his approach to the use of offensive language to Naylor's. How do the two works converge? diverge? What is the effect of each work on the reader?

INCIDENT

Once riding in old Baltimore
Heart-filled, head-filled with glee,
I saw a Baltimorean
Keep looking straight at me.
Now I was eight and very small,
And he was no whit bigger,
And so I smiled, but he poked out
His tongue, and called me, "Nigger."
I saw the whole of Baltimore
From May until December
Of all the things that happened there
That's all that I remember.

SUMMING UP: CHAPTER 10

1. In her essay on the N-word, Gloria Naylor defines a term we all understand but might have difficulty defining. One way she approaches this definition is through negation—that is, by explaining what the word is *not*. Write an essay that defines by negation another term that is understood but difficult to explain—for example, *privacy, the blues, class, happiness,* or *success.*

2. Gilb's essay attempts a complicated definition of a complicated concept, pride. In what way do you disagree with his definition? Write your own definition of pride, referring to Gilb's essay in forging your own definition.

3. Gloria Naylor argues that a word is defined by "consensus." That is, the members of a community agree about how to use a word, despite outside definitions. On your campus find examples of words defined by "consensus." Choose a word whose meaning on campus might surprise people like your parents, and write an essay defining that word.

4. Look back over the titles of all the essays in this and previous chapters of this book. Choose one word or phrase from any title (for example, "The Struggle to Be an All-American Girl," "Salvation," "Night Walker," "In the Jungle"), and write an essay defining that term *subjectively* (from your personal viewpoint).

5. Imagine a conversation between the students identified by Nicholas Handler and those identified by Thomas Friedman. Remember that the writers are attempting to identify the same generation. Write an essay in which you explore what each group would say to the other.

6. Compare and contrast Gloria Naylor's treatment of race with Dagoberto Gilb's. What do you think is the difference between their definitions?

✳ FROM SEEING TO WRITING

Examine this 1934 photograph of a street scene in Harlem, the section of New York City that is famous as a center of African American culture. Use the photograph as the basis for an extended definition of a key term or concept—for example, *community, culture, city,* or *race*. In writing your essay, refer specifically to elements in the photograph that support your thesis. Use those writing strategies that serve best to develop your extended definition.

CHAPTER 11

Argumentation and Persuasion

WHAT ARE ARGUMENTATION AND PERSUASION?

When we use *argumentation,* we aim to convince someone to join our side of an issue. We want the readers to change their views and adopt ours. We also use *persuasion* when we want a person to take action that will advance our cause. Both argumentation, which appeals to reason, and persuasion, which appeals to emotions, aim to convince an audience to agree with your position. Argument and persuasion often work hand in hand.

In everyday life we hear the word *argument* used as a synonym for *fight.* In writing, however, an argument is not a brawl but a train of thought directed toward a well-focused goal. Usually an argument has a topic that can be debated, and an argument should reflect the ethical and critical standards that apply to debate. Although argument naturally includes emotion and even passion, a good argument avoids mere emotional appeals. A good argument appeals to reason. Consequently, argument relies on logic more than do other kinds of writing. At the same time, all writing—analysis, narrative, even description—can be said to be a form of argument. Whatever we write, we want the reader to get our point, and if possible to see it our way. This proposition can be reversed, as well. Just as all writing includes some form of argument, so, too, argumentation draws on all the writers' tools that you have learned so far. In preparing your argumentative essay, you will be able to rehearse and refine the skills you have learned to this point.

The first step in arguing successfully is to state your position clearly. This means that a good thesis is crucial to your essay. For argumentative or persuasive essays, the thesis is sometimes called a *major proposition,* or a *claim.* Through your major proposition, you take a definite position in a debate, and by taking a strong position, you give your essay its argumentative edge. Your readers must know what your position is and must see that you have supported your main idea with convincing minor points. The weakest arguments are those in which the writer tries to take both sides and as a result persuades no one. As you will see in the reading selections, writers often concede or yield a point to the opposition, but they do so only to strengthen the side that they favor.

Writing arguments should make you even more aware of the need to think about audience. In particular, in writing you need to think about the people who will make up their minds on the basis of your evidence. As you consider how to present your case, think about what kind of language, what kinds of examples, and what general tone will speak most persuasively to your audience. As well, keep in mind that readers are rarely persuaded simply by assertion; you can't just tell them something is true. You need to show them through well-organized support of the main and minor points that support your major proposition or claim. In this respect you might say that there are two audiences for an argumentative essay: the actual, living audience of readers; and something that you might see as the "court of standards"—the rules of logic and of evidence. The actual audience is in fact more likely to be convinced of your case if it follows these rules and meets the standards for debate. Moreover, an essential feature of argument is credibility. An excellent way to establish and sustain your credibility is to follow the rules of logic and of evidence faithfully.

Evidence or support can come from many sources. Among the most powerful forms of evidence are facts, whether these are drawn from the historical record, from reliable statistical sources, or from personal experience. Another common form of evidence is expert opinion. If, for example, you are writing an essay about cleaning up pollution in a river, you may want to rely on statements from scientists or environmental engineers to support your point. Indeed, you may have come to your own conclusions on the basis of authoritative information or opinion.

In addition to evidence, writers often depend on analysis of the opponent's points to advance the writer's own arguments. Finally, a writer can of course use narrative, description, comparison and contrast, illustration, process, cause and effect, classification, and definition to persuade.

Because we use argument in everyday life, we may think it is easy to argue in writing—but just the opposite is true. If we are arguing with someone in person, we can *see* our opponent's response and quickly change our direction. In writing, we can only imagine the opponent and so must carefully prepare evidence for all possible responses. Moreover, although the evening news may expose us to arguments, about abortion clinics, increasing the minimum wage, or accusations of sexual harassment, we often see only what media experts call "sound bites," tiny fragments of information. We may see just a slogan as a picket sign passes a camera. We may hear only a few sentences out of hours of testimony. We seldom see or hear the entire argument. When we turn to writing arguments ourselves, we need to remember to develop a complete and detailed and *rational* argument.

This does not mean that written arguments lack emotion. Rather, written argument channels that emotion into a powerful eloquence that can endure much longer than a shouting match. The writer states the major proposition, or point he or she wants to make, and keeps it firmly in front of the reader. To do this, a writer must have a clear sense of purpose and audience and plan the argument accordingly.

A wide range of topics—and of purposes and intended audiences—is possible. For example, a writer may want to argue that the U.S. government should grant amnesty to illegal aliens who have been in the country for at least two years. He may write to his member of Congress to persuade her to take action on a proposed bill. Or the writer may want to convince a group of readers, such as readers of the local newspaper, that something is true—that single fathers make excellent parents, for example, or that wife abuse is an increasingly serious crime in our society.

Whatever the writer's topic, the keys to a good argument are

- a clear and effective major proposition or claim
- a reasonable tone
- an abundance of evidence
- an avoidance of personal attacks

ORGANIZATION OF THE CHAPTER

Because of the nature of argumentation, we have organized this chapter differently from the others so as to highlight more than usual the issues—the claims, ideas, techniques—raised in the selections. Since argument typically implies an opposing or differing viewpoint, we start by providing a set of pro and con essays on a topic of current interest: can torture ever be justified? However, in order to help readers understand that issues are often complex and lend themselves to multiple viewpoints, we have grouped additional essays under three sets of perspectives: on identity, the "Mommy Wars," and political rights.

Here are the selections you find in this chapter:

Arguments Pro and Con: Can Torture Be Justified?

Mirko Bagaric, *A Case for Torture*
John McCain, *Torture's Terrible Toll*

Perspectives on Identity: Who Are We, and How Are We Formed?

Jonathan Kozol, *Are the Homeless Crazy?*
Richard Rodriguez, *The American Community*
Ronald Takaki, *The Harmful Myth of Asian Superiority*

Perspectives on the "Mommy Wars": Should Mothers Work?

Linda Hirshman, *Off to Work She Should Go*
Susan Cheever, *Baby Battle*
Anna Quindlen, *The Good Enough Mother*

Perspectives on Political Rights: Are We Truly Free?

Molly Ivins, *Get a Knife, Get a Dog, but Get Rid of Guns*
Martin Luther King Jr., *I Have a Dream*
Orlando Patterson, *Jena, O. J., and the Jailing of Black America*

HOW DO WE READ ARGUMENTS?

Try to find out something about the background and credentials of the writer. In what way is he or she an expert on the topic?

Is the proposition presented in a rational and logical way? Is it credible and presented accurately and fairly? What reasons (or minor propositions) are used to support the writer's claim, and are they convincing?

Has the writer presented ample reliable evidence to back up the proposition? (If you look at the headlines on supermarket tabloid newspapers that try to persuade us that aliens have been keeping Elvis Presley alive on Mars, you will see why it is important to be able to evaluate a writer's evidence before accepting the proposition!)

Does the writer consider the counterarguments and deal effectively with the opposition?

HOW DO WE WRITE ARGUMENTS?

State a clear major proposition, and stick to it.

Convince readers of the validity of your thesis by making an essay plan that introduces *minor propositions*. These are assertions that help clarify the reasons you offer to support your main idea.

Use *refutation*. This is a technique in which you anticipate what an opponent will say and answer the objection ahead of time. Another technique is *concession*. You yield a small point to your opponent but at the same time claim a larger point on your own side. Using these techniques makes your argument seem fairer. You acknowledge that there *are* at least two sides to the issue. Moreover, these devices help you make your own point more effectively.

Be aware of these pitfalls:

- Avoid personal attacks on your opponent, and don't let excessive appeals to emotion damage the tone of your argument.
- Avoid hasty generalization—that is, using a general statement about a subject without properly supporting it.
- Avoid drawing a conclusion that does not follow from the evidence in your argument.
- Avoid faulty analogies—that is, comparing two things or situations that are not really comparable.

Writing the Draft

Begin the rough draft. State your thesis or main proposition boldly.

Back up all minor propositions with

- statistics
- facts

- testimony from authorities
- personal experience

Find a reliable listener and read your essay aloud. Encourage your listener to refute your points as strongly as possible.

Revise the essay, taking into account your listener's refutations. Find better support for your weakest points. Write a new draft.

Revise the essay carefully. Read it aloud again if possible. Prepare a final copy.

A STUDENT PARAGRAPH: ARGUMENTATION AND PERSUASION

In the following paragraph, the student begins quite forcibly by stating his position on custody battles during divorce cases—in other words, in an argumentative mode. Examine the simple but effective way he provides evidence for his position.

Main proposition; "outrageous" a cue for sympathy	The outcomes of custody battles during divorce proceedings exemplify the outrageous prejudice against fathers in our culture. Recently, the *Houston Chronicle* reported on the outcome of a child custody case the
Cites authority to support main proposition	paper had followed for nearly six months. In the case, both father and mother wanted sole custody of their only child. The mother, a defense attorney at a high-
Case study provides evidence	flying Houston firm, worked 60–70 hours a week; she had maintained this schedule from the time the child, now six, was two months old. She frequently spent at least one weekend day at the office; she traveled on business as many as 10 weeks out of the year. The father, a freelance writer who worked at home, was acknowledged by both spouses to be the child's primary caretaker, and to have filled this role from the time the child was two months old and the wife returned to work. He typically woke the child, prepared breakfast, helped her choose clothing to wear, packed her a lunch, and walked her to school. He picked her up from school, accompanied her on playdates or took her to play in the park, made dinner for them both, helped the child with her homework, bathed her, read her a story,

and put her to sleep. The mother ordinarily arrived home from work after the child was already asleep, and often left for work before the child was awake. Guess who got custody? The mother, of course. Sadly, judges persist in assuming that mothers are always the better—the more "natural"—caretaker. This assumption leads them all too often to award custody to the mother, despite evidence in many cases that the child has been raised primarily by the father, and would be better off continuing in his care.

Identification of opposition: conservative judges

Refutation and conclusion that reinforces main proposition

www.mhhe.com/
shortprose

To learn more about using argumentation, click on
Writing > Writing Tutor: Arguments

ARGUMENTS PRO AND CON: CAN TORTURE BE JUSTIFIED?

Word of American soldiers torturing prisoners in 2003 at the Abu Ghraib prison in Baghdad, Iraq, shocked the country as well as the international community of nations. Obscene photographs of contorted prisoners with members of the military smiling beside them—could this be the America of human rights, so long admired by the rest of the world and one of our proudest achievements as a democratic society? It wasn't until two years later that the government officially acknowledged to the United Nations that prisoners were in fact subjected to torture at Abu Ghraib—and also by some reports since 2002 in Cuba at Guantanamo Bay, the holding center for suspected terrorists.

A cry of outrage resounded across the globe. As one of the writers in this section, Mirko Bagaric, states, "The formal prohibition against torture is absolute—there are no exceptions to it." Truth be told, however, torture has an ugly history among nations right up to the present day. Yet the explosive news of the United States as an agent of prisoner mistreatment has led to an ongoing, serious conversation among commentators and political analysts about the uses of torture. In the administration of George W. Bush, much attention focused on the government-accepted practice of "waterboarding," in which, as Senator John McCain describes it in his essay, "a prisoner is restrained and blindfolded while an interrogator pours water on his face and into his mouth—causing the prisoner to believe that he is being drowned." So torture is still in the news, and America's support of torture in philosophy and practice continues to stimulate writers, politicians, and policy makers.

The two writers here take opposite positions on torture. You can tell from the titles who is on which side: McCain's piece is called "Torture's Terrible Toll"; Bagaric's, "A Case for Torture." But the two writers bring supporting evidence for their positions. No matter what your view of the controversy, read the two selections with an eye to whether the writers make their points fairly and whether the evidence they provide is valid in the context of acceptable argumentation strategies.

A Case for Torture

Mirko Bagaric

Mirko Bagaric was born in Croatia. He holds a number of degrees, including an LLB and a PhD, and is professor of law and former head of the Law School at Deacon University in Australia. Bagaric writes on law and moral and political philosophy and is the author of twenty books, including *How to Live: Being Happy and Dealing with Moral Dilemmas* (2006) and *Torture: When the Unthinkable Is Morally Permissible* (2006), which he coauthored with Julie Clarke. Here he deals with the moral dilemma of torture and finds that the belief that torture is always wrong is misguided.

PREREADING: THINKING ABOUT THE ESSAY IN ADVANCE

Under what conditions would you find torture acceptable, if any? Make a list of situations that might lead to torture and explain your responses to the possible use in each instance.

Words to Watch

prevalence (par. 1)   frequency
deplored (par. 1)   condemned; criticized
verging (par. 3)   bordering on
floodgates (par. 8)   a gate that controls the flow of water
reprehensible (par. 11)   in the wrong; blameworthy
vacuous (par. 16)   empty-headed; stupid

1   Recent events stemming from the "war on terrorism" have highlighted the prevalence of torture. This is despite the fact that torture is almost universally deplored. The formal prohibition against torture is absolute—there are no exceptions to it.

2   The belief that torture is always wrong is, however, misguided and symptomatic of the alarmist and reflexive responses typically emanating from social commentators. It is this type of absolutist and short-sighted rhetoric that lies at the core of many distorted moral judgements that we as a community continue to make, resulting in an enormous amount of injustice and suffering in our society and far beyond our borders.

Torture is permissible where the evidence suggests that this 3 is the only means, due to the immediacy of the situation, to save the life of an innocent person. The reason that torture in such a case is defensible and necessary is because the justification manifests from the closest thing we have to an inviolable right: the right to self-defence, which of course extends to the defence of another. Given the choice between inflicting a relatively small level of harm on a wrongdoer and saving an innocent person, it is verging on moral indecency to prefer the interests of the wrongdoer.

The analogy with self-defence is sharpened by considering the 4 hostage-taking scenario, where a wrongdoer takes a hostage and points a gun to the hostage's head, threatening to kill the hostage unless a certain (unreasonable) demand is met. In such a case it is not only permissible, but desirable for police to shoot (and kill) the wrongdoer if they get a "clear shot." This is especially true if it's known that the wrongdoer has a history of serious violence, and hence is more likely to carry out the threat.

There is no logical or moral difference between this scenario 5 and one where there is overwhelming evidence that a wrongdoer has kidnapped an innocent person and informs police that the victim will be killed by a co-offender if certain demands are not met.

In the hostage scenario, it is universally accepted that it is per- 6 missible to violate the right to life of the aggressor to save an inno- cent person. How can it be wrong to violate an even less important right (the right to physical integrity) by torturing the aggressor in order to save a life in the second scenario?

There are three main counter-arguments to even the above 7 limited approval of torture. The first is the slippery slope argu- ment: if you start allowing torture in a limited context, the situa- tions in which it will be used will increase.

This argument is not sound in the context of torture. First, 8 the floodgates are already open—torture is used widely, despite the absolute legal prohibition against it. Amnesty International has recently reported that it had received, during 2003, reports of torture and ill-treatment from 132 countries, including the United States, Japan and France. It is, in fact, arguable that it is the exis- tence of an unrealistic absolute ban that has driven torture beneath the radar of accountability, and that legalization in very rare cir- cumstances would in fact reduce instances of it.

9   The second main argument is that torture will dehumanize society. This is no more true in relation to torture than it is with self-defence, and in fact the contrary is true. A society that elects to favour the interests of wrongdoers over those of the innocent, when a choice must be made between the two, is in need of serious ethical rewiring.

10   A third counter-argument is that we can never be totally sure that torturing a person will in fact result in us saving an innocent life. This, however, is the same situation as in all cases of self-defence. To revisit the hostage example, the hostage-taker's gun might in fact be empty, yet it is still permissible to shoot. As with any decision, we must decide on the best evidence at the time.

11   Torture in order to save an innocent person is the only situation where it is clearly justifiable. This means that the recent high-profile incidents of torture, apparently undertaken as punitive measures or in a bid to acquire information where there was no evidence of an immediate risk to the life of an innocent person, were reprehensible.

12   Will a real-life situation actually occur where the only option is between torturing a wrongdoer or saving an innocent person? Perhaps not. However, a minor alteration to the Douglas Wood* situation illustrates that the issue is far from moot. If Western forces in Iraq arrested one of Mr Wood's captors, it would be a perverse ethic that required us to respect the physical integrity of the captor, and not torture him to ascertain Mr Wood's whereabouts, in preference to taking all possible steps to save Mr Wood.

13   Even if a real-life situation where torture is justifiable does not eventuate, the above argument in favour of torture in limited circumstances needs to be made because it will encourage the community to think more carefully about moral judgements we collectively hold that are the cause of an enormous amount of suffering in the world.

14   First, no right or interest is absolute. Secondly, rights must always yield to consequences, which are the ultimate criteria upon which the soundness of a decision is gauged. Lost lives hurt a lot more than bent principles.

15   Thirdly, we must take responsibility not only for the things that we do, but also for the things that we can—but fail to—prevent. The retort that we are not responsible for the lives lost through a

*Douglas Wood, an Australian construction engineer, was captured and held hostage in Iraq from May 1 to June 15, 2005.

decision not to torture a wrongdoer because we did not create the situation is code for moral indifference.

Equally vacuous is the claim that we in the affluent West have 16 no responsibility for more than 13,000 people dying daily due to starvation. Hopefully, the debate on torture will prompt us to correct some of these fundamental failings.

BUILDING VOCABULARY

Bagaric has used several words that are useful in legal situations but serve in other contexts as well. Check these words in a dictionary and write definitions for each.

1. injustice (par. 2)
2. defensible (par. 3)
3. justification (par. 3)
4. inviolable (par. 3)
5. wrongdoer (par. 3)
6. co-offender (par. 5)
7. aggressor (par. 6)
8. prohibition (par. 8)
9. punitive (par. 11)
10. retort (par. 15)

THINKING CRITICALLY ABOUT THE ESSAY

Understanding the Writer's Ideas

1. What does Bagaric believe is "misguided and symptomatic of the alarmist reflexive responses typically emanating from social commentators"?
2. When, according to the writer, is torture permissible?
3. What "inviolable right" allows torture, according to Bagaric?
4. What kind of scenario does the writer point out to support his view? How does that scenario compare with a kidnapping scenario?
5. What does the writer believe is an appropriate response in the kinds of situations identified in question 4 above?
6. What is the "slippery-slope" argument?
7. How does the writer address the argument that "torture will dehumanize society"?

   8. What does Bagaric indicate as the third counterargument against the use of torture?
   9. What is the "Douglas Wood" situation?
   10. What does the writer believe we must take responsibility for?

Understanding the Writer's Techniques

   1. State Bagaric's major premise in your own words. Where does he himself state it in the essay?
   2. Bagaric uses an *analogy* (see Glossary) beginning in paragraph 5. What does he compare to what? Is the analogy effective? Why or why not?
   3. In the first paragraph, what reason did you think the writer had for placing the words "war on terrorism" in quotation marks? Where else does he use quotation marks—and for what reason, do you think?
   4. Bagaric argues mainly through *refutation* (see Glossary). What arguments does he refute? Do you find his arguments convincing—in other words, has he laid out logical reasons for readers to agree with him? Explain your answer.
   5. The writer uses illustration strategies in the essay, enumerating items almost in a list (first . . . , second . . . , third . . .). Where does he do this? How effective is this kind of presentation?
   6. What is your reaction to the supporting data in paragraph 8? Other than the example of Douglas Wood (par. 12), Bagaric offers no other specific supporting detail. How does that fact influence the argument?
   7. The writer raises a question in paragraph 12 and then answers it. What is your reaction to this writing strategy?

Exploring the Writer's Ideas

   1. Bagaric indicates the situations in which he believes torture is permissible. Do you agree with him? Why or why not?
   2. Do you agree that the right to self-defense is an inviolable right (par. 3)? Why or why not? Do you believe that this right also "extends to the defense of another"? Why or why not?
   3. Do you accept the point that "Torture is permissible . . . to save the life of an innocent person" (par. 3)? Explain your response.

4. Which of the three counterarguments do you think Bagaric refutes most effectively? Why?

5. Do you agree with the writer that people must take responsibility not only for what they do but also what they can, but fail to, prevent? Why or why not? Other than the point Bagaric makes, what situation can you imagine in which someone could have taken responsibility for preventing something from happening but wouldn't?

6. Do you agree that rights must always yield to consequences? Why or why not?

IDEAS FOR WRITING

Prewriting

Make a list of the reasons you have for either accepting or opposing the use of torture.

Guided Writing

Write an original essay called "A Case for Torture" or "A Case Against Torture" in which you argue for or against the use of torture in a situation or situations that you define.

1. State clearly your major proposition about whether or not torture is justifiable.

2. Provide evidence to support your argument. Use data or examples from what you've read or seen in the news, as appropriate.

3. Use an analogy that makes your argument clear.

4. Argue mainly through refutation—that is, explain what people who oppose your point of view would say and then refute their arguments.

5. Use illustration strategies as Bagaric has, enumerating some of your arguments as he does.

Thinking and Writing Collaboratively

Form groups and discuss this point made in the essay: "no right or interest is absolute." What does Bagaric mean by the statement? What examples can group members provide to support or oppose the point?

Writing About the Text

Write a brief essay about Bagaric's use of analogy and other figures of speech in his essay.

More Writing Projects

1. Write a journal entry about the right to self-defense. What do you think this right entails?
2. Write an extended paragraph on the idea from the essay of the West's "fundamental failings." Do you agree that the debate on torture may prompt us to correct some of them?
3. Write an argumentative essay in which you take a position on the first counterargument that Bagaric attempts to refute: "If you start allowing torture in a limited context, the situations in which it will be used will increase."

Torture's Terrible Toll

John McCain

John Sidney McCain III was born on August 29, 1936, and since 1986 has been the senior U.S. Senator from Arizona. He attended the U.S. Naval Academy and graduated in 1958. As a naval aviator during the Vietnam War, he was shot down on his twenty-third bombing mission in 1967 and badly injured. He then endured five and a half years as a prisoner of war in North Vietnam, including periods of torture, before he was released in 1973. McCain ran for president of the United States in 2008 on the Republican ticket. His political career, marked by conservatism, nonetheless reflects his maverick approach to problems and his willingness to defy the Republican Party line on many issues. McCain is the author or coauthor of several books, including *Faith of My Fathers* (1999), *Worth the Fighting For: A Memoir* (2002), and *Why Courage Matters: The Way to a Braver Life* (2004). This essay, which appeared in *Newsweek* in 2005, grew out of the political fallout in the Bush administration's support of certain kinds of torture in extracting information from enemy prisoners.

PREREADING: THINKING ABOUT THE ESSAY IN ADVANCE

What does the title of McCain's essay make you think of? What do you believe he means by the "terrible toll" of torture?

Words to Watch

partisan (par. 1)   political; biased
vigilance (par. 1)   watchfulness; caution
latitude (par. 2)   leeway; freedom; room to maneuver
deceptive (par. 3)   misleading
sociopath (par. 4)   someone with a serious personality disorder marked by aggressive and antisocial behavior
inherently (par. 5)   fundamentally; essentially
existential (par. 5)   relating to human existence
in extremis (par. 13)   in desperate circumstances
enshrine (par. 14)   preserve; protect
onerous (par. 15)   difficult; burdensome

1   The debate over the treatment of enemy prisoners, like so much of the increasingly overcharged partisan debate over the war in Iraq and the global war against terrorists, has occasioned many unserious and unfair charges about the administration's intentions and motives. With all the many competing demands for their attention, President Bush and Vice President Cheney have remained admirably tenacious in their determination to prevent terrorists from inflicting another atrocity on the American people, whom they are sworn to protect. It is certainly fair to credit their administration's vigilance as a substantial part of the reason that we have not experienced another terrorist attack on American soil since September 11, 2001.

2   It is also quite fair to attribute the administration's position—that U.S. interrogators be allowed latitude in their treatment of enemy prisoners that might offend American values—to the president's and vice president's appropriate concern for acquiring actionable intelligence that could prevent attacks on our soldiers or our allies or on the American people. And it is quite unfair to assume some nefarious purpose informs their intentions. They bear the greatest responsibility for the security of American lives and interests. I understand and respect their motives just as I admire the seriousness and patriotism of their resolve. But I do, respectfully, take issue with the position that the demands of this war require us to accord a lower station to the moral imperatives that should govern our conduct in war and peace when they come in conflict with the unyielding inhumanity of our vicious enemy.

3   Obviously, to defeat our enemies we need intelligence, but intelligence that is reliable. We should not torture or treat inhumanely terrorists we have captured. The abuse of prisoners harms, not helps, our war effort. In my experience, abuse of prisoners often produces bad intelligence because under torture a person will say anything he thinks his captors want to hear—whether it is true or false—if he believes it will relieve his suffering. I was once physically coerced to provide my enemies with the names of the members of my flight squadron, information that had little if any value to my enemies as actionable intelligence. But I did not refuse, or repeat my insistence that I was required under the Geneva Conventions to provide my captors only with my name, rank and serial number. Instead, I gave them the names of the Green Bay Packers' offensive line, knowing that providing them false information was sufficient to suspend the abuse. It seems probable to me that the terrorists we interrogate under less than humane standards of

treatment are also likely to resort to deceptive answers that are perhaps less provably false than that which I once offered.

Our commitment to basic humanitarian values affects—in 4 part—the willingness of other nations to do the same. Mistreatment of enemy prisoners endangers our own troops who might someday be held captive. While some enemies, and Al Qaeda surely, will never be bound by the principle of reciprocity, we should have concern for those Americans captured by more traditional enemies, if not in this war then in the next. Until about 1970, North Vietnam ignored its obligations not to mistreat the Americans they held prisoner, claiming that we were engaged in an unlawful war against them and thus not entitled to the protections of the Geneva Conventions. But when their abuses became widely known and incited unfavorable international attention, they substantially decreased their mistreatment of us. Again, Al Qaeda will never be influenced by international sensibilities or open to moral suasion. If ever the term "sociopath" applied to anyone, it applies to them. But I doubt they will be the last enemy America will fight, and we should not undermine today our defense of international prohibitions against torture and inhumane treatment of prisoners of war that we will need to rely on in the future.

To prevail in this war we need more than victories on the 5 battlefield. This is a war of ideas, a struggle to advance freedom in the face of terror in places where oppressive rule has bred the malevolence that creates terrorists. Prisoner abuses exact a terrible toll on us in this war of ideas. They inevitably become public, and when they do they threaten our moral standing, and expose us to false but widely disseminated charges that democracies are no more inherently idealistic and moral than other regimes. This is an existential fight, to be sure. If they could, Islamic extremists who resort to terror would destroy us utterly. But to defeat them we must prevail in our defense of American political values as well. The mistreatment of prisoners greatly injures that effort.

The mistreatment of prisoners harms us more than our ene- 6 mies. I don't think I'm naive about how terrible are the wages of war, and how terrible are the things that must be done to wage it successfully. It is an awful business, and no matter how noble the cause for which it is fought, no matter how valiant their service, many veterans spend much of their subsequent lives trying to forget not only what was done to them, but some of what had to be done by them to prevail.

7   I don't mourn the loss of any terrorist's life. Nor do I care if in the course of serving their ignoble cause they suffer great harm. They have pledged their lives to the intentional destruction of innocent lives, and they have earned their terrible punishment in this life and the next. What I do mourn is what we lose when by official policy or official neglect we allow, confuse or encourage our soldiers to forget that best sense of ourselves, that which is our greatest strength—that we are different and better than our enemies, that we fight for an idea, not a tribe, not a land, not a king, not a twisted interpretation of an ancient religion, but for an idea that all men are created equal and endowed by their Creator with inalienable rights.

8   Now, in this war, our liberal notions are put to the test. Americans of good will, all patriots, argue about what is appropriate and necessary to combat this unconventional enemy. Those of us who feel that in this war, as in past wars, Americans should not compromise our values must answer those Americans who believe that a less rigorous application of those values is regrettably necessary to prevail over a uniquely abhorrent and dangerous enemy. Part of our disagreement is definitional. Some view more coercive interrogation tactics as something short of torture but worry that they might be subject to challenge under the "no cruel, inhumane or degrading" standard. Others, including me, believe that both the prohibition on torture and the cruel, inhumane and degrading standard must remain intact. When we relax that standard, it is nearly unavoidable that some objectionable practices will be allowed as something less than torture because they do not risk life and limb or do not cause very serious physical pain.

9   For instance, there has been considerable press attention to a tactic called "waterboarding," where a prisoner is restrained and blindfolded while an interrogator pours water on his face and into his mouth—causing the prisoner to believe he is being drowned. He isn't, of course; there is no intention to injure him physically. But if you gave people who have suffered abuse as prisoners a choice between a beating and a mock execution, many, including me, would choose a beating. The effects of most beatings heal. The memory of an execution will haunt someone for a very long time and damage his or her psyche in ways that may never heal. In my view, to make someone believe that you are killing him by drowning is no different than holding a pistol to his head and firing a blank. I believe that it is torture, very exquisite torture.

Those who argue the necessity of some abuses raise an impor- 10
tant dilemma as their most compelling rationale: the ticking-
time-bomb scenario. What do we do if we capture a terrorist who
we have sound reasons to believe possesses specific knowledge of
an imminent terrorist attack?

In such an urgent and rare instance, an interrogator might well 11
try extreme measures to extract information that could save lives.
Should he do so, and thereby save an American city or prevent
another 9/11, authorities and the public would surely take this into
account when judging his actions and recognize the extremely dire
situation which he confronted. But I don't believe this scenario
requires us to write into law an exception to our treaty and moral
obligations that would permit cruel, inhumane and degrading treatment. To carve out legal exemptions to this basic principle of human
rights risks opening the door to abuse as a matter of course, rather
than a standard violated truly in extremis. It is far better to embrace
a standard that might be violated in extraordinary circumstances
than to lower our standards to accommodate a remote contingency,
confusing personnel in the field and sending precisely the wrong
message abroad about America's purposes and practices.

The state of Israel, no stranger to terrorist attacks, has faced 12
this dilemma, and in 1999 the Israeli Supreme Court declared
cruel, inhumane and degrading treatment illegal. "A democratic,
freedom-loving society," the court wrote, "does not accept that
investigators use any means for the purpose of uncovering truth.
The rules pertaining to investigators are important to a democratic
state. They reflect its character."

I've been asked often where did the brave men I was privileged 13
to serve with in North Vietnam draw the strength to resist to the best
of their abilities the cruelties inflicted on them by our enemies. They
drew strength from their faith in each other, from their faith in God
and from their faith in our country. Our enemies didn't adhere to
the Geneva Conventions. Many of my comrades were subjected to
very cruel, very inhumane and degrading treatment, a few of them
unto death. But every one of us—every single one of us—knew and
took great strength from the belief that we were different from our
enemies, that we were better than them, that we, if the roles were
reversed, would not disgrace ourselves by committing or approving
such mistreatment of them. That faith was indispensable not only to
our survival, but to our attempts to return home with honor. For without our honor, our homecoming would have had little value to us.

14   The enemies we fight today hold our liberal values in contempt, as they hold in contempt the international conventions that enshrine them. I know that. But we are better than them, and we are stronger for our faith. And we will prevail. It is indispensable to our success in this war that those we ask to fight it know that in the discharge of their dangerous responsibilities to their country they are never expected to forget that they are Americans, and the valiant defenders of a sacred idea of how nations should govern their own affairs and their relations with others—even our enemies.

15   Those who return to us and those who give their lives for us are entitled to that honor. And those of us who have given them this onerous duty are obliged by our history, and the many terrible sacrifices that have been made in our defense, to make clear to them that they need not risk their or their country's honor to prevail; that they are always—through the violence, chaos and heartache of war, through deprivation and cruelty and loss—they are always, always, Americans, and different, better and stronger than those who would destroy us.

BUILDING VOCABULARY

Locate the following words in the paragraphs indicated and determine the meaning of the words from the *context clues*. (See Glossary.) Use a dictionary to check your definitions.

1. tenacious (par. 1)
2. atrocity (par. 1)
3. nefarious (par. 2)
4. unyielding (par. 2)
5. inhumanely (par. 3)
6. reciprocity (par. 4)
7. malevolence (par. 5)
8. valiant (par. 6 and 14)
9. abhorrent (par. 8)
10. indispensable (par. 13)

THINKING CRITICALLY ABOUT THE ESSAY

Understanding the Writer's Ideas

1. To what does McCain attribute the fact that America has not had another terrorist attack on our soil since September 11, 2001?

2. What was the Bush and Cheney administration's position on allowing interrogators latitude in questioning prisoners?

3. What does McCain believe results from the mistreatment of prisoners?

4. What did McCain himself provide to his captors when they asked for the names of the members of his flight squadron?

5. What, according to the writer, compelled the North Vietnamese to decrease their mistreatment of prisoners of war?

6. What does the writer see as our greatest strength as a country?

7. What is waterboarding? What does McCain think about it as a strategy for getting information from captured enemies?

8. What is the "ticking-time-bomb scenario"? How does McCain feel about an interrogator's use of extreme measures in this circumstance?

9. What was Israel's dilemma regarding cruel treatment of prisoners? How did the Israelis resolve that dilemma?

10. What, according to McCain, gave American prisoners of war in North Vietnam the strength to resist the cruelties inflicted by the enemy?

Understanding the Writer's Techniques

1. What is McCain's argument in this essay? What, in other words, is his major proposition?

2. What minor proposition does he introduce to clarify the reasons he offers to support the main idea?

3. How do McCain's personal experiences make him an appropriate authority to write about the uses of torture? Or do you think that these experiences do not necessarily make him an expert on the subject? Explain your response.

4. In what ways does the writer deal with opposing arguments to his position? How, for example, does he treat President Bush and Vice President Cheney, both of whom disagree with McCain? What tone does he assume in addressing their positions?

5. McCain uses a highly sophisticated vocabulary throughout the essay. Why do you think he chose such a formal level of diction? How do you think *Newsweek*'s readers, the direct audience for this piece, would respond to "Torture's Terrible Toll"?

6. The writer seems to change his mind about torture in regard to the "ticking-time-bomb scenario." What is your response to this

apparent contradiction to the major premise of his essay? Does his position here seem reasonable? Or do you find it unacceptably inconsistent with his argument? Explain your answer.

Exploring the Writer's Ideas

1. McCain says that "the abuse of prisoners harms, not helps, our war effort." Do you agree with him? Why or why not?
2. How would you define "cruel, inhumane or degrading" in regard to questioning prisoners? Is the definition self-evident? Or does it require careful enumeration? Explain your response.
3. What is your reaction to waterboarding as an interrogation strategy?
4. McCain believes that the way a country treats prisoners is a direct reflection of the country's honor and that government must take the high road in assuring a commitment to moral principles. Why might you agree with him? disagree with him? If his point is correct, why would any country torture prisoners?

IDEAS FOR WRITING

Prewriting

Write nonstop for ten or fifteen minutes on another area in which you believe the government should or should not limit its right to act in a way that might be viewed as morally offensive.

Guided Writing

Write an argumentative essay in which you argue for or against limiting the government's power in some arena other than questioning prisoners of war. Build your essay around the moral principles inherent in the government's actions. For example, you might write about the government's ability to remove people from their homes when public works take precedence; to send back to their own countries illegal immigrants; to allow drilling for oil in ecologically sensitive areas like national parks or waterways close to shorelines; to refuse to allow the use of marijuana in treating painful medical conditions. There are others, certainly. The point is to decide whether or not the government's actions are justifiable and to make a strong case for your argument.

1. Begin your essay respectfully by indicating what those who oppose your argument might say.
2. Assert your major proposition early in the essay.
3. Give examples of how the government's power regarding the issue you have chosen does or does not serve its citizens.
4. Identify the moral issues involved in the government's action.
5. Discuss one exception to your major premise, and make a case briefly for allowing the government to act in an opposite way within a special instance.
6. End your essay by reiterating your position and making another reference to moral principles.

Thinking and Writing Collaboratively

Form groups and read drafts of each other's Guided Writing essays. Have the writers in your group made the major proposition clear? Does the paper incorporate the suggestions indicated for writing the essay?

Writing About the Text

McCain writes about a highly emotional topic in a very calm and reasonable manner. Write an essay in which you analyze how he achieves this balance between explosive topic and rational presentation.

More Writing Projects

1. Write a journal entry about the uses of torture in arenas other than military.
2. Write an extended paragraph to address the idea from the essay that despite "the violence, chaos and heartache of war" fought by our country, those who fight it are "always, always, Americans, and different, better, and stronger than those who would destroy us."
3. Write an argumentative essay about McCain's notion that with terrorists we are in a war of ideas and that we need more than victories in the battlefield.

PERSPECTIVES ON IDENTITY: WHO ARE WE, AND HOW ARE WE FORMED?

Who am I? Am I a unique individual, with certain physical and emotional traits and with the habits and tastes that I myself have chosen to develop? Or am I the product of a certain group, community, nation, race, religion? Am I who I feel myself to be on the inside? Or am I the person others perceive me to be? These are among the most charged issues about which we, as Americans, tend to argue. But how can we discuss issues of identity fairly and reasonably? How can we persuade others of the rightness of our own views and the limits of theirs? As you read the following selections, pause to reflect not only about what the writer has to say but also about *how* the writer says it. What approaches do you find most persuasive? Which rhetorical devices appeal to you most? What can you take from these essays for your own use in your own essays?

Are the Homeless Crazy?

Jonathan Kozol

Mixing Patterns

Jonathan Kozol was educated at Harvard University and Magdalen College, Oxford. He rose to national prominence with his startling account of his experience as a teacher in an urban school, *Death at an Early Age* (1967). Writing frequently about inequities in education and in American society, Kozol has reached wide audiences with best-selling books such as *Rachel and Her Children: Homeless Families in America* (1989), *Savage Inequalities: Children in America's Schools* (1992), and *Letters to a Young Teacher* (2007). This selection, derived from "Distancing the Homeless," appeared originally in the *Yale Review* in 1988. Kozol examines the idea that much of the homelessness of the late 1980s resulted from the release of patients from mental hospitals in the 1970s. The essay discusses how we tend to impose a disturbing identity on those outside the circle of social respectability.

www.mhhe.com/
shortprose

To learn more about Kozol, click on
**More Resources > Chapter 11 >
Jonathan Kozol**

PREREADING: THINKING ABOUT THE ESSAY IN ADVANCE

What are your views of the homeless in American society? Should we classify the homeless as crazy, lazy, unfortunate, or abject failures? Why or why not?

Words to Watch

deinstitutionalized (par. 1)   let inmates out of hospitals, prisons, and so forth
conceding (par. 2)   acknowledging; admitting to
arson (par. 4)   the crime of deliberately setting a fire
subsidized (par. 5)   aided with public money
destitute (par. 6)   very poor
afflictions (par. 7)   ills; problems
stigma (par. 7)   a mark of shame or discredit
complacence (par. 7)   self-satisfaction

bulk (par. 10)   the main part
de facto (par. 11)   actually; in reality
resilience (par. 12)   ability to recover easily from misfortune
paranoids (par. 13)   psychotic people who believe everyone is persecuting them
vengeance (par. 14)   retribution; retaliation

1   It is commonly believed by many journalists and politicians that the homeless of America are, in large part, former patients of large mental hospitals who were deinstitutionalized in the 1970s—the consequence, it is sometimes said, of misguided liberal opinion that favored the treatment of such persons in community-based centers. It is argued that this policy, and the subsequent failure of society to build such centers or to provide them in sufficient number, is the primary cause of homelessness in the United States.

2   Those who work among the homeless do not find that explanation satisfactory. While conceding that a certain number of the homeless are or have been mentally unwell, they believe that, in the case of most unsheltered people, the primary reason is economic rather than clinical. The cause of homelessness, they say with disarming logic, is the lack of homes and of income with which to rent or acquire them.

3   They point to the loss of traditional jobs in industry (2 million every year since 1980) and to the fact that half of those who are laid off end up in work that pays a poverty-level wage. They point out that since 1968 the number of children living in poverty has grown by 3 million, while welfare benefits to families with children have declined by 35 percent.

4   And they note, too, that these developments have occurred during a time in which the shortage of low-income housing has intensified as the gentrification of our major cities has accelerated. Half a million units of low-income housing are lost each year to condominium conversion as well as to arson, demolition, or abandonment. Between 1978 and 1980, median rents climbed 30 percent for people in the lowest income sector, driving many of these families into the streets. Since 1980, rents have risen at even faster rates.

5   Hard numbers, in this instance, would appear to be of greater help than psychiatric labels in telling us why so many people become homeless. Eight million American families now use half or more of their income to pay their rent or mortgage. At the same time, federal support for low-income housing dropped from

$30 billion (1980) to $7.5 billion (1988). Under Presidents Ford and Carter, 500,000 subsidized private housing units were constructed. By President Reagan's second term, the number had dropped to 25,000.

In our rush to explain the homeless as a psychiatric problem 6 even the words of medical practitioners who care for homeless people have been curiously ignored. A study published by the Massachusetts Medical Society, for instance, has noted that, with the exceptions of alcohol and drug use, the most frequent illnesses among a sample of the homeless population were trauma (31 percent), upper-respiratory disorders (28 percent), limb disorders (19 percent), mental illness (16 percent), skin diseases (15 percent), hypertension (14 percent), and neurological illnesses (12 percent). Why, we may ask, of all these calamities, does mental illness command so much political and press attention? The answer may be that the label of mental illness places the destitute outside the sphere of ordinary life. It personalizes an anguish that is public in its genesis; it individualizes a misery that is both general in cause and general in application.

There is another reason to assign labels to the destitute and 7 single out mental illness from among their many afflictions. All these other problems—tuberculosis, asthma, scabies, diarrhea, bleeding gums, impacted teeth, etc.—bear no stigma, and mental illness does. It conveys a stigma in the United States. It conveys a stigma in the Soviet Union as well. In both nations the label is used, whether as a matter of deliberate policy or not, to isolate and treat as special cases those who, by deed or word or by sheer presence, represent a threat to national complacence. The two situations are obviously not identical, but they are enough alike to give Americans reason for concern.

The notion that the homeless are largely psychotics who 8 belong in institutions, rather than victims of displacement at the hands of enterprising realtors, spares us from the need to offer realistic solutions to the deep and widening extremes of wealth and poverty in the United States. It also enables us to tell ourselves that the despair of homeless people bears no intimate connection to the privileged existence we enjoy—when, for example, we rent or purchase one of those restored town houses that once provided shelter for people now huddled in the street.

What is to be made, then, of the supposition that the home- 9 less are primarily the former residents of mental hospitals, persons who were carelessly released during the 1970s? Many of them are, to be sure. Among the older men and women in the streets and shelters, as many as one-third (some believe as many as one-half) may be chronically disturbed, and a number of these people were deinstitutionalized during the 1970s. But to operate on that assumption in a city such as New York—where nearly half the homeless are small children whose average age is six—makes no sense. Their parents, with an average age of twenty-seven, are not likely to have been hospitalized in the 1970s, either.

10   A frequently cited set of figures tells us that in 1955 the average daily census of non-federal psychiatric institutions was 677,000, and that by 1984 the number had dropped to 151,000. But these people didn't go directly from a hospital room to the street. The bulk of those who had been psychiatric patients and were released from hospitals during the 1960s and early 1970s had been living in low-income housing, many in skid-row hotels or boardinghouses. Such housing—commonly known as SRO (single-room occupancy) units—was drastically diminished by the gentrification of our cities that began in the early '70s. Almost 50 percent of SRO housing was replaced by luxury apartments or office buildings between 1970 and 1980, and the remaining units have been disappearing even more rapidly.

11   Even for those persons who are ill and were deinstitutionalized during the decades before 1980, the precipitating cause of homelessness in 1987 is not illness but loss of housing. SRO housing offered low-cost sanctuaries for the homeless, providing a degree of safety and mutual support for those who lived within them. They were a demeaning version of the community health centers that society had promised; they were the de facto "halfway houses" of the 1970s. For these people too—at most half of the homeless single persons in America—the cause of homelessness is lack of housing.

12   Even in those cases where mental instability is apparent, homelessness itself is often the precipitating factor. For example, many pregnant women without homes are denied prenatal care because they constantly travel from one shelter to another. Many are anemic. Many are denied essential dietary supplements by recent federal cuts. As a consequence, some of their children do not live to see their second year of life. Do these mothers sometimes show signs of stress? Do they appear disorganized, depressed, disordered? Frequently. They are immobilized by pain, traumatized by fear. So it is no surprise that when researchers enter the scene

to ask them how they "feel," the resulting reports tell us that the homeless are emotionally unwell. The reports do not tell us that we have *made* these people ill. They do not tell us that illness is a natural response to intolerable conditions. Nor do they tell us of the strength and the resilience that so many of these people retain despite the miseries they must endure.

A writer in the *New York Times* describes a homeless woman 13 standing on a traffic island in Manhattan. "She was evicted from her small room in the hotel just across the street," and she is determined to get revenge. Until she does, "nothing will move her from that spot. . . . Her argumentativeness and her angry fixation on revenge, along with the apparent absence of hallucinations, mark her as a paranoid." Most physicians, I imagine, would be more reserved in passing judgment with so little evidence, but this reporter makes his diagnosis without hesitation. "The paranoids of the street," he says, "are among the most difficult to help."

Perhaps so. But does it depend on who is offering the help? Is 14 anyone offering to help this woman get back her home? Is it crazy to seek vengeance for being thrown into the street? The absence of anger, some psychiatrists believe, might indicate much greater illness.

"No one will be turned away," says the mayor of New York 15 City, as hundreds of young mothers with their infants are turned from the doors of shelters season after season. That may sound to some like a denial of reality. "Now you're hearing all kinds of horror stories," says the President of the United States as he denies that anyone is cold or hungry or unhoused. On another occasion he says that the unsheltered "are homeless, you might say, by choice." That sounds every bit as self-deceiving.

The woman standing on the traffic island screaming for 16 revenge until her room has been restored to her sounds relatively healthy by comparison. If 3 million homeless people did the same, and all at the same time, we might finally be forced to listen.

BUILDING VOCABULARY

1. Throughout this essay, Kozol uses medical and psychiatric *jargon* (see Glossary). List the medical or psychiatric terms or references that you find here. Then look up any five in the dictionary and write definitions for them.

2. Explain in your own words the meanings of the following phrases. Use clues from the surrounding text to help you understand.
   a. sufficient number (par. 1)
   b. primary cause (par. 1)
   c. poverty-level wage (par. 3)
   d. median rents (par. 4)
   e. low-income housing (par. 5)
   f. sheer presence (par. 7)
   g. intimate connection (par. 8)
   h. chronically disturbed (par. 9)
   i. skid-row hotels (par. 10)
   j. precipitating cause (par. 11)
   k. low-cost sanctuaries (par. 11)
   l. mutual support (par. 11)
   m. demeaning version (par. 11)
   n. natural response (par. 12)
   o. intolerable conditions (par. 12)
   p. angry fixation (par. 13)

THINKING CRITICALLY ABOUT THE ESSAY

Understanding the Writer's Ideas

1. According to Kozol, who has suggested that the deinstitutionalizing of mental-hospital patients is the major cause of homelessness? Does he agree? If not, what does he identify as the major causes?
2. In the opening paragraph, what two groups does Kozol link together? Why? What relation between them does he suggest?
3. In New York City, what percentage of the homeless are children? What is the average age of their parents? In the past twenty years, has the number of children living in poverty increased or decreased? What about welfare payments to families with children? How has this affected the homelessness situation?
4. What are "gentrification" and "condominium conversion" (par. 4)? How have they affected homelessness?
5. Explain the meaning of the statement: "Hard numbers, in this instance, would appear to be of greater help than psychiatric labels in telling us why so many people become homeless" (par. 5).

6. List in descending order the most common illnesses among the homeless. From what does Kozol draw these statistics? What is his conclusion about them?

7. In your own words, summarize why Kozol feels that journalists and politicians concentrate so heavily on the problems of mental illness among the homeless.

8. What are SROs? Explain how they figure in the homeless situation.

9. What is meant by the "press" (par. 6)? What are "halfway houses" (par. 11)?

10. What is Kozol's attitude toward former President Reagan? toward former New York City Mayor Ed Koch? Explain your answers with specific references to the beginning and ending of the essay.

11. Summarize in your own words the *New York Times* story to which Kozol refers. According to the *Times* reporter, why did the homeless woman mentioned refuse to move from the traffic island? Does Kozol agree with the reporter's interpretation? Explain.

12. In one sentence, state in your own words the opinion Kozol expresses in the last paragraph.

Understanding the Writer's Techniques

1. Which sentence states the *major proposition* of the essay?

2. Describe Kozol's argumentative purpose in this essay. Is it primarily to *convince* or to *persuade*? Explain.

3. In paragraph 1, the author uses a particular verbal construction that he doesn't repeat elsewhere in the essay. He writes: "It is commonly believed . . ."; "it is sometimes said . . ."; and "It is argued . . ." Why does he use the "it is" construction? What effect does it have? How does he change that pattern in paragraph 2? Why?

4. In paragraph 2, Kozol uses the phrase "mentally unwell" instead of the more common "mentally ill," and he uses "unsheltered people" instead of "homeless people." Why does he use these less-expected phrases? Does he use them again in the essay? Why or why not?

5. *Cynicism* adds an edge of pessimism or anger to a statement that might otherwise be perceived as *irony* (see Glossary). In

the sentence, "The cause of homelessness, they say with dis-arming logic, is the lack of homes and of income with which to rent or acquire them" (par. 2), the clause set off by commas might be considered cynical. Why? Find and explain several other examples of cynicism in this essay. Are they effective? Are they justified?

6. Identify the *minor proposition* statements in this essay. How do they add *coherence* (see Glossary) to the essay?

7. How important is Kozol's use of *statistics* in this essay? Why does he use them?

8. What is the difference between *refutation* (see Glossary) and *negation*? Kozol uses refutation as a major technique in this essay. Analyze his use of refutation in paragraphs 1 and 2. List and discuss at least three other instances where he uses refutation. Where in the essay does he specifically use negation?

9. Characterize the overall *tone* of the essay. How and why does Kozol develop this tone? Who is the intended *audience* for this essay? What is the *level of diction*? How are the two connected? What assumption about the audience is implied in the last sentence of paragraph 8?

10. Writers often use *rhetorical questions* in order to prompt the reader to pay special attention to an issue, but rhetorical questions are usually not meant to be answered. Evaluate Kozol's use of rhetorical questions in paragraph 12. What is the effect of the one-word answer, "Frequently"? Where else does he use rhetorical questions? What message does he attempt to convey with them?

11. Returning to the thesis in the course of an essay is often an effective technique to refocus the reader's attention before beginning a new analysis or a conclusion. Explain how Kozol uses this technique in paragraph 11 to make it a key turning point in the essay.

12. Although Kozol cites various studies and authorities, he makes little use of *direct quotations*. Why? Identify and analyze the three instances where he *does* use direct quotations. How does it help to convey his attitude toward the material he's quoting?

13. Evaluate Kozol's conclusion. How does he establish an aura of unreality in paragraphs 15 and 16? Why does he do so? Does he effectively answer the title question? Explain.

> ✳ MIXING PATTERNS
>
> Kozol draws on a number of rhetorical strategies to advance his argument. How effective is his use of *cause-and-effect analysis* in paragraphs 1 through 6. In paragraph 12, how does Kozol revise the more commonly cited causal relation between homelessness and mental illness? How effective is Kozol's use of *comparison* in paragraph 7? In what ways does he use *illustration*? How is his use of illustration in the last paragraph different from his other uses of it?

Exploring the Writer's Ideas

1. In small groups, discuss your own experiences, both positive and negative, with homeless people.
2. If possible, conduct an interview with one or more homeless people. Try to find out:
   a. how they became homeless
   b. how long they've been homeless
   c. what they do to survive
   d. whether they feel there may be an end to their homelessness

   Write a report based on your interviews and share it with your classmates.
3. This essay is an excerpt from a much longer essay entitled "Distancing the Homeless," published in the *Yale Review.* How is the theme of that title expressed in this essay?
4. Kozol presents an impressive array of statistics. Working in small groups, compile as many other statistics about homelessness as possible. Each group should then draw a subjective conclusion from the data and be prepared to present and defend it to the class as a whole.
5. Read the following description of New York City's Bowery district:

   Walk under the El at night and all you feel is a sort of cold guilt. Touched for a dime, you try to drop the coin and not touch the hand, because the hand is dirty; you try to avoid the glance, because the glance accuses. This is not so much personal menace as universal—the cold menace of unresolved human suffering and poverty and the advanced stages of the disease alcoholism. On a summer night the drunks sleep in the open. The sidewalk is a free bed, and there are no lice. Pedestrians step along and over and around the still forms as though walking on a battlefield among the dead. In doorways, on the steps of the savings bank, the bums lie sleeping it off. Standing sentinel at each sleeper's head is the empty bottle from which he drained his release. Wedged in the crook of his arm is the paper bag containing his things.

This description is from E. B. White's 1949 essay "Here Is New York." This selection is but one small indication that the current problem of homelessness is nothing new. Try to find other examples, either written or visual, that indicate homelessness is a long-standing social issue. (You may want to contact such organizations as the Coalition for the Homeless and the Salvation Army.)

In your own experience, how have the conditions of homelessness changed in your own environment over the past five years? the past one year?

IDEAS FOR WRITING

Prewriting

Draft a brief outline arguing for or against a specific issue of campus concern—for example, date rape, political correctness, drugs or alcohol, or AIDS counseling. In your outline, list at least three main reasons that support the position you are advocating.

Guided Writing

Choose a controversial local issue about which you hold a strong opinion that is not the generally accepted one. (For example, you might write about a decision by the town council to build a new shopping mall on an old vacant lot; the limiting of public library hours in order to save money; a decision to open a halfway house in your neighborhood; and so forth.) Write an essay that will convince the reader of the validity of your stance on the issue.

1. Begin your essay with a discussion of the commonly held opinion on this issue. Use the verbal construction "it is" to help distance you from that opinion.

2. In the next section, strongly refute the commonly held opinion by stating your major proposition clearly and directly.
3. Develop your opinion by the use of comparative statistics.
4. While trying to remain as objective as possible, establish a slightly cynical edge to your tone.
5. If appropriate, include some jargon related to the issue.
6. Explain and refute the causal logic (cause-and-effect analysis) of the common opinion.
7. About midway through the essay, return to the thesis in a paragraph that serves as a "pivot" for your essay.
8. Link ideas, statistics, and opinions by means of well-placed minor proposition statements.
9. Continue to refute the common opinion by
   a. using rhetorical questions
   b. citing and showing the invalidity of a recent media item on the issue
   c. lightly ridiculing some of the "big names" associated with the common opinion on the issue
10. Conclude your essay with a somewhat unrealistic, exaggerated image that both reinforces your opinion and invokes the reader to reexamine the issue more closely.

Thinking and Writing Collaboratively

In groups of four to five, discuss the alternatives or the opposition viewpoint to the arguments presented in your Guided Writing essay. Jot down notes, and then incorporate the opposition viewpoint—and your refutation or answer to it—in your final draft.

Writing About the Text

Write an essay in which you evaluate Kozol's use of statistics. Which do you find most impressive? Which do you find less than convincing? How do statistics advance the essay's thesis? What other kinds of statistics might Kozol have used?

More Writing Projects

1. In your journal, freewrite about this topic: the homeless. Do not edit your writing. Write nonstop for at least fifteen minutes. When you finish, exchange journal entries with another

student in the class. How do your responses compare? contrast?

2. Do you think it is correct to give money to panhandlers? Write a paragraph in which you state and defend your opinion.

3. Write an essay in the form of a letter to your local chief executive (mayor, town supervisor, and so forth) in which you express your opinion about the local homeless situation. Include some specific measures that you feel need to be enacted. Draw freely on your journal entry in question 1 of this exercise.

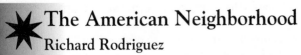

The American Neighborhood
Richard Rodriguez

Mixing Patterns

Richard Rodriguez, the son of Mexican immigrants, was born in San Francisco in 1944. As a young boy he moved to a white neighborhood in California's capital, Sacramento. He is the author of *Hunger of Memory: The Education of Richard Rodriguez* (1982), *Days of Obligation: An Argument with My Mexican Father* (1992), and *Brown: The Last Discovery of America* (2002). He has published widely in popular magazines and journals, including the *American Scholar, Change, College English, Harper's, Mother Jones,* and *Time*. Rodriguez holds a BA from Stanford University and an MA from Columbia University. In this essay, he explores the relation between religious variety and neighborhood, and he sees the interdependence of the two as a great asset to American life.

PREREADING: THINKING ABOUT THE ESSAY IN ADVANCE

How would you describe the neighborhood in which you grew up or lived in for most of your life? What qualities would you identify as key features of your neighborhood: race, religion, social factors, economics, or something else? What bound the people together, other than the fact that they lived side by side?

Words to Watch

tic (par. 1)   twitch; spasm
dispense (par. 3)   distribute
inexplicable (par. 4)   cannot be explained
proximity (par. 8)   closeness
firebrands (par. 11)   agitators; troublemakers
dogmatic (par. 12)   rigid; strict; inflexible
astigmatic (par. 12)   characteristic of blurred vision
abrogation (par. 13)   formal end to an agreement
ambivalence (par. 13)   presence of two opposing ideas at the same time
mundane (par. 14)   ordinary; everyday
lewd (par. 15)   vulgar; coarse

relativism (par. 18)   the belief that concepts like good and evil are not absolute but change from culture to culture and situation to situation

antagonists (par. 23)   rivals; opponents

1 I confided to an interviewer my regret at never having been appraised or even dismissed by critics as a "Catholic writer," despite the fact that so much of my writing concerns religion. That aspect of my writing is ignored by the secular world as a kind of tic—but also ignored by the church, because I am the son of an intellectual tradition within the church that no longer exists, I guess.

2   The interviewer was surprised by my dilemma, but surprised from a different angle: Are you *still* a Catholic?

3   To which I answered, oh, well. I go to 7:30 Mass with the man who has been, for more than 20 years, my companion—*companion*! I belong to a church that hasn't enough charity to give us a word. I am nevertheless desperate for the sacraments my sinful church dispenses. And, as a sinner, I am eligible for every sacrament except, of course, marriage.

4   A few years ago, I was invited to spend a week at Yeshiva University. At first sight, the campus seemed to me a fortress against the neighborhood—a working-class Dominican neighborhood on Manhattan's upper West Side—and against the world, an impulse that as a Catholic of a certain age I did not find inexplicable or even unattractive.

5   Not enough is written or said about the impact of the American neighborhood—officially secular; informally tolerant of many faiths. Today's American neighborhood is without historical precedent: Methodists living next door to Muslims who live next door to pagans who live next door to Catholics who live next door to Orthodox Greeks who share the shade of a huge Magnolia with Buddhists who live next door to Orthodox Jews. Et cetera. Yeshiva University in a Dominican New York neighborhood.

6   Religions traditionally thrive on suspicion and separation. So, there is a crisis in religion resulting from our American neighborliness: Neighborhood kids are playing in the houses of their friends where they happen to see Confucian shrines they do not understand, except as the shrines partake of the recognizably devotional, which everyone understands. So the kids become cultural Confucians, in some sense.

Neighbors invite neighbors to weddings or graduations and 7
bar mitzvahs and whatnot. At first, the watchers from behind lace
curtains only notice when their neighbors are "swarming." But
neighbors eventually come to recognize "swarming" as religious
festivals—Happy Ramadan!—and on those festival days begin
themselves to feel a bit of a spiritual uplift, as one unconsciously
does who hears the Angelus tolled, or used to.

From proximity, from shared lives, comes ever-increasing 8
familiarity. And then, of course, the birds and the bees. The children of the neighborhood are eventually going to fall in love. The
great crisis of American Judaism today, for example, is occasioned
by love. Jews are falling in love with non-Jews and vice-versa.

If you were a Buddhist and I were in love with you, I would 9
hop onto your lotus. Love trespasses. Dogma is seen as matter-
ing less when affection enters the soul. Subversive love overrules
dogma and orthodoxy, and this all begins when we see for ourselves that our neighbors aren't so bad.

But already back in the 1950s, my eyes were open to the com- 10
mon decency around me. My parents noticed, for example, the
goodness of our closest neighbors, a family of Mormons. And their
praise was not wasted on me. How, I wondered, was it that people
so decent, so generous to us, were not Catholics? From such a
question without an easy answer in the Baltimore Catechism does
the world reveal itself truly to a child's imagination as seductively
round.

The firebrands of any age do not wish anyone to notice that 11
the neighbors are not so bad. The firebrands of any age do not wish
the Catholic altar society and the Presbyterian altar guild to hook
up with the sewing circle at the Chan Buddhist Temple or with the
Baptist Choir Breakfast Committee.

Even as a child I did not believe non-Catholics were damned, 12
but I perceived, only through observation and common sense,
such could not be the case and all such dogmatic statements must
be errors in perception or understanding on someone's part. (I was
told as a child that animals feel no pain.) It wasn't until relatively
recently I came to believe that my church's estimation of me was
also flawed, astigmatic.

I find myself in a one-sided battle against various bishops of 13
my church, and at what I perceive is their abrogation of moral
example. I do not expect the church to bless my union with another
man, but I do expect the church—at a time of sexual scandal within,

at a time of extraordinary example of love and fidelity on the part of gay couples—to admit at least ambivalence or puzzlement or pause at all the church does not understand about the mystery of love. The church is no longer my teacher, maybe because my life doesn't teach the church.

14   And yet, and yet, the most influential document describing the intersection of my religious and mundane life was composed, 40 years ago, by an assembly of princes of the church at the Second Vatican Council. *Gaudium et Spes* described how Catholics must and should live in a spirit of exchange with the world beyond church doors; learning from the world, as well as teaching the world.

15   So, I am at Mass. Seven-thirty a.m. Sunday. Distracted from the homily as I sift through what the world has taught me about God this week. What have I learned? I saw lesbians getting married at City Hall! People waiting in lines that extended all the way around the block, in the rain, for a sacrament. I saw a man—a Muslim—in Golden Gate Park at prayer at midday. I read a book on Andy Warhol; Warhol's brilliant notion of the Incarnation evident within his notions about celebrity. I watched, I listened, as a friend dying of AIDS exchanged several lewd and very funny jokes in his hospital room with a young Buddhist nun, the chaplain at a Catholic hospital.

16   I wrote, in my most recent book, *Brown,* of the end of black or white America—the collapse of race. With the success of the Negro Civil Rights movement in the 1960s, and with the reform of immigration laws, a decade later, allowing for the globalization of the American city, there has come a freedom to love brownly, without regard to race.

17   If I were to write an addendum to *Brown,* it would be about the browning of religion, about how America's religious life is being transformed by our new American marriages. The African-Korean daughter is unwilling to choose between parents; no longer willing to "identify" racially with only one parent, as children of racially mixed marriage were once encouraged to do. And, she is unwilling to choose one faith tradition over another. She becomes a formulation I have used so often since I first heard her say it: "Baptist Buddhist." We can all claim a version of Baptist Buddhist. Abortion Catholic. Gay Mormon. Movie queen Kabbalist.

18   As my third-grade nun could have told you, there is danger from religious intermarriage. Relativism is the heresy to rival

modernism—or rather, relativism is an aspect of modernism. One belief is as good as another, nothing is clear, nothing is wrong or right, just different, or just the same. Distinction is useless. Joss, mangoes, ancestor worship. The human soul is made to seek God.

But in this time of marriage, the religions that will grow stron- 19 ger are those capable of syncretism, as the Spanish colonial church grew stronger by embracing a brown Virgin Mary, who dressed as an Aztec princess.

Don't tell me you don't know what I am talking about. You 20 have a cousin who married a Mormon and it turned out all right, didn't it? You have a lesbian aunt, don't you? Yes, you do.

There have been times in the history of the world when reli- 21 gious traditions have flowed into one another, fed one another from secret streams. Medieval Jew, Muslim and Christian in Spain. Yugoslavia before the fall. San Francisco.

But the brown future of Catholicism may be nothing at all like 22 what those of us who call ourselves "liberal" Catholics imagine or wish for. I celebrate as brown the marriage of two gay men. But why then does it anger me to see, in the morning paper, the cardinal of New York seated at a White House ceremony along-side various right-wing Protestant activists, like the Rev. Jerry Falwell? Has Roman Catholicism come to this? Is the church unable to distinguish our understanding of various public issues of the day from right-wing Protestantism? Thousands of years of subtlety—the exegesis of love, after all—descends to this?

But by the time I have had my second cup of green tea, I think 23 more brownly that perhaps right-wing Catholicism is finding itself strengthened by its association with right-wing Protestantism—a new neighborliness among old theological antagonists. Nothing like the brown future I imagined. But, then, Brown, nevertheless.

BUILDING VOCABULARY

1. To advance his argument about religion and neighborhoods, Rodriguez has drawn on words that we often use in religious contexts but are applicable in many other contexts as well. Check these words in a dictionary and write definitions for them, partic-ularly as they apply to writing about topics other than religion.

    a. sacrament (par. 3)

    b. secular (par. 5)

    c. tolerant (par. 5)
    d. pagans (par. 5)
    e. shrines (par. 6)
    f. devotional (par. 6)
    g. orthodoxy (par. 9)
    h. fidelity (par. 13)
    i. homily (par. 15)
    j. exegesis (par. 22)

2. Divide the class into groups. Ask each group to explore and identify three or four of the following religions and religion-based activities. Share definitions with the rest of the class.
    a. Catholic
    b. Mass
    c. Methodists
    d. Muslims
    e. Orthodox Greeks
    f. Buddhists
    g. Orthodox Jews
    h. Confucian
    i. Bar mitzvah
    j. Ramadan
    k. Mormons
    l. Baptist
    m. Second Vatican Council
    n. *Gaudium et Spes*
    o. The Incarnation
    p. Kabbalist
    q. Protestant

THINKING CRITICALLY ABOUT THE ESSAY

Understanding the Writer's Ideas

1. What surprises Rodriguez about how critics have appraised him and his work? How does he respond to the question an interviewer asked him?

2. What fault does the writer find with his church in regard to his personal relations with the man who has been his companion for twenty years?

3. What impresses the writer most about American neighborhoods?

4. What does Rodriguez indicate as the great crisis of American Judaism?

5. What was there about the 1950s that opened the writer's eyes to the common decency around him?

6. How, according to the writer, have various bishops he knows abrogated moral example?

7. What does Rodriguez believe that the church doesn't understand?

8. What did the Second Vatican Council and *Gaudium et Spes* say?

9. What thoughts distract the writer from the homily at the 7:30 a.m. Sunday Mass?

10. How is America's religious life being transformed, according to the writer? What does the African Korean daughter label herself?

11. What does Rodriguez say he wrote about in his book *Brown*?

12. What danger does the writer cite about intermarriage? Who taught him about this danger?

13 What angers Rodriguez about the picture that he sees in the morning papers?

14. What association does Rodriguez see between right-wing Catholicism and right-wing Protestantism?

Understanding the Writer's Techniques

1. What is Rodriguez's argument in this essay? Where does he come closest to stating it in a thesis sentence?

2. What evidence does the writer provide to support his argument? Where do you find the details very specific? Where do you note general ideas that might benefit from more specificity?

3. The writer asks a number of questions throughout the piece. How well does this strategy suit the essay? Look especially at paragraph 20. What does the forceful address to the reader through a series of questions contribute to the essay? Why does the writer then go on to answer the questions himself?

4. Explain the irony in paragraphs 6 and 7. How does irony contribute to the essay? How does it influence the writer's tone? Would you say that Rodriguez's tone is mostly angry, resigned,

happy, puzzled, suspicious—or something else? Support your response with direct references to the text.

5. What do the personal details of the writer's mental state at Sunday Mass contribute to the essay?

6. The writer uses a number of fragments, often, but not always, one-word sentences. Look especially at paragraph 17. What do the fragments contribute to the essay? Where else do you find fragments in the selection?

7. This essay appeared in the *National Catholic Reporter,* a periodical clearly directed at Catholics. How do you think the writer's sense of his audience contributed to the essay? Rodriguez, evidently a Catholic himself, identifies some negative elements in Catholicism as he sees it. Why do you think the writer would seek to publish a piece critical of the religion in a magazine for Catholics?

8. Where does the writer use figurative language? Identify metaphors and similes of note. What does Rodriguez mean by this humorous figure in paragraph 9: "If you were a Buddhist and I were in love with you, I would hop onto your lotus"?

9. What is your reaction to the many religious-based words and concepts in the essay? How important are they in making Rodriguez's point? Has the writer provided readers with clear definitions of the major terms—or would you have preferred that he ascribe more detailed meanings for key words? Explain your answer.

10. What is your response to the conclusion of the essay, especially the last paragraph? Does it surprise you? Why or why not?

✳ MIXING PATTERNS

Rodriguez draws heavily on narration, description, and definition to advance his argument. In what ways do these patterns contribute to the essay? Consider especially the strategy of definition, which is indispensable to the writer's development of the last part of the essay. What words and (or) concepts does he define? How does his definition of the word *brown,* for example, differ from your understanding of the word?

Exploring the Writer's Ideas

1. Rodriguez lives in an openly gay relationship with another man, and he is critical of how his religion treats him and his partner. Do you think that his criticism is justified? Why or why not? What is wrong with the church's identification of Rodriguez's partner as a *companion,* do you think? What word do you imagine that Rodriguez would prefer? How do you think religions in general should treat nonheterosexual unions?

2. The writer sees extraordinary benefits in the "browning" of America's religions and praises the informal tolerance he finds in neighborhoods. Based on your own experience, do you find his enthusiasm warranted? Why or why not?

3. Rodriguez writes that religions "traditionally thrive on suspicion and separation." Why might you agree or disagree with this statement?

4. What point does Rodriguez make about the document from the Second Vatican Council? How does the *Gaudium et Spes* resonate with current religious practice?

5. What does Rodriguez mean by "the collapse of race"? Do you agree with him on this point? Why or why not?

6. Why is Rodriguez so impressed with the woman who calls herself a "Baptist Buddhist"? Do you think that the integration of religions in the manner of personal identity is a good or bad thing? Explain your answer.

7. Clearly the writer is addressing the reader in paragraph 17. How do the questions he asks there reflect features of your own life? Rodriguez certainly doesn't believe that every reader could answer these questions in the affirmative. Why, then, does he ask them?

8. What does Rodriguez mean by the phrase "a new neighborliness among old theological antagonists"? Why does this situation surprise him? In what ways do you find it surprising? How are the two religions that the writer indicates antagonists?

IDEAS FOR WRITING

Prewriting

Write nonstop for ten or fifteen minutes on the neighborhood in which you grew up, especially in regard to the role that religion played in your community.

Guided Writing

Write an argumentative essay called "My American Neighborhood" in which you show the community in which you grew up and, in particular, in regard to the role that religion played in helping to define the neighborhood.

1. Open your essay with a brief anecdote about religion and your neighborhood.
2. Identify the religion or religions that characterized the people in your neighborhood.
3. Briefly identify a ceremony that you attended in the course of religious practice.
4. Show how people of different religions in your neighborhood interacted—or did not interact.
5. Deal with how your community viewed intermarriages between people of differing faiths.
6. Conclude your paper with an assertion about the value of your neighborhood's view and practice of religion. Is it still relevant today?

Thinking and Writing Collaboratively

Form groups and read and respond to the questions Rodriguez identifies in paragraph 20. How would each member of your group respond to each question?

Writing About the Text

Unity and coherence are essential elements in good writing. Check the Glossary for a review of the two terms. Then, write an essay in which you explain how Rodriguez achieves—or does not achieve—unity and coherence in his essay "The American Neighborhood."

More Writing Projects

1. Write a journal entry about your experiences with a religion other than your own.
2. Write an extended paragraph to address this statement from the essay: "From proximity, from shared lives, comes ever-increasing familiarity."

3. Rodriguez deals with what many would consider unconventional unions, particularly intermarriages of people of different cultures and faiths and relations between gay men and women. Write an essay in which you argue for or against unconventional unions and how religions should treat them.

The Harmful Myth of Asian Superiority
Ronald Takaki

Ronald Takaki, whose grandparents were Japanese plantation workers in Hawaii, is Professor of Ethnic Studies at the University of California, Berkeley. He received his PhD from Berkeley in 1967 and
has since published widely in the area of ethnic studies. His works
include *Pau Hana: Plantation Life and Labor in Hawaii* (1983)
and *Strangers from a Different Shore: A History of Asian Americans* (1989). His most recent publication is *Hiroshima* (2001). In
this selection, written in 1990, Takaki argues that stereotyping Asian
Americans as uniformly successful not only belies the facts but also
is a veiled form of racist attack on other American ethnic groups, in
particular African Americans.

Mixing Patterns

PREREADING: THINKING ABOUT
THE ESSAY IN ADVANCE

How are we to gauge whether the American dream is truly available to all Americans? Is race a factor? How do you account for
the success of some recent immigrants in the face of the poverty
of many who have lived in the United States for generations? Is
the success of some immigrants used unfairly to bolster racial stereotyping, for example, by appealing to the argument: if they can
do it, why can't you?

Words to Watch

ubiquity (par. 2)   presence everywhere
pundits (par. 3)   authoritative opinion-shapers
superfluous (par. 3)   unnecessary
acquiring (par. 5)   obtaining
median (par. 12)   a number or value in a set (say, the set of all
   incomes) such that there are an equal number of greater and
   lesser numbers or values
paragons (par. 12)   models of excellence
exacerbates (par. 15)   worsens

1 Asian Americans have increasingly come to be viewed as a
"model minority." But are they as successful as claimed? And for
whom are they supposed to be a model?

Asian Americans have been described in the media as "exces- 2
sively, even provocatively" successful in gaining admission to
universities. Asian American shopkeepers have been congratu-
lated, as well as criticized, for their ubiquity and entrepreneurial
effectiveness.

If Asian Americans can make it, many politicians and pundits 3
ask, why can't African Americans? Such comparisons pit minorities against each other and generate African American resentment
toward Asian Americans. The victims are blamed for their plight,
rather than racism and an economy that has made many young
African American workers superfluous.

The celebration of Asian Americans has obscured reality. For 4
example, figures on the high earnings of Asian Americans relative to Caucasians are misleading. Most Asian Americans live in
California, Hawaii, and New York—states with higher incomes
and higher costs of living than the national average.

Even Japanese Americans, often touted for their upward mo- 5
bility, have not reached equality. While Japanese American men
in California earned an average income comparable to Caucasian
men in 1980, they did so only by acquiring more education and
working more hours.

Comparing family incomes is even more deceptive. Some 6
Asian American groups do have higher family incomes than
Caucasians. But they have more workers per family.

The "model minority" image homogenizes Asian Americans 7
and hides their differences. For example, while thousands of
Vietnamese American young people attend universities, others are
on the streets. They live in motels and hang out in pool halls in
places like East Los Angeles; some join gangs.

Twenty-five percent of the people in New York City's China- 8
town lived below the poverty level in 1980, compared with 17 percent of the city's population. Some 60 percent of the workers in
the Chinatowns of Los Angeles and San Francisco are crowded
into low-paying jobs in garment factories and restaurants.

"Most immigrants coming into Chinatown with a language 9
barrier cannot go outside this confined area into the mainstream
of American industry," a Chinese immigrant said. "Before, I was
a painter in Hong Kong, but I can't do it here. I got no license, no
education. I want a living; so it's dishwasher, janitor, or cook."

Hmong and Mien refugees from Laos have unemployment 10
rates that reach as high as 80 percent. A 1987 California study

showed that three out of ten Southeast Asian refugee families had been on welfare for four to ten years.

11   Although college-educated Asian Americans are entering the professions and earning good salaries, many hit the "glass ceiling"—the barrier through which high management positions can be seen but not reached. In 1988, only 8 percent of Asian Americans were "officials" and "managers," compared with 12 percent for all groups.

12   Finally, the triumph of Korean immigrants has been exaggerated. In 1988, Koreans in the New York metropolitan area earned only 68 percent of the median income of non-Asians. More than three-quarters of Korean greengrocers, those so-called paragons of bootstrap entrepreneurialism, came to America with a college education. Engineers, teachers, or administrators while in Korea, they became shopkeepers after their arrival. For many of them, the greengrocery represents dashed dreams, a step downward in status.

13   For all their hard work and long hours, most Korean shopkeepers do not actually earn very much: $17,000 to $35,000 a year, usually representing the income from the labor of an entire family.

14   But most Korean immigrants do not become shopkeepers. Instead, many find themselves trapped as clerks in grocery stores, service workers in restaurants, seamstresses in garment factories, and janitors in hotels.

15   Most Asian Americans know their "success" is largely a myth. They also see how the celebration of Asian Americans as a "model minority" perpetuates their inequality and exacerbates relations between them and African Americans.

BUILDING VOCABULARY

This selection draws on concepts from economics and sociology. Define the terms below:

a.   cost(s) of living (par. 4)
b.   the national average (par. 4)
c.   the poverty level (par. 8)
d.   unemployment rates (par. 10)
e.   welfare (par. 10)

THINKING CRITICALLY ABOUT THE ESSAY

Understanding the Writer's Ideas

1. Why have Asian Americans been viewed as a "model minority"?
2. What's wrong with such a categorization, according to Takaki?
3. How has the "celebration of Asian Americans . . . obscured reality" (par. 4)?
4. How does the "model minority" image homogenize Asian Americans?
5. What is the consequence of the language barrier faced by Chinese immigrants?
6. How has the "triumph" of Korean immigrants been "exaggerated" (par. 12)?

Understanding the Writer's Techniques

1. What is the writer's thesis statement?
2. The writer begins by stating the view he is going to oppose, and asks two questions to probe the opposing view. How does he answer these two questions? What evidence does he use in each case?
3. Categorize the examples the writer uses to show that the "celebration of Asian Americans has obscured reality" (par. 4).
4. Much of Takaki's supporting evidence is in the form of examples. How does he develop his essay and maintain coherence?
5. What do you think is the writer's strongest piece of evidence for his point of view? What is the weakest? What is his strongest argument? His weakest?
6. Takaki saves the word *myth* for last. Does that decision strengthen his use of the word to sum up his essay? Is the conclusion effective?

✳ MIXING PATTERNS

How does the writer solve the problem of definition that his essay involves, that is, the definition of "Asian American"? How do comparison and contrast and classification operate as strategies in Takaki's essay?

Exploring the Writer's Ideas

1. Is the writer's reliance on example excessive? Are some of his examples more persuasive than others? Are some of his examples liable to other interpretations? Is it a problem for his argument that he does *not* give certain examples, such as the statistics on Asian American admissions to universities? What other strategies might the writer have considered as alternatives to the one he chose? Explain your answers.

2. African Americans often identify themselves as a coherent group. Orlando Patterson (see pages 505–508), for example, uses statistics and examples to support this viewpoint. Why is it appropriate (or inappropriate) to do the same with Asian Americans?

3. Takaki cites examples and statistics about Asian Americans that seem, unintentionally, to be very positive. He says, for example, that Asian Americans work long hours, cooperate as families, have entered the professions, and have higher family incomes than whites. Are these examples a contradiction of his thesis? Why or why not?

IDEAS FOR WRITING

Prewriting

Is it fair to make any generalizations about "groups," or do groups simply consist of individuals who should be judged on their own merits? Write down ideas about the two sides of this question.

Guided Writing

Write an essay titled "The Harmful Myth of _____." Make your myth a positive perception that nonetheless can have negative repercussions for those inside or outside the group. For example, the myth that all Ivy League students are brainy might be a positive perception that leads people to undervalue the academic achievements of other students or, say, the athletic achievements of Ivy League students.

1. Begin by stating the myth. Raise two questions that expose the myth as distorting the reality.

2. Indicate kinds of negative repercussions the myth can have.
3. Use four examples to demonstrate that the reality is more complex than the myth allows. In discussing these examples, and elsewhere in your essay, draw on strategies of definition, comparison and contrast, and classification—as needed—to advance your thesis.
4. End by restating how the myth obscures the reality and can be used negatively.

Thinking and Writing Collaboratively

Debate the question of whether a focus on ethnic or racial identification is a positive or negative phenomenon in the context of our multiethnic society. One half of the class should prepare the case that such a focus is harmful because, for example, it obscures differences within the group and discourages the appreciation of individuals as individuals. The other half should make the case that such a focus is beneficial because, for example, solidarity within a group can promote the economic and political progress of the individuals within the group.

Writing About the Text

Write an essay that explores the question of success as Takaki sees it. What is "success"? What are the main factors that make a person successful in America today? How important is the individual's race or ethnicity in success? How does race or ethnicity play a role?

More Writing Projects

1. Many essays in *The Short Prose Reader* are by members of minority ethnic or racial groups. How do these essays influence your reading of Takaki? How does your reading of Takaki affect your appreciation for these other essays? Write journal entries that answer these questions.
2. Write a one-paragraph portrait of a city street, either your own street or one you have visited recently. Choose one with a clear ethnic identity. What ethnic groups are represented? What effect has each group had on the life of this street?

3. Interview Asian American immigrants in your community, town, or city about their notion of the American Dream. Did they have an idea of the American Dream before they arrived in the United States? What do they think of the American Dream now? Has being part of the American Dream changed their identity? Write an essay based on the interviews.

PERSPECTIVES ON THE "MOMMY WARS": SHOULD MOTHERS WORK?

Since the modern women's movement began in the 1960s, women have brought new powers of activity and imagination to our society and culture. Many would argue without fierce opposition that the struggle for equality with men still continues today. Yet we can point to unmistakable signs of progress. The U.S. Department of Labor reports that the number of working women has risen from 5.1 million in 1900, to 18.4 million in 1950, to 66.9 million in 2006. Women accounted for 18 percent of the labor force in 1900 and 46.3 percent in 2006. Whereas in 1900 only 20.4 percent of all women worked, in 2006, almost 60 percent worked. The number of working women is projected to reach nearly 76 million by 2014.

Pressures on women who wish to remain part of the workforce have not diminished, however, especially in regard to those who elect to have children. For many years, women opted for employment as well as motherhood, arranging to have their children supervised by nannies, babysitters, grandparents, relatives, or day care centers, for example. The freedom to choose to work and have children produced a new set of accomplishments and anxieties. Should a woman work full or part time and still be able to do an effective job of mothering? Should a woman work at all if she has young children?

Recent data from the Pew Foundation, a respected research-oriented think tank, points to women's diminishing interest in full-time work. In a 2007 survey, among working mothers with minor children (ages 17 and under), just one in five (21 percent) said that full-time work is the ideal situation for them, down from the 32 percent who said this in 1997. Six in ten (up from 48 percent in 1997) of today's working mothers say part-time work would be their ideal, and another one in five (19 percent) says she would prefer not working at all outside the home.

What, in fact, is best for mother and child in this age of personal choice? The three selections in this section provide varying perspectives on the importance of a stay-at-home mother and a working mother. Linda Hirshman, a strong advocate for equality at home between men and women, insists that women must return to the workforce after childbirth. Susan Cheever identifies the conflict between mothers who work and those who stay at home to rear their children. And, using her own mother as an example, Anna Quindlen identifies those qualities that she believes are important in being a good mother without turning "motherhood into martyrdom."

Off to Work She Should Go

Linda Hirshman

Born in 1944 in Cleveland, Ohio, Linda Redlick Hirshman is a lawyer and the author of *The Woman's Guide to Law School* (1999), *Hard Bargains: The Politics of Sex* (1998), and, most recently, *Get to Work: A Manifesto for Women of the World* (2006). She holds a law degree from the University of Chicago and a PhD in philosophy. Hirshman has written for a variety of periodicals, including *Glamour, Tikkun, Ms.,* and the *Boston Globe,* and has served as Distinguished Professor of Philosophy and Women's Studies at Brandeis University. Hirshman regularly argues that women should demand that their husbands participate in rearing their children. In this essay of 2007, she examines the phenomenon of women leaving the workforce.

PREREADING: THINKING ABOUT THE ESSAY IN ADVANCE

Why might a woman who works give up her job during motherhood? Is this a good or bad idea? Explain your reasoning.

Words to Watch

number crunchers (par. 1)   colloquial term for professionals who interpret data and statistics

exodus (par. 4)   mass departure; flight

opt-out (par. 4)   avoid; refuse to take part

1   The United States Bureau of Labor Statistics recently published its long-awaited study, "Trends in Labor Force Participation of Married Mothers of Infants." "In recent years," the number crunchers reported, "the labor force participation of married mothers, especially those with young children, has stopped its advance."

2   Sixty percent of married mothers of preschool children are now in the work force, four percentage points fewer than in 1997. The rate for married mothers of infants fell by about six percentage points, to 53.5 percent. The bureau further reports that the declines "have occurred across all educational levels and, for most groups, by about the same magnitude."

3   In sum, sometime well before the 2000 recession, wives with infants and toddlers began leaving the work force. And they stayed out even after the economy began to revive.

For several years, experts have been arguing about the 4 "opt-out" revolution—the perception that there has been an exodus of young mothers from the work force. Heather Boushey of the Center for Economic and Policy Research called the opt-out revolution a myth, and asserted that married mothers don't drop out any more than other women in a bad economy. The new report is strong evidence that something really is going on.

Why are married mothers leaving their jobs? The labor bureau's 5 report includes some commonsense suggestions, but none that fully explains the situation. New mothers with husbands in the top 20 percent of earnings work least, the report notes. As Ernest Hemingway said, the rich do have more money. So they also have more freedom to leave their jobs. But why do they take the option? It's easier in the short term, sure, but it's easier to forgo lots of things, like going to college or having children at all. People don't—nor should they—always do the easier thing.

The authors also speculate that the pressure of working and run- 6 ning a household is great. They do not say, however, that working hours have increased as participation has declined. Educated women, they report, work 42.2 hours a week on average and those with professional degrees, 45—hardly the "80-hour week" of legend.

Poorer mothers can less afford child care, and because they 7 earn less, their opportunity costs of not working are lower, the authors suggest. But for these women, lost income cuts deeper. And this factor, like the average number of hours worked, has not changed since 1997.

What has changed in the last decade is that the job of mother- 8 hood has ramped up. Mothers today spend more time on child care than women did in 1965, a time when mothers were much less likely to have paying jobs, family scholars report.

The pressure to increase mothering is enormous. For years, 9 women have been on the receiving end of negative messages about parenting and working. One conservative commentator said the lives of working women added up to "just a pile of pay stubs." When the National Institute of Child Health reported recently that long hours in day care added but a single percentage point to the still-normal range of rambunctious behavior in children, newspaper headlines read, "Day Care, Behavior Problems Linked in Study."

Should we care if women leave the work force? Yes, because 10 participation in public life allows women to use their talents and to powerfully affect society. And once they leave, they usually cannot regain the income or status they had. The Center for Work-Life Policy, a research organization founded by Sylvia Ann Hewlett of Columbia, found that women lose an average of 18 percent of their earning power when they temporarily leave the work force. Women in business sectors lose 28 percent.

11   And despite the happy talk of "on ramps" back in, only 40 percent of even high-powered professionals get back to full-time work at all.

12   That the most educated have opted out the most should raise questions about how our society allocates scarce educational resources. The next generation of girls will have a greatly reduced pool of role models.

13   But what is to be done? Organizations like Moms Rising and the Mothers Movement Online have stepped up the pressure for reforms like flexible work hours and paid parental leave. Such changes probably would help lower-income women in the most unforgiving workplaces. But they are unlikely to affect the behavior of the highly educated women with the highest opt-out rates.

14   We could make an effort to change men's attitudes. Sociologists have found that mothers (rich and poor) still do twice the housework and child care that fathers do, and even the next generation of males say they won't sacrifice work for home. But in the short term, it might be easier to change the tax code.

15   In most American marriages, wives earn less than their husbands. Since the tax code encourages joint filing (by making taxes lower for those who do), many couples figure that the "extra" dollars the wife brings in will be piled on top of the husband's income and taxed at the highest rates, close to 50 percent, according to estimates made by Ed McCaffery, a tax professor at the University of Southern California. Considering the cost of child care, couples often conclude that her working adds nothing to the family treasury.

16   If married couples were taxed as the separate income earners they often are, women would be liberated from some of the pressure to reduce their "labor force participation," as the labor bureau would say.

17   Labor statistics are always couched in such dry language, but it reveals a powerful reality: working mothers, rich and poor, struggle with their competing commitments. Now that we have seen the reality, it is time to address it.

BUILDING VOCABULARY

For each word in italics, choose the letter of the word or phrase that most closely matches its meaning.

1. about the same *magnitude* (par. 2)
   a. number of women
   b. extent
   c. critics
   d. declines
2. *"opt-out"* revolution (par. 4)
   a. choose to leave
   b. choose to enroll
   c. choose to consider
   d. hard attitude
3. *forgo* lots of things (par. 5)
   a. give up
   b. purchase
   c. desire
   d. stimulate
4. *speculate* that the pressures of working (par. 6)
   a. imply
   b. write
   c. investigate
   d. guess
5. the job of motherhood has *ramped up* (par. 8)
   a. declined
   b. lost status
   c. reversed itself
   d. gradually increased
6. *rambunctious* behavior (par. 9)
   a. hard to control
   b. adorable
   c. effective
   d. depressing
7. women in business *sectors* (par. 10)
   a. clothing
   b. meetings
   c. zones
   d. lunches
8. *allocates* scarce educational resources (par. 12)
   a. distributes
   b. criticizes

    c. allows

    d. denies

9. reduced *pool* of role models (par. 12)

    a. water supply

    b. game

    c. supply

    d. rate

10. *couched* in such dry language (par. 17)

    a. left to sleep

    b. presented

    c. implied

    d. spelled out

THINKING CRITICALLY ABOUT THE ESSAY

Understanding the Writer's Ideas

1. What fact did the Bureau of Labor Statistics' study report?
2. What data from the study does Hirshman present?
3. What is the "opt-out" revolution? How does Hirshman define it? What does Heather Boushey think of the opt-out revolution? Who is Heather Boushey, and why should we be interested in her opinion?
4. What commonsense suggestions does the Bureau of Labor Statistics provide, according to Hirshman? Why does the writer feel that the suggestions do not fully explain the situation?
5. What, according to the writer, has changed in the last decade in regard to motherhood?
6. Why should we care if women leave the workforce, according to Hirshman?
7. How, according to the writer, would attempts to change men's attitudes fare?
8. What does Hirshman think the tax code has to do with women who work or choose to leave work?

Understanding the Writer's Techniques

1. What is the central argument in this essay? What is the relation between the problem and possible solutions?
2. What specific questions does Hirshman raise? What is your reaction to raising questions as an essay-writing strategy?

3. Why does Hirshman present so many data-based observations? How does this strategy improve readers' acceptance of her argument?

4. What is your view of the title? In what ways is it an allusion to the seven dwarves from the Snow White fairy tale who sing, "Hi ho, hi ho, it's off to work we go"? Or do you think that Hirshman did not intend to have readers make that association?

5. What is your view of the conclusion? Is Hirshman trying to persuade readers to take some course of action? Has she convinced you? Why or why not?

Exploring the Writer's Ideas

1. Hirshman believes that even reforms in working hours and parental leaves will not "affect the behavior of highly educated women with the highest opt-out rates." Why might you agree or disagree with her?

2. What efforts could we make that might change men's attitudes about their roles in a marriage with children? Hirshman believes that this strategy will not work. Do you think it could work? Why or why not?

3. The writer asserts, "People don't—nor should they—always do the easier thing." What examples, other than those Hirshman offers, might you provide to support this notion? What examples could you provide to challenge it?

4. The point about fixing the tax code to make it more reasonable for mothers to work seems logical. Why has it not happened, do you think?

IDEAS FOR WRITING

Prewriting

Freewrite on what the role of men in households with children should be so that women have more flexibility to return to work.

Guided Writing

Write an argumentative essay called "Off to the Household He Should Go" in which you argue about what and how men should contribute to managing households with children so that women can return to work.

1. Open your essay with data about men who do not participate in rearing their children and in performing household chores regularly.
2. State your argument clearly in a thesis sentence.
3. Provide further data in the essay to support your point.
4. Explain why certain proposed recommendations for keeping men involved in household management will not work.
5. Identify strategies that you think will work for changing the current situation as you see it.
6. Raise questions in your essay and attempt to answer them.

Thinking and Writing Collaboratively

In groups of three or four, discuss the concept of the "opt-out revolution." Is the word *revolution* appropriate to identify the phenomenon? What other groups opt out and for what reasons? (Think of high school or college students, men in high-paying, high-pressure jobs, aspiring actors or musicians.)

Writing About the Text

Hirschman uses a variety of informal phrases in the essay, such as *opt-out, ramp up, something really is going on,* and *high-powered.* Why does she use these phrases instead of adopting a more formal writing style? What does her use of these expressions tell you about her view of the audience for her essay? Write an essay in which you answer these questions.

More Writing Projects

1. Write a journal entry about the remark the writer cites from Hemingway: "the rich do have more money."
2. In an extended paragraph, explain the interactions of parents and children regarding work and household responsibilities in a family or families that you know or have read about or seen in the media.
3. Write an essay about what you see as the effect on American culture and economy of women leaving and not returning to the workforce.

Baby Battle

Susan Cheever

Susan Cheever was born July 31, 1943, in New York City. She is the daughter of John Cheever, the Pulitzer Prize–winning short story writer and novelist. Cheever graduated from Brown University and was a Guggenheim Fellow. She teaches in the Bennington College MFA program and at the New School. Her books include *My Name is Bill—Bill Wilson: His Life and the Creation of Alcoholics Anonymous* (2004); *Home Before Dark* (1999), a memoir about her father; *American Bloomsbury: Louisa May Alcott, Ralph Waldo Emerson, Margaret Fuller, Nathaniel Hawthorne, and Henry David Thoreau: Their Lives, Their Loves, Their Work* (2006); and five novels, including *Looking for Work* (1981) and *Doctors and Women* (1987). Her most recent book is *Desire: Where Sex Meets Addiction* (2008). In this selection Cheever explores the phenomena of what she calls Stay-at-Home Mothers as opposed to Working Mothers and Women Without Children.

(sidebar: **Mixing Patterns**)

PREREADING: THINKING ABOUT THE ESSAY IN ADVANCE

Before you read, consider the title of this essay, "Baby Battle." What does the title make you think of? What do you think the essay will be about based on the title?

Words to Watch

entitlement (par. 4)   right or privilege
slalom (par. 10)   zigzag
encumbered (par. 13)   burdened; hindered
progeny (par. 14)   children; offspring
fatuous (par. 18)   silly; pointless
Lamaze (par. 18)   an instructional program in birthing for mothers and fathers expecting a child
burgeoning (par. 18)   growing; rapidly increasing
hapless (par. 23)   unfortunate; unlucky
effusively (par. 27)   overly enthusiastic and expressive in emotions
caul (par. 29)   membrane, usually the membrane surrounding the amniotic fluid that protects the child in the womb
patriarchal (par. 31)   characteristic of rule by men

1   There is a war going on in the streets of New York City.

2   Platoons of mothers in bicycle shoes and designer sweats wheel divisions of gleaming, clanking strollers down the sidewalks, chattering into their cell phones and blocking the passage of other pedestrians. These are the Stay-at-Home Mothers.

3   Their adversaries, the Working Mothers and the Women Without Children, straighten their sleek success suits and try to stay out of the way.

4   "It's not just the strollers," said a Working Mother friend recently as we barely escaped being mowed down by a squadron of juice-cup-wielding Stay-at-Home Mothers. "It's the stroller *entitlement.*"

5   The Stay-at-Homes hang together as if they are from a different planet than the mothers who chose to go on working, or the mothers who *have* to go on working. They regroup in the playgrounds, brushing the crumbs off their strollers, Björns, and tricycles. If a toddler under a nanny's care has an accident or a tantrum, the Stay-at-Homes cluck and shake their heads knowingly. *That child needs a mother.*

6   Women without children are whipsawed by hostility from both camps. The Working Moms look down on the Stay-at-Home Moms: *What on earth do they do all day? How can they be so dependent?* The Stay-at-Home Moms feel sorry for the Working Moms: *Do they know what they're missing?*

7   Why are children such a divisive force between women?

8   What happened to the good old days when women used to fight with men?

9   Last week, a mother and her toddler were in my local supermarket in the evening, at a time when few children are there. The toddler was mounted on a tricycle with a metal handle protruding about three feet at a forty-five-degree angle from the seat. The purpose of the handle—parental control—had apparently been forgotten. As the toddler sped down the aisles, the handle brought down a paper-towel display and threatened the eggs. "Gabby! *Gabby!* GAB-RI-ELLE!!" the mother's voice escalated as she looked the other way and manically loaded her cart with an assortment of Lunchables, Dunkaroos, and other junk foods manufactured to temporarily pacify and ultimately enrage our country's children.

10 As little Gabby approached my shopping cart, she began to slalom, sending the handle zooming from side to side and

knocking loaves of freshly baked bread into the aisle. Clouds of choking flour rose around us as I dodged flying baguettes. I was about to grab little Gabby and summon her irresponsible mother.

Flashback.   11

Only a few years ago, I *was* that mother.   12

Before that, as a single woman twenty-five years ago, I   13
fiercely protected my single rights. I had a great job and I did what I pleased. I was thrilled not to be encumbered by a family. When the people in the apartment next door bought a piano for their little girl, and her endless practices bothered me, *I hired a lawyer to limit her practice time.* Why should families have more rights than single people? I chose to be single. They chose to have children. Therefore I was as entitled to my silence and freedom as they were entitled to their family.

I looked down on women with children as fools, dupes who had   14
fallen for a myth created for the purpose of their own oppression. Women with children were trapped, dependent on their husbands for money and for whatever else they still had the brains to need. Just the presence of a child seemed to reduce intelligent women to blithering idiots. Once at the gynecologist's office I watched as a group of chic, smart, professional women kicked off their Chanel sling-backs, left their briefcases unattended, and crawled around on the filthy floor making goo-goo faces at someone's sluglike progeny.

"Ohhh, she's so adooorable," cooed a real estate tycoon.   15

"And look at that face!" squawked a Citibank vice president.   16

I was appalled. Even if I ever had a child—and for most of   17
my twenties and thirties it was the last thing I imagined doing—I would never, ever, behave like that.

Marriage and pregnancy at the age of thirty-eight didn't   18
change me. I was amazed at the fatuous way people spoke about childbirth in my Lamaze class. "I want to share Cathy's pain," one of the husbands intoned. The leader nodded approvingly while I burst out laughing. Even my husband smiled. We flunked Lamaze. When strangers cooed at me and reached out for my burgeoning stomach, I wanted to bite them.

"Oh, it's such a celebration," gushed one friend with a new   19
baby, a woman who had formerly been a brilliant journalist. She and I had once spent two hours searching for the perfect lip gloss—a pale pink called *Prrr.* She used to be *fun.* Now she appeared to

be drooling. As I watched her change her baby, exclaiming over its small green excrement, I took a vow. I would have the baby—there was no way to avoid that now—but I would never lose my mind. I planned for full-time help. I signed a contract for a new book. I rented an office.

20   Then I had my baby, my Sarah.

21   The moment I held her in my arms, I became a different person. You could say that I joined the human race. For the first time in my life, my connection with someone else sliced through the web of defenses, fear, and pride that had separated me from the world. I had been married twice, but holding Sarah was my first experience of love. My heart seemed to melt. My mind no longer interested me. This tiny baby became the center of my world. I crossed over.

22   As soon as I got home from the hospital I went out and bought the biggest, most expensive stroller I could find. I wanted my precious girl to be safe. With her tucked into the stroller, I resented anyone else on the sidewalk. Everything seemed like a threat to the only being I had ever loved. I took Sarah everywhere with me, even in places where she wasn't allowed. To me it seemed criminal that my baby wasn't supposed to be with me at all times. Why should she have to be alone with a strange babysitter instead of at the movies with me? I took her to expensive restaurants and delighted when she threw the foie gras on the floor and smeared her adorable face with *quenelles de brocket*. Other diners frowned at us; I ignored them.

23   On airplanes, where baby Sarah was particularly fussy, I demanded extra help from the staff and often threw enough of a tantrum to get an extra seat—no one wanted to be close to us anyway, not even my husband. I personally took the time to explain to hapless complainers that my child was a *child,* and that people who were not enchanted by the noise of children were uptight, intolerant puritans who had probably never had an orgasm. *Weren't you ever a child yourself?* I would hiss. If someone suggested that I might think about controlling my daughter, I would lean over them menacingly. *So you think I'm a bad mother?* These confrontations never ended well.

24   As a mother I felt like the keeper of the flame, a woman who had been entrusted with something infinitely sacred. I had done nothing to earn the gift of this child. Watching her sleep I sometimes felt enveloped in a golden cloud of unconditional grace.

I kept on working—I had signed the book contract—but I slowed way down, and my old Armani success suits are still gathering dust in the back of the closet. Suddenly, I looked with pity on people who had never had children. How sad. They had never loved. They didn't know what they were missing.

My baby daughter is twenty-two now, and although she 25 remains at the center of my life she has also developed a life of her own. My beloved son is fourteen. I've had decades of being a mother first and a writer second. I kept on working when my children were born, partly because I didn't have the luxury of having to decide whether to be a stay-at-home or a working mother. I took a professional hit and lost a lot of the sharpness and brashness that were my trademarks. I spent hours on the floor oohing and aahing over tiny hands and feet. I wrote and edited among the blocks and plastic castles in the pediatrician's waiting room and missed deadlines to attend parents' meetings. My lip gloss was whatever I could find at the bottom of a bag filled with lunch passes, old homework papers, and half-empty juice boxes.

Lately though, as my children become adults, I am noticing 26 a change. I have become dependent on getting eight hours of sleep a night. I get regular haircuts and spend more money than I should on clothes. For the first time in a long time I'm annoyed by children like little Gabby and the way their mothers defend them. I'm crossing back over. I can almost feel it. I'm changing sides again.

Why does having children, while bringing out our most lov- 27 ing, effusively maternal selves, simultaneously ignite our fears and turn us against one another? After all, women with children— whether they work or stay at home—might get together to make this world a better place for all women with children.

What's all this anger really about? 28

For one thing, we're too sleep-deprived to be tolerant or tem- 29 perate. I remember the caul of exhaustion I lived in as the mother of young children. In those days the most erotic thing a man could say to me was "Why don't you just go back to sleep." My idea of lingerie was earplugs and a sleep mask—neither of which blocked out my children clamoring for my attention.

Women do the lion's share—perhaps it should be called 30 the woman's share—of the child care and household work in this country. A recent National Labor Bureau study shows that women who work still spend twice as much time as men on child care and housework. We live with the results of half a revolution: Women have earned the right to work as hard as men do, but men did not take over half the work at home. Every woman knows her pediatrician's telephone number; I have yet to meet a man who does.

31   What worsens our predicament is that women lack core representation in our government. Photographs of the Senate still look like "Class of 1970" men's college-reunion photos. One of the great mysteries of modern politics is that women, who comprise more than half the population, still comprise less than 20 percent of the government. More women vote than men, but we don't vote for one another. Certainly gender is not the defining reason to vote for or against anyone, but if more women voted for women, at least we would be governed by those who have walked in our flip-flops and pushed our strollers and hunched over our changing tables at 4 A.M. Have we been so indoctrinated by a patriarchal society that we secretly think men are more fit to govern? Are we so hardwired by advertising and fairy tales that we assume the best child care always comes from a mother even if she's a resentful nervous wreck?

32   Working and stay-at-home moms today are like the famous psychology experiment in which too many rats are put in a cage with too little food. The rats *have* had enough sleep, nevertheless, they kill one another. The stakes in the baby battle are high—nothing is more precious than our children and being able to provide for them and ourselves. The level of resources is low. There isn't much support for women who work—support like office child care, flexible hours, and reasonable maternity leaves. There isn't much support for women who stay home—like tax breaks, financial protection in case of divorce, subsidized medical care, or even licensed child care. Kennels are more strictly regulated than child-care agencies; veterinarians get paid more than pediatricians; men who can hire better lawyers tend to walk away with more advantageous divorce decrees than their ex-wives who have spent two decades with zeros on their income tax forms.

33   No wonder every woman who has made a different choice seems like an enemy. What if you are right? What if I am wrong? What if in working we are damaging our children by being absent and preoccupied? What if by staying home we are sacrificing our

independence and our ability to financially take care of our children and hurting them in another way?

And so we fight.   **34**

BUILDING VOCABULARY

Cheever uses a number of words that connote offensive action. Write definitions for each of the words. Then explain why Cheever has chosen this language for her essay. (Look again at the title of the essay as well.)

1. platoons (par. 2)
2. adversaries (par. 3)
3. squadron (par. 4)
4. whipsawed (par. 6)
5. hostility (par. 6)
6. divisive force (par. 7)
7. oppression (par. 14)
8. brashness (par. 25)
9. ignite (par. 27)
10. indoctrinated (par. 31)

THINKING CRITICALLY ABOUT THE ESSAY

Understanding the Writer's Ideas

1. Who are the women in the "war on the streets"? How does Cheever distinguish them from each other?
2. Which women does the writer initially identify as the aggressors? Who are the victims?
3. Who is Gabby? Why does Cheever mention her?
4. How did Cheever feel about families when she was a single woman? when she was married and pregnant? after she had her child?
5. What specific actions for her child did the writer take after her daughter Sarah was born?
6. Now that her children are adults, what changes does Cheever note about her own behavior?
7. How does the writer explain the anger of women who turn against each other?

8. How do men figure into the equation of anger?

9. In what ways does the government represent a roadblock to women?

10. What kind of support does Cheever see as absent in the "opt-out" revolution?

Understanding the Writer's Techniques

1. The first paragraph is just one sentence long. What is your reaction to it? Why has Cheever chosen to write such a brief opening? How does the second paragraph in the essay explain the point she has made in this introductory paragraph? How does the opening paragraph interact with the essay's title? the very last paragraph?

2. Cheever builds to her main argument. In the first part of the essay she argues about the relations among different groups of women. Later, she proposes ways to improve women's predicament. Where in the essay does she state the first part of the argument? the second? What would you say, then, was her major proposition? State it in your own words.

3. Where does Cheever provide evidence for her argument? How do you feel about the details drawn from her own life experiences? What other kinds of supporting detail does she offer?

4. Like other writers throughout this book, Cheever uses questions as strategies for engaging readers' attention. But by any measure, the questions here seem quite numerous. In fact, in the next to the last paragraph (par. 33) we read four consecutive questions. What is your reaction to these and other questions throughout the essay? Identify them by checking them off in the margin or by making a list. How does Cheever answer the questions that she raises, if at all? How would you answer them?

5. Whom would you say is Cheever's audience for this piece? How do you know?

6. Cheever uses humor throughout the essay. Which examples of humor do you think best serve her argument?

7. The writer presents several direct quotes uttered by various people. What do the quotes add to the essay—Gabby's mother's statement, for example, or the statement from the Citibank vice president?

8. Cheever says that after the birth of her children, she "took a hit and lost the sharpness and brashness" that were her "trademarks." Would you agree that this essay lacks sharpness and brashness? Why or why not? Support your opinion with direct references to the text.

✳ MIXING PATTERNS

Cheever draws on several rhetorical patterns to build her argument. Where and how does she use classification? narrative? comparison and contrast? Do you find her cause-and-effect reasoning valid? What is your reaction to these various modes in a single essay?

Exploring the Writer's Ideas

1. In regard to the war that Cheever sees in the streets: is this a war found only in New York City? Why? Where else might you find similar conflict? Is the conflict exclusively an urban phenomenon? Explain your response.
2. Discuss your responses to this question that Cheever raises: "Why should families have more rights than single people?"
3. Cheever argues that "there isn't much support for women who work." Why might you agree or disagree with this statement?

IDEAS FOR WRITING

Prewriting

Make two columns on a sheet of paper, and make a numbered list to indicate under each the value for women of joining the workforce and the value of staying at home to rear their children.

Guided Writing

Write an argumentative essay in which you weigh the options for women after they have children: returning to work or being stay-at-home moms. Be sure to take a position on the matter.

1. Open and close your essay with an attention-getting one-sentence paragraph.

2. Clearly state your major proposition, or claim, at a key point in your essay.
3. Draw on your personal experience or the experience of people you know.
4. Provide relevant data and any other details to support your argument.
5. Use humor to advance your position.
6. Draw on at least two other patterns as you develop your argument—for example, you could choose from narration, comparison and contrast, classification, or cause or effect.
7. Raise questions in your essay and attempt to answer them.
8. Give your essay a provocative title.

Thinking and Writing Collaboratively

Bring to class your draft in response to the Guided Writing activity. In small groups, read each other's essays. What suggestions can you make to help improve your classmates' efforts?

Writing About the Text

Write an essay about the language Cheever uses in this essay. She makes many references to popular culture (the references to designer products, for example) and relies on many colloquial and informal expressions to advance her position. How effective are these strategies? If you could speak with the writer, what would you tell her about your response to her language?

More Writing Projects

1. Write a journal entry about how our society addresses the needs of single people in a world more focused on families.
2. Write a well-developed paragraph on the responsibilities of parents to supervise their children in public settings like restaurants, supermarkets, doctors' offices, and airplanes.
3. Write an essay to address this question from Cheever's essay: "Why are children such a divisive force between women?"

The Good Enough Mother

Anna Quindlen

Anna Marie Quindlen was born in Philadelphia on July 8, 1952. She graduated in 1970 from South Brunswick High School in South Brunswick, New Jersey, and completed a bachelor's degree at Barnard College in New York City. Quindlen writes a biweekly column for *Newsweek* and often criticizes what she sees as the fast-paced and materialistic character of modern American life. Much of her personal writing focuses on her mother, who died at the age of 40 from ovarian cancer, when the writer was 19 years old. Quindlen's nonfiction books include *How Reading Changed My Life* (1998), *Being Perfect* (2005), and *Good Dog. Stay.* (2007). Three of her best-selling novels became movies: *One True Thing* (1997) was a popular feature film for which Meryl Streep received an Academy Award nomination as best actress; *Black and Blue* (1998) and *Blessings* (2002) became television movies. Quindlen is married and the mother of three children. In this column for *Newsweek*, which appeared in 2005, Quindlen identifies what she sees as the most important elements in rearing children.

PREREADING: THINKING ABOUT THE ESSAY IN ADVANCE

What are the qualities of a good mother from your point of view? How would you feel about someone calling a mother you know "a good enough mother"? Is it okay to be just "good enough"? Why or why not?

Words to Watch

pernicious (par. 3)   harmful; evil
malleable (par. 5)   flexible; impressionable
credulous (par. 5)   gullible; trusting
vulnerable (par. 5)   weak; defenseless
improbable (par. 6)   not likely
disparate (par. 7)   dissimilar; different
omnipresent (par. 9)   everywhere; all-pervading
roundelay (par. 10)   medieval dance in a circle
prodigies (par. 10)   geniuses
addled (par. 11)   confused

expiate (par. 12)   apologize for; make up for
incandescent (par. 12)   glowing; shining

1   There was a kind of carelessness to my childhood. I wandered away from time to time, rode my bike too far from home, took the trolley to nowhere in particular and back again. If you had asked my mother at any given time where I was, she would likely have paused from spooning Gerber's peas into a baby's mouth or ironing our school uniforms and replied, "She's around here somewhere."

2   By the new standards of mothering, my mother was a bust. Given the number of times I got lost when I was young, she might even be termed neglectful. There's only one problem with that conclusion. It's dead wrong. My mother was great at what she did. Don't misunderstand: she didn't sit on the floor and help us build with our Erector sets, didn't haul us from skating rink to piano lessons. She couldn't even drive. But where she was always felt like a safe place.

3   The idea that that's enough is a tough sell in our current culture, and not simply because if one of my kids had been found wandering far from our home there would have been a caseworker and a cop at the door. We live in a perfection society now, in which it is possible to make our bodies last longer, to manipulate our faces so the lines of laughter and distress are wiped out. We believe in the illusion of control, and nowhere has that become more powerful—and more pernicious—than in the phenomenon of manic motherhood. What the child-care guru D. W. Winnicott once called "the ordinary devoted mother" is no longer good enough. Instead there is an über-mom who bounces from soccer field to school fair to play date until she falls into bed at the end of the day, exhausted, her life somewhere between the Stations of the Cross and a decathlon.

4   A perfect storm of trends and events contributed to this. One was the teeter-totter scientific argument of nature versus nurture. When my mother was raising kids, there was a sub rosa assumption that they were what they were. The smart one. The sweet one. Even the bad one. There was only so much a mother could do to mold the clay she'd been dealt.

5   But as I became a mother, all that was changing. Little minds, we learned from researchers, were infinitely malleable, even before birth. Don't get tense: tense moms make tense infants. (That news'll make you tense!) In a prenatal exercise class, I remember

lying on the mat working on what was left of my stomach muscles, listening to the instructor repeating, "Now hug your baby." If I had weak abs, did that mean my baby went unhugged? Keeping up with the Joneses turned into keeping up with the Joneses' kids. Whose mothers, by the way, lied. I now refuse to believe in 9-month-olds who speak in full sentences. But I was more credulous, and more vulnerable, when I had a 9-month-old myself.

This craziness sounds improbable in the face of the feminist revolution that transformed the landscape of America during our lifetime. But at some level it is the fruit of that revolution, a come-uppance cleverly disguised as a calling. Every time we take note of the fact that work is not a choice but an economic necessity—"most women have to work, you know"—it's an apology for freedom. How better to circumvent the power of the new woman than with the idea of mothering not as care but as creation? Every moment for children was a teachable moment—and every teachable moment missed was a measure of a lousy mom. 6

My baby-boomer friends and I were part of the first generation of women who took for granted that we would work throughout our lifetime, and like most pioneers we made it up as we went along. In 1976, Dr. Spock revised his bible of child care to say that it was all right if we worked and had children as well. There was a slapdash approach to melding these disparate roles, usually reflected in the iconic woman at a business meeting with spit-up on her shoulder. My first sitter was the erstwhile manager of a cult punk band. She was a good sitter, too. We got by. 7

But quicker than you could say nanny cam, books appeared, seminars were held and modern motherhood was codified as a profession. Professionalized for women who didn't work outside the home: if they were giving up such great opportunities, then the tending of kids needed to be made into an all-encompassing job. Professionalized for women who had paying jobs out in the world: to show that their work was not bad for their kids, they had to take child rearing as seriously as dealmaking. (Fathers did not have to justify themselves; after all, no man has ever felt moved to say that most guys have to work, you know.) 8

It's not just that baking for the bake sale, meeting with the teachers, calling the other mothers about the sleepover and looking at the SAT camp made women of both sorts crazy, turning stress from an occasional noun into an omnipresent verb and adverb. A lot of this was not particularly good for kids. If your 9 mother has been micromanaging your homework since you were 6, it's hard to feel any pride of ownership when you do well. You can't learn from mistakes and disappointments if your childhood is engineered so there aren't any.

10   So much has been written about how the young people of America seem to stay young longer now, well into the years when their grandparents owned houses and had families. But their grandparents never had a mother calling the teacher to complain about a bad grade. And hair-trigger attention spans may be less a function of PlayStation and more a function of kids who never have a moment's peace. I passed on the weekend roundelay of kiddie-league sports so our three could hang out with one another. I told people I hoped it would cement a bond among them, and it did. But I really wanted to be reading rather than standing on the sidelines pretending my kids were soccer prodigies. Maybe I had three children in the first place so I wouldn't ever have to play board games. In my religion, martyrs die.

11   Our oldest child wrestled custody of his life away from me at a fairly early age, perhaps inspired by an epic bout in which I tried to persuade him to rewrite a perfectly good fourth-grade paper to turn it into an eighth-grade paper. Perhaps I'd been addled by the class art projects, some of which looked like the work of a crack graphics design team—and were. I asked the other day about his memories of my mothering. "You sorta freaked out during the college application process," he noted accurately. But then he wrote, "What I remember most: having a good time." You can engrave that on my headstone right this minute.

12   There's the problem with turning motherhood into martyrdom. There's no way to do it and have a good time. If we create a never-ending spin cycle of have-tos because we're trying to expiate senseless guilt about working or not working, trying to keep up with the woman at school whose kid gets A's because she writes the papers herself, the message we send our children is terrible. By our actions we tell them that being a mom—being their mom—is a drag, powered by fear, self-doubt and conformity, all the things we are supposed to teach them to overcome. It just becomes a gloss on that old joke: Enough about me. What about you? How do you make me feel about myself? The most incandescent memories of my childhood are of making my mother laugh. My kids did the same for me. A good time is what they remember long after toddler programs and art projects are over. The rest is just scheduling.

BUILDING VOCABULARY

Quindlen has used a number of hyphenated words in this essay.
Write definitions of those listed below.

1. child-care (par. 3)
2. über-mom (par. 3)
3. teeter-totter (par. 4)
4. come-uppance (par. 6)
5. baby-boomer (par. 7)
6. spit-up (par. 7)
7. all-encompassing (par. 8)
8. hair-trigger (par. 10)
9. kiddie-league (par. 10)
10. never-ending (par. 12)
11. have-tos (par. 12)
12. self-doubt (par. 12)

THINKING CRITICALLY ABOUT THE ESSAY

Understanding the Writer's Ideas

1. What characteristics of mothering does Quindlen ascribe to her own mother?
2. What are the qualities of the "perfection society" that the writer identifies?
3. What is an "über-mom? What functions does she perform? How does she compare with "the ordinary devoted mother"? What "storm of trends and events" contributed to the change from one kind of mother to the other, according to Quindlen?
4. What did the feminist movement assert about working and motherhood, according to the writer? Who is Dr. Spock, and what did he contribute to the conversation?
5. What, according to the writer, changed the notion of stress?
6. Why did Quindlen give up "the weekend roundelay of kiddie-league sports"?
7. What memories of Quindlen's mothering did her son note in response to her question?
8. What joke does Quindlen tell at the end of the essay?

Understanding the Writer's Techniques

1. In what ways does the title of the essay engage the reader? How does the title contradict the way we ordinarily think of mothers?

2. What is Quindlen's argument here? Where does she state it most clearly? How does her claim in the essay interact with the essay's title?

3. Quindlen draws on both formal and informal language in the essay, in some cases within the same paragraph or sentence. For example, look at this sentence in paragraph 7: "There was a slapdash approach to melding these disparate roles, usually reflected in the iconic woman at a business meeting with spit-up on her shoulder." What examples of formal and informal language can you identify in the sentence? What is the effect on the reader? Would you say the effect is shocking, ordinary, surprising, predictable, unfortunate—or something else? Explain your response.

4. In what ways does Quindlen draw on her personal experiences to provide support for her argument? Do you find the supporting detail convincing? Why or why not?

5. How does the writer use comparison and contrast strategies in the essay?

6. *Newsweek* is a national publication with a wide readership, and this selection appeared in one of Quindlen's columns. How do you think the writer's view of readership, that is, the audience, affected the style of the piece? Would you call Quindlen's style journalistic, ordinary, explosive, cool, or something else? Explain your response.

7. How effective are Quindlen's transitions in the essay? Look at the first sentence of each paragraph and identify the way in which the writer links that paragraph to the previous paragraph or paragraphs.

8. What does the joke in the last paragraph contribute to the essay? How does it help the writer reach her conclusion?

Exploring the Writer's Ideas

1. What does Quindlen mean in paragraph 3 when she writes "We live in a perfection society now"? Do you agree with her? Why or why not? In what ways does the demand for perfection in our society extend beyond the issue of child rearing?

2. What does the writer mean by "the teeter-totter scientific argument of nature versus nurture"? What is your view of this argument? Which side would you take?

3. Quindlen implies that parents pay too much attention to their children's needs and daily activities. Why might you agree or disagree with her on this point? Do some kids "never have a moment's peace" because of their parents' interference? Explain. In what ways is the issue an exclusively middle- or upper-class phenomenon?

4. Quindlen ultimately says about children that "a good time is what they remember." How important do you think "having a good time" is in a child's upbringing?

IDEAS FOR WRITING

Prewriting

Make a list of the qualities that you think would earn someone the label "good enough father."

Guided Writing

Write an argumentative essay called "The Good Enough Father" in which you identify the qualities of fatherhood that you believe children remember.

1. Open your essay with a brief description of your childhood or the childhood of someone you know and the father's role in that childhood.

2. Explain how a father today is different from the kind of father you remember.

3. State your argument in a well-developed thesis sentence.

4. Explain how our "perfection society" makes demands on fathers today and their responsibilities as parents.

5. Show whether today's father has a positive or negative effect on children.

6. Draw on your personal experience or the experience of people you know in order to support your claim.

7. Deal with the notion of "having a good time" and the father's role in assuring it.

8. Try to tell a relevant joke.

Thinking and Writing Collaboratively

Write down the various responsibilities that mothers have in bringing up young children. In small groups, discuss your lists. Which elements does the group believe are most important?

Writing About the Text

Quindlen uses some lively and vivid adjectives in this selection. Write your own essay analyzing the writer's dramatic and emotional diction. Focus on the adjectives, but feel free to discuss whatever words you like. Explain why you think Quindlen uses the words she does.

More Writing Projects

1. Write a journal entry about the value—or lack of value—in structuring the after-school lives of children by means of play dates, music lessons, gymnastics, and so on.
2. Write a well-developed paragraph expressing your views about Winnicott's label "the ordinary devoted mother" (par. 3).
3. Write an essay to address the notion that "the young people in America seem to stay young longer now."

PERSPECTIVES ON POLITICAL RIGHTS:
ARE WE TRULY FREE?

Issues of political rights arise from conflicting conceptions of freedom, government, progress, and human welfare. Men and women over the centuries have argued passionately about politics. Is freedom the freedom to be left to my own devices—and thus, freedom from government interference in my life (individual rights)? Or is freedom being treated fairly and equally—and thus, freedom sustained by government so I can run my life as I please (civil rights)? What is the appropriate balance between the individual and the State? In the United States these issues often arise in the context of the law, specifically the Bill of Rights and in the Constitution in general. In the selections that follow, look carefully at the arguments and how they draw on American law and American tradition even as they attempt to change that tradition or to apply it to unprecedented situations. Broadly speaking, these essays use irony, reason, and rhetorical insights to advance their views. Which do you find most persuasive, and why? What can you take from these essays for use in your own essays?

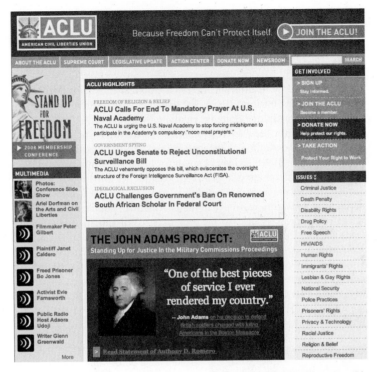

Organizations like the ACLU work to extend and defend civil rights. How does this screenshot from their Web site support this position?

American Civil Liberties Union, Inc. Used with permission.

Get a Knife, Get a Dog, but Get Rid of Guns

Molly Ivins

Born in Monterey, California, in 1944, political columnist Molly Ivins grew up in Houston, Texas. She graduated from Smith College and from the prestigious Columbia University School of Journalism. Ivins's column for the Fort Worth *Star-Telegram* was syndicated in 113 newspapers. Author of the best-selling *Molly Ivins Can't Say That Can She?* (1990), Ivins is known for her brash, amusing writing. Her titles alone are provocative. Consider her 2004 work *Who Let the Dogs In?: Incredible Political Animals I Have Known*. In addition to appearing regularly in major American publications, she wrote about press issues for the American Civil Liberties Union. Ivins died in 2007; that year, her last book, *Bill of Wrongs: The Executive Branch's Assault on America's Fundamental Rights* was published. This selection from her *Nothin' but Good Times Ahead* (1993) attacks "gun nuts" in a spirited, wry, and sometimes angry tone. As a professional writer for popular audiences, Ivins is alert to the need to be both persuasive and entertaining. Keep an eye out for how she manages to achieve these goals.

www.mhhe.com/
shortprose

To learn more about Ivins, click on
**More Resources > Chapter 11 >
Molly Ivins**

PREREADING: THINKING ABOUT THE ESSAY IN ADVANCE

Stop a moment to explore your attitudes toward guns. Can you say *why* you think what you do? Are your opinions based on reliable evidence? Are your opinions well-reasoned?

Words to Watch

ricochet (par. 3)   bounce off a surface
civil libertarian (par. 4)   a person who believes strongly in freedom of speech and action
infringed (par. 5)   violated
perforating (par. 6)   making holes in
lethal (par. 8)   deadly
wreak . . . carnage (par. 8)   cause great bloodshed

martial (par. 12)   warlike
literally (par. 13)   actually
psychosexual (par. 13)   having to do with the emotional aspects
    of sexuality
psyches (par. 14)   emotional makeup

1 Guns. Everywhere guns.

2 Let me start this discussion by pointing out that I am not anti-gun. I'm pro-knife. Consider the merits of the knife.

3 In the first place, you have to catch up with someone in order to stab him. A general substitution of knives for guns would promote physical fitness. We'd turn into a whole nation of great runners. Plus, knives don't ricochet. And people are seldom killed while cleaning their knives.

4 As a civil libertarian, I, of course, support the Second Amendment. And I believe it means exactly what it says:

5 *A well-regulated militia being necessary to the security of a free state, the right of the people to keep and bear arms shall not be infringed.* Fourteen-year-old boys are not part of a well-regulated militia. Members of wacky religious cults are not part of a well-regulated militia. Permitting unregulated citizens to have guns is destroying the security of this free state.

6 I am intrigued by the arguments of those who claim to follow the judicial doctrine of original intent. How do they know it was the dearest wish of Thomas Jefferson's heart that teenage drug dealers should cruise the cities of this nation perforating their fellow citizens with assault rifles? Channeling?

7 There is more hooey spread about the Second Amendment. It says quite clearly that guns are for those who form part of a well-regulated militia, that is, the armed forces, including the National Guard. Their reasons for keeping them away from everyone else get clearer by the day.

8 The comparison most often used is that of the automobile, another lethal object that is regularly used to wreak great carnage. Obviously, this society is full of people who haven't enough common sense to use an automobile properly. But we haven't outlawed cars yet.

9 We do, however, license them and their owners, restrict their use to presumably sane and sober adults, and keep track of who sells them to whom. At a minimum, we should do the same with guns.

In truth, there is no rational argument for guns in this society.   10
This is no longer a frontier nation in which people hunt their own
food. It is a crowded, overwhelmingly urban country in which letting people have access to guns is a continuing disaster. Those
who want guns—whether for target shooting, hunting, or potting
rattlesnakes (get a hoe)—should be subject to the same restrictions
placed on gun owners in England, a nation in which liberty has
survived nicely without an armed populace.

The argument that "guns don't kill people" is patent nonsense.   11
Anyone who has ever worked in a cop shop knows how many
family arguments end in murder because there was a gun in the
house. Did the gun kill someone? No. But if there had been no
gun, no one would have died. At least not without a good foot race
first. Guns do kill. Unlike cars, that is all they do.

Michael Crichton makes an interesting argument about tech-   12
nology in his thriller *Jurassic Park*. He points out that power without discipline is making this society into a wreckage. By the time
someone who studies the martial arts becomes a master—literally
able to kill with bare hands—that person has also undergone years
of training and discipline. But any fool can pick up a gun and kill
with it.

"A well-regulated militia" surely implies both long training   13
and long discipline. That is the least, the very least, that should be
required of those who are permitted to have guns, because a gun
is literally the power to kill. For years I used to enjoy taunting my
gun-nut friends about their psychosexual hang-ups—always in a
spirit of good cheer, you understand. But letting the noisy minority
in the NRA force us to allow this carnage to continue is just plain
insane.

I do think gun nuts have a power hang-up. I don't know what   14
is missing in their psyches that they need to feel they have the
power to kill. But no sane society would allow this to continue.

Ban the damn things. Ban them all.   15

You want protection? Get a dog.   16

BUILDING VOCABULARY

1. Identify the following:
    a. the Second Amendment (par. 4)
    b. the judicial doctrine of original intent (par. 6)

> **c.** Michael Crichton's *Jurassic Park* (par. 12)
> **d.** NRA (par. 13)

2. This is an essay that argues a certain point of view. It therefore wishes to undermine opposing ideas. List five words or phrases in this essay that aim to strengthen the writer's position by making fun of or otherwise undermining the opposition.

THINKING CRITICALLY ABOUT THE ESSAY

Understanding the Writer's Ideas

1. Why does the writer devote her first three paragraphs to the knife?
2. In your own words, state the writer's interpretation of the Second Amendment.
3. What is the point of comparing guns and cars?
4. In the view of the writer, was there ever an argument for the unlimited access to firearms?
5. What is the writer's response to the argument that "guns don't kill people," it is people using guns who do?
6. Why does the writer allude to *Jurassic Park*?

Understanding the Writer's Techniques

1. What is the *tone* (see Glossary) of this essay? How does the tone support the writer's argument?
2. What is the rhetorical effect of beginning the essay by a discussion of knives? How does the first sentence frame this discussion?
3. This essay lists and responds to the main arguments in *favor* of unlimited sale and possession of guns. Identify these positive arguments in the order they are presented.
4. Why does Ivins present the arguments for guns in the order that she does?
5. In addition to responding to arguments by the opposition, the writer puts forward her own arguments against guns. Identify these in the order that she presents them.
6. How does the concluding paragraph reinforce the writer's argument?

Exploring the Writer's Ideas

1. Is the writer too "argumentative"? That is, does she overstep credibility by mocking those who oppose her views? Explain your opinion.
2. Meddling with amendments to the Constitution is a serious matter, for these provisions have governed the nation well for hundreds of years. Does the writer do justice to the gravity of the documents whose meaning she is interpreting? Could she advance her argument in a less provocative way? Explain.
3. Do Ivins's arguments regarding militias persuade you? If so, explain why. If not, explain why not.
4. Write a response to the writer's taunt that progun advocates must have something "missing in their psyches."

IDEAS FOR WRITING

Prewriting

Using the same tone as the writer, write a few sentences in support of guns.

Guided Writing

Write an essay in which you mock a well-established but controversial position, such as the advocacy of unlimited access to pornography on the grounds of free speech or the appropriateness of sex education in elementary schools.

1. Begin the essay with a bold mocking statement that puts those opposed to your view on the defensive. Make sure you can usefully return to the example or tactic of your opening at other points in your essay.
2. State the main argument for the opposition point of view, preferably one referring to its basis in law.
3. Refute this argument by short, dismissive sentences and examples.
4. State two or three other arguments for the opposing point of view, again using short, pointed, and mocking retorts.
5. End your essay by a return, in the form of a pithy summary, to the ploy of your opening paragraph.

Thinking and Writing Collaboratively

Divide the class arbitrarily in two. Assign one group the progun position, and the other the antigun position. Have each group take the writer's main points and amplify or refute them.

Writing About the Text

Ivins states in paragraph 10, "In truth, there is no rational argument for guns in this society." How well has she supported this argument? What examples or details best support it? Has the essay convinced you to accept her argument? Why or why not? Address these questions in an essay that analyzes "Get a Knife, Get a Dog, but Get Rid of Guns."

More Writing Projects

1. Visit a firing range and interview some people there about their views on guns. Write an outline for an essay about your visit.
2. Read the debates that led to the original adoption of the Second Amendment. Write an extended paragraph that reflects on the relevance or irrelevance of the arguments of that time to our own.
3. Write an essay that argues for a favored solution of your own to the problem of violence in our society.

I Have a Dream
Martin Luther King Jr.

Martin Luther King Jr. (1929–1968), American clergyman and Nobel Prize winner, was one of the main leaders of the civil rights movement of the 1960s and a passionate advocate of nonviolent protest. His assassination in 1968 became an international rallying cry in the struggle for racial justice. A native of Atlanta, Georgia, King was educated at Morehouse College and Boston University. In 1957 King helped to found the Southern Christian Leadership Conference, and he soon led a series of protests throughout the South to desegregate the society. In 1963 King organized the now-legendary March on Washington, at the conclusion of which, standing before the Lincoln Memorial, he delivered the "I Have a Dream" speech, printed below, to an audience of more than 200,000 people. Immediately adopted into the canon of great American oratory, King's speech, with its distinctive use of religious language and emotional allusion to American images of freedom, merits careful attention as an example of powerful and historic argument.

www.mhhe.com/ **shortprose**   To learn more about King, click on **More Resources > Chapter 11 > Martin Luther King Jr.**

PREREADING: THINKING ABOUT THE ESSAY IN ADVANCE

The essay's title is in the present tense: the speaker *has* a dream. How would the essay be different if King's title used the past tense? It's unlikely that you have not heard of Martin Luther King Jr., or of this essay. But it was originally not an essay: it was a speech on a highly public occasion. What expectations does King raise by speaking of a dream rather than, say, a goal, or an ambition, or a purpose?

Words to Watch

symbolic (par. 1)   representative
emancipation (par. 1)   liberation
proclamation (par. 1)   official publication

unalienable (par. 3)   incapable of being surrendered or taken
  away
interposition (par. 16)   interference
nullification (par. 16)   the impeding by a state of federal law
prodigious (par. 21)   vast

1   Five score years ago, a great American, in whose symbolic shadow
we stand, signed the Emancipation Proclamation. This momentous
decree came as a great beacon light of hope to millions of Negro
slaves who had been seared in the flames of withering injustice. It
came as a joyous daybreak to end the long night of captivity.

2   But one hundred years later, we must face the tragic fact that
the Negro is still not free. One hundred years later, the life of the
Negro is still sadly crippled by the manacles of segregation and
the chains of discrimination. One hundred years later, the Negro
lives on a lonely island of poverty in the midst of a vast ocean
of material prosperity. One hundred years later, the Negro is still
languishing in the corners of American society and finds himself
an exile in his own land. So we have come here today to dramatize
an appalling condition.

3   In a sense we have come to our nation's capital to cash a check.
When the architects of our republic wrote the magnificent words of
the Constitution and the Declaration of Independence, they were
signing a promissory note to which every American was to fall
heir. This note was a promise that all men would be guaranteed the
unalienable rights of life, liberty, and the pursuit of happiness.

4   It is obvious today that America has defaulted on this promissory note insofar as her citizens of color are concerned. Instead
of honoring this sacred obligation, America has given the Negro
people a bad check; a check which has come back marked "insufficient funds." But we refuse to believe that the bank of justice is
bankrupt. We refuse to believe that there are insufficient funds in
the great vaults of opportunity of this nation. So we have come to
cash this check—a check that will give us upon demand the riches
of freedom and the security of justice. We have also come to this
hallowed spot to remind America of the fierce urgency of *now*.
This is no time to engage in the luxury of cooling off or to take the
tranquilizing drugs of gradualism. *Now* is the time to make real the
promises of Democracy. *Now* is the time to rise from the dark and
desolate valley of segregation to the sunlit path of racial justice.
Now is the time to open the doors of opportunity to all of God's

children. *Now* is the time to lift our nation from the quicksands of racial injustice to the solid rock of brotherhood.

It would be fatal for the nation to overlook the urgency of the 5 moment and to underestimate the determination of the Negro. This sweltering summer of the Negro's legitimate discontent will not pass until there is an invigorating autumn of freedom and equality. 1963 is not an end, but a beginning. Those who hope that the Negro needed to blow off steam and will now be content will have a rude awakening if the nation returns to business as usual. There will be neither rest nor tranquility in America until the Negro is granted his citizenship rights. The whirlwinds of revolt will continue to shake the foundations of our nation until the bright day of justice emerges.

But there is something that I must say to my people who stand 6 on the warm threshold which leads into the palace of justice. In the process of gaining our rightful place we must not be guilty of wrongful deeds. Let us not seek to satisfy our thirst for freedom by drinking from the cup of bitterness and hatred. We must forever conduct our struggle on the high plane of dignity and discipline. We must not allow our creative protest to degenerate into physical violence. Again and again we must rise to the majestic heights of meeting physical force with soul force. The marvelous new militancy which has engulfed the Negro community must not lead us to a distrust of all white people, for many of our white brothers, as evidenced by their presence here today, have come to realize that their destiny is tied up with our destiny and their freedom is inextricably bound to our freedom. We cannot walk alone.

And as we walk, we must make the pledge that we shall march 7 ahead. We cannot turn back. There are those who are asking the devotees of civil rights, "When will you be satisfied?" We can never be satisfied as long as the Negro is the victim of the unspeakable horrors of police brutality. We can never be satisfied as long as our bodies, heavy with the fatigue of travel, cannot gain lodging in the motels of the highways and the hotels of the cities. We cannot be satisfied as long as the Negro's basic mobility is from a smaller ghetto to a larger one. We can never be satisfied as long as a Negro in Mississippi cannot vote and a Negro in New York believes he has nothing for which to vote. No, no, we are not satisfied, and will not be satisfied until justice rolls down like waters and righteousness like a mighty stream.

I am not unmindful that some of you have come here out of 8 great trials and tribulations. Some of you have come fresh from narrow jail cells. Some of you have come from areas where your quest for freedom left you battered by the storms of persecution and staggered by the winds of police brutality. You have been the veterans of creative suffering. Continue to work with the faith that unearned suffering is redemptive.

9   Go back to Mississippi, go back to Alabama, go back to South Carolina, go back to Georgia, go back to Louisiana, go back to the slums and ghettos of our northern cities, knowing that somehow this situation can and will be changed. Let us not wallow in the valley of despair.

10   I say to you today, my friends, that in spite of the difficulties and frustrations of the moment I still have a dream. It is a dream deeply rooted in the American dream.

11   I have a dream that one day this nation will rise up and live out the true meaning of its creed: "We hold these truths to be self-evident; that all men are created equal."

12   I have a dream that one day on the red hills of Georgia the sons of former slaves and the sons of former slaveowners will be able to sit down together at the table of brotherhood.

13   I have a dream that one day even the state of Mississippi, a desert state sweltering with the heat of injustice and oppression, will be transformed into an oasis of freedom and justice.

14   I have a dream that my four little children will one day live in a nation where they will not be judged by the color of their skin but by the content of their character.

15   I have a dream today.

16   I have a dream that one day the state of Alabama, whose governor's lips are presently dripping with the words of interposition and nullification, will be transformed into a situation where little black boys and black girls will be able to join hands with little white boys and white girls and walk together as sisters and brothers.

17   I have a dream today.

18   I have a dream that one day every valley shall be exalted, every hill and mountain shall be made low, the rough places will be made plain, and the crooked places will be made straight, and the glory of the Lord shall be revealed, and all flesh shall see it together.

19   This is our hope. This is the faith with which I return to the South. With this faith we will be able to hew out of the mountain of despair a stone of hope. With this faith we will be able to transform the jangling discords of our nation into a beautiful symphony

of brotherhood. With this faith we will be able to work together, to pray together, to struggle together, to go to jail together, to stand up for freedom together, knowing that we will be free one day.

This will be the day when all of God's children will be able to 20 sing with new meaning

> My country, 'tis of thee,
> Sweet land of liberty,
> Of thee I sing:
> Land where my fathers died,
> Land of the pilgrims' pride,
> From every mountain-side
> Let freedom ring.

And if America is to be a great nation this must become true. So 21 let freedom ring from the prodigious hilltops of New Hampshire. Let freedom ring from the mighty mountains of New York. Let freedom ring from the heightening Alleghenies of Pennsylvania!

Let freedom ring from the snowcapped Rockies of Colorado! 22

Let freedom ring from the curvaceous peaks of California! 23

But not only that; let freedom ring from Stone Mountain of 24 Georgia!

Let freedom ring from Lookout Mountain of Tennessee! 25

Let freedom ring from every hill and molehill of Mississippi. 26 From every mountainside, let freedom ring.

When we let freedom ring, when we let it ring from every vil- 27 lage and every hamlet, from every state and every city, we will be able to speed up that day when all of God's children, black men and white men, Jews and Gentiles, Protestants and Catholics, will be able to join hands and sing in the words of the old Negro spiritual, "Free at last! free at last! thank God almighty, we are free at last!"

BUILDING VOCABULARY

King's speech is highly metaphorical. Rewrite the words in italics below in simple declarative language:

a. "slaves who had been *seared in the flames of withering* injustice" (par. 1).

b. "the Negro *lives on a lonely island of poverty in the midst of a vast ocean of material prosperity*" (par. 2).

c. "We refuse to believe that *there are insufficient funds in the great vaults of opportunity* of this nation" (par. 4).

d. *"from the quicksands of racial injustice to the solid rock of brotherhood"* (par. 4).

THINKING CRITICALLY ABOUT THE ESSAY

Understanding the Writer's Ideas

1. Who is the "great American" King speaks about in the first sentence of his essay?
2. What is the "appalling condition" that King says he and his followers have come to Washington to dramatize?
3. What does King mean when he says "we have come to our nation's capital to cash a check" (par. 3)?
4. Why does King emphasize the word *now* in par. 4?
5. What does King advise as proper for his followers as they stand "on the warm threshold" of justice?
6. How does King respond to the charge that his demands are insatiable?
7. Summarize in one sentence the point King makes in paragraphs 10–18.
8. How does King connect his faith and hope with the tradition of American patriotism?
9. Why does King end his speech with a passage from a Negro spiritual?

Understanding the Writer's Techniques

1. What aspects of King's address illustrate that it is a speech and not an essay? What is the purpose of King's speech?
2. King casts the purpose of the March on Washington in surprisingly monetary terms. The Constitution and Declaration of Independence were, he says, a "promissory note" on which America has "defaulted." But King has come to Washington "to cash this check." In what ways is this extended metaphor appropriate to advance King's cause? Or do you think it is too much to do with money and demeans his cause?
3. King, a preacher, makes abundant use of biblical allusion and biblical language to make his points. In paragraph 2, for

example, King speaks of the Negro as being an "exile in his own land." How does this analogy appeal to Judeo-Christian tradition? What other examples of biblical allusion or biblical language do you find especially effective?

4. What is King's thesis? Where does he state it?

5. To whom do you think King addressed this speech? Support your answer by quoting pertinent passages.

6. How does King, as an orator, seek to move his audience? Why, for example, does he open his speech with the words "Five score" instead of "One hundred"?

7. Why does King include the opening of "My Country, 'Tis of Thee"? Why does he refer to so many different places in his final paragraphs? What is especially significant in his choice of Mississippi for his final geographical reference?

8. What argumentative strategies does King use? Which do you find most effective?

9. How does repetition affect the essay? Cite some examples and explain why you think King used repetition as he did.

10. How do the final words of the speech form an especially effective conclusion?

Exploring the Writer's Ideas

1. In the opening paragraphs of his speech, King uses metaphors related to money and payment in explaining the reason for his speech. Later in the speech, however, he calls upon a whole new set of references as he talks about his dream, a dream that doesn't seem to have much to do with money at all. Explain why you think that these two parts of his speech do or do not fit well together.

2. Do you think that King would today advocate the kind of non-violent protest, known as "passive resistance," that he advocated in 1963 (par. 6)? Do you think that passive resistance would succeed in obtaining justice for people struggling for their rights today, within the United States or outside of it? Explain your answers.

3. Few ideas in American life are more powerful than the idea that "all men are created equal" (par. 11). But how does King intend us to understand that phrase? Does he mean that all people are entitled to the same things? Why does he not mention women? And can we achieve this entitlement? Does King

mean that we are all equal in the eyes of God? If so, what does that imply for political equality? economic equality? Should the government of the United States ensure that all people in the nation enjoy economic equality? Explain your thinking.

4. Do you find King's intensely religious way of speaking, with its echoes of biblical language and its heavy use of biblical metaphors, a strength or a weakness of his speech? Explain your answer.

IDEAS FOR WRITING

Prewriting

How should our democracy settle social or political grievances? Jot down some ideas about how you would go about changing some common practice or law that many people find oppressive—say, the laws that establish the age at which young people can drink; or the laws about marriage between people of the same sex; or . . . .

Guided Writing

Write a speech intended to stir your classmates to conduct a sit-in or other protest at the college administration building, the mayor's or governor's offices, or a similar location to call attention to an injustice that you think affects many people.

1. Begin by making an allusion to a famous American or famous alumnus or alumna, with the purpose of showing that this person acted to correct an injustice.
2. Then note that many years have passed and yet today injustices remain.
3. In metaphorical language, indicate the injustice that you want to rouse your audience to oppose.
4. Say that the moral high ground demands action—but action that avoids violence.
5. Emphasize King's notion that "unearned suffering is redemptive" (par. 8).
6. In your concluding paragraph or paragraphs, paint a picture of what you dream will come to pass.
7. Conclude the essay with an emotional sentence or phrase from a hymn or spiritual or popular patriotic or protest song.

Thinking and Writing Collaboratively

Almost half a century has passed since King delivered this famous speech. In small groups discuss whether his dream has been realized. Jot down the evidence for and against the view. Compare the conclusion arrived at by your group with the conclusions of the other groups in the class.

Writing About the Text

Argument depends mainly on reason. But clearly King does not mainly rely on reason. He often appeals directly to emotion. Is there then an inherent conflict between the fairly cool and objective standards of argument and the inevitably emotional methods of persuasion? Write an essay that considers whether in King's speech, his rational arguments support or undermine his more emotional writing, his methods of persuasion; and whether, on the other hand, the emotional passages of the essay tend to support or undermine the passages that rely more on reason.

More Writing Projects

1. Will social inequality always exist, or can we eliminate it? In your journal, record your responses to this question.
2. Write a paragraph about King's conception of justice based on what you can reasonably conclude from the references and metaphors of his speech.
3. On the basis of some research, write an essay in which you describe the picture of America in 1963 that emerges from King's speech, and do research to determine whether that picture was or was not accurate.

Jena, O. J. and the Jailing of Black America

Orlando Patterson

Orlando Patterson is John Cowles Professor of Sociology at Harvard University. He earned a PhD in sociology from the London School of Economics and is the author of *Slavery and Social Death* (1982) and *The Ordeal of Integration* (1997). His book *Freedom in the Making of Western Culture* (1991) won the National Book Award for nonfiction. Patterson served as Special Advisor for Social Policy and Development to Prime Minister Michael Manley of Jamaica. The author of three novels, he has written for the *New York Times,* in which this selection appeared as an op-ed piece on September 30, 2007. He also has written for *Time, Newsweek, The New Republic,* and the *Washington Post.*

PREREADING: THINKING ABOUT THE ESSAY IN ADVANCE

What do you think Patterson means by the phrase "the Jailing of Black America" as part of the title in his essay?

Words to Watch

grievous (par. 1)   serious; grave

gulag (par. 5)   originally, a prison or labor camp in Russia for government dissenters

draconian (par. 6)   unjustly harsh or severe

punitive (par. 6)   disciplinary; relating to punishment

tabloids (par. 8)   newspapers focused on sensational or scandalous reports

estranged (par. 9)   separated; on bad terms

malevolent (par. 10)   mean; spiteful; wicked

iconic (par. 10)   characterized by fame

felonious (par. 10)   criminal; illegal

misogyny (par. 11)   hatred of women

1   The miscarriage of justice at Jena, La.—where five black high school students arrested for beating a white student were charged with attempted murder—and the resulting protest march tempts us to the view, expressed by several of the marchers, that not much

has changed in traditional American racial relations. However, a remarkable series of high-profile incidents occurring elsewhere in the nation at about the same time, as well as the underlying reason for the demonstrations themselves, make it clear that the Jena case is hardly a throwback to the 1960s, but instead speaks to issues that are very much of our times.

What exactly attracted thousands of demonstrators to the small 2 Louisiana town? While for some it was a simple case of righting a grievous local injustice, and for others an opportunity to relive the civil rights era, for most the real motive was a long overdue cry of outrage at the use of the prison system as a means of controlling young black men.

America has more than two million citizens behind bars, the 3 highest absolute and per capita rate of incarceration in the world. Black Americans, a mere 13 percent of the population, constitute half of this country's prisoners. A tenth of all black men between ages 20 and 35 are in jail or prison; blacks are incarcerated at over eight times the white rate.

The effect on black communities is catastrophic: one in three 4 male African-Americans in their 30s now has a prison record, as do nearly two-thirds of all black male high school dropouts. These numbers and rates are incomparably greater than anything achieved at the height of the Jim Crow era. What's odd is how long it has taken the African-American community to address in a forceful and thoughtful way this racially biased and utterly counterproductive situation.

How, after decades of undeniable racial progress, did we end 5 up with this virtual gulag of racial incarceration?

Part of the answer is a law enforcement system that unfairly 6 focuses on drug offenses and other crimes more likely to be committed by blacks, combined with draconian mandatory sentencing and an absurdly counterproductive retreat from rehabilitation as an integral method of dealing with offenders. An unrealistic fear of crime that is fed in part by politicians and the press, a tendency to emphasize punitive measures and old-fashioned racism are all at play here.

But there is another equally important cause: the simple fact 7 that young black men commit a disproportionate number of crimes, especially violent crimes, which cannot be attributed to judicial bias, racism or economic hardships. The rate at which blacks commit homicides is seven times that of whites. Why is this? Several incidents serendipitously occurring at around the same time as the march on Jena hint loudly at a possible answer.

8   • In New York City, the tabloids published sensational details of the bias suit brought by a black former executive for the Knicks, Anucha Browne Sanders, who claims that she was frequently called a "bitch" and a "ho" by the Knicks coach and president, Isiah Thomas. In a video deposition, Thomas said that while it is always wrong for a white man to verbally abuse a black woman in such terms, it was "not as much . . . I'm sorry to say" for a black man to do so.

9   • Across the nation, religious African-Americans were shocked that the evangelical minister Juanita Bynum, an enormously popular source of inspiration for churchgoing black women, said she was brutally beaten in a parking lot by her estranged husband, Bishop Thomas Weeks.

10   • O. J. Simpson, the malevolent central player in an iconic moment in the nation's recent black-white (as well as male-female) relations, reappeared on the scene, charged with attempted burglary, kidnapping and felonious assault in Las Vegas, in what he claimed was merely an attempt to recover stolen memorabilia.

11   These events all point to something that has been swept under the rug for too long in black America: the crisis in relations between men and women of all classes and, as a result, the catastrophic state of black family life, especially among the poor. Isiah Thomas's outrageous double standard shocked many blacks in New York only because he had the nerve to say out loud what is a fact of life for too many black women who must daily confront indignity and abuse in hip-hop misogyny and everyday conversation.

12   What is done with words is merely the verbal end of a continuum of abuse that too often ends with beatings and spousal homicide. Black relationships and families fail at high rates because women increasingly refuse to put up with this abuse. The resulting absence of fathers—some 70 percent of black babies are born to single mothers—is undoubtedly a major cause of youth delinquency.

13   The circumstances that far too many African-Americans face—the lack of paternal support and discipline; the requirement that single mothers work regardless of the effect on their children's care; the hypocritical refusal of conservative politicians to put their money where their mouths are on family values; the recourse by male youths to gangs as parental substitutes; the ghetto-fabulous culture of the streets; the lack of skills among black men for the jobs and pay they want; the hypersegregation of blacks into impoverished

inner-city neighborhoods—all interact perversely with the prison system that simply makes hardened criminals of nonviolent drug offenders and spits out angry men who are unemployable, unreformable and unmarriageable, closing the vicious circle.

Jesse Jackson, Al Sharpton and other leaders of the Jena demonstration who view events there, and the racial horror of our prisons, as solely the result of white racism are living not just in the past but in a state of denial. Even after removing racial bias in our judicial and prison system—as we should and must do—disproportionate numbers of young black men will continue to be incarcerated.   14

Until we view this social calamity in its entirety—by also acknowledging the central role of unstable relations among the sexes and within poor families, by placing a far higher priority on moral and social reform within troubled black communities, and by greatly expanding social services for infants and children—it will persist.   15

BUILDING VOCABULARY

Try to determine the meanings of these words from the word parts that make them up, and write the definitions of the words. Then check a dictionary to see if your meanings are correct.

a. miscarriage (par. 1)
b. throwback (par. 1)
c. incomparably (par. 4)
d. counterproductive (par. 4)
e. disproportionate (par. 7)
f. indignity (par. 11)
g. hypocritical (par. 13)
h. hypersegregation (par. 13)
i. unreformable (par. 13)
j. unmarriageable (par. 13)

THINKING CRITICALLY ABOUT THE ESSAY

Understanding the Writer's Ideas

1. What happened in Jena, Louisiana? How does the writer explain the attraction to the city of thousands of demonstrators? Which reason does he feel was the real motive?

2. What data does Patterson offer to support his contention that the use of the prison system to control black men is outrageous?

3. How, according to the writer, does the law enforcement system itself contribute to the disproportionate number of black males sent to prison?

4. What three high-profile incidents does Patterson provide to support his notion that judicial bias, racism, or economic hardship is not fully responsible for all the imprisonment of black men?

5. What does the writer believe "has been swept under the rug for too long in black America"?

6. What particular circumstances faced by African Americans "interact perversely" with the prison system to create "hardened criminals out of nonviolent drug offenders"?

Understanding the Writer's Techniques

1. What is the main argument in Patterson's essay? Where do you think he comes closest to stating it directly?

2. What is the effect of the single sentence paragraph (par. 5)?

3. What is the value of Patterson's presentation of key events as a bulleted list? Is this an effective rhetorical strategy? Why or why not?

4. The writer draws on names and events, some of which he identifies briefly and others not at all: Jena, Lousiana; Jim Crow; Anucha Brown Sanders; Isaiah Thomas; Bishop Thomas Weeks; O. J. Simpson; Jesse Jackson; Al Sharpton. Identify these references. Why does Patterson include them in his essay? What does this strategy tell you about his view of the audience?

5. Paragraph 13 provides a number of examples, all separated by semicolons. What is your reaction to this listing of details? Should Patterson have elaborated on any of them? Or do you feel that the mere listing provides enough of an insight into the negative circumstances faced by many African Americans?

6. The writer uses highly charged language in some places to make his point. What is the emotional effect on the reader of words and phrases like *catastrophic* (par. 4), *cry of outrage* (par. 2), *virtual gulag of racial incarceration* (par. 5)? What other vocabulary can you identify that Patterson has used for emotional effect?

7. In what ways does this essay reflect cause-and-effect strategies? illustration?

8. Why does the writer present a series of data in paragraph 3? How do the data support Patterson's argument?

9. Patterson asks three questions and then attempts to answer them. What is the effect of this question-and-answer strategy on the reader?

10. What is your opinion of the concluding paragraph of the essay? How does it contribute to Patterson's argument?

Exploring the Writer's Ideas

1. Patterson states that our country's enforcement system focuses too much on drug offenses and other crimes likely to be committed by blacks. Why might you agree or disagree with his opinion? In what ways could we relax rules about drug offenses and at the same time assure that drug crimes have appropriate consequences?

2. The writer challenges the notion that "not much has changed in traditional American racial relations" and acknowledges instead "decades of undeniable racial progress." Why might you agree or disagree with his argument here? What would you consider the highlights of racial progress in America over the last twenty or thirty years? In what ways could the country make further progress?

3. Patterson writes forcefully about abuses directed against black women. What does he mean in paragraph 12 by "a continuum of abuse"? How does the use of verbal abuse, such as "hip-hop misogyny," contribute to physical abuse? Do you agree with the cause-and-effect relation that Patterson identifies here?

IDEAS FOR WRITING

Prewriting

Make a list of what you see as the main features of the "crisis of relations" in American families, no matter what their race or ethnic background. Share your list with other members of the class in small groups. How do the items on your list compare and contrast with those of the other writers in your group?

Guided Writing

Write an argumentative essay about what you see as "the crisis in relations between men and women of all classes."

1. Begin with one or two current newsworthy events that indicate some element of the crisis as you see it. Establish your argument based on these events.
2. Use data to dramatize your argument.
3. Identify other features of the crisis or expand on the essential element that you have already indicated.
4. Raise questions in your essay as Patterson does in his, and try to answer the questions that you raise.
5. In your conclusion, suggest ways to correct the crisis—the "social calamity" as Patterson sees it.

Thinking and Writing Collaboratively

In groups of three or four, discuss the "other crimes" that Patterson alludes to in paragraph 6. Which crimes do you think he means are the crimes likely to be committed by black males and for which the society punishes them unfairly?

Writing About the Text

Write an essay in which you analyze Patterson's use of questions as an essay technique. Identify the key questions he raises and the responses he provides. Explain why you think he uses this strategy and how it affects readers.

More Writing Projects

1. Write a journal entry about lyrics in hip-hop music. What is your reaction to the abusive language directed at women?
2. In an extended paragraph, write about your view of the relation between economic class and crime.
3. Write an essay in which you argue about ways to improve the justice system so that it doesn't unjustly penalize blacks, other minorities, and the poor.

SUMMING UP: CHAPTER 11

1. Keep a journal in which you record your thoughts on, and observations of, homelessness in your part of the country. Try to gather specific data from reading, local television, interviews, or direct observation. Try to answer the following questions:
   a. How many are male? female?
   b. How many are children?
   c. How many are elderly?
   d. How many appear to be mentally ill?
   e. What are the causes of their homelessness?
   Using the data you gather, along with your observations, present your position on homelessness in a letter to the editor of your campus or local newspaper.

2. Write an essay in which you compare and contrast the three essays included in the section Perspectives on the "Mommy Wars": Should Mothers Work? Which of the writers makes the strongest argument?

3. Invite a local expert to class to speak on a current controversial issue. You might want to think about inviting a scholar from your school, a legislator (local, state, or federal), or a newspaper reporter. Then, write an essay in support of, or in opposition to, the speaker's opinion.

4. Justify the inclusion of the essays by Kozol, Ivins, Rodriguez, and Quindlen under the category "Argumentation and Persuasion." Treat the major issues they raise, their positions on these issues, their minor propositions, their use of evidence, and their tone. Finally, establish the degree to which you are persuaded by their arguments.

5. Exchange with a classmate an essay that you've each written for one of the Guided Writing exercises in this chapter. Even if you agree with your partner's opinion, write a strongly worded response opposing it. Be sure you touch on the same, or similar, major and minor propositions.

6. Fill in the blanks in the following essay topic as you please, and use it as the major proposition in a well-developed argumentation–persuasion paper. Draw on the expository writing skills you have studied throughout the book. "I am very concerned about _____, and I believe it's necessary to _____ ."

7. What are the similarities and differences that you detect in the essays by Hirshman, Cheever, and Quindlen?

8. In what ways are the essays by Martin Luther King Jr. and Orlando Patterson complementary? In what ways are they different? Write an essay in which you compare the two selections.

9. Write an essay that seeks to reconcile the views of Mirko Bagaric and John McCain.

10. The United States was once known as a "melting pot," meaning that the great thing about American life was that everyone could be assimilated into one nation regardless of race, creed, or religion. Today, we talk about diversity instead. Write an essay that explores the implications of this change in attitudes, using the selections in this and other chapters as resources for your argument.

11. Critics identify John McCain and Richard Rodriguez as "conservative" writers. Argue for or against the proposition that their conservatism prevents them from presenting their arguments in a fair and balanced way.

12 Critics consider Anna Quindlen and Molly Ivins "liberal" or "progressive" writers. Argue for or against the proposition that their liberalism prevents them from arguing in a fair or accurate way.

13. Reread the essays by Kozol, Takaki, and Quindlen, and then select your favorite. Write about why you think your choice is the best essay about identity in this chapter.

14. Mirko Bagaric and John McCain take opposite points of view on the matter of torture. How do their writing styles compare? In what ways are they similar? In what ways are they different? Write an essay to explore these questions.

15. Quindlen and Ivins use various comic strategies to advance their arguments. Analyze these comic elements in a comparative essay.

✳ FROM SEEING TO WRITING

What is the protestor's argument, and how does he advocate it?
Do you support or oppose his decision to engage in civil disobedience? Take your own stand on a specific environmental issue, and
state your main proposition. Offer three reasons to support your
position, and supply evidence for each. Deal with the opposing
viewpoints. In your conclusion, either support or reject the use of
civil disobedience as a way of advancing your viewpoint.

APPENDIX:
A Guide to Research and Documentation

WHAT ARE RESEARCH AND DOCUMENTATION?

A *research* paper grows out of careful investigation of books, periodicals, online resources, and other documents and texts to support a thesis. Research writing can be a form of problem-solving or a careful investigation of a subject. You may identify a problem, form a hypothesis (an unproven thesis, theory, or argument), gather and organize information from various sources, assess and interpret data, evaluate alternatives, reach conclusions, and provide documentation. Other research writing projects may involve the discovery or revision of facts, theories, or applications. In either kind of research paper, your purpose is to demonstrate how other researchers approach a problem and how you treat that problem. A good research paper subtly blends your ideas and the ideas or discoveries of others. In research writing, you become part of a larger academic, social, or cultural conversation. You synthesize ideas that have already been made public—carefully documenting the sources of those ideas—and you contribute your own unique insights and conclusions.

Documentation refers to the rules and conventions by which academic researchers acknowledge the sources on which their work is based. As you research your subject, you will use documentation to note carefully where you find your information so that readers of your work can retrace your sources. Documentation also allows you to give proper credit to the work of other writers. Not providing full and accurate documentation can leave you open to charges of plagiarism.

THE RESEARCH PROCESS

The research process involves thinking, searching, reading, writing, and rewriting. The final product—the research paper—is the result of your discoveries about your topic as well as your contribution to the ongoing academic conversation about your topic. More than any other form of college writing, the research paper evolves gradually through a series of stages. As you develop as a writer and researcher, you will probably adapt this process according to your own strengths and style. As a beginning researcher and writer, however, you may find that a more methodical approach to this process will help you structure your library work as well as your writing.

PHASE I: CHOOSING AND LIMITING A TOPIC

- Browsing
- Limiting the topic

PHASE II: GATHERING AND ORGANIZING DATA

- Developing a working bibliography
- Assessing and evaluating sources
- Taking notes
- Developing a thesis
- Organizing your notes and writing an outline

PHASE III: WRITING THE PAPER

- Drafting
- Incorporating sources
- Revising your draft
- Preparing the final manuscript

PHASE IV: DOCUMENTING SOURCES

PHASE I: CHOOSING AND LIMITING A TOPIC

Although you may receive a very specific research topic from your professor, you are far more likely to meet your first research challenge before you even set foot in the library: what will you write about? One of the great challenges of academic research is learning how to ask the kind of question that will lead to a terrific research topic. You can save time, effort, and anxiety if you approach your research project as a problem to be investigated and solved, a controversy to take a position on, or a specific question to be answered. As a basis for your research, you need at least a hunch or a calculated guess—an idea that will lead to a strong hypothesis or working thesis.

- Before you can formulate a hypothesis, you need to start with a general idea of what subject you want to explore, what your purpose is going to be, and how you plan to select and limit a topic from your larger subject area.

To find and limit that topic, you'll want to begin with some preliminary browsing in the library.

Browsing

When you *browse,* you inspect, informally, books and articles in your general area of interest. These points will help you browse in the library as you explore a topic idea:

- The *library reference section* provides encyclopedias, almanacs, and other reference books for an overview of your area of interest. These resources may be print, online, or on CD-ROM. General reference resources can be useful for background reading and an introduction to your topic. However, these general resources should only be the beginning of your research—do not rely exclusively on these sources, which may not be the most up-to-date or in-depth.
- The *library catalog* lists information by author, title, subject, and key word. It will suggest possible subtopics under the general topic heading and also give you an idea of how many books have been written about your topic. Your library may have both a card catalog and an online catalog; if so, your browsing will be more fruitful if you use both. Ask your

reference librarian for guidance on using both the online and
card catalogs.

- In your catalog browsing, you will notice that books on your
topic most likely share a *call number,* or have call numbers
within the same range. Go to that area of your library where
books with these call numbers are shelved. Because library
classification systems group all books on similar topics near
one another, you have many approaches to your topic at your
fingertips. Select books that have the most recent copyright
dates, which you'll find on the first few pages of the book
(ten years is a good boundary). Examine the table of contents, the index, the glossary, and the appendices. Look at the
illustrations, if there are any. Read a paragraph or two from the
preface or introduction.

- A *periodical index* is an alphabetical listing (usually annual) of
authors, titles, and subjects of articles in magazines, journals,
or newspapers. Some *databases,* which your library may have
on CD-ROM or online, may also provide summaries or complete texts of articles. Indexes are both general (covering major
newspapers, journals, and magazines, and a wide range of
topics) and very subject-specific. Ask your reference librarian
for indexes specific to your subject. Like a library catalog, an
index or database shows you at a glance the kinds of subtopics
current writers have addressed as parts of larger topics. Reading over the titles of current articles, you can see a variety of
approaches to your topic.

- *Search engines* online can help you find a broad range of
information about your general topic—but that very broad-
ness of information can be overwhelming. Your instructor
may be able to recommend useful sites, as can your reference
librarian. Search engines such as Google, Firefox, Dogpile,
and HotBot hunt through vast numbers of pages at Web sites,
seeking those that mention key words that you specify.
Browsing through the "hits" you get through such a search
engine can give you a spectrum of ideas about your topic.
However, you will probably want to check with your instructor about any Web sites you may wish to use as a basis for
your research. Print out the first page of the Web site, which
will give you the URL (the site's address); you can then ask
your instructor to visit the Web site and evaluate its reliability
as a source.

For more help with locating sources, click on
Research > Using the Library
Research > Using the Internet
Research > Discipline-Specific
Resources

Limiting the Topic

The first step in research writing is to *limit* your research to a *researchable topic*. Such a topic is appropriate in scope for your assignment, promises an adventure for you in the realm of ideas, and interests your audience. Developing a hypothesis, or a question that requires more than a simplistic answer, will lead to a researchable topic. The following chart shows examples of general topics narrowed to researchable topics.

NARROWING THE TOPIC			
Too General	*Still Broad*	*Less Broad*	*Narrow Enough*
Teaching	teaching number concepts	teaching number concepts to children	teaching number concepts at home to children under five
Religion	religious customs	ancient religious customs in North America	Anasazi religious customs in America's Midwest
Pollution	fighting air pollution	fighting air pollution in California	the government's role in fighting air pollution in Los Angeles
World War II	effects of WWII	effects of WWII in the United States	economic effects of WWII in Detroit

After your first effort to limit your topic as a result of browsing and of some preliminary thinking, you should expect to limit your topic even further. Two further strategies for narrowing your topic are *freewriting* and *feedback*. Try the following freewriting exercise:

1. Why does this topic interest me so strongly?
2. What do I already know about this topic?

3. What three or four questions do I have about this topic, based on my preliminary browsing?

4. What are my opinions about problems related to this topic?

Sharing your freewriting with other students in a discussion group, with your instructor, or with some other friendly reader will give you additional insight into your topic.

PHASE II: GATHERING AND ORGANIZING MATERIAL

Developing a Working Bibliography

The purpose of compiling a working bibliography is to keep an accurate record of all the sources you consulted with all the critical information about them. If you are required to do so, you can prepare a list of works cited (see pages A-19 to A-24) from the data in your working bibliography. Although you may wish to keep your working bibliography as a computer document, you may find it more useful and efficient to use 4 by 6-inch index cards. Index cards allow you to do the following:

• Arrange the cards easily in alphabetical order as sources are added or deleted (your final bibliography will be alphabetically organized)

• Make quick notes to yourself about your first impressions of the materials to help you decide later whether to return to the source for closer study

• Carry them easily to the library for quick notes, where a computer is not always convenient

Use a standard form for your working bibliography, whether you use cards or computer entries, to simplify the task of preparing your final Works Cited or References section.

INFORMATION FOR A WORKING BIBLIOGRAPHY

Record the following information for a book:

1. Name(s) of author(s)
2. Title of book, underlined
3. Place of publication

(continued)

4. Publisher's name
5. Date of publication
6. Call number or location in library

Record the following information for an article in a periodical:

1. Name(s) of author(s)
2. Title of article, in quotation marks
3. Title of periodical, underlined
4. Volume number or issue number
5. Date of publication
6. Page numbers on which article appears
7. Call number or location in library

For online sources, record all of the above information as well as the complete URL (site address) and date of access online.

Sample working bibliography card: Article

Gladwell, Malcolm. "Examined Life." The New Yorker
17 Dec. 2001: 86–92.

Assessing and Evaluating Sources

At this phase in the research process, you will have amassed a variety of sources and perspectives. Your task now is to revisit those articles, books, Web sites, and other sources—using your working bibliography as a constant guide. Begin by *skimming* your sources. Skimming is not random or casual reading, but a careful examination of the material to sort out the useful sources from those that aren't helpful. For a book, check the table of contents and index for information on your topic; then determine whether the information is relevant to your topic (your hypothesis, question, or problem). For an article, see if the abstract or topic sentences in the body of the essay apply to your topic.

Online sources require careful and critical evaluation on your part. In general, librarians have recommended or chosen the books that you find in your school library. In addition, editors and experts in the field have for the most part reviewed books and articles in print. To the contrary, unbiased or authoritative experts may or may not have examined materials located on the Web. When in doubt, ask your instructor or a reference librarian.

EVALUATING PRINT AND ONLINE SOURCES

1. Is the source directly relevant to your topic? Does it confirm your hypothesis, answer your question, or propose a solution to your problem?
2. Does the source present relatively current information, especially for research in the social and natural sciences?
3. Does the source indicate the author's expertise (background, education, other publications)? Do other writers refer to this author as a reliable expert?
4. Does the source provide information comparable to that in other reputable sources?
5. Does the source supply notes, a bibliography, or other information to document its own sources?
6. Does an online source identify its author? Is the site sponsored by a particular business, agency, or organization? Is contact information provided for the author or sponsor?
7. Does an online source supply useful, appropriate links? Are the links current and relevant? Are many of the links broken? (Many broken links indicate that the site has not been recently updated.)

www.mhhe.com/
shortprose

For more help with assessing and evaluating sources, click on
Research > CARS Source Evaluation Tutor

Taking Notes

Once you have assembled relevant, useful sources, you can begin to read these sources more closely and take detailed notes. Accurate, well-chosen notes will help you build your research essay. You want to select and summarize the general ideas that will form the outline of your paper, to record specific evidence to support your ideas, and to copy exact statements you plan to quote for evidence or interest.

Many researchers find it useful to take notes on 4 by 6-inch cards. By keeping your notes on cards, you can easily rearrange information from different sources; compare ideas from different sources; and build a visual outline when it's time to draft your research essay.

There are three kinds of notes that you can take as you do your research:

- *Summaries* of material keep track of specific facts, overall perspectives, reminders of what particular sources provide.
- *Paraphrases* of material compel you to think carefully about what you read so that you can express it in your own words. Paraphrase helps you to summarize specific ideas and arguments without having to copy out, word for word, a particular source.
- *Direct quotations* are exact copies of an author's own words. Use direct quotations for ideas and concepts that are concise, specific, and that state the author's opinion or conclusion.

GUIDELINES FOR TAKING NOTES ON YOUR TOPIC

1. Write the author's last name, the title of the book or article, and the page number on each index card. Be sure that you also have an entry for this source in your working bibliography. This will help you accurately document your sources and save you time later.
2. Copy only one idea, group of closely related facts, or quote on each card. This will make it easier for you to organize the information when you begin to draft your research essay.

(continued)

3. List a subtopic at the top of the card. This will permit you to arrange your cards into groups, which can then serve as the basis of your outline. Keep a separate list of these subtopics, and be sure that you don't use a new term for each card!
4. If applicable, add your own ideas to each card—perhaps using a different color ink, or on the reverse side of the card.

The sample cards below illustrate each of these note-taking strategies.

1: Sample note card: Summary

Subtopic	*N.A.T./college admissions*
Author/title	*Gladwell, "Examined Life"*
Page number(s)	*86–88*
Summary	*The University of California in 2001 proposed using measures other than the N.A.T. when considering students for admission, because a study of UC students found that the N.A.T was the least reliable measure of potential student success.*

2: Sample note card: Paraphrase

Subtopic	*N.A.T./college admissions*
Author/title	*Gladwell, "Examined Life"*
Page number(s)	*86–88*
Paraphrase	*A University of California study showed that achievement tests like the N.A.T. 99 were far more likely than the N.A.T. in predicting student success. High school grade point averages were also found by the study to be a more reliable way to determine student success. The study was based on the records of UC students from 1996–1999. Achievement tests were found, overall, to be more fair to students because they measure what students have already learned.*

3: Sample note card: Direct Quotation

Subtopic	*N.A.J./college admissions*
Author/title	*Gladwell, "Examined Life"*
Page number(s)	*86–88*
Direct quotation	*Gladwell quotes Richard Atkinson, the president of the University of California: "Achievement tests are fairer to students because they measure accomplishment rather than promise ... they tell students that a college education is within the reach of anyone with the talent and determination to succeed."*

Developing a Thesis

As you read your material and take notes, you should start developing ideas for your proposal or thesis. You began your research with a *hypothesis*—an unproven idea, hunch, or question that guided your reading and helped you to narrow your topic. Your *thesis* is the main idea of your research essay. Although your thesis may change a bit as you draft your research paper and continue to think about different ideas and perspectives, writing your thesis down before you begin your outline will give you a solid foundation for your outline and draft.

HYPOTHESIS	THESIS
Fashion magazines promote an unrealistic body image.	The self-esteem of adolescent girls determines how they respond to unreal images of women in fashion magazines.

Organizing Your Notes and Writing an Outline

Because you must organize all of this material you have gathered in a clear, logical way, an outline is especially valuable for a research essay. Plan to spend as much time as you can in drafting your outline and organizing your evidence, as this will make the actual writing of your research essay much more efficient. Your instructor may require you to submit an outline at some stage of writing the research essay; be sure that you understand the required format. You may also find it useful to ask your instructor, or fellow students, to review your outline and make suggestions. A good outline should allow a reader to follow easily the lines of your argument and see how each piece of evidence will fit in to the final essay.

THE ORGANIZING PROCESS

1. Gather all your note cards. Be sure they include source information (p. A-9).
2. Group your note cards by subtopic. Can any subtopics be combined? Are any subtopics so large that you can divide them further?
3. Do any note cards duplicate each other? Set aside any cards which, within a subtopic grouping, duplicate information.
4. Are there any subtopics that include just one or two cards, or that don't seem to "fit" anywhere? Set those aside.
5. Number your note cards within each subtopic. Use capital letters for each subtopic, followed by a dash and a numeral for the card number (the first subtopic's cards would be numbered A-1, A-2; the next subtopic's cards would be B-1, B-2; and so on). This will help you save time as you write your rough draft.
6. Do not throw away any note cards. Even if you don't see an obvious place for a card in your outline, you never know what might prove useful as you write. Set those cards aside for now.
7. Do not feel obliged to use every note card when you write your paper. You may be overwhelmed by the number of note cards you have—but you probably won't use every single quotation, paraphrase, and piece of information in your final paper.

This grouping of cards by subtopic should provide you with the basic structure of an outline. If your instructor requires a formal outline, follow the guidelines provided. If not, follow these basic principles as you arrange your note cards within each subgrouping:

I. (Most important points)
  A.
  B. (Next most important point)
    1.
    2.
    3. (Supporting points)
      a.
      b. (Relevant details, minor points)

www.mhhe.com/
shortprose

For more help with outlining, click on
Writing > Outlines
Writing > Outlining Tutor

PHASE III: WRITING THE PAPER

As you begin the third phase of the research process, keep in mind that your research paper will be a formal essay, not a collection of notes. You should be prepared to take your research effort through multiple drafts, each time reconsidering the relevance and "fit" of your evidence.

Drafting

For your rough draft, concentrate on filling in the shape of your outline. Take the time to organize your note cards in the topic order of your outline. In this way you will be able to integrate notes and writing more efficiently.

Remember that your outline is a *guide* for your writing—you are not obliged to adhere to it. As you write, you may find subtle points taking on new importance, or additional evidence that needs to be included. Your purpose in writing a rough draft is to work out the shape and content of your research essay, and you should expect to make many changes and adjustments as you write.

You may choose to incorporate direct quotations from your notes into the rough draft. Some writers prefer to save time by indicating in the draft which note card to return to later in order to copy out the entire paraphrase or quote. If you have numbered your note cards as suggested above, you might find this a valuable time-saving strategy.

As you work through your outline, organizing your sources, you must contribute your own commentary. You will arrange details in an effective order, sort out conflicting claims and interpretations, and solve problems. Writing the rough draft of a research paper is much more complex than a mere transcription of facts and quotations. The process of writing is an effort to work in a logical way from the introduction and the statement of your thesis, through the evidence, to the outcome or conclusion that supports everything that has come before.

You may not use every note card in your rough draft. Again, set aside those that you do not use, or that do not seem to fit. *Do not throw away any note cards!* At the same time, you may find as you write that you need further information on a particular point. Try to phrase that "missing" information in the form of questions, and write those questions on a separate piece of paper. Consult your working bibliography and all of your note cards (those you are using as well as those you have set aside). Can you answer your questions from sources you already have? If not, what sources will you consult (or return to) in order to get the information you need?

www.mhhe.com/
shortprose

For more help with drafting, click on
Writing > Drafting and Revising

Incorporating Sources

As you draft, you will refer to your note cards for ideas as well as information. Introducing that information—hard facts, paraphrases, or direct quotations—into the flow of your own writing requires that you make it clear to your reader that the following information or words come from a different source. At the same time, you do not want to interrupt the flow of your own argument by randomly dropping in chunks of outside information. Gracefully incorporating research sources into your essay supports your own ideas without confusing the reader. Think of this as a kind of conversational skill; by including other voices in your research essay and clearly identifying each of those voices, you are allowing your "listener"—your reader—to take part in the ongoing academic "conversation" about your research topic. For example:

Recently, some colleges and universities have reconsidered the
importance of S.A.T. scores in admissions decisions. "Seventy-five

years ago, the S.A.T. was instituted because we were more interested, as a society, in what a student was capable of learning than
in what he had already learned. Now, apparently, we have changed
our minds ..." (Gladwell 88).

In revision, this writer used paraphrase to help make the transition
from her argument to Gladwell's observation:

> Discussing the recent decision by the University of California
> to use measures other than the S.A.T. in admissions decisions,
> Malcolm Gladwell points out that "seventy-five years ago, the
> S.A.T. was instituted because we were more interested, as a society,
> in what a student was capable of learning than in what he had already
> learned" (Gladwell 88), whereas today's educators realize that it is
> more fair to assess what students have already accomplished.

Using conversational verbs rather than simply "says" or "writes"
can enliven your introduction of sources without confusing your
reader. The writer above uses the verb phrase "points out." Other
possibilities include:

> Malcolm X forcefully argues that . . .
> Annie Dillard vividly describes . . .
> David Sedaris suggests that . . .
> Gina Barreca compares the results of . . .
> Katha Pollitt admits that . . .

You will notice that this system does not rely on footnotes or
end notes to give credit to the source of information. When you
write your research essay and incorporate outside sources, be sure
to include the author's last name and the page number on which
you found the ideas to which you are referring. You must provide
this information for paraphrases and factual information as well
as direct quotations. For more information on in-text citation, see
p. A-18 of this appendix.

www.mhhe.com/
shortprose

For more help with paraphrasing,
summarizing, and quoting, click on

**Research > Avoiding Plagiarism >
Summarize/Paraphrase**

**Research > Avoiding Plagiarism >
Using Quotations**

**Research > Incorporating Source
Information**

**Research > Using Sources
Accurately**

Revising Your Draft

In your rough draft you thought and wrote your way through your problem or hypothesis, considering different kinds of evidence and various points of view. In revision, you rethink and rewrite in order to give better form and expression to your ideas. Your instructor may ask you to share your rough draft with other students, which allows you to test the structure of your argument and the strength of your evidence. Even if you are not required to share your paper in class, you might find it very helpful to exchange drafts with another student for comment and feedback at this stage.

GUIDELINES FOR REVISING YOUR RESEARCH WRITING

1. Does my title clearly indicate the topic of my essay? Does it capture my reader's interest?
2. Does my opening paragraph clearly establish and limit my topic?
3. Is my thesis statement clear, limited, and interesting?
4. Do all my body paragraphs support the thesis? Is there a single topic and main idea for each paragraph? Is there sufficient evidence in each paragraph to support the main idea?
5. Are there clear and effective transitions linking my ideas within and between paragraphs?
6. Do I incorporate evidence gracefully and logically? Do I acknowledge other people's ideas properly? Do I clearly indicate the sources of facts and evidence?
7. Is my conclusion strong and effective? Does it clearly and obviously echo my thesis statement?
8. If I share my paper with a student reader, does that reader have any questions about my argument or my evidence? What further information would my reader suggest I add?
9. Are my sentences grammatically correct and complete? Have I varied my sentences effectively?
10. Is my use of punctuation correct?
11. Are all words spelled correctly? Have I printed out and read through my paper to catch any spelling errors that a computerized "spell-check" function might miss?

|  www.mhhe.com/ **shortprose** | For more help with revising your essay, click on **Writing > Drafting and Revising** |

Preparing the Final Manuscript

Leave time in your research writing to prepare a neat, clean manuscript. Consult your instructor for the required format, and carefully follow those guidelines for your final manuscript. Store your word processor file on a backup disk, and print or duplicate an extra copy for your own records.

PHASE IV: DOCUMENTING SOURCES

Documenting your sources throughout your paper and in a section called Works Cited tells your audience just how well you have conducted your research. It offers readers the opportunity to check and review the same sources you used in writing your paper. Failure to provide proper documentation for your paper can have very serious consequences, including charges of *plagiarism*. Plagiarism, or the use of material without giving proper credit to the source, is considered a kind of intellectual theft. The disciplinary consequences of plagiarism in academic writing can range from a failing grade for that assignment to dismissal from the college. The consequences for plagiarism in the workplace are even more severe, ranging from dismissal from a job to criminal charges.

MATERIALS THAT REQUIRE DOCUMENTATION

1. Direct quotations
2. Paraphrased material
3. Summarized material
4. Any key idea or opinion adapted and incorporated into your paper
5. Specific data (whether quoted, paraphrased, or tabulated)
6. Disputed facts
7. Illustrations (maps, charts, graphs, photographs, etc.)

	For more help with documenting sources, click on
www.mhhe.com/ **shortprose**	**Research > Avoiding Plagiarism > Using Copyrighted Materials**
	Research > Bibliomaker

In-Text Citations, in the Style of the Modern Language Association (MLA), Seventh Edition (2009)

Briefly identifying sources in the text of your paper, either as part of your sentence or within parentheses, is the most common method of indicating sources. In MLA style, include the author's name and the page number of the source. Then list complete information alphabetically by author or title (if the source has no specific author) in the Works Cited section.

GUIDELINES FOR PARENTHETICAL (IN-TEXT) DOCUMENTATION

1. Give enough information so that the reader can readily identify the source in the Works Cited section of your paper.
2. Give the citation information in parentheses placed where the material occurs in your text.
3. Make certain that the complete sentence containing the parenthetical documentation is readable and grammatically correct.

The following examples illustrate how to cite a source in the text. The MLA guidelines require you to include the author's last name and the page number where the quotation or information is located. If you state the author's name in the text, do not repeat it in the citation. Other professional organizations, such as the American Psychological Association (APA), require alternate citation styles.

Page Number(s) for a Book

The play offers what many audiences have found a satisfying conclusion (Hansberry 265–76).

Garcia Marquez uses another particularly appealing passage as the opening of the story (105).

Page Number(s) for an Article in a Journal or Magazine

Barlow's description of the family members includes "their most notable strengths and weaknesses" (18).

Section and Page Number(s) for a Newspaper Article

A report on achievement standards for high school courses found "significant variation among schools" (Mallory B1).

Page Number(s) for a Work Without an Author

Computerworld has developed a thoughtful editorial on the issue of government and technology ("Uneasy Silence" 54).

Works Cited List

To prepare your Works Cited list of sources, simply transcribe those bibliography cards or entries that you actually used to write the paper. The Works Cited page is a separate page at the end of your research paper (see p. A-31 for an example).

GUIDELINES FOR THE WORKS CITED LIST

1. Use the title Works Cited. Center this title at the top of the page. Do not underline this title, type it in an italic font, or place it in quotation marks. Use upper and lower case.
2. Arrange the list of sources alphabetically according to the author's last name or according to the title of the work if there is no author. Ignore *A, An,* or *The.*
3. List alphabetically according to title other works by the same author directly under the first entry for the author's name.
4. For works by more than one author, list the entry under the last name of the first author, giving other writers' names in regular order (first name, middle, last).
5. Begin each entry at the left margin. Indent everything in an entry that comes after the first line by one-half inch or five spaces. Use the hanging indent feature of your software to achieve this.
6. Double-space every line.
7. Punctuate with periods after the three main divisions in most entries: author, title, and publishing information.

	For more help with documenting sources, click on
www.mhhe.com/ **shortprose**	**Research > Avoiding Plagiarism > Using Copyrighted Materials**
	Research > Bibliomaker
	Research > Links to Documentation Sites

Book by One Author

Notice the punctuation and underlining in the basic entry for a book.

> Fonda, Jane. *My Life So Far.* New York: Random, 2005. Print.
> Michaelis, David. *Schulz and Peanuts: A Biography.* New York: Harper, 2007. Print.

Several Books by One Author

If you use several books by one author, list the author's name in the initial entry. In the next entry or entries, replace the name with three hyphens.

> Friedman, Thomas L. *The Lexus and the Olive Tree.* New York: Anchor, 2000.
> ---. *The World Is Flat: A Brief History of the Twenty-first Century.* New York: Farra, 2006. Print.

Book with Two or Three Authors or Editors

List the names of several authors in the sequence in which they appear in the book. Begin with the last name of the author listed first because it is used to determine the alphabetical order for entries. Then identify the other authors by first and last names.

> Brown, Nathan, and Sheryle A. Proper. *The Everything Paying for College Book.* Avon: Adams, 2005. Print.

Work with More than Three Authors or Editors

Name all those involved, or list only the first author or editor followed by *et al.,* for "and others."

Nordhus, Inger, Gary R. VandenBos, Stig Berg, and Pia
Fromholt, eds. *Clinical Geropsychology*. Washington: APA,
1998. Print.
Nordhus, Inger, et al., eds. *Clinical Geropsychology*. Washington:
APA, 1998. Print.

Work with Group or an Organization as Author

National PTA. *National Standards for Parent/Family Involvement
Programs*. Chicago: National PTA, 1997. Print.

Work Without an Author

The New York Times Guide to Essential Knowledge. New York:
St. Martins, 2004. Print.

Work in a Collection of Pieces All by the Same Author

Coetzee, J. M. "Nadine Gordimer." *Inner Workings: Literary Essays
2000–2005*. New York: Viking, 2007. 244–56. Print.

Work in an Anthology

Kolbert, Elizabeth. "Butterfly Lessons." *The Best American Science
Writing 2007*. Ed. Gina Kolata. New York: Harper, 2007. 234–51.
Print.

Work Translated from Another Language

Tolstoy, Leo. *War and Peace*. Trans. Richard Pevear and Larissa
Volokhonsky. New York: Knopf, 2007. Print.

New Edition of an Older Book

Wharton, Edith. *The Custom of the Country*. 1913. NY Public Library
Collector's Edition. New York: Doubleday, 1998. Print.

Entry from a Reference Volume

Treat less common reference books like other books, including place of publication, publisher, and date. For encyclopedias, dictionaries, and other familiar references, simply note the edition and its date. No page numbers are needed if the entries appear in alphabetical order in the reference volume.

"Civil War." *World Book:* 2008 ed. Print.

Minton, John. "Worksong." *American Folklore: An Encyclopedia.* Ed. Jan Harold Brunvand. New York: Garland, 1996. Print.

Article in a Journal with Pagination Continuing Through Each Volume

Seitz, David. "Making Work Visible." *College English.* 67 (2004): 210–21. Print.

Article in a Journal with Pagination Continuing Only Through Each Issue

Add the issue number after the volume number.

Pinkowski, Jennifer. "A City by the Sea." *Archaeology* 59.1 (2006): 46–49. Print.

Article in a Weekly or Biweekly Periodical

Collins, Lauren. "The Other Obama." *The New Yorker* 10 Mar. 2008: 88–97. Print.

Kuchment, Anita. "A Tough Balancing Act." *Newsweek* 21 Feb. 2005: 61–62. Print.

Article in a Monthly or Bimonthly Periodical

If an article in a magazine or a newspaper does not continue on consecutive pages, follow the page number on which it begins with a plus sign.

Leslie, Jacques. "The Last Empire." *Mother Jones* Jan.–Feb. 2008: 28+. Print.

Article in a Daily Newspaper

Tam, Pui-Wang. "In Silicon Valley, A Flight to Safety." *Wall Street Journal* 7 March 2008: A1+. Print.

Article with No Author

"Spanish Customs." *The Economist* 1–7 March 2008: 55. Print.
"People in the News." *US News and World Report* 11 Jan. 1999:
16. Print.

Editorial in a Periodical

Gannon, Mary. "Studies in Writing." Editorial. *Poets and Writers*
Nov.–Dec. 2007: 6. Print.

Letter Written to the Editor of a Periodical

West, Bing. "Securing Iraq." Letter. *Foreign Affairs* Jan.–Feb.
2008: 199. Print.

Film, Videotape

Start with the title, italicized. Then include any actor, producer, director, or other person whose work you wish to emphasize. Or simply list the italicized title of the recording. Note the form cited—videocassette, film, and so forth.

No End in Sight. Ferguson, Charles, writer, dir. and prod. Magnolia
Home Entertainment, 2007. DVD.
Visions of the Spirit: A Portrait of Alice Walker. By Elena Featherston.
Women Make Films, 1989. Videocassette.

Programs on Radio or Television

"Greek Tragedy Now." *What's the Word.* WBGC, New York, 27 Apr.
2005. Radio.

CD or Other Recording

Identify the format of the recording.

Basie, Count. "Sunday at the Savoy." Rec. 11–12 May 1983.
88 Basie Street. Pablo Records, 1984. LP.
Schwartz, Stephen. *Wicked a New Musical: Original Broadway Cast
Recording.* Decca Broadway, 2003. CD.

Published or Personal Interview

Doctorow, E. L. Personal interview. 16 May 2007.
Previn, Andre. Interview with Jed Distler. "A Knight at the Keyboard."
Piano and Keyboard. Jan.–Feb. 1999: 241–29. Print.

Book, Article, or Other Source Available Online

Besides author and title, add any translator or editor, the publisher or sponsor of the site, the date of electronic publication or last update, and the medium of publication (Web). Conclude with the date on which you visited the electronic site where the source is located.

> Land-Webber, Ellen. *To Save a Life: Stories of Jewish Rescue.* 1999. Web. 27 Apr. 2008.
>
> Latham, Ernest. "Conducting Research at the National Archives into Art Looting, Recovery, and Restitution." *National Archives Library.* National Archives and Records Administration. 4 Dec. 1998. Web. 27 Apr. 2008.
>
> Marvell, Andrew. "Last Instructions to a Painter." Ed. Bob Blair, Jon Lachelt, Nelson Miller, and Steve Spanoudis. *Poet's Corner.* 31 Aug. 2003. Web. 27 Apr. 2008.
>
> Wollstonecraft, Mary. "A Vindication of the Rights of Women: With Strictures on Political and Moral Subjects." Ed. Steven van Leeuwen. *Bartleby.com* Columbia U. Jan. 1996. Web. 27 Apr. 2008.

Magazine Article Available Online

> Sivy, Michael. "Three Bargains for Uncertain Times." *money.cnn .com. Money.* 21 Apr. 2005. Web. 27 Apr. 2008.

Database Available Online

> Van Leeuwen, Steven, Ed. *Bartleby Library. Bartleby.com.* 1999. Web. 27 Apr. 2008.

Newspaper Article Available Online

> Meyer, Jeremy P. "Kids Eating Up Chef's Classes." *denverpost.com.* 17 Oct. 2008. Web. 22 Oct. 2008.

Article from an Electronic Journal

> Warren, W. L. "Church and State in Angevin Ireland." *Chronicon: An Electronic History Journal* 1 (1997): 6 pars. Web. 27 Apr. 2008.

Electronic Posting to a Group

> Faris, Tommy L. "Tiger Woods." *H-Net: Humanities & Social Sciences Online Posting.* 3 Sept. 1996. Web. 27 Apr. 2008.

SAMPLE STUDENT RESEARCH PAPER

Yeager 1

Frances Yeager
Professor Richard Kelaher
Expository Writing
June 3, 2008

Who Wants to Be a Cover Girl?: Media
and Adolescent Body Image

In our consumer-focused society, the average
American encounters between 400 and 600 advertisements per day. One in every 11 of those advertisements
contains a message directly related to beauty (Wolf 35).
And yet many Americans—especially adolescents—are
not critical about the power that the advertising media
holds. For so many young people, advertisements are
the ultimate determining judgment of what is *chic* and
what is *passé*. This holds especially true for women.
Research has shown that girls are more inclined to
become vulnerable to the ideal body images projected
by the media than boys are. Many studies conducted
on this issue have concluded that our culture places
more importance on physical beauty in the assessment of women and girls than it does on boys or men.
According to Naomi Wolf, females of all ages have been
"consistently taught from an early age that their self-
worth is largely dependent on how they look. The fact
that women earn more money than men in only two job
categories, those of modeling and prostitution, serves to
illustrate this point" (50). Writers like Hargreaves make
the point very clear: Unrealistic images of the female
body in advertising and the media can lead to distorted
body image and eating disorders in young women
immersed in our media culture.

Title clearly
defines topic.

All lines
double-spaced.

Opening
establishes
common audi-
ence experience
and interests.

Last sentence of
paragraph is the
thesis statement.

Specific evi-
dence to sup-

port thesis is introduced.

Summarized information is correctly cited.

Advertisements—print and other media—also require citation. All illustrations require credit lines, unless you provide all information in the text or take photo yourself (as here).

Certainly, the print media geared towards young women seems to confirm this argument. A study of five popular fashion and beauty magazines geared variously towards women between the ages of 13 and 40 (*Seventeen, Cosmopolitan, Glamour,* and *Teen Vogue*), found that approximately 65 percent of their advertising consisted of products and services directly related to beauty (Stice and Shaw 289). Most of these advertisements used one or more of the following in their ads: models, sexual images, celebrities or other icon figures, and images of happiness, popularity, success, and love.

Consider, for example, two typical advertisements (shown below) that appeared in the women's magazines *Cosmopolitan* and *Allure* in April 2005. Both ads use popular singers in sexy poses to sell products. The ad on the left, featuring Christina Aguilera, shows the singer in tight jeans draped in a titillating manner across a police car; except for the text at the bottom, it's not clear that readers would know the ad was for Skechers footwear. The ad on the right, featuring Britney Spears, emphasizes romance; note the barely visible man in the background, which suggests that women who "dare" to wear Curious, Britney's new fragrance, will find love.

Yeager 3

In a study comparing forty eight issues of the four most popular women's magazines with the four most popular men's magazines, there was a total of sixty three diet food ads for women and one diet food ad for men (Mellin, Scully, and Irwin). What is even more disconcerting is that in the magazines geared more towards teens and young adults (*Seventeen, Teen Vogue*), this same study found that the average of sexual images and ads related to sex was much higher than in magazines geared for older women (*Cosmopolitan, Paper, Glamour*). The magazines targeted to adolescent girls and young women also used icons and celebrities more often to sell products, as well as popularity gimmicks, implying that "popular" people buy *this* product and people who have fun use *that* product.

> Online source does not need a page number for in-text citation.

A typical advertisement from the May 2001 issue of the teen magazine *Seventeen* is for the shampoo "Herbal Essence" (15). The ad features a picture of the popular singer Britney Spears, with a caption reading: "Does this look like a girl who stays home on Friday nights to wash her hair? YES!" The clear implication is that even famous—and famously sexy—young girls clear their calendar to shampoo with "Herbal Essence," and therefore young girls who idolize Britney Spears should do so as well. (Of course, the older sisters of *Seventeen* readers are targeted by a much more explicit television campaign for "Herbal Essence," implying that washing with the shampoo is an "organic" experience—but with a blatant implication that it's really "orgasmic." One commercial even featured "sex expert" Dr. Ruth Westheimer praising the "organic" pleasures of the shampoo.)

Television, magazines, and other popular media seem at once to create and perpetuate our culture's values for beauty, and what is currently found acceptable for body shape and size, style, and attitude. Magazines, television ads, billboards, music videos, and movies all reveal images of tall, thin, tanned, and beautiful young people, linking them smoothly to other images of love, success, happiness, prestige, popularity, and wealth for women. It has been found that "repeated exposure to the thin ideal via the various media can lead to the internalization of this ideal" (Richins 75), and Stice and Shaw find that, to women who have internalized these ideals, the fantasy begins to seem an attainable goal. Studies also suggest that exposure to the idealized images lowered women's satisfaction with their own attractiveness; and that immediately after viewing these images women began to experience shame, guilt, body dissatisfaction, depression, and stress (Richins 83). These results leave women even more vulnerable to ever-enticing advertisements selling them happiness, beauty and confidence in a bottle of shampoo or tube of lipstick.

The direct quote, from a print source, is immediately cited with a page number. The paraphrased online study is identified by the authors' names in the text.

This paragraph summarizes the conclusions of two studies, demonstrating the *cause* and *effect* of the author's thesis (unreal media images—the "cause"—can lead to eating disorders—the "effect.").

For many young women, the effort to remake themselves in the idealized images perpetuated by the media becomes life-threatening. A 1991 study that tracked the incidents of anorexia nervosa over a fifty-year period found that the incidents of the disease among American females aged 10 to 19 reflected directly changes in fashion and its ideal body image. Many of the subjects also stated that they felt the greatest pressure of body weight ideals primarily from the media, with additional but lesser influence from peers and family. Even more devastating is that these results of the media's influence do not only affect adolescents and adults, but also children (Lucas et al). A study conducted by the American Association of University Women (1990) found that girls who had a negative body image were three times as likely as boys to believe that others perceived them negatively. The study also established that a negative body image has been directly linked to a higher risk of suicide for girls, and not boys.

A 1997 study by the Kaiser Family Foundation finds that young women are receiving conflicting views and reflections of their bodies and social roles. In some circumstances, "women are shown being self-reliant and

Yeager 5

using intelligence, honesty and efficiency to achieve their goals," and magazines "reinforce these messages by encouraging their readers to rely on themselves and resolve situations in honest and direct ways." However, many other television shows targeted to adolescent females broadcast "stereotypical messages about appearance, relationships and careers, as well as more subtle signals about girls' value and importance" (Signorelli). Commenting on these findings, a study for the Vanier Institute of the Family notes that it has been discovered that the more television girls and young women watch, the more likely they would be to create a hypothetical female television character "who is rich and thin, concerned about popularity, clothes, money, and looking attractive, and who wants to be a model or a famous actress" (Moscovitch). These conflicting messages can have a powerful and confusing influence on young women at a vulnerable stage of their development.

> The study, published electronically, does not require a page number for in-text citation.

> Moscovitch's article is also published electronically.

Young women—and young men, too—want to be popular. But an increasing body of evidence suggests that young women in particular believe that the route to popularity and success depends on their physical beauty, and their ability to meet rigid definitions of "beauty" perpetuated by the media. Cynical advertising campaigns exploit this anxiety among young women, encouraging them to buy beauty-related products to make them as popular, beautiful, and successful as Britney Spears or the latest supermodel. Everyone wants to look in the mirror and be happy with what they see, but the fact is few young women are happy when they are comparing themselves to the covers of *Teen Vogue* or *In Style*. The fashion world knows this, the advertising companies know this, and they also know that most women will pay a large price for a temporary fix of their shame and self-dissatisfaction. Women are sold on a quick pick-me-up with the latest lipstick, or the new and trendy jeans.

> Paragraph reminds readers of author's thesis and key points.

A-30

Conclusion makes a prediction based on assembled evidence. The author's language is strong, but she has amassed enough evidence to support her opinion.

The research cited above suggests that the media's strong influence on women and girls wreaks havoc on the mental, physical, and emotional condition of America's female population. As the media and advertising companies continue to sell to the insecurities that the media itself created, the cycle of distorted body image and associated eating disorders will continue.

Works Cited

American Association of University Women. *Short-changing Girls, Shortchanging America: Full Data Report*. Washington, D.C.: American Association of University Women, 1990. Print.

Curious, Britney's New Fragrance. Advertisement. *Allure* April 2005: 27. Print.

Hargreaves, D. "Idealized Women in TV Ads Make Girls Feel Bad." *Journal of Social and Clinical Psychology* 21 (2002): 287–308. Print.

Herbal Essences by Clairol. Advertisement. *Seventeen* May 2001: 15. Print.

Lucas, A. R., C. M. Beard, W. M. O'Fallon, and L. T. Kurland. "50-Year Trends in the Incidence of Anorexia Nervosa in Rochester, Minn.: A Population-Based Study." *American Journal of Psychiatry* 148:7 (1991): 917–922. Print.

Mellin, L. M., S. Scully, and C. E. Irwin. "Disordered Eating Characteristics in Preadolescent Girls: Meeting of the American Dietetic Association." Las Vegas: 1986. Abstract. *About-Face.org*. 1996–2001. Web. 15 May 2008.

Moscovitch, Arlene. "Electronic Media and the Family." The Vanier Institute of the Family. 1998. Web. 20 May 2008.

Richins, M. L. "Social Comparison and the Idealized Images of Advertising." *Journal of Consumer Research* 18 (1991): 71–83. Print.

Signorelli, Nancy. "A Content Analysis: Reflections of Girls in the Media." *The Kaiser Family Foundation*. April 1997. Web. 20 May 2008.

Pagination continues from body of paper.

Title centered.

All entries double-spaced.

All entries in alphabetical order by author.

First line at left margin; subsequent lines indented 5 spaces or one-half inch (one hit on "tab" key).

Skechers Footwear. Advertisement. *Cosmopolitan* April
    2005: 65. Print.
Stice, E., and H. E. Shaw. "Adverse Effects of the Media-
    Portrayed Thin Ideal on Women and Linkages to
    Bulimic Symptomatology." *Journal of Social and
    Clinical Psychology* 13 (1994): 288–308. Print.
Wolf, Naomi. *The Beauty Myth*. New York: Doubleday,
    1992. Print.

For another sample research essay using MLA-style documentation, click on

**Research > Sample Research
            Paper > Sample
            Paper in MLA Style**

For additional sample research essays using other documentation styles, click on

**Research > Sample Research
            Paper > Sample
            Paper in APA Style**

**Research > Sample Research
            Paper > Sample
            Paper in CMS Style**

**Research > Sample Research
            Paper > Sample
            Paper in CSE Style**

www.mhhe.com/
shortprose

Glossary

Abstract and concrete   are ways of describing important qualities of language. Abstract words are not associated with real, material objects that are related directly to the five senses. Such words as *love, wisdom, patriotism,* and *power* are abstract because they refer to ideas rather than to things. Concrete language, on the other hand, names things that can be perceived by the five senses. Words like *table, smoke, lemon,* and *half-back* are concrete. Generally you should not be too abstract in writing. It is best to employ concrete words naming things that can be seen, touched, smelled, heard, or tasted in order to support your more abstract ideas.

Allusion   is a reference to some literary, biographical, or historical event. It is a "figure of speech" (a fresh, useful comparison) used to illuminate an idea. For instance, if you want to state that a certain national ruler is insane, you might refer to him as a "Nero"—an allusion to the emperor who burned Rome.

Alternating method   in comparison and contrast involves a point-by-point treatment of the two subjects that you have selected to discuss. Assume that you have chosen five points to examine in a comparison of the Volkswagen Jetta (subject A) and the Honda Accord (subject B): cost, comfort, gas mileage, road handling, and frequency of repair. In applying the alternating method, you would begin by discussing cost in relation to A + B; then comfort in relation to A + B; and so on. The alternating method permits you to isolate points for a balanced discussion.

Ambiguity   means uncertainty. A writer is ambiguous when using a word, phrase, or sentence that is not clear. Ambiguity usually results in misunderstanding, and should be avoided in essay writing. Always strive for clarity in your compositions.

Analogy   is a form of figurative comparison that uses a clear illustration to explain a difficult idea or function. It is unlike a formal comparison in that its subjects of comparison are from different categories or areas. For example, an analogy likening "division of labor" to the activity of bees in a hive makes the first concept more concrete by showing it to the reader through the figurative comparison with the bees.

Antonym   is a word that is opposite in meaning to that of another word: *hot* is an antonym of *cold; fat* is an antonym of *thin; large* is an antonym of *small.*

Argumentation   is a type of writing in which you offer reasons in favor of or against something (see Chapter 11).

Audience   refers to the writer's intended readership. Many essays (including most in this book) are designed for a general audience, but a writer may also try to reach a special group. For example, William Zinsser in his essay "Simplicity" (pp. 30–39) might expect to appeal more to potential writers than to the general reading public. Similarly, Elizabeth Wong's "The Struggle to Be an All-American Girl" (pp. 143–150) could mean something particularly special to young Chinese Americans. The intended audience affects many of the writer's choices, including level of diction, range of allusions, types of figurative language, and so on.

Block method   in comparison and contrast involves the presentation of all information about the first subject (A), followed by all information about the second subject (B). Thus, using the objects of comparison explained in the discussion of the "alternating method," you would for the block method first present all five points about the Volkswagen. Then you would present all five points about the Honda. When using the block method, remember to present the same points for each subject, and to provide an effective transition in moving from subject A to subject B.

Causal analysis   is a form of writing that examines causes and effects of events or conditions as they relate to a specific subject (see Chapter 8).

Characterization   is the description of people. As a particular type of description in an essay, characterization attempts to capture as vividly as possible the features, qualities, traits, speech, actions, and personality of individuals.

Chronological order   is the arrangement of events in the order that they happened. You might use chronological order to trace the history of the Vietnam War, to explain a scientific process, or to present the biography of a close relative or friend. When you order an essay by chronology, you are moving from one step to the next in time.

Classification   is a pattern of writing in which the author divides a subject into categories and then groups elements in each of those categories according to their relation to each other (see Chapter 9).

Clichés   are expressions that were once fresh and vivid, but have become tired and worn from overuse. "I'm so hungry that I could eat a horse" is a typical cliché. People use clichés in conversation, but writers generally should avoid them.

Closings   or "conclusions" are endings for your essay. Without a closing, your essay is incomplete, leaving the reader with the feeling that something important has been left out. There are numerous closing possibilities available to writers: summarizing main points in the essay; restating the main idea; using an effective quotation to bring the essay to an end; offering the reader the climax to a series of events; returning to the introduction and echoing it; offering a solution to a problem; emphasizing the topic's significance; or setting a new frame of reference by generalizing from the main thesis. Whatever type of closing you use, make certain that it ends the essay in a firm and emphatic way.

Coherence   is a quality in effective writing that results from the careful ordering of each sentence in a paragraph, and each paragraph in the essay. If an essay is coherent, each part will grow naturally and logically from those parts that come before it. Coherence depends on the writer's ability to organize materials in a logical way, and to order segments so that the reader is carried along easily from start to finish. The main devices used in achieving coherence are transitions, which help to connect one thought with another.

Colloquial language   is language used in conversation and in certain types of informal writing, but rarely in essays, business writing, or research papers. There is nothing wrong with colloquialisms like *gross, scam,* or *rap* when used in conversational settings. However, they are often unacceptable in essay writing—except when used sparingly for special effects.

Comparison/contrast   is a pattern of essay writing treating similarities and differences between two subjects (see Chapter 7).

Composition   is a term used for an essay or for any piece of writing that reveals a careful plan.

Conclusion   (See *Closings*)

Concrete   (See *Abstract and concrete*)

Connotation/denotation   are terms specifying the way a word has meaning. Connotation refers to the "shades of meaning" that a word might have because of various emotional associations it calls up for writers and readers alike. Words like *American, physician, mother, pig,* and *San Francisco* have strong connotative overtones to them. With denotation, however, we are concerned not with the suggestive meaning of a word but with its exact, literal meaning. Denotation refers to the "dictionary definition" of a word—its exact meaning. Writers must understand the connotative and denotative value of words, and must control the shades of meaning that many words possess.

Context clues   are hints provided about the meaning of a word by another word or words, or by the sentence or sentences coming before or after it. Thus in the sentence, "Mr. Rome, a true *raconteur,* told a story that thrilled the guests," we should be able to guess at the meaning of the italicized word by the context clues coming both before and after it. (A *raconteur* is a person who tells good stories.)

Definition   is a method of explaining a word so that the reader knows what you mean by it (see Chapter 10).

Denotation   (See *Connotation/denotation*)

Derivation   is how a word originated and where it came from. Knowing the origin of a word can make you more aware of its meaning, and more able to use it effectively in writing. Your dictionary normally lists abbreviations (for example, O.E. for Old English, G. for Greek) for word origins and sometimes explains fully how they came about.

Description   is a type of writing that uses details of sight, color, sound, smell, and touch to create a word picture and to explain or illustrate an idea (see Chapter 3).

Dialogue   is the exact duplication in writing of something people say to each other. Dialogue is the reproduction of speech or conversation; it can add concreteness and vividness to an essay, and can also help to reveal character. When using dialogue, writers must be careful to use correct punctuation. Moreover, to use dialogue effectively in essay writing, you must develop an ear for the way other people talk, and an ability to create it accurately.

Diction   refers to the writer's choice or use of words. Good diction reflects the topic of the writing. Malcolm X's diction, for example, is varied, including subtle descriptions in standard diction and conversational sarcasms. Levels of diction refer both to the purpose of the essay and to the writer's audience. Skillful choice of the level of diction keeps the reader intimately involved with the topic.

Division   is that aspect of classification (see Chapter 9) in which the writer divides some large subject into categories. For example, you might divide *fish* into saltwater and freshwater fish; or *sports* into team and individual sports. Division helps writers to split large and potentially complicated subjects into parts for orderly presentation and discussion.

Effect   is a term used in causal analysis (see Chapter 8) to indicate the outcome or expected result of a chain of happenings. When dealing with the analysis of effects, writers should determine whether they want to work with immediate or final effects, or both. Thus, a writer analyzing the effects of an accidental nuclear explosion might choose to analyze effects immediately after the blast, as well as effects that still linger.

Emphasis   suggests the placement of the most important ideas in key positions in the essay. Writers can emphasize ideas simply by placing important ones at the beginning or at the end of the paragraph or essay. But several other techniques help writers to emphasize important ideas: (1) key words and ideas can be stressed by repetition; (2) ideas can be presented in climactic order, by building from lesser ideas at the beginning to the main idea at the end; (3) figurative language (for instance, a vivid simile) can call attention to a main idea; (4) the relative proportion of detail offered to support an idea can emphasize its importance; (5) comparison and contrast of an idea with other ideas can emphasize its importance; and (6) mechanical devices like underlining, capitalizing, and using exclamation points (all of which should be used sparingly) can stress significance.

Essay   is the name given to a short prose work on a limited topic. Essays take many forms, ranging from a familiar narrative account of an event in your life to explanatory, argumentative, or critical investigations of a subject. Normally, in one way or the other, an essay will convey the writer's personal ideas about the subject.

Euphemism   is the use of a word or phrase simply because it seems less distasteful or less offensive than another word. For instance, *mortician* is a euphemism for *undertaker; sanitation worker* for *garbage collector.*

Fable   is a story with a moral. The story from which the writer draws the moral can be either true or imaginary. When writing a fable, a writer must clearly present the moral to be derived from the narrative, as Rachel Carson does in "A Fable for Tomorrow" (see pp. 260–266).

Figurative language,   as opposed to *literal,* is a special approach to writing that departs from what is typically a concrete, straightforward style. It involves a vivid, imaginative comparison that goes beyond plain or ordinary statements. For instance, instead of saying that "Joan is wonderful," you could write that "Joan is like a summer's rose" (a *simile*); "Joan's hair is wheat, pale and soft and yellow" (a *metaphor*); "Joan is my Helen of Troy" (an *allusion*); or use a number of other comparative approaches. Note that Joan is not a rose, her hair is not wheat, nor is she some other person named Helen. Figurative language is not logical; instead, it requires an ability on the part of the writer to create an imaginative comparison in order to make an idea more striking.

Flashback   is a narrative technique in which the writer begins at some point in the action and then moves into the past in order to provide necessary background information. Flashback adds variety to the narrative method, enabling writers to approach a story not only in terms of straight chronology, but in terms of a back-and-forth movement. However, it is at best a very difficult technique and should be used with great care.

General/specific words   are necessary in writing, although it is wise to keep your vocabulary as specific as possible. General words refer to broad categories and groups, while specific words capture with more force and clarity the nature of a term. The distinction between general and specific language is always a matter of degree. "A woman walked down the street" is more general than "Mrs. Walker walked down Fifth Avenue," while "Mrs. Webster, elegantly dressed in a muslin suit, strolled down Fifth Avenue" is more specific than the first two examples. Our ability to use specific language depends on the extent of our vocabulary. The more words we know, the more specific we can be in choosing words.

Hyperbole   is obvious and intentional exaggeration.

Illustration   is the use of several examples to support an idea (see Chapter 6).

Imagery   is clear, vivid description that appeals to our sense of sight, smell, touch, sound, or taste. Much imagery exists for its own sake, adding descriptive flavor to an essay, as when Suzanne Berne in "My Ticket to the Disaster" writes, "Light reflecting off the Hudson River vaults into the site, soaking everything—especially on an overcast morning—with a watery glow." However, imagery can also add meaning to an essay. For example, when Orwell writes at the start of "A Hanging," "It was in Burma, a sodden morning of the rains. A sickly light, like yellow tinfoil, was slanting over the high walls into the jail yard," we see that the author uses imagery to prepare us for the somber and terrifying event to follow. Writers can use imagery to contribute to any type of wording, or they can rely on it to structure an entire essay. It is always difficult to invent fresh, vivid description, but it is an effort that writers must make if they wish to improve the quality of their prose.

Introductions   are the beginning or openings of essays. Introductions should perform a number of functions. They should alert the reader to the subject, set the limits of the essay, and indicate what the *thesis* (or main idea) will be. Moreover, they should arouse the reader's interest in the subject, so that the reader will want to continue reading into the essay. There are several devices available to writers that aid in the development of sound introductions.

1. Simply state the subject and establish the thesis. See the essay by William Zinsser (pp. 30–39).

2. Open with a clear, vivid description that will become important as your essay advances. Save your thesis for a later stage, but indicate what your subject is. See the essay by George Orwell (pp. 165–176).

3. Ask a question or a series of questions, which you might answer in the introduction or in another part of the essay. See the Takaki essay (pp. 455–461).

4. Tell an anecdote (a short, self-contained story of an entertaining nature) that serves to illuminate your subject. See the Staples essay (pp. 220–227).

5. Use comparison or contrast to frame your subject and to present the thesis. See the Goode essay (pp. 280–286).

6. Establish a definitional context for your subject. See the Ingrassia essay (pp. 273–279).

7. Begin by stating your personal attitude toward a controversial issue. See the Ivins essay (pp. 490–495).

These are only some of the devices that appear in the introductions to essays in this book. Writers can also ask questions, give definitions, or provide personal accounts—there are many techniques that can be used to develop introductions. The important thing to remember is that you *need* an introduction to an essay. It can be a single sentence or a much longer paragraph, but it must accomplish its purpose—to introduce readers to the subject, and to engage them so that they want to explore the essay further.

Irony   is the use of language to suggest the opposite of what is stated. Writers use irony to reveal unpleasant or troublesome realities that exist in life, or to poke fun at human weaknesses and foolish attitudes. For instance, in Orwell's "A Hanging," the men who are in charge of the execution engage in laughter and lighthearted conversation after the event. There is irony in the situation and in their speech because we sense that they are actually very tense—almost unnerved—by the hanging; their laughter is the opposite of what their true emotional state actually is. Many situations and conditions lend themselves to ironic treatment.

Jargon   is the use of special words associated with a specific area of knowledge or a specific profession. It is similar to "shop talk" that members of a certain trade might know, but not necessarily people outside it. For example, the medical jargon in Kozol's essay helps him defend his opinion on a nonmedical subject. Use jargon sparingly in your writing, and be certain to define all specialized terms that you think your readers might not know.

Journalese   is a level of writing associated with prose types normally found in newspapers and popular magazines. A typical newspaper article tends to present information factually or objectively; to use simple language and simple sentence structure; and to rely on relatively short paragraphs. It also stays close to the level of conversational English without becoming chatty or colloquial.

Metaphor   is a type of figurative language in which an item from one category is compared briefly and imaginatively with an item from another area. Writers create metaphors to assign meaning to a word in an original way.

Narration   is telling a story in order to illustrate an important idea (see Chapter 4).

Objective/subjective   writing refers to the attitude that writers take toward their subject. When writers are objective, they try not to report their own personal feelings about their subject. They attempt to control, if not eliminate, their own attitude toward the topic. Thus in the essay by Diamond (see pp. 245–252) we read about globalization, but he doesn't try to convince us that globalization is good or bad. Many essays, on the other hand, reveal the authors' personal attitudes and emotions. In

Frisina's essay, the author's personal approach to the process of reading seems clear. She takes a highly subjective approach to the topic. Other essays, such as Kozol's (see pp. 432–443), blend the two approaches to help balance the author's expression of a strong opinion. For some kinds of college writing, such as business or laboratory reports, research papers, or literary analyses, it is best to be as objective as possible. But for many of the essays in composition courses, the subjective touch is fine.

Order is the manner in which you arrange information or materials in an essay. The most common ordering techniques are *chronological order* (involving time sequence); *spatial order* (involving the arrangement of descriptive details); *process order* (involving a step-by-step approach to an activity); *deductive order* (in which you offer a thesis and then the evidence to support it); and *inductive order* (in which you present evidence first and build toward the thesis). Some rhetorical patterns such as comparison and contrast, classification, and argumentation require other ordering techniques. Writers should select those ordering principles that permit them to present materials clearly.

Paradox is a statement that *seems* to be contradictory but actually contains an element of truth. Writers use it in order to call attention to their subject.

Parallelism is a variety of sentence structure in which there is "balance" or coordination in the presentation of elements. "I came, I saw, I conquered" is a good example of parallelism, presenting both pronouns and verbs in a coordinated manner. Parallelism can also be applied to several sentences and to entire paragraphs. It can be an effective way to emphasize ideas.

Personification is giving an object, thing, or idea lifelike or human qualities. Like all forms of figurative writing, personification adds freshness to description, and makes ideas vivid by setting up striking comparisons.

Point of view is the angle from which a writer tells a story. Many personal or informal essays take the *first-person* (or "I") point of view, as the essays by Malcolm X, Hughes, Orwell, and others reveal. The first-person "I" point of view is natural and fitting for essays when the writer wants to speak in a familiar and intimate way to the reader. On the other hand, the *third-person* point of view ("he," "she," "it," "they") distances the reader somewhat from the writer. The third-person point of view is useful in essays where writers are not talking exclusively about themselves, but about other people, things, and events, as in the essays by Kozol and Carson. Occasionally, the *second-person* ("you") point of view will appear in essays, notably in essays involving process analysis where the writer directs the reader to do something; part of Ernest Hemingway's essay (which also uses a third-person point of view) uses this strategy. Other point-of-view combinations are possible when a writer wants to achieve a special effect—for example, combining *first-* and *second-person* points of view. The position that you take as a writer depends largely on the type of essay you write.

Prefix   is one or more syllables attached to the front of another word in order to influence its meaning or to create a new word. A knowledge of prefixes and their meanings aids in establishing the meanings of words and in increasing the vocabulary that we use in writing. Common prefixes and their meanings include *bi-* (two), *ex-* (out, out of), *per-* (through), *pre-* (before), *re-* (again), *tele-* (distant), and *trans-* (across, beyond).

Process analysis   is a pattern of writing that explains in a step-by-step way the methods for doing something or reaching a desired end (see Chapter 5).

Proposition   is the main point in an argumentative essay. It is like a *thesis,* except that it usually presents an idea that is debatable or can be disputed.

Purpose   refers to what a writer hopes to accomplish in a piece of writing. For example, the purpose may be *to convince* the reader to adopt a certain viewpoint (as in Quindlen's "The Good Enough Mother," pp. 480–487), *to explain* a process (as in Hemingway's "Camping Out," pp. 195–202), or to allow the reader *to feel a dominant impression* (as in Ackerman's "Farewell to Summer and Its Buzzing Creatures," pp. 107–112). Purpose helps a writer to determine which expository technique will dominate the essay's form, as well as what kinds of supporting examples will be used. Purpose and *audience* are often closely related.

Refutation   is a technique in argumentative writing in which you recognize and deal effectively with the arguments of your opponents. Your own argument will be stronger if you can refute—prove false or wrong—all opposing arguments.

Root   is the basic part of a word. It sometimes aids us in knowing what the larger word means. Thus if we know that the root *doc-* means "teach," we might be able to figure out a word like *doctrine. Prefixes* and *suffixes* are attached to roots to create words.

Sarcasm   is a sneering or taunting attitude in writing. It is designed to hurt by ridiculing or criticizing. Basically, sarcasm is a heavy-handed form of irony, as when an individual says, "Well, you're exactly on time, aren't you" to someone who is an hour late, and says it with a sharpness in the voice, designed to hurt. Writers should try to avoid sarcastic writing and to use more acceptable varieties of irony and satire to criticize their subject.

Satire   is the humorous or critical treatment of a subject in order to expose the subject's vices, follies, stupidities, and so forth. Barry, for instance, satirizes stereotyped ideas of men and women, exposing them as empty concepts. Satire is a better weapon than sarcasm in the hands of the writer because satire is used to correct, whereas sarcasm merely hurts.

Sentimentality is the excessive display of emotion in writing, whether it is intended or unintended. Because sentimentality can distort the true nature of a situation, writers should use it cautiously, or not at all. They should be especially careful when dealing with certain subjects, for example the death of a loved one, the remembrance of a mother or father, a ruined romance, the loss of something valued, that lend themselves to sentimental treatment. Only the best writers—like Hughes and others in this text—can avoid the sentimental traps rooted in their subjects.

Simile is an imaginative comparison using *like* or *as*. When Orwell writes, "A sickly light, like yellow tinfoil, was slanting over the high walls into the jail yard," he uses a vivid simile in order to reinforce the dullness of the scene.

Slang is a level of language that uses racy and colorful expressions associated more often with speech than with writing. Slang expressions like "Mike's such a dude" or "She's a real fox" should not be used in essay writing, except when the writer is reproducing dialogue or striving for a special effect. Hughes is one writer in this collection who uses slang effectively to convey his message to the reader.

Subjective (See *Objective/subjective*)

Suffix is a syllable or syllables appearing at the end of a word and influencing its meaning. As with prefixes and roots, you can build vocabulary and establish meanings by knowing about suffixes. Some typical suffixes are *-able* (capable of), *-al* (relating to), *-ic* (characteristic of), *-ion* (state of), *-er* (one who), which appear often in standard writing.

Symbol is something that exists in itself but also stands for something else. As a type of figurative language, the symbol can be a strong feature in an essay, operating to add depth of meaning, and even to unify entire essays.

Synonym is a word that means roughly the same as another word. In practice, few words are exactly alike in meaning. Careful writers use synonyms to vary word choice, without ever moving too far from the shade of meaning intended.

Theme is the central idea in an essay; it is also often termed the *thesis*. Everything in an essay should support the theme in one way or another.

Thesis is the main idea in an essay. The *thesis sentence,* appearing early in the essay, and normally somewhere in the first paragraph, serves to convey the main idea to the reader in a clear way. It is always useful to state your central idea as soon as possible, and before you introduce other supporting ideas.

Title for an essay should be a short, simple indication of the contents of your essay. Titles like "Salvation" (pp. 151–154) and "Pride" (pp. 383–385) convey the central subjects of these essays in brief, effective ways. Others, such as "I Have a Dream" (pp. 496–500) and "Night Walker" (pp. 220–223), also convey the central idea, but more abstractly. Always provide titles for your essays.

Tone is the writer's attitude toward his or her subject or material. An essay writer's tone may be objective, ironic ("Let It Snow"), comic ("Catfish in the Bathtub"), nostalgic ("Farewell to Summer and Its Buzzing Creatures"), or a reflection of numerous other attitudes. Tone is the "voice" that you give to an essay; every writer should strive to create a "personal voice," or tone, that will be distinctive throughout any type of essay under development.

Transition is the linking of one idea to the next in order to achieve essay *coherence*. Transitions are words that connect these ideas. Among the most common techniques to achieve smooth transition are (1) repeating a key word or phrase; (2) using a pronoun to refer back to a key word or phrase; (3) relying on traditional connectives like *thus, for example, moreover, therefore, however, finally, likewise, afterward,* and *in conclusion;* (4) using parallel structure (see *Parallelism*); and (5) creating a sentence or an entire paragraph that serves as a bridge from one part of your essay to the next. Transition is best achieved when the writer presents ideas and details carefully and in logical order. Try not to lose the reader by failing to provide adequate transition from idea to idea.

Unity is that feature in an essay where all material relates to a central concept and contributes to the meaning of the whole. To achieve a unified effect in an essay, the writer must design an introduction and conclusion, maintain a consistent tone and point of view, develop middle paragraphs in a coherent manner, and always stick to the subject, never permitting unimportant elements to enter. Thus, unity involves a successful blending of all elements that go into the creation of a sound essay.

Vulgarisms are words that exist below conventional vocabulary, and are not accepted in polite conversation. Always avoid vulgarisms in your own writing, unless they serve an illustrative purpose.

Credits

PHOTOS

Page 66: © Jacob A. Riis/Stringer/Getty Images; **p. 67:** © Mary Kate Denny/PhotoEdit, Inc.; **p. 101:** © Mario Anzuoni/Reuters/Corbis; **p. 137:** © James Marshall/The Image Works; **p. 178:** John Moore/AP Photo; **p. 254:** Ric Feld/AP Photo; **p. 318:** Photo by Three Lions/Getty Images; **p. 324:** © Kim Kulish/Corbis; **pp. 349, 350, 351, 352, 353:** Courtesy of Balch Institute of Collections/Historical Society of Pennsylvania; **p. 354:** Courtesy of S & P Company, Mill Valley, CA, and the J. Walter Collection at the John Hartman Center for Sales, Advertising and Marketing History, Duke University; **p. 406:** © Culver Pictures, Inc.; **p. 514:** © Bob Daemmrich/Stock Boston; **p. A-26:** Brooke Pleasanton.

COLOR INSERT PHOTOS

Page 1: © Chris Carlson/AP Photo; **p. 2:** © Images.com/Corbis; **p. 3:** Kevin Fleming/Corbis; **p. 4:** Photograph by Anita Kunz, © Condé Nast Publications; **p. 5:** © The Winchester Star, Scott Mason/AP Photo; **p. 7:** Rick Gayle/Corbis; **p. 8:** © National Fluid Milk Processor Promotion Board.

TEXT

Ackerman, Diane. "Farewell to Summer and Its Buzzing Creatures" by Diane Ackerman from *The New York Times*, September 7, 2002. Reprinted by permission of the William Morris Agency.

Bader, Eleanor J. "Homeless on Campus" by Eleanor J. Bader from *The Progressive*, July 2004. Reprinted by permission from The Progressive, 409 East Main St., Madison, WI 53703, www.progressive.org.

Bagaric, Mirko. "A Case for Torture" by Mirko Bagaric from www.theage.au, May 17, 2005. Reprinted by permission of the author.

Baker, James T. "How Do We Find the Student in a World of Academic Gymnasts and Worker Ants?" by James T. Baker from *Chronicle of Higher Education*, 1982. Reprinted by permission of the author.

Barry, Dave. "Punch and Judy" by Dave Barry (original title: "Neither Man Nor Rat Can Properly Fold the Laundry"), *Miami Herald*, July 2, 2000. Copyright 2000 by Dave Barry. Reprinted by permission of the author. No duplication, all rights reserved.

Berne, Suzanne. "My Ticket to the Disaster" by Suzanne Berne from *The New York Times*, April 21, 2002. This article appeared in *The New York Times* as "Where Nothing Says Everything." Copyright © 2002 The New York Times. All rights reserved. Used by permission and protected by the copyright laws of the U.S. The printing, copying, redistribution, or retransmission of the material without permission is prohibited.

Bryson, Bill. "Your New Computer" from *I'm a Stranger Here Myself* by Bill Bryson, copyright © 1999 by Bill Bryson. Used by permission of Broadway Books, a division of Random House, Inc., and Doubleday Canada. Published in Canada as *Notes from a Big Country*. Copyright © 1998 by Bill Bryson.

Carson, Rachel. "A Fable for Tomorrow" from *Silent Spring* by Rachel Carson. Copyright © 1962 by Rachel L. Carson, renewed 1990 by Roger Christie. Reprinted by permission of Houghton Mifflin Harcourt Publishing Company. All rights reserved. And by permission of Francis Collin, Trustee.

Cheever, Susan. "Baby Battle" copyright © 2006 by Susan Cheever, from *Mommy Wars*, edited by Leslie Morgan Steiner. Used by permission of Random House.

Cofer, Judith Ortiz. "Volar" by Judith Ortiz Cofer is reprinted with permission from the publisher of *The Year of Our Revolution* by Judith Ortiz Cofer, 1998 (© 1998 Arte Público Press–University of Houston).

Crews, Harry. "Why I Live Where I Live" by Harry Crews from *Esquire*. Copyright © 1980 Harry Crews. Reprinted by permission of John Hawkins & Associates, Inc.

Diamond, Jared. "Globalization Rocked the Ancient World Too" by Jared Diamond from *Los Angeles Times*, September 14, 2003. Used with permission of the author.

Dillard, Annie. "In the Jungle" from *Teaching a Stone to Talk: Expeditions and Encounters* by Annie Dillard. Copyright © 1982 by Annie

Ingrassia, Michele. "The Body of the Beholder" by Michele Ingrassia. From *Newsweek*, April 24, 1995, pp. 66–67. © 1995.

Ivins, Molly. "Get a Knife, Get a Dog, but Get Rid of Guns" from *Nothin' But Good Times Ahead* by Molly Ivins, copyright © 1993 by Molly Ivins. Used by permission of Random House, Inc.

King, Martin Luther Jr. "I Have a Dream" by Martin Luther King Jr. Reprinted by arrangement with the Estate of Martin Luther King Jr., c/o Writers House as agent for the proprietor New York, NY. Copyright 1963 Martin Luther King Jr., copyright renewed 1991 Coretta Scott King.

King, Stephen. "Why We Crave Horror Movies" by Stephen King. Reprinted With Permission. © Stephen King. All rights reserved. Originally appeared in *Playboy* (1982).

Kingston, Maxine Hong. "Catfish in the Bathtub" from *The Woman Warrior* by Maxine Hong Kingston, copyright © 1975, 1976 by Maxine Hong Kingston. Used by permission of Alfred A. Knopf, a division of Random House, Inc., and the Sandra Dijkstra Literary Agency.

Kozol, Jonathan. "Are the Homeless Crazy?" by Jonathan Kozol from *Yale Review*, 1988. Reprinted by permission of the author.

Lee, Jennifer. "I Think, Therefore IM" by Jennifer Lee from *The New York Times*, May 19, 2002. Copyright © 2002 The New York Times. All rights reserved. Used by permission and protected by the copyright laws of the U.S. The printing, copying, redistribution, or retransmission of the material without permission is prohibited.

Mailer, Norman. "One Idea" by Norman Mailer from *Parade* Magazine, January 23, 2005. © 2005 The Norman Mailer Estate. Initially published in *Parade* Magazine. All rights reserved. Reprinted with permission.

Malcolm X. From *The Autobiography of Malcolm X* by Malcolm X and Alex Haley, copyright © 1964 by Alex Haley and Malcolm X. Copyright © 1965 by Alex Haley and Betty Shabazz. Used by permission of Random House, Inc. and by Random House Group Ltd.

McCain, John. "Torture's Terrible Toll" by John McCain from *Newsweek*, November 25, 2005. © 2005 Newsweek, Inc. All rights reserved. Used by permission and protected by the copyright laws of the U.S. The printing, copying, redistribution, or retransmission of the material without permission is prohibited.

Index of Authors and Titles

The Short Prose Reader, Eleventh Edition, Powered by
@ www.mhhe.com/shortprose

IF YOU NEED HELP WITH . . .	SEE THESE PAGES IN THE TEXT . . .	AND FOLLOW THIS CLICK PATH IN CATALYST.
Argument essay	407	Writing ➤ Writing Tutor: Arguments
Body paragraphs	105, 142, 181, 219, 258, 292, 328, 374	Writing ➤ Paragraph Patterns
Cause-and-effect essay	289	Writing ➤ Writing Tutor: Causal Analysis
Classification essay	325	Writing ➤ Writing Tutor: Classification
Comparison-and-contrast essay	255	Writing ➤ Writing Tutor: Comparison/Contrast
Concluding paragraphs	10	Writing ➤ Conclusions
Coordination	10	Editing ➤ Coordination and Subordination
Definition essay	370	Writing ➤ Writing Tutor: Definition
Descriptive essay	102	Writing ➤ Writing Tutor: Description
Documentation styles	A-18	Research ➤ Bibliomaker Research ➤ Links to Documentation Sites Research ➤ Sample Research Papers
Documenting sources	A-17	Research ➤ Bibliomaker Research ➤ Links to Documentation Sites
Drafting	4, A-13	Writing ➤ Drafting and Revising
Evaluating sources	A-7	Research ➤ CARS Source Evaluation Tutor
Illustration essay	216	Writing ➤ Writing Tutor: Exemplification
Internet, locating sources	A-4	Research ➤ Using the Internet
Library, locating sources	A-3	Research ➤ Using the Library
Mixed pattern essay	11	Writing ➤ Writing Tutor: Blended Essay
Narrative essay	138	Writing ➤ Writing Tutor: Narration
Outlining	A-11	Writing ➤ Outlines Writing ➤ Outlining Tutor
Paraphrases, incorporating	A-15	Research ➤ Avoiding Plagiarism Research ➤ Incorporating Source Information Research ➤ Using Sources Accurately
Plagiarism, how to avoid	A-14, A-17	Research ➤ Avoiding Plagiarism
Prewriting	2	Writing ➤ Prewriting
Process analysis essay	179	Writing ➤ Writing Tutor: Process Analysis
Quotations, incorporating	A-14	Research ➤ Avoiding Plagiarism Research ➤ Incorporating Source Information Research ➤ Using Sources Accurately
Resources, locating	A-3	Research ➤ Discipline-Specific Resources Research ➤ Using the Internet Research ➤ Using the Library
Redundancies and repetition	10	Editing ➤ Eliminating Redundancies
Revising	7, A-16	Writing ➤ Drafting and Revising
Subordination	10	Editing ➤ Coordination and Subordination
Summaries, incorporating	A-15	Research ➤ Avoiding Plagiarism Research ➤ Incorporating Source Information Research ➤ Using Sources Accurately